Black Music of Two Worlds

▲▼▲▼▲▼▲▼▲▼▲▼▲▼▲▼▲▼▲▼▲▼▲▼▲▼▲▼▲▼▲▼▲▼▲▼▲

Black Music

of

Two Worlds

African, Caribbean, Latin, and African-American Traditions

Second Edition

John Storm Roberts

THOMSON
———*———
™
SCHIRMER

Australia • Canada • Mexico • Singapore • Spain
United Kingdom • United States

Library of Congress Catalog Card Number: 98-6587

ISBN: 0-02-864929-X

Wadsworth/Thomson Learning
10 Davis Drive
Belmont CA 94002-3098
USA

For information about our products, contact us:
Thomson Learning Academic Resource Center
1-800-423-0563
http://www.wadsworth.com

For permission to use material from this text, contact us by
Web: http://www.thomsonrights.com
Fax: 1-800-730-2215
Phone: 1-800-730-2214

Printed in the United States of America
10 9 8 7 6 5 4 3 2

Library of Congress Cataloging-in-Publication Data
Roberts, John Storm.
Black music of two worlds: African, Caribbean, Latin, and African-American
traditions / John Storm Roberts.— 2nd ed. p. cm. Discography : p. Includes
bibliographical references (p.   ) and index. ISBN 0-02-864929-X
1. Blacks—Music—History and criticism. 2. Afro-Americans—Music—History and criticism.
3. Music—Africa—History and criticism. 4. Music—America—African influences. 1. Title.
ML 3556.R6 1998
780'.89'96—dc21   98-6587
                                   CIP
                                   MN

To my wife,
Anne Needham,
for everything and
a good deal more.

Contents

Contents

Foreword

When I first came across this book, in the early 1970s, the timing couldn't have been better. At that moment I was straddling what seemed like an unbridgeable divide. Beckoning from one side was a rather obscure academic subspecialization called ethnomusicology, which I had only recently discovered; tugging from the other was the music of the millions, which I was loath to relinquish. The moment I laid eyes on *Black Music of Two Worlds*, the apparent divide evaporated.

I suspect the book had a similar effect on others. Few may dream of a career in ethnomusicology, but who hasn't stopped at one time or another to ponder where the musical sounds we take for granted in our daily lives come from, or how long they have been around? In most parts of the world today, one cannot pose these basic questions without conjuring up an enormously complicated history of cultural exchange. At the heart of this history lies the transatlantic slave trade and its ongoing repercussions. So profound an imprint has the music of people of African descent made on the dominant popular styles of the Western Hemisphere (and, by extension, the rest of the globe) that any serious attempt to locate the sources of today's mass-mediated musics almost inevitably leads, through a maze of little-known rural and urban folk traditions, back to the African continent.

Despite this history, most people in the United States and Europe remain woefully ignorant about African music. Because the authentic musical expressions of Africa have for so long been ignored by the musical powers-that-be in the West, they have until recently remained inaccessible to all but the most persevering researchers. To be sure, many writers on jazz or the blues have recognized the need to follow the stylistic strands back beyond Storyville or the Mississippi Delta to the other side of the ocean; some have even made good use of the findings of Africanist anthropologists or ethnomusicologists, or carried out careful scholarly research of their own. But for the majority of commentators on the urban black music of the twentieth century, the traditional musics of Africa and the neo-African musics of the diaspora have remained little more than fodder for the occasional footnote speculating on connections with a mythic past.

Among those who, in contrast, have devoted their careers to the study of traditional African music, we tend to see the reverse—a lack of regard for the sounds of the city, on either side of the ocean. Indeed, there was a time not so long ago when most ethnomusicologists viewed these new urban musics of mixed African and European parentage as a threat to the integrity of supposedly pristine "primitive" or "tribal" musical cultures. (In fact, trendy music journalists, hindered by their own prejudices, were no quicker than protectionist ethnomusicologists to wake up to the emerging urban popular styles of Africa.)

To sum up the situation as the 1970s opened: For jazz and blues buffs in the United States and Europe (not to mention rock critics), the older African and Afro-Caribbean traditions that had fed into American popular styles were too far out of the mainstream to command much attention; for academic purists, on the other hand, the newer, hybrid sounds of Africa and the diaspora were simply too "common"—which is to say, too popular—to deserve study. Meanwhile, an unprecedented explosion of new African and African-influenced musical idioms was about to rock the planet.

Along came *Black Music of Two Worlds*. When it appeared in 1972, there was nothing quite like it. Here was a book about black music that excluded no genre from consideration, no matter how "traditional" or how "popular." No music was too rude or remote, nor was any too slick or cosmopolitan. All were treated with equal seriousness and respect: The urbanizing *cumbia* of the Atlantic coast of Colombia and the rustic *currulao* of the Pacific coast; the digging songs and *tambo* drumming of backcountry Jamaica and the rocksteady and reggae of downtown Kingston; the traditional *bomba* and *plena* of Puerto Rico and the industrial-strength *pachanga* of Latin New York; the calypso hits of Port of Spain and the sacred rhythms of a Shango temple in the hills above; the ecstatic ring shout of a Sea Islands congregation and the exploratory improvisations of a Manhattan jazz club; the polyrhythms of traditional drum ensembles from the hinterland of Ghana and the modern highlife of guitar bands from Accra; and dozens of other musical traditions large and small, from *abakwá* to zydeco.

That the book paid equal attention to music of greatly differing social registers made perfect sense given the constant feedback between rural traditional and urban popular forms of music—as well as religious and secular ones—over the last several decades, both in Africa and the Americas. Yet, no one had taken the trouble to present so balanced and inclusive a picture before. Nor had many authors been so ambitious in their geographical coverage. In *Black Music of Two Worlds*, John Storm Roberts took the bold step of attempting to span the full range of African and diasporic musics—the entire universe of black music—between the covers of a single slim volume. The "two worlds" of the title are actually broken down into several smaller "black music" macrocosms—Latin America, Central America, the Caribbean, North America, and the various musical subregions of Africa—each displaying a startling complexity of its own. In sketching out the outlines of all these and teasing out the relationships between them, Roberts managed to convey as clearly as any writer before or since the fundamental connectedness of all the far-flung branches of this great musical family. Few others possessed the sheer breadth of knowledge needed to pull off an undertaking of this scale.

As if these accomplishments weren't enough, the book is richly intuitive and full of original ideas. Roberts repeatedly reminds us that underlying Africa's tremendous musical diversity are certain "generalized" patterns and widely shared "attitudes." When he contends that these abstract patterns and attitudes were able to survive and resurface in the Americas in new guises, even in those parts of Afro-America where more obvious African musical continuities are absent, he anticipates what was to become (during the 1980s and 1990s) a dominant trend in anthropological and ethnomusicological thinking about cultural creolization. Cultural continuity, Roberts recognizes, can exist at several levels, and those manifestations that lie closest to the surface are not necessarily the most interesting or significant ones. In one of my favorite passages, he argues, in effect, that boogie-woogie piano, despite being an entirely original African-American creation, displays a fundamentally African deep structure (though he never uses this term to describe it); this deep-level Africanness, he points out, reflects a history of inter-African cultural synthesis and regeneration that is shared by black musics across the Western Hemisphere.

"Boogie-woogie," he writes, "must surely represent the purest example of how various African strands in a culturally mixed music can come together to produce music that, though nonexistent in Africa, is non-African only in that it is played on a piano and usually makes a nod in the direction of three-chord harmonies." A page later he picks up the thread again: "The point about boogie-woogie is that for a brief spell it brought together a number of Africanisms, all of which had been present in the United States in more diffused forms, and thus produced an eerie doppelgänger of African music." The subtle approach to African cultural continuities exemplified by this passage remains all too rare today, though its basic premises are now widely accepted by scholars specializing in musics of the African diaspora. When writing of the parallels between early jazz drumming and the music of Caribbean fife-and-drum bands, both of which succeeded in marrying European genres and instrumentation with African-derived "rhythmic attitudes," Roberts proves similarly insightful.

Roberts was also ahead of many of his colleagues in his insistence on the importance of adaptation and change to musical and cultural survival. As he himself puts it, "cultural survival is not the antonym of change but depends on it." "The crux of the matter," he observes, "lies in what one means by 'survival.' Nothing, from an amoeba to a planet, can survive without adapting itself to new circumstances. Indeed, adaptation is a prime sign of life." This positive attitude toward change pervades the entire book, and is part of what makes it so refreshing. It also helps to explain the author's sensitivity to the vast creative potential of musical shifts in Africa and the Caribbean that few fans and critics of the more mainstream styles of black popular music at the time even knew were occurring. Long before the term "world music" was invented as a shorthand for "modernized" or "Westernized" exotic musics with the potential to appeal to formula-weary European and U.S. record buyers, John Storm Roberts was preaching the pleasures of many of these same musics. For instance, at a time when most of the pop music press remained disdainful, if not entirely unaware, of Jamaican popular music (neither Bob Marley nor any of the other Wailers yet having hit it big outside the Caribbean), *Black Music of Two Worlds* recognized the vital interplay of tradition and innovation in ska, rocksteady, and reggae, celebrating the latter as "the Caribbean's only entirely new musical form in this century." But the most dramatic evidence of the book's prescience is the entire section devoted to popular musics of postcolonial Africa. It wasn't until the 1980s and 1990s that these vibrant new sounds from the Mother Continent began to capture the attention of large numbers of adventurous listeners outside of Africa and to be seen as hip in places such as Paris, London, and New York (thanks largely to the efforts of a handful of established pop producers and rock stars in "discovering" and promoting African talent in the West). By the mid-1990s, a number of rock critics were even touting African popular music (somewhat quixotically) as the wave of the future—the new center of creative gravity that would finally dislodge America's hegemonic grip on the world of mass-marketed music.

In the more than two and a half decades since *Black Music of Two Worlds* first saw print, a great deal of new research has appeared, and much more is now known about both of the musical worlds it explores than was known back then. What was then a major challenge—the idea of presenting a comprehensive overview of so vast a topic—now seems an impossibility. Given the explosion of new musical developments in Africa, Europe, and the Americas over the last couple of decades, not to mention the recent proliferation of relevant recordings, books, and articles, there is no way a single book—even this newly revised edition—could accomplish anything like complete coverage. But this updated volume, like its predecessor, offers a picture that is still about as close to comprehensive as you'll find. More importantly, it does justice to those slices of black musical life it singles out for scrutiny, combining a hardheaded critical sense with an undisguised passion for the boundless creative energy unleashed by the meeting of diverse musical worlds in the context of the African diaspora. Like the author, we should learn never to underestimate this energy, whether manifested among the rural folk, the urban masses, the conservatory-trained elites, or the ranks of million-selling recording artists. The very least we stand to gain by following this lead and opening up to the full range of black musical expression is increased musical enjoyment and a renewed appreciation of just how deep and extensive the roots of the sounds that most of us nowadays take for granted actually are.

KENNETH BILBY

Dr. Kenneth Bilby is an expert on the neo-African musics of Jamaica, French Guiana, and Suriname. He has also done extensive research on non-Maroon musical traditions in Jamaica, such as Kumina, Gumbay, Revival, and Mento. He coauthored *Caribbean Currents: Caribbean Music from Rumba to Reggae* with Peter Manuel and Michael Largey and has published many other monographs. He has produced several albums from his own field recordings, including *From Kongo to Zion: Three Black Musical Traditions from Jamaica* and *Drums of Defiance: Maroon Music from the Earliest Free Black Communities of Jamaica.* He also contributed as recordist and researcher to several titles in Mickey Hart's "The World" series, and is now coeditor, with Morton Marks, of the "Caribbean Voyage" reissue series of Alan Lomax's historic Lesser Antilles recordings made in 1962. Dr. Bilby holds an M.A. in anthropology from Wesleyan University and a Ph.D. in anthropology from Johns Hopkins University and is currently a Research Associate in the Department of Anthropology at the Smithsonian Institution in Washington, D.C.

Preface to the 1998 Edition

Since I wrote the first edition of this book a quarter of a century ago, the situation has totally changed, in part—so people younger and more knowledgeable than I have been kind enough to tell me—as a result of the original edition of *Black Music of Two Worlds.* Whatever the reason, an enormous amount of research has been done all over the African and Afro-American musical world.

In addition, the area I was covering has changed enormously in the last quarter-century. In fact most of the major Afro-American styles of the present were then unborn. Rap, Trinidadian soca, French Antillean zouk, were all half a decade away; Haitian mini-jazz and Jamaican reggae were in their adolescence. And the international awareness of pretty much all non–U.S. Afro-American music was just about nil.

What a difference twenty-five years makes! Back then I was concerned with emphasizing African roots that were then grossly underestimated. Now they tend, if anything, to be overstated, to the extent that it would be nice to see more work done in the countries that supplied the European side of the Afro-American equation, and on the European (particularly English and French) elements without which African-American music would no more have existed than it would without its Africanisms.

At the time it first came out, *Black Music of Two Worlds* didn't fit into the way any of its subject areas were considered, let alone taught. As a result I had the impression it had sunk rapidly and pretty much without trace, leaving behind only a few rueful anecdotes. I found out much later that the book's different way of looking at its subject was in fact influencing a number of students, some of whom were to become the new generation of scholars, who have taken aspects of my work far farther than any one person could attempt, proving me right in much of what I argued and wrong in some of it (more right than wrong, I'm happy to say).

A book of this scope is inevitably based to a very large extent on other people's work. So much so, in fact, that the conventional academic battery of footnotes and sources would end up looking like one of those eighteenth-century biblical commentaries with a trickle of text along the top of each page above several inches of elucidative pontificating. Where suitable I have credited other writers in the text, and recognized the help of many other people in the acknowledgments. Otherwise you may take it as a matter of course that pretty much everything in this book is based on a mix of the books and articles in the bibliography, recordings in the discography, conversations, interviews and correspondence with people thanked in the acknowledgments, my own research, and my distillation of all this raw material, for whatever these last two elements are worth. Only in a few areas (notably Latin influences on ragtime and jazz) has my own work been in territory still largely ignored by others. Yet with all the admirable detailed research that has been done in the last quarter-century, the overview that attempts to pull it all together is still largely missing. This edition, like the first one, attempts to remedy that situation.

Preface to the 1972 Edition

In any book covering a field as wide as this one, a good deal must be left out, and a good deal must be touched on very rapidly. Above all, boundaries have to be set. I have not dealt with the "white" styles of U.S. music containing very important black elements, whether folk music, country-and-western, or rock. These are essentially black-influenced white styles, just as many of the styles I have described in this book are white-influenced black styles. In an area such as this, any definition can have holes picked in it. I have therefore deliberately used terms such as "black" or "Afro-American" in a broad, sometimes vague, sense covering the Americas as a whole, and "African-American" to refer to U.S. citizens.

The concept of black music is an imprecise and changing one. To be more precise is to be too precise. Black music, in this book, is music created *mainly* by people who call themselves black, or music containing significant elements derived from Africa, whoever plays it. At times I have probably strayed beyond these definitions. But the importance of considering the Afro-American musical area as a whole in relation to both Africa and Europe is so great that it seems to me worth the risk of some inconsistencies and even apparent self-contradictions.

It is worth mentioning what this book is *not*. It is not a straightforward history of Afro-American music. Too much is unknown about the black music of South America and the Caribbean for a history to be written about it; and there are already many histories of black musical forms of the United States. In view of this, I have tackled the different regions rather differently: I have included rather less straight description of styles in the United States than other countries. The facts about black U.S. music are pretty well known, but the question of Africanisms is still a much-argued one. The opposite is true of South America and the Caribbean.

The Afro-American musical area is one with a common background—the encounter of African and European music. The early chapters of this book deal with aspects of this encounter seen as a single phenomenon with effects that resembled or differed from each other for regional reasons. By the late nineteenth and early twentieth centuries, however, its component areas had developed very differently in many respects. The second part, therefore, looks at the music of the various regions separately.

Folksinger Josh White is said to have remarked, when asked a question about folk music, "I ain't never heard no horse sing." Afro-American music includes folk music, urban popular music, and occasionally bubble-gum music. Too many books have been published condemning one or another style for reasons that boil down to the fact that the author has not liked them. I hope I have avoided this. On the other hand, criticism of individual pieces of music seems to me perfectly valid. I got involved in Afro-American and African music because I thought it marvelous—and I still do. If this has led me astray at any point, I can only quote Mary Frances, in Brumsic Brandon's cartoon strip *Luther:* "I got just as much right to be wrong as anybody else."

Errors of enthusiasm are one thing; errors of fact are another. If I have made many of the latter, I may perhaps comfort myself by remembering the obvious mistakes I have encountered in the works of famous authorities of all sorts. I hope the reader will therefore approach this modest effort in the same spirit as that shown by a Jamaican Revival Zion pastor who, interrupted once at length by a mentally afflicted member of his congregation, observed, "Wise people can learn from the words of foolish ones."

Acknowledgments

So many people have been so helpful in so many ways, both when I was writing the first draft and during the revisions for the second edition, that it seems wrong to select—but I owe a special debt of gratitude to the following:

Kenneth Bilby, Ph.D., for commentary, information, photographs and for the kind words in his preface to the second edition;

Mr. and Mrs. Eustace Brissett of Barton Court, Saint James Parish, Jamaica, for their warmth and hospitality;

Richard Carlin of Schirmer Books for commissioning the second edition and editing it with tact and insight, and to the (as always anonymous) publisher's reader who supplied significant comments and questions;

David Carp for extraordinary generosity with remarkable primary Latin research;

Tony Cox, who suggested and produced the BBC African Service series that was the germ of it all;

Walter Danylak of Tandy Service Department for going beyond the call of duty to rescue parts of this manuscript from a potentially disastrous harddrive crash;

Jim Farrington of Wesleyan University in particular, and many other music librarians in general;

Philip Harrington, photographer, for a great deal of technical help and general kindness;

Dr. Donald Hill of SUNY Oneonta for photos, information, and encouragement;

Michael Kieffer for the supply of many rare recordings and for discographical information;

David Lewiston, for more technical help and general encouragement;

Mrs. Stephanie Lloyd, Douglas, and Sandra, of Long Pond Estate, Jamaica, and Clem Lloyd of New York;

Alfred McLarty, who helped find singers and organize recordings in Maryland, Jamaica, as well as singing superbly himself;

Tomás Morel, of the Museo Folklórico Tomás Morel in Santiago de los Caballeros, Dominican Republic;

Jane Roberts for typing, editing, proofreading, and assisting in the research for the first edition, as well as for general exhortation;

Carey Robinson, of the Jamaica Broadcasting Corporation;

Dr. Manuel Rueda, Director of the Dominican Conservatory of Music, eminent folklorist, musician, poet, and dramatist;

Max Salazar of New York, whose unpublished study of Latin Jazz confirmed much of what I believed, and taught me more;

Dr. Aaron Segal, for introductions that proved very fruitful;

Richard Spottswood for discographical help and supplying a copy of an extremely rare jazz-biguine;

Bob Stack, for a great deal of help and for his loan of Latin records;

Mr. and Mrs. Bob Staples of Maryland, Jamaica, for warmth, hospitality, and help (as well as for employing, and introducing us to, Alfred McLarty);

His Excellency Dr. Adolph Thompson, Jamaican Ambassador to the Dominican Republic, and Mrs. Thompson, for their hospitality;

Bernard Vega, for putting us on the rightest of tracks in Santo Domingo;

Jeremy Verity of the BBC External Services, for sharing his Jamaican expertise and contacts;

The Walker family: Boysie and Jean in Philadelphia; Mas' Aaron, Mrs. Walker, and Valerie at Chatham, Saint James, Jamaica;

Mr. and Mrs. Tim Williams of Dover, Massachusetts, who came to the rescue so that we could do field research without our two children;

all the authors and experts quoted or cited in this book and many others not cited, who provided insights beyond their written work:

all those who lent me photographs, who are identified under the photos themselves;

all the people in many record companies, from whom it would be wrong to single out individuals; and

most of all, all those who ever made the music that this book is about.

Introduction: Africa, Europe, and Islam

The subject of this book is the meeting of three apparently very different musical traditions to create a fourth, and the development of this fourth tradition into a range of new styles of great richness and international impact. By the end of the book, we shall have explored all these musical traditions in varying detail. But first it is worth taking a look at some of the main differences and similarities among African, European, and Arabic musical styles.

It is important to get away from the idea—a slightly bizarre hangover from the old "Dark Continent" nonsense, added to a touch of Rousseau's "noble savage"—that African music was for centuries cut off from the rest of the world; that it existed in some limbo or cultural Garden of Eden, unsullied by outside influences, until the colonial era, when it was raped by outside forces; and that it has never been the same since. In fact, Africa has always been in contact with other parts of the world. An anonymous ancient Greek wrote around the tenth century B.C. about the East African coast in the *Periplus of the Erythrean Sea,* and ancient Greek musical instruments, have been found near Khartoum. Chinese plates of the thirteenth century have been dug up in Mombasa. North Africa was an area of myriad musical influences; it had heard Phoenician, Greek, Roman, and Byzantine music before falling to invaders who brought an Arabic music containing elements of Coptic, Syrian, Egyptian, and Persian music (and, some think, even Indian). North Africa was always linked to the sub-Saharan savanna by the trade caravans that constantly crossed the Sahara; the savanna civilizations had contact with those further south; and so on. Even groups in the interior of the heavily forested central region had contacts with their neighbors on either side, and thus a pipeline for cultural practices, particularly in the great period of the Kongo kingdom (corresponding to the European thirteenth to seventeenth centuries). And there was over the centuries a gradual migratory drift westward and southward: one (though only one) of the groups that make up the Abaluhya of western Kenya is pretty well established to have vestigial links with a clan in Cameroun.

There were also early links with Europe. When the Arabs invaded Spain (with a Moor at their head), they founded European Islamic kingdoms, the last of which was cast out seven hundred years later, in 1492, the year Columbus arrived in the New World. And there were always links between Muslim Spain and Muslim black Africa through North Africa. When the Arab dynasties in Spain were threatened, they called for help from the Almoravides, who came from the area that is now Niger. In fact, Islamic music, in its part-African Moorish form, is a highly important link between the musical worlds of Europe, West Africa, and parts of the New World. Moreover, Islam has been spreading in most parts of Africa (except the South) for a thousand years—it had a foothold on the East African coast barely two centuries after the official date of its founding—and with it the basic elements of Arab-derived music. Islam in fact was the first profound foreign influence on African music, and has so far had a far greater effect than the Western elements about which cultural purists fret.

Africa is a huge continent, measuring about 11,700,000 square miles (roughly four times the size of the United States). It has around 250 million indigenous inhabitants belonging to at least four major racial divisions and forming at least 2,000 tribal groups, speaking between 800 and 2,400 tongues, depending on one's definition of what is a language and what is only a dialect. Every one of these units has its own customs, including its own music. Still, there is a certain unity underlying this bewildering diversity of peoples. Tribes and languages belong to a smaller number of groups or families: about 600 fall within the Bantu language family of southern, East, and parts of Central Africa, for instance. And the larger regions of underlying similarity are reflected in the music, which can be divided into regional groupings in a number of ways.

The most obvious division is into East, West, Central, and southern Africa. But you can subdivide the major areas, so that in West Africa you have a wooded, coastal strip with one set of characteristics, and behind it the savanna lands with another (including a high degree of Muslim influence). Or you can differentiate those groups that sing in thirds from those which A. M. Jones calls the "fourth-fifth-octave peoples." Each of these regions, and even each tribe within each region, has its own musical styles, and ethnomusicologists—and anybody tired of the persistent Western treatment of a huge and enormously diverse continent as if it were a single unit—tend to stress the differences. But certain basic musical elements transcend local differences (and even the biggest difference of all, that between Muslim-influenced and older traditional idioms). And it is these that are most significant for the music of the New World.

Taking the continent as a whole, the single most important form of musical accompaniment is probably handclapping. Drums are found in most cultures, though their use varies a good deal in importance, and Africa has a wide range of other musical instruments, compared with most other musical cultures. But the human voice is nevertheless of overriding importance; call-and-response singing is by far the most common form of group vocal technique. African music is often built up by the use of relatively short musical phrases, often repeated, or of longer lines made up of phrases never repeated in just the same form. Rhythm and, more generally, a percussive approach are fundamental. And above all, music is a communal functional expression to a far greater degree than in most other parts of the world.

Traditional African music differs from European music in that it tends to be more directly tied to function. Up to a point, all music anywhere has a function: to accompany worship or courtship; to make work go better; or simply to give pleasure. Yet there is no doubt that in Africa it is more closely bound up with the details of daily living than in Europe. There is an immense amount of music for special purposes. All continents have lullabies for putting babies to sleep, of course, but in the Fon area of Dahomey (now Benin) there is a song children learn to sing on the loss of their first tooth. The Akin of Ghana have a song of derision aimed at habitual bed wetters sung at a special ritual designed to cure enuresis. Punishment for wrongdoing frequently has its own music: the Akin have special drums, played to accompany a petty thief while he is paraded through town with whatever he stole in his hands; and the Bagman of Cameroun have some eerie and impressive music to be played when a court official is taken to be hanged. Examples of the social use of music are endless, and they permeate the modern urban music of Africa as well as more traditional rural forms.

The way in which music interconnects with everyday life is underscored by an anecdote told by the Ghanaian musicologist Atta Annan Mensah. He tells of a middle-aged woman trader who had just returned from a long journey and was telling members of her family about it. "As she came to the more exciting part of her narration, she burst into song, and her audience . . . joined in with a refrain."

This very close connection between music and every aspect of life goes much deeper than the existence of songs for special purposes. The Camerounian writer Francis Bebey has pointed out that, because of it, some groups—he mentions the Douala of Cameroun, but the same holds true for the Swahili language—have no indigenous word for music. There are words for musical forms, like "song" or "tune," but the idea of "music" itself has never been abstracted from the things to which it belongs. "The musical art is so much a part of man himself that he has seen no purpose in giving it a separate name," as Bebey puts it. Moreover, the word for a major division of music is often also the name of an instrument. In Swahili, for instance, *ngoma* (the generic word for drum) tends to mean dance music in general. Music in general is *muziki,* taken from Europe.

Music is very closely involved in religious practice. Whereas it is not essential to Christian rituals—however much it may add to their impressiveness—many African ceremonies simply could not take place at all without the appropriate music. To give just one example, the spirits are summoned by the drums in both Yoruba and Dahomeyan ceremonial, each by its own special rhythms. No drums, no spirits—and no ritual.

An equally important aspect of African music is that it is only part of a greater artistic whole. Africans feel that they should make no distinction, for instance, between music and dance, that they should avoid the European habit of separating the two and talking as if one *accompanied* the other. For them, the sound of music is only one element in a total experience, which may include the sight of costumes, the sensation of dancing, and so on. The Ghanaian musicologist J. H. Kwabena Nketia says, "Music-making is an activity with a dramatic orientation." Performance attitudes, bodily movements, costumes, audience response, and so on are all a part of it.

Another deep-seated principle of African music is its relationship to speech. The word has been conceived as fundamentally powerful in many philosophies—not least to the ancient Greeks, and in Christianity, as the opening of the Gospel according to St. John makes clear. A Dogon legend tells that it was through the drum that God gave Man the gift of speech. Words are so powerful, even magical, that African songs tend to be oblique in reference and obscure in meaning, whereas European folk lyrics usually proceed in an orderly narrative fashion. It may seem paradoxical in a continent with such a variety of musical instruments, but virtually all African music is conceived vocally. In Uganda, for instance, there is a great body of xylophone music; every piece has its lyrics, which are known by the musicians even though they are never sung. The same is true of many other parts of Africa.

Twin talking drums in a Ghanaian orchestra. The master drummer is watching a distant dancer whose bodily movement his drumming is directing.
Photo: Ghana Information Services

   Many instruments in some way are used to imitate the human voice. The most famous of the "talking" instruments are the talking drums of many West and Central African tribes, which send messages by imitating the inflections of the speaking voice, but there are many others. The Jabo of Liberia have talking xylophones, whose players sit in the marketplace and keep up a barrage of musical comment on the scene around them. The Nigerian Ibo use flutes and a trumpetlike instrument in the same way. Jean-Baptiste Obama observes that "the principal and essential traits of African music, its melodic, harmonic and rhythmic characteristics, are all linked to the making of the essentially 'speaking' instrument." Moreover, this tradition sometimes moves into contemporary urban dance music. The American ethnomusicologist John Miller Chernoff cites a moment in a Ghanaian highlife recording in which bassist Jerry Hansen uses his instrument to make a quite explicit comment on a young woman dancing near the band. And according to John F. Carrington (cited by

Chernoff), listeners to a trumpet solo in a popular Congolese dance piece also interpreted it as "speaking."

Though music is so closely related to religious and social activity, Africans frequently sing to amuse each other or themselves, or to pass away a quiet hour. The essential fact is that music—communal or private—is interwoven with every part of African life. You might expect from this that every African is a musician. It is true that, growing up in a society where music—and rhythmic music at that—is so fundamental, most Africans display a considerable rhythmic sense. It is also true that in most African societies everybody takes part in certain sorts of music. But this does *not* mean that everybody or anybody can take over the lead drum in a major social dance, or any of the drums, for that matter. As Chernoff—who has learned to play in several Ghanaian traditions—brings out in his book *African Rhythm and African Sensibility*, West African master drummers are highly skilled musicians who take years to learn their art.

On the other hand, in most places the audience does not simply stand around and admire the "professionals." The music envisages roles for both skilled and unskilled musicians. The skilled musicians may drum and lead the singing, while the other participants sing choral parts and add to the general rhythmic effect by handclapping, dancing, and so on. Moreover, the "basic" underlying pulse of complex drummed pieces may be supplied not by the musicians, who are "playing around" it, but by the dancers.

Besides these semiprofessional musicians—whose musical skill determines their place in community functions—some African societies have fully professional musicians. This is especially true of Muslim groups and others influenced by them, and in general peoples with a chiefly system of government and an established court. Generally called *griots* (a name given to them during the seventeenth century by French explorers, mimicking several local names for hereditary bards), they provide music for various occasions. Some are employed at princely courts; others specialize in work music and praise music, often associated with a guild. The Hausa of northern Nigeria, for example, have *griots* who sing nothing but songs praising the products of certain butchers. There are *griots* who provide music to lighten the farmers' work and others who travel around to meet an indispensable need at weddings and other ceremonies. Importantly, the *griots* are guardians of the tribe's history, which they often chant or sing in epics somewhat similar to the medieval European *chansons de geste*, and are often the exponents of major instrumental traditions, like the West African harp-lute, the *kora*.

The very close relationship between music and social religious life has had a number of effects on the music itself. The concept of music as a purely

Gambian *kora* player Jali Nyama Suso, a virtuoso of a Sahelian string tradition that, according to Paul Oliver, fed early into styles that were to contribute to the formation of the blues.
Photo by Roderic Knight

aesthetic experience is foreign to much of traditional Africa. Africans get plea-sure from their music, but the aesthetic element—the whole purpose of a Brahms symphony—is for them a by-product. Africans and Europeans judge music differently. In Africa, music is not so much "good" as "effective," that is, right for its purpose. Thus Bebey says of singing: "African voices are . . . what the total nature of the music demands of them: clear to sing of the bride newly brought into the community, hushed to sing of something which one would have preferred to keep quiet, mocking in satire . . . harsh or soft, piercing or tender depending on the time and the place." A "beautiful voice" in the European sense is an accident, not the main point.

The aim, in Bebey's words, is not to make agreeable sounds but to "live the actions of everyday life by means of sound." Singing, moreover, is everybody's art in a way that can never be true of musical instruments, which demand some technical ability. Anybody is a potential singer; a "fine voice" does not count, because the criteria for choosing a singer are social, not musical. The singer may be the priest, or he may be the oldest man in the age group.

The wide range of vocal tone in African music has partly to do with use and is partly regional or ethnic. In Ghana, the Akin use an "open" voice quality, whereas the Frafra like a more intense tone, probably of Islamic and thus ultimately Middle Eastern origin. The effect of Islamic influence is particularly obvious in the singing of the Yoruba of southwestern Nigeria, whose traditional vocal sound is open-throated and undecorated but who use tight, high tones in Muslim-associated styles like *apala* and the women's *waka* music. Other groups prefer a near- or true falsetto. Instrumental tone, for some reason, is less varied. There is a definite liking for a buzz tone, shown, for example, in the attachment of little bits of metal to the prongs of the hand-piano (also called the thumb or finger-piano; another name for the *lamella-phone*) to give a slight rattling quality. (This deliberate choice of "dirty" tones is significant in the consideration of New World black music.) Bebey associates the search for unusual, burred, "dirty" tone in both vocal and instrumental music with a desire to bring music as close as possible to natural sound, while creating musical instruments that will supply melody and percussion at the same time. (As with everything else about African music, it's important to remember that they don't apply universally. The *kora* has a notably "clean" sound, and of two East African finger-pianos that I own, one has buzzing devices and the other has a singularly sweet and—in the European sense— "pure" tone.)

The similarities in African music extend to form as well as use and practice. The stresses of the sung melody are generally placed between the main beats of the percussion rhythm, though sometimes the melody has a quite different rhythm from its accompaniment, in line with the African liking for cross-rhythms, rhythmic interplay, and the use of differing meters at one time, what is called polymeter. Except in areas of Islamic influence, melodic lines on the whole are rather short, particularly for instruments like xylophones (and drums, for that matter) which often build their music out of the repetition of short melodic–rhythmic (melorhythmic) patterns, blending and contrasting

Part of a Chopi village xylophone orchestra in Mozambique. The origin of the xylophone is uncertain, but it traveled to the New World with slave ships, as did the name it bore, and still bears, in many Bantu languages, marimba.

Photo by Hugh Tracey

with each other, and perhaps with a more complex, improvised primary (lead) instrument or singer.

By far the most common form of group singing in most parts of Africa is the call-and-response style, in which a lead singer sings a line, or a phrase, and a group answers it. This is quite different from the common European form of a verse of several lines followed (or not) by a chorus. For one thing, the European verse is complete in itself, while the African call by itself is only half of the equation; it needs the response before it is complete. Moreover, though the lead singer is very important and has a good deal of freedom to improvise, in many areas it is the chorus's response that is considered the essential part of the tune. Historically, the call-and-response technique overrode many other differences. Muslim groups tended to adopt longer melody lines with Middle-East-derived melismas (ornaments fitting several notes to one syllable), but the same call-and-response form was often adapted. It also evolved into an overlapping form, particularly among groups that used a longer melody line, where the chorus would chime in before the end of the solo line, creating a remarkable wavelike effect.

Though call-and-response singing was more common in Europe at one time than it is now (some scholars see it as linked to tribal and communal ways of living), by the time African and European music met in the New World it had survived in European usage only in a few forms, such as church litanies and ballad refrains. European folk music's most typical feature, the division into regular "verses," came from the equally typical tendency of European poetry to be divided into regular groups of lines, most often two, four, or eight. The musical form tended to follow the poetic divisions, so that most songs—unlike songs on a call-and-response pattern—were series of neat packages of four, six, eight, or twelve lines, separated by pauses or joined by a bit of instrumental filling-in. This important link between European verse and music was maintained down to quite small details like connections between musical and verbal stress, and between length of syllable and length of musical note. Take the accentuation of these lines from a British border ballad:

> Oh whát's the blóod that's ón your swórd, my són Dávid,
> Oh són Dávid?
> Whát's the blóod that's ón your swórd,
> Oh són now téll me trué?

Different singers may place the stress differently in some particulars, but it will never cut right across the verbal stress. That is to say, the words strongly affect the music, which is by no means the case in much of Africa. As a fairly

obvious example, Western newcomers to African urban music are disconcerted to find definitely gloomy themes sung to the jauntiest of melodies.

Despite the non-African's conception of African music being dominated
by drums, the African instruments most often used by the greatest number of
people in the greatest variety of societies are the human voice and the human
hands, used for clapping. Drums are essential to the music of some groups,
especially in West and western Central Africa. They are highly important in
many others. But some groups never use drums, and many use them only
moderately. Besides drums, Africa has stringed instruments, wind instruments, rattles, gongs, xylophones—in fact, examples of almost every kind of
instrument known. Some instruments are very simple: a collection of stones
that give musical notes, a xylophone made of a few logs laid across the knees.
Many others are highly sophisticated. But, crude or intricate, they are always
beautifully adapted to their purpose.

Though Africa is far more than a land of drums, there *is* something behind
the general idea that African music is "percussive." But what is percussive is
not just a dominant group of instruments. Alan Merriam stresses this:

> It seems to be the totality of the musical concept which sees
> rhythm and percussive effect as the deep, basic organizational princi-
> ple underlying African music. Drums and drumming, the use of idio-
> phones, the forceful and dynamic vocal attack, and other
> characteristics reflect this principle; it is African music which is essen-
> tially rhythmic and percussive in effect, and the devices used simply
> reflect the principle.

Perhaps the most important formal element of rhythm in African music is that
instead of having a single meter, either duple (two or four beats) or triple
(three or six*), a performance puts two or more different meters together
(polyrhythm), as if one drummer were playing in waltz time and another in
march time simultaneously, for example. Rhythm is also based on contrasting
recurrent beats with irregular patterns.

Rhythm as a musical fundamental cannot be overemphasized. Its use is
highly sophisticated and far from the old "savage drumming" stereotype.
Meaningful sounds are the basis of African music, as they are of any other
music, but there seems to be value not only in the sounds themselves but also,
to use musicologist Nketia's words, "in their arrangement in orderly sequences
or patterns of rhythm." In traditional music, at least in the "drumming tribes"

---

* One version of the latter rhythm, written as 6/8 in European scores, is technically duple. But in nonart
and non-Western music, its effect is usually triple.

of West Africa such as the Yoruba and the Ewe, rhythm is basic to enjoyment. Pieces with almost no "tune" in a Western sense are enjoyed if there is sufficient rhythmic interest. As A. M. Jones put it in an article in *Africa* magazine, "Rhythm is to the African what harmony is to the European, and it is in the complex interweaving of contrasting rhythmic patterns that he finds his greatest aesthetic satisfaction."

This rhythmic emphasis led in the past to the cliché that African music is long on rhythm and short on melodic variety and harmony. Like any cliché, this is not totally untrue, but it's not very helpful either, because it assumes European attitudes as a norm. The African approach to melody differs from the European, but only a rash or ignorant person would argue that it is more limited. As for harmony, that is a question of definitions. Certainly there is nothing anywhere in the world to compare with the extraordinary richness of European classical harmony. But classical music aside, European music isn't really all that harmonically rich, especially if you restrict yourself to northwest Europe and ignore the very large part of the continent whose music shares with Africa a strong Islamic element—not just Spain and Portugal, but the Balkans. Even most written popular music keeps its harmonies pretty simple. In fact, sounding more than one note at a time in choral singing is certainly no less widespread in African music than in European folk music taken as a whole. In fact, choral singing is arguably *less* common in European folk music—certainly in music from the areas that were to affect the New World—than in African music.

With exceptions, African choirs generally sing by using parallel melodic lines a third, a fourth, a fifth, or an octave above or below the "basic" tune. But the whole concept of thirds, fifths, and so on is European. It is useful for description, but it has nothing to do with the way Africans themselves conceive of what they are doing when they sing—nor indeed with the way most Europeans think of it. This kind of musical analysis is strictly a conservatory-derived phenomenon. While it is useful, it has to be handled gingerly when dealing with any music that is not "art-music" in the Western sense.

Harmony, in the sense of a theoretical progression of chords with a formal relationship basic to the structure of a piece of music, is not known in Africa. But the supposed complexity of European harmony is overstated. Outside of classical and classically derived music (and even here the complexity was a nineteenth-century creation), the basic chord progressions are mostly fairly simple.

The African approach to singing includes the use of a large number of ornamental devices, of which two of the most common are the slide up to the first note of a phrase, and the slide down off the last note. Notes are often "bent," and some songs are almost shouted rather than sung. Singing techniques vary from tribe to tribe, and the use of decoration in singing is connected with Arab-Berber influences in Islamic Africa. For the moment it is necessary to remember only that singing techniques are highly flexible and varied.

This is in sharp contrast to Europe, where—apart from conservatory standards of tonal purity—different regions have tended to adopt a single type of vocal tone and stick to it. Alan Lomax has divided singing styles in Europe into "Old European," "Modern European," and "Eurasian." The "Eurasian" style, high-pitched, strident, and harsh, is typical of Spain and Portugal and is suited to long, ornamented styles; it is probably an Arabism. Though a similar sound is also found in parts of France and the British Isles, notably in Celtic music, there is a plausible theory that it is the remnants of an "educated" medieval performance style brought back from Palestine by the Crusaders.

The other style relevant to our concerns is the "Modern European" found in most of France and England, the area of ballads and lyrical love songs. It tends to be associated with solo or unison singing; is harsh, strained, and usually less emotional than the "Eurasian" type; and shows a greater interest in the words than in the music.

North African Islamic music differs from the music of the Middle East, itself very varied in a number of ways, some of which (especially a greater emphasis on rhythm instruments) may be the result of influence from black Africa. Because it influenced both Iberian music and much of the music of West and East Africa—partly through trade and neighborly contacts of various sorts, but mainly through the spread of Islam—it is important to the development of New World black music. The Muslim call to prayer is heard five times a day, seven days a week, wherever Islam is practiced. It has been heard for hundreds of years in many parts of Africa. Although relatively simple, its lengthy, highly decorated, very characteristic Arabic melodic approach found its way into much African music. This melodic element was perhaps the most fundamental influence of Arabic music on African. There are others similarities between North African and black African music, such as a liking for percussion and syncopation, which made mutual influence easy. There has always been much travel between Arab and black Muslim areas. In the Middle Ages, Timbuktu (in present-day Mali) was a great university city, and there was as much moving about within the Arab Muslim world as there was in medieval Europe. But it is important to realize that African Islamic music, wherever it came from, is finally just that: *African.* One of the remarkable things about it is that the styles of every Muslim African country are, once you get familiar with them, so very different from each other, even though they

The three-way traffic of African, Arab, and South European music has been a hidden factor in the New World also. Versions of the big frame drums played by these Moroccan women show up in Brazil and Puerto Rico, perhaps via Spain.
Photo courtesy of United Nations

share the same theoretical elements (an indication of the limitations of theory). There is no mistaking Somali music for coastal Kenyan or for Sudanese, even though all three countries border on each other, and the same is true of every other African country.

There has tended to be argument—with an undertone of cultural and racial politics—about the extent to which Spanish music has been influenced by the eight centuries of Islamic rule. There seems to be little doubt, however, that in southern Spain the influence of Islam was immense. For eight hundred years Spain was culturally as well as spiritually divided in two: the so-called Mozarabic kingdoms, of which Seville was the musical capital, and the Christian area centered in Zaragoza. As a result, while some Spanish music, particularly northern, is closely tied to France and Europe in general, the music of southern Spain is still more or less heavily Arab. Some of the Arab characteristics of southern Spanish music include a rhythmic approach that is quite different from northern Europe, a liking for recitative singing without obvious metric structure and with a great deal of ornament; a harsh, nasal singing tone; and a number of individual elements like the highly decorated syllable with which a singer may introduce a song (usually "ay-y-y-y-y" in Spain and "ah-ah-h-h-ah" in Arab music). Incidentally, a Moorish "double-reed" called the *rheita* is found among the Spaniards (where it is called a *gaita*) and the West Africans (the Hausa call it *algaita*).

The picture is complicated by the fact that Spanish-Moorish music developed into a high form of its own during the eight centuries of Islam in Iberia, in part under Jewish and Gypsy (and thus ultimately Indian) influence. It was taken back to North Africa when the Spanish Moors left Europe, where it proceeded to influence Moorish music and thus probably Islamic black African music (and still exists under the name of "Maghrebi-Andalus" music). The Moorish element is also present in Portugal, colonizer of Brazil, although to a lesser degree. And to complicate matters further, there seem to be traces of pre-Islamic North African Berber music in some Mediterranean countries, including southern Portugal and Sardinia. Thus North Africa, parts of West Africa, and important parts of Spain and Portugal share certain common cultural traits, even though they have gone their own ways for five centuries. (In case you think that the Arab influence in Spain would have died out over such a long span of time, remember that songs written by Provençal troubadours eight hundred years ago are still sung by Catalonian peasants.)

If we cannot trace exact Arabic survivals in Spain, this is partly because Arab music was never written down, so we could never find an original score with which to compare modern southern Spanish music. Moreover, Spain, after having spent eight hundred years in the Arab world, has spent five hundred in the European, so changes are bound to have occurred. Besides, musical evidence is not necessarily the best evidence of musical survival. We know enough from working on African and other non-European music to be highly suspicious of printed transcriptions. So much of the essence of all folk music gets left out in the writing. Better evidence of Arab influence in Spain lies in written accounts of the popularity of Moorish traveling singers and dancers or of the fisherman who at the siege of Calatanazor sang a complaint consisting of alternate Arabic and Spanish verses. Countless surviving accounts show a degree of social interpenetration so great that it is inconceivable that musical interpenetrations should *not* have taken place. And indeed earlier Spanish attempts to argue otherwise were clearly part of an attempt to cling to European culture. (The formal Spanish *Usted*—"You"—seems very clearly derived from the Arabic honorific "Ustad"; the old theory that it is an elision of *Vuestra Merced*—"Your Grace"—appears to be simply Eurocentric denial.) Now that Spain is rediscovering its Arabic elements, my guess is that the complex roots of its music will also be honored.

The debt of the whole of European music to Arabic influence is far greater than we usually realize. The surprisingly large range of musical instruments introduced from the Islamic world includes the guitar, the fiddle, and drums of all sorts. One clear link between North Africa and the Iberian Peninsula lies in rhythm. In northern Europe, especially Britain and France, rhythm has tended toward relative simplification. Much of its folk music has gravitated toward common meters such as 4/4, 2/4, 6/8, and 3/4, whereas many British and some French ballads once used "free" rhythms that changed every bar or two. But except for the old "free-meter" ballads, most northern European folk music tends to have a basic beat and to stick to it; any syncopation takes a simple form, in which the melody places a weak beat against a strong beat of the underlying rhythm (as is quite common in Scots music). This is usually a passing effect, and it does not affect the underlying pulse. The relative rhythmic simplicity is also true of northwestern European dance music, in sharp contrast to Spanish and Portuguese dance music, which goes in for very complex rhythms (if not cross-rhythms like African music) and for the use of a number of different meters in succession, especially 3/4 and 6/8 (which are closely related in practice, even though European music theory describes one as a triple meter and the other as duple).

Another area of relative similarity between African and European music is the use of scales. European folk music uses a wide variety of scales, and even preserves the older modes, which—to put it crudely—had different notes going up than coming down, and whose melodies often ended on a note that a scalar approach wouldn't admit. A tune starting with a C, for example, might close on a D, one tone up. The "academic" scales of seven basic notes (so-called diatonic scales) are by no means the only possibilities open to the musician. You can perfectly well have a song in a scale of only one note, and it needn't even be particularly dull. Melody is only part of what makes a song attractive. Rhythm and elements in the way it's presented—like vocal tone—are also important. Similarly, you can have songs using much smaller intervals than a semitone, the smallest note used in academic music. Much Eastern music, for example, uses "microtones" far smaller even than a "quarter-tone," and a more-or-less even scale of these microtones would have far more than seven notes. Many European scales are what is called "pentatonic," having five basic notes; others have six, yet others seven. On the whole it is the older songs that used "gapped" scales—scales with fewer notes than the diatonic scale.

Although there was once much argument about the "African scale," it is pretty much universally accepted that, in the words of the American musicologist Alan Merriam, it is "essentially a natural diatonic. At the same time, no brief is held for a universal African scale, for it is clear that intervals and their arrangement vary from culture to culture." Neither European nor African music makes much formalized or regularized use of microtones, though neither Africans nor European folksingers necessarily use notes that are at

Carnival costumes in Luanda, Angola, show similarities with festival costumes widespread in the New World—an example of a largely European contribution to the meeting of cultures on both continents.
Courtesy of Centro de Informaçao e Turismo de Angola

European "concert pitch." Moreover, different cultures, even different singers, will make the gap between two semitones fractionally larger or smaller—notably the third and seventh notes, the famous "blue notes" of African-American music, which also tend to be flattened slightly by English as well as African traditional singers!

Scales built from notes at European concert pitch are not the only scales possible, and "out of tune" has meaning only within a particular musical culture. A South African, John Ngcobo, once said on a BBC radio program: "When I first heard the Western scale . . . I thought it was terrible—quite out of pitch. And you can see small African schoolchildren today looking really hurt when they have to sing sharps and flats." But it should be clear by now that, though Europeans and Africans find each other's music strange at first, their musical cultures are far closer together than either is to Chinese or even Indian music. And the similarities as well as the differences are important in the story of what happened when African and European music met in the New World.

Traditions Preserved
Neo-African Music

As LeRoi Jones remarked in *Blues People* back in the 1970s, "Undoubtedly, none of the African prisoners broke out into 'St. James's Infirmary' the minute the first of them was herded off the ship"—which is not surprising, because the title and many of the lyrics originated in Ireland! In fact, it took many years of mutual influence between the descendants of the African slaves and the descendants of the European pioneers whom they met in the New World for what we understand as "Afro-American" music in all its richness to develop; in fact, the process is still going on today.

There are really two sorts of Afro-American music, although they overlap with one another. The first is the subject of this chapter, the "neo-African" music whose elements are still totally or very largely African. The origins of this music are fairly easy to establish by comparison with present-day Africa or, at times, because its practitioners themselves still remember where it came from. The second sort, though it was developed either completely or largely by Afro-Americans and though it really forms a continuum with neo-African music, consists of various blends of European and African ingredients, all of which have been molded into a new and original music. The African origins of this music are more difficult to pinpoint, because even when we can still isolate African strands they are so changed as to have become broadly "African" rather than narrowly Yoruba, Ashanti, Congo-Angolan, or whatever. We then have to try to find out what parts of Africa the slaves in a particular area came from.

The great majority of slaves were from three main cultural regions: (1) the coastal rainforest area of West Africa, which includes the Yoruba, Ewe,

Ashanti, Fon, Ibo, and other major Nigerian, Dahomeyan, and Ghanaian tribes; (2) the savanna belt, which lies from the coast at Guinea across and to the north of the Sudanese rainforest area and includes such largely Muslim groups as the Wolof of the former Senegambia, the Malinke of Guinea, the Hausa and Fulani of northern Nigeria and its surroundings, and the Mandingo, who cover a wide area including Senegambia and what is now Sierra Leone; and (3) the Congo-Angolan area, populated largely by people of another language and culture group, the Bantu.

These groups were brought in different proportions to different parts of the Americas at different times, partly reflecting political upheavals in Africa itself. For instance, in the mid-sixteenth century the old Jolof empire was in the process of breaking up violently. As a result, a large number of Wolof were to be found in sixteenth-century America, though they were never again to form a significant part of the slave trade. During the nineteenth century, there was a great increase in the number of Yoruba enslaved because of the Yoruba wars, which lasted for much of the century, and for the first time a fairly large number of Hausa caught in the local civil wars ended up in the New World.

African politics was not the only explanation for the ethnic makeup of the slave population. Different slaving powers had a greater presence in some parts of Africa than in others, even before the main colonial era. The Portuguese were politically active in parts of Congo-Angola from the six-teenth century on, for instance, and the British were powerful along the Gold Coast and the Bights of Benin and Biafra. So more Bantu were taken to Brazil and the Spanish areas, whereas British possessions in the West Indies and North America had many Fanti and Ashanti from what is now Ghana. In the sixteenth century, England drew more than 70 percent of its slaves from the Gold Coast while Spain drew only 9 percent. These factors partly explain why black music in different parts of the New World shows influences from different African regions. Besides the people brought directly from Africa, many slaves were taken first to one area, then eventually moved to another, which certainly had a significance in the development of the blended cultures of the New World. And though the overwhelming majority of Africans were brought to the New World as slaves, not all were: some 9,000 Yoruba traveled to Trinidad in the 1850s as indentured labor.

Another fairly important element in the way music developed in different countries had to do with the local economies, even in neighboring countries colonized by the same European power. Peter Manuel, in *Caribbean Currents*, observes that the differences between Puerto Rican and Cuban music stemmed partly from the fact that Puerto Rico grew tobacco and coffee rather than sugar and therefore needed less slave labor, so there were proportionally fewer Africans in Puerto Rico. At one extreme, the Cayman Islands had no plantations, so pretty much all the slaves were domestic servants. Attempts to establish a direct link of this kind may be complicated further: Not only were the British Virgin Islands a plantation economy, but a rebellion on Tortola shortly after Emancipation caused all the whites to leave. Tortola was therefore essentially an entirely African-American island for much of the nineteenth century. Yet the music of both the Caymans and Tortola contains no local neo-African forms, and Tortola in particular preserves a wealth of British ballads.

A third factor ties the United States to the anglophone and francophone West Indies in a way that History 101 teaches us, but whose musical significance we sometimes miss. Until 1776, what were to become the original thirteen states were British, and so were many Caribbean islands. Certain big landowners operated estates in both Virginia and the West Indies, and various accounts make it clear that slaves (particularly domestic servants) might travel back and forth with the families they served. And what was true for British America was even truer for the French West Indies and the large part of the future United States involved in the Louisiana Purchase (1803) which, we also tend to forget, covered an area much larger than the current Louisiana and joined the United States later than the English-speaking east. There were in fact close links between the south-central United States—Louisiana itself, but also Missouri and elsewhere—and Haiti (until it freed itself) and Martinique, Guadeloupe, and the smaller islands that were French at the time. The cultural ties between the West Indies and the continental United States, in other words, were extremely close for a third or more of the history of European settlement—and a crucial third at that.

Myths about the slaves totally losing their culture on arrival in the New World have been pretty well exploded. What is not always realized is that—as the musicologist Dena Epstein points out—slaving ships at times collected and brought with them African instruments to accompany the forced dancing onboard ship. And planters in both the West Indies and the United States appear actively to have encouraged music-making among new arrivals on the equally practical basis that people in deep depression don't work very well in any conditions, and that familiar music—and the company of earlier arrivals from the same group—helped newcomers to adjust. This kind of practicality, along with the permitting or even encouraging of dancing and other recreation, may have been purely self-interested. But it explains better than the notion of consistent cultural repression how African music survived for at least the first generation and then transmuted first into neo-African and then "creolized" or Afro-American idioms.

In the very early days, as far as can be established, the various African ethnic groups maintained their music fairly separate to the extent that they could. Blending took place mainly during the nineteenth century. The Brazilian folklorist Oneyda Alvarenga says that "only at the end of the nineteenth century did authentic Brazilian music begin to emerge." Nowhere else did the various elements ever produce a uniform "national" music, least of all in the United States. Meanwhile, differing African tribal musics blended in the New World to form neo-African musics that were almost entirely African-derived, and yet non-African, for they were not to be heard in Africa.

What African music did survive in the Americas, either in a pure form or in new amalgams? Perhaps the easiest survivals to recognize are the large numbers of musical instruments of African origin still found in the New World. Drums of various kinds play an important part in neo-African music, and many display African characteristics. "Peg drums" use an African method for attaching the skins to the body of the drum and for tuning, a system of pegs that stick out from the sides of the drum near the head to which cords from the drumhead are attached. The pegs are hammered in to tighten the drumhead.

I do not believe it is a coincidence that the drums in so much of the black music of the Caribbean and South America come in sets of two or of three, given that two or three is also the most common number for the "core group" of drums in most West African styles, including those of the Yoruba and the Ewe. In the "round drum" music of the coastal Barlovento region of Venezuela, three drums are used, the *pujao, cruzado,* and *corrido.* In the "big drum" dances of the same area, two are used, the *mina* and the *curveta* (or *curbata*). All these are single-headed drums, tall, usually held between the musician's legs. The *curveta* stands upright on three feet carved of one piece with the body, like some drums from the Congo.

Playing styles show strong African traits, too, including the use of a small stick in one hand while the drumhead is muted with the other hand, or with the drummer's heel if he is sitting on his instrument, to give a wider range of notes. Another, even more striking Africanism is to have a second man beat a counter-rhythm on the side of the drum with a pair of small sticks. A *tambo* drummer whom I interviewed and recorded in the Jamaican village of Wakefield, Trelawney Parish, told me categorically that his music came from his Congolese grandmother. While the details of his family tradition had obviously become garbled, his style of drumming and singing seemed to contain definite Bantu elements, besides more generalized Africanisms such as muting his drum with his heel. His son used a pair of *cata 'ticks* to beat out a second rhythm on the *tambo.*

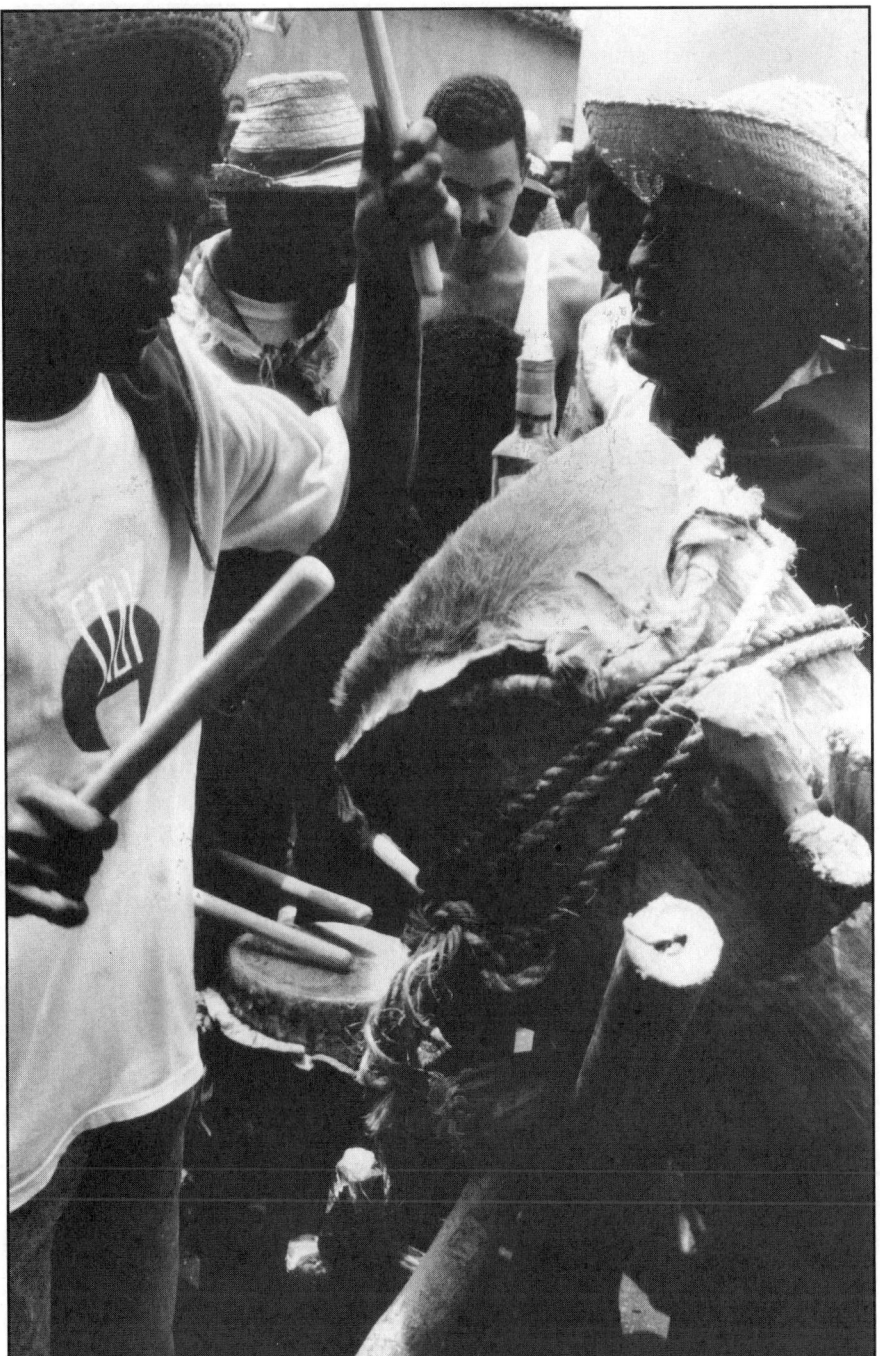

The big Afro-Venezuelan tambor mina and its smaller partner the *culo 'e puya* or *curbata* are typical of New World drums still built and played very much as their predecessors were in West Africa.

Photo by Lise Waxer

Tambo drumming in Jamaica: The drummer mutes his drum with his heel—a technique that originated in Africa—while his son beats out a second rhythm on the side of the drum.
Photo by John Storm Roberts

Sticks called *catá* are used to beat the side of the *bonko* drum in the Cuban Abakwá rhythm. In the most famous of Afro-Cuban styles, the street-rumba, *palitos* ("little sticks") are used to tap a counter-rhythm on the side of one of the two conga drums. The *bomba* dance of Puerto Rico uses two drums, the *burlador* and the *requinto*. A second man squats in front of the *burlador* and plays on its side with sticks; the same method is used by Congoloese drummers. Moreover, if you spell the Cuban and Jamaican names for these sticks with a "k" instead of a "c" they take on a remarkably Bantu look. If anybody has tracked the *cata 'ticks* to their original tongue I haven't heard of it, but in Bantu languages as far apart as Swahili and Lingala, *kata* is a verb root meaning "to cut," including secondary senses of cutting across or against something (as in the Swahili *kata maji*, "go against the current"). Indeed, cutting across the main rhythm is exactly the function of the *cata 'ticks* and their Cuban equivalent.

African-derived drums and their music are in fact extremely widespread in the Caribbean. The *gwo ka* (big drum) of Guadeloupe is not only a roots voices-and-percussion style, but the main percussion instrument involved. Its Martinican analog, the *ka* or *tanbo belé* (*belé* drum) is a crucial part of Martinican *belé*, a dance (or at least a name) found pretty much everywhere that Caribbean French creole is spoken, including Trinidad, where it is called *belair*. Nor are all the African-derived percussion instruments in existence today headed drums (membranophones): a type of log- or slit-drum (a log hollowed out to provide a resonator when beaten) is still in use in the form of the *ti-bois* ("little wood") of Martinique. Interestingly, slit-drums and the various forms of maraca-style shakers—unlike those with a lattice of beads loosely woven on the outside like the Cuban *chekeré*—were described by early travelers as being the basic instrumentation used in Amerindian religious ceremonies. Slit-drums are fairly common in Africa, and rattles of various sorts even more so. So their New World versions may very well represent a multicultural survival.

Besides these major styles, Trinidad has had various forms that are less well known (as well as dances, like the limbo, that have had moments of fame) but often nearer to an African tradition. Some are directly associated with African sources. The *congo* is a *patois* song and dance form with a three-drum accompaniment, *chantwell* (solo singer), and chorus. It is used by people of Congolese descent for weddings and baptisms. Similar is the *yarraba*, a dance music for people of Yoruba descent using three or four drums, *claves* (sticks), *chac-chac* (West African rattles), *chantwell*, and chorus. Trinidad also has Yoruba-derived, Shango Rada cult music, which is more important in Haiti. The Rada cult hymns use three drums, sticks, an iron (like the West African gong), *chac-chac*, *chantwell*, and chorus.

The already-mentioned *belé* (*belaire*) dance, found in Tobago, Grenada, and Carriacou as well as Trinidad and Martinique, is a partly religious (or magical) and partly social form. In Tobago it can be both, and so too in Grenada, where it is connected with ancestor ceremonies and can also be a vehicle for songs of derision. All forms use drums and other percussion and call-and-response singing. In Martinique, where it is the major traditional form, it comes in three rhythms: *biguine-belair, grand belair,* and *bélia.* A style maintained by the traditional musician Ti-Raoul Grivalliers and revivalists (of whom the late Eugène Mona was one of the most important), the *belair* includes the *calenda* also found in Trinidad and Cajun Louisiana—which seems to have preserved it from the days before the Louisiana Purchase (when it was often mentioned as a slave dance)—and a war dance called the *ladja.* Like so many other neo-African forms, the *belair's* lyrics include a great deal of social commentary as well as proverbial wisdom and plain common sense.

The importance of the wake for the dead is as great in Trinidad and the neighboring islands as elsewhere in black America. There are a number of musical forms associated with it; many are creolized, but some are non-African in form or spirit. For example, Trinidad and Tobago have the *bongo,* a mostly sung style often of social commentary, which in Tobago at least has the function of placating the spirits. "Sings," which punctuate storytelling, are found on all four islands and are basically a way of passing the time at wakes. "Pass play" songs have the same use and are also sung by children.

Given its unusual history and long independence, it is not surprising that Haiti has kept the most Africanisms in its music of almost any Caribbean island. Not only is it rich in neo-African forms, but much of the Afro-American music of Haiti has a higher degree of Africanism than occurs elsewhere. Haitian secular music includes all the folk forms found in the other countries: work songs, play songs, story songs, songs of protest and ridicule, political songs, and secret society music. All of it springs from a principally or entirely African tradition. Besides folk music, Haiti has a number of Carnival and dance styles, the best known being the *méringue* (*mereng* in creole).

Work songs of the New World often preserve a large degree of Africanism, and Haitian work songs are no exception. They are frequently associated with the *combite,* a communal field work party similar to those common in some parts of Africa and in other parts of the Caribbean. Whether the *combite* is a direct survival from Africa or developed because of Haitian conditions is sometimes argued; as with most New World Africanisms, the question is beside the point. For people faced with the suitable conditions to develop a communal approach to harvesting and other large farming jobs is natural. But for people descended from Africans to organize a work pattern that is also something of a picnic—with a band and a vocalist to spur on the farmers and jeer at the idle, and a hierarchy of officers to perform various well-defined functions, from planning the work to hushing chatterers—and to do so quite independent of the fact that their ancestors took a similar highly individual approach to organizing work, is less likely. It is much more plausible that elements of traditions and attitudes were handed down among a people very conscious of tradition and revived when it seemed useful to do so.

Anyway, the work songs are there, and there is also work music, not identical to that played by Hausa *griots* to encourage their local farmers, but having the same function and some of the same ingredients. Besides, many work songs are more directly functional in that they regulated the actual flow of activity. (Incidentally, the Haitian workers sometimes use a falsetto voice in a way widely popular in Africa and America.)

Songs of social criticism are widespread in Haitian folk music. Some make use of a proverb, like "Zamis Loin Moin," which suggests that friends nearby are a two-edged knife. A considerable degree of indirection and allusion is common. Reflections about a Haitian President named Alexis Nord are put by the singer into the mouth of his wife, Cece, who praises him for nongovernmental virtues:

> Cece said Alexis Nord is a fine man all over! [three times]
> Cece said he will quit whenever he sees fit.
> Cece said Uncle Nord is a fine man all over.

The indirect, multilevel praise-with-humor song is far from European tradition.

Another very important Africanism common to Haiti and all other Afro-American areas (including the inner cities of the United States) is the necessity of a good, indeed a splendid, funeral, and the holding of a social wake as part of a long series of death rituals. In Haiti as elsewhere, wakes mix religious and secular elements and are an occasion for games, storytelling, and songs. Many of the traditional tales told at Haitian country funerals contain songs, like the Jamaican Anancy stories and their African prototypes. Many of the play songs come from these story cycles, and they become even more allusive when taken out of that context.

Carnival music is as much a part of Haitian life as it is of Brazilian or Trinidadian, though the scale of festivities is more modest. Carnival street dances include the *rara* and the *mascaron*. The *rara* is associated with the descendants of the single-note trumpets of Africa, called *vaccines* in Haiti. The music, a gay and highly skilled hooting, is underlined by the tapping of sticks on the sides of the bamboo *vaccine* trumpets (a variation on the African-derived tendency to use an instrument for two purposes at once). *Vaccine* orchestras of three or four instruments move through Haitian villages, followed by dancers, during Holy Week festivities. *Rara* music is often sung as

Haitian *vaccines,* single-note wooden instruments played in sequence, are direct descendants of an instrument and technique found in many parts of Africa (notably the area now known as the Central African Republic). The nearest musician is tapping a second rhythm on the side of the instrument, a common African-derived technique.
Photo by Alfred Métraux, by courtesy of Ed. de la Baconnière

well, providing an occasion for praising local officials and other popular figures. Not all *rara* bands are made up of *vaccines;* other groups use drums, trumpets, whistles, and so on. Another form of festival song is the *mayousse,* which may be heard in Holy Week, on All Saints' Day, and on lesser occasions. The marimba, Haiti's version of the African hand-piano, is quite popular for *mayousse* music.

If the drums and drum groups of so many areas are obviously based on African models, so are many features of the music they play. There is almost always a lead drum, which improvises, along with one or two others, which play repeated sequences. Where there is only one drum, as in Jamaican *tambo,* it sounds rather thin without the support of subsidiary drums. This thinness, also characteristic of the recordings of Haitian virtuoso Ti-Roro, underlines the point that drum music is communal. A lead drum without its supporting cast is a bit like a piano played without a left-hand part.

Old accounts often mention instruments of all sorts that have exact parallels in Africa. An architect named Benjamin Latrobe, who visited New Orleans in 1819, provided a long description of a dance he happened upon, which is interesting despite the author's disapproving tone:

> The music consisted of two drums and a stringed instrument. An old man sat astride of a cylindrical drum about a foot in diameter, and beat it with incredible quickness with the edge of his hand and fingers. The other drum was an open staved thing held between the knees and beaten in the same manner. . . . The most curious instrument, however, was a stringed instrument which no doubt was imported from Africa. On top of the finger board was the rude figure of a man in sitting posture, and two pegs behind him to which the strings were fastened. The body was a calabash.

Further on, Latrobe described more instruments: "One, which from the color of the wood seemed new, consisted of a block cut into something of the form of a cricket bat with a long and deep mortice down the center. . . . In the same orchestra was a square drum, looking like a stool . . . also a calabash with a round hole in it, the hole studded with brass nails, which was beaten by a woman with two short sticks." The descriptions match the kind of slit-drum used by a large number of tribes from the West Coast and the Congo; a common form of small harp-lute found pretty much all over the continent; another drum with its own feet (square drums are found in Ghana, though there is evidence that they were in fact developed in the Caribbean and taken back to Ghana by returning freed slaves); and a calabash used as a percussion instrument. This last suggests a strong continuation of tradition; its brass studs and the fact that it was a woman's instrument are both features of calabashes played by the Hausa and other groups.

African-derived instruments other than drums still exist in many parts of the New World (though not in the United States). Less well-known than Latrobe's reference to African instruments in the Western Hemisphere is a mention of the marimba, or xylophone, in *A True and Exact History of the Island of Barbadoes, written by Richard Ligon, Gent,* published in 1673. Ligon came across a slave called Macow, "sitting on the ground, and before him a piece of large timber, upon which he had laid cross, six billets, and having a handsaw by him, would cut the billets by little and little till he had brought them to the

The marimba of the Colombian Pacific coast carries not only its African name but also a central role in a music high in African content. This is part of a rural *currulao* group.
Photo by David Lewiston

tunes, he would fit them to; I took the stick out of his hand, and tryed the sound, finding the six billets to have six distinct notes." Macow, in other words, was building himself a marimba of a very common six-tone variety.

The marimba mentioned in Ligon's book is still a major feature of music in Mexico and other parts of Central and South America, and most people probably think it is an Amerindian instrument. It used to be more widespread; it was found in Brazil until the nineteenth century, for instance. Where it is still found, the music played on it is usually Indian, but a fine Nonesuch disc of black music recorded mainly in Colombia by David Lewiston presents marimbas combined with drums in fiery neo-African *currulaos* from the Colombian Pacific coast. Unlike marimba music elsewhere in the Americas, these *currulaos* seem almost purely African, despite Spanish lyrics. The scales of the marimbas themselves are not standard European ones. These marimbas are normally played by two men standing facing each other, one playing the melody, the other plays a bass line, another apparently African trait. The staggered entry of the instruments is also typically African: the marimba plays an introduction, the lead drum comes in, then one of the rhythm drums, then the others.

More remarkably—given the general impression that very little in the way of African instruments made it to North America—Dena Epstein cites several descriptions of xylophones in the United States. Most refer to them as "bal-afo," which suggests a Manding origin. Epstein devotes four pages to the instrument, and many of her examples are from the West Indies (including Saint Vincent and Jamaica). But she also cites descriptions of a "barrafou" in 1775 and a "barrafoo" in 1776 Virginia.

Two unusual instruments of purely African origin are the so-called mos-quito drum, or earthbow, found in Haiti and the Dominican Republic (where it is called *gayamba*), and the stamping tubes known as *quitiplas* in Colombia and Venezuela and *ganbo* in Haiti. The earthbow is a stringed instrument built of a bent sapling, a cord, and a hole in the earth covered with animal hide, which acts as the resonator. Stamping tubes are differing lengths of hollow bamboo tapped on the ground in sequence by a group of men. Descendants of African wind instruments are found in the already described *vaccines* of Haiti, one-note bamboo trumpets that the players blow in sequence to produce a highly rhythmic (and highly communal) music. Similar instruments are found in several African countries.

African-derived stringed instruments also have their place in the Americas. Sir Hans Sloan, writing of Jamaica in 1688, describes a gourd with a neck strung with horsehair, like one of the instruments Latrobe saw, and a "hollowed timber strung with parchment" (that is, a little drum) having a bow for its neck. Many African stringed instruments are made of gourds, and so were the early U.S. banjos, which were undoubtedly African-inspired at the outset but have changed a good deal since. Under various versions of the name—often "banjar" in the United States and anglophone Caribbean, "banza" in the French-speaking islands—the banjo was reported very early in the New World: by 1678 in Martinique, 1689 in Jamaica, and the United States by the mid-eighteenth century. It was, moreover, regarded from the start as an archetypal "African" instrument. The contemporary shape seems (as Robert Cantwell mentions in his *Bluegrass Breakdown*) to have stemmed from stretching the skin resonator over the hoop of a cheesebox. The use of a little drum as a resonator for a stringed instrument, essentially the effect of the cheesebox banjo, is extremely common in Africa too. The one- and two-stringed fiddles are frequently made the same way. Sloan's two-stringed instruments are no longer found in Jamaica, but in the 1920s Helen H. Roberts met some people who said they remembered them. (She did find the *cumbe,* a small square drum on two legs rather like what Latrobe saw in New Orleans, as well as sheep's jawbones used as rattles or scrapers.)

An instrument whose background is African but whose function has changed in the New World is the hand- or thumb-piano, which many Bantu groups in Africa call marimba, just as they do the xylophone. It is a little box

The Caribbean *marimbula* is a much-enlarged descendant of the African thumb-piano, with metal (or occasionally wooden) tines that are plucked to produce a note. This version comes from the Dominican Republic, but it was once common in Cuba—so much so that the Jamaicans call it a rumba-box.

Photo by John Storm Roberts

or board with metal prongs fastened to it, each of which sounds a different note when plucked. Small versions of them were seen in New Orleans and Trinidad in the nineteenth century and are still occasionally found in Cuba, but much more common is a large version made of a packing case with four to eight metal keys. It is found in country districts of Haiti, Puerto Rico, Cuba, the Dominican Republic, Jamaica, and Trinidad. In the Spanish-speaking countries it is called the *marimbula* or *marimbola*. In Jamaica it is the *rumba-box*, and in Trinidad the *basse-en-boîte* (box-bass). The *marimbula* is not always used in highly traditional music: it was the standard bass for the Cuban *sones* groups that were to sweep the world in the 1930s; as late as 1972, I recorded a Dominican *merengue* group that used one.

Another instrument of African origin that has become familiar to the more experimental American jazz fans through the work of Brazilian percussionists like Airto Moreira and Dom Um Romao is the musical bow, of which there are several versions in Brazil alone. The Brazilian instruments—and the most common names, *berimbau* and *urucungu*—are generally accepted as being of Congo-Angolan origin, but they are widespread in several parts of Africa. Though the *berimbau* is the only well-known New World musical bow, it still crops up in the Caribbean—in Curaçao where it is known as a *benta*, for example, and in Grenada where it is called a *cocoa-lute*. It was also more widespread in the past. In her definitive study *Sinful Tunes and Spirituals*, Epstein cites an eighteenth-century comment, by one William Beckford, of a "bender" in Jamaica that was clearly a musical bow, and even a U.S. report from 1858 Mississippi (the only written example she found of a musical bow in the United States; Alan Lomax in his *The Land Where the Blues Began* notes that Napoleon Strickland of Mississippi, among others, played a "Diddley Bow," the common North American name for the traditional musical bow).

Besides the actual musical instruments from Africa (also including a wide range of maracalike instruments, rhythm bells like the *agogó* of Cuba and Brazil, and countless others), many culture patterns relating to music are still strongly African. The role of the lead drummer in Africa includes giving directions to the dancers on sacred and secular occasions, a function widespread in the New World too. In the *tamborito* of Panama, the *repicador*, the smallest drum, summons the dancers and directs their movements. And the lead drum in many traditions—including Colombia's "national" dance, the *cumbia*—is even called the *llamador*, or caller.

Another intriguing Africanism in New World drums is that percussion instruments are often given sexual attributes. In the Colombian *cumbia* and *currulao*, among other forms, one of each pair of drums is called male and the other female. The same is true of the Puerto Rican *bomba* drums. And in the double-headed Dominican *tambora,* not in itself an African survival, one of the heads is made of male and the other of female goatskins. This male/female concept of instruments is clearly African. Not only are whole classes of instruments seen as male or female (drum = male, calabash percussion = female, for example) but the Dogon of Mali (who have the continent's most complex musical metaphysic) explain triple rhythms as male and duple as female. Significantly, in most parts of Africa music without both duple and triple rhythms is not regarded as "complete."

How has so much that was African survived in a fairly pure state? In part because musical survivals have been associated with both religious and social survival. Except in areas too small for them to flourish or where persistent persecution was more successful than usual (as in Jamaica), powerful and important cults kept African religions alive in the New World, either in a relatively pure state or blended with non-African faiths. The neo-African cults, impressive in their own right, are among the main preservers of neo-African music in the Western Hemisphere, principally because the major role of music in African religions persists in Afro-American cults.

The best known of these are not merely still functioning, but have taken on a new lease of life in the cities, including the cities of the United States. They are Haitian *vaudou* or *voudon* (voodoo), the Cuban and Puerto Rican Lucumí or Santería, and (in their native land) the great range of Brazilian cults that variously blend African, European, and Amerindian elements.

The reputation of voodoo has suffered from sensationalist writings perpetrated by whites prepared to believe anything of a religion belonging not just to blacks, but to *independent* blacks, to which is added Hollywood's and TV's eye for a piece of apparently spooky exoticism. In fact, like similar cults in other parts of the Americas, it is a complex system that accommodates and integrates various beliefs, philosophies, social conditions, and cultural and artistic elements. The breadth of African influences in Haitian voodoo is obvious from the names of the various "mysteries" that the religion takes in: Ibo, Bambara, Congo, Mayombe, Congo Mandragues, Mandragues Go-Roug, Mali, Badagri, Caplaou, and Conga. The Dahomeyan religion in voodoo is dominant, and other African cultures have become subordinate to the Dahomeyan Fon culture.

The religious music of the Afro-American cults is often almost indistinguishable from the music of the parent faiths in West Africa. The rhythms, the drum techniques and even specific patterns, and the overall structures are basically the same. The main differences are an occasional tendency to use longer melody lines divided into more European-style verses and, where the African scales are not similar to European scales, to adapt them somewhat.

The continuation of African music in the cults is not solely a result of religious music's universal tendency to conservatism; it is music's absolutely essential role in the cults, just as it has in West African faiths. The spirits are summoned by specific drum rhythms, and if the rhythms are altered too much, the spirits will stay away. The drums are the voice of the god as well; cult dancers in Guiana dance facing the drums for that reason.

The songs of the cults are ritual praises to the different spirits, hence the wording seems to be more important than the melody. The basic style of the singing in the Yoruba cults of Brazil, the *candomblé*, is virtually that of western Nigeria. Both incorporate the call-and-response form and the special group technique called heterophony, which is almost singing in unison except that individuals slightly alter the main line from time to time. The result is a sound immediately recognizable and remote from European styles.

Where the songs of the New World neo-African cults are solo, the melody line is fairly long and complex; the call-and-response phrases are repeated many times. Other pure Africanisms include the practice whereby the soloist ends the song as well as beginning it, which would be quite unbalanced to European minds; a chorus replying with unvarying phrases to a leader's part that is improvised and rarely repeated; the use of a hard tone in the women's voices and a frequent, passing falsetto by both male and female singers; polyrhythmic rather than polyphonic music, giving drums such importance that the vocal is an accompaniment to the percussion rather than the other way round; and the use of more than one meter simultaneously, so that the vocals are often in triple time while the drumming is in duple time.

Alan Merriam summed up the main African features of Brazilian cult music as "the metronome sense, dominance of percussion, the use of polymeter, the off-beat phrasing of melodic accents, and the overlapping call-and-response pattern." There is a Library of Congress recording of Afro-Brazilian cult music that gives fine examples of all these characteristics.

Others besides the big Brazilian and Cuban cults have preserved strongly African music. Richard Waterman, who has studied the music of the Trinidadian Shango cult (named after the Yoruba god of thunder and introduced not by slaves, but by Yoruba contract workers in the 1850s), points out that it too contains a bedrock feature of African music: "use of patterns of combinations of duple with triple time which include simultaneous and coterminous duple and triple measures, duple accent applied to triple meter, and triple accent applied to duple meter."

Except in Haiti, where the Fon dominates, and in Cuba, where the multitude of cults includes some important Bantu ones, the Yoruba beliefs have tended to dominate neo-African religions. In Brazil and Cuba, at least, there have been Muslim cults as well, but most of them ended up joining the larger Yoruba groups. Most neo-Yoruba cults are like that of Cuba, where it is called Lucumí. The Lucumí worship a series of spirit-gods, or *orisha,* most of which are also found in western Nigeria and Benin; they are called *loa* in the Haitian cults originating with the Fon, indicating more of a linguistic than a religious difference. (England's "God" and France's "Dieu" are not different deities.) They include Ogun (Gun in Fon), god of the mountains; Obatala, god of iron and war; Yemaya, goddess of the sea; and many others. The songs of Lucumí worship are in a Yoruba pure enough to be mostly understood by Yoruba speakers from Africa, and the remembered vocabulary is large enough that anthropologist Lydia Cabrera compiled a fair-sized dictionary of it. The most important ritual drums are called *batá,* and their players *olu-batá,* in both Africa and Cuba; in both places there are three of them, with a similar relationship to one another. Much of the religious symbolism is preserved, including the association of the colors red and white with Shango.

In most places where they have been preserved, the African cults have been associated with the cult houses known as "saint's houses" (*ilé-ocha* in Yoruba). The priests and acolytes there undergo training that can last as long as a year and which is clearly important in handing on African traditions. Of course, a great deal of change has occurred in the Afro-American cults, but the African cults are not static, either. In some instances, the American cults perpetuate traditions lost in Africa, just as Canadian French and American English preserve words and phrases forgotten in Europe. The Society of Hunters associated with the god Oshossi has been preserved in Bahia, Brazil, but is forgotten in the Yoruba area of Nigeria, where it originated.

The Bahia region, which has so many saint's houses that its chief town, Salvador, was known as "the Rome of the Africans," is in fact a major center of Yoruba religion in the New World. Bahia has tended to preserve more purely African elements, both sacred and secular, than any other area. The anthropologist Melville J. Herskovits, on a 1941–42 visit there, heard a priestess give an impromptu speech in Yoruba, which would demand a much better knowledge of the language than the recitation of set prayers. (How many Roman Catholic priests can give a good after-dinner speech in Latin these days?) Bahia's strongly African cast had to do with patterns of agriculture and slavery in Brazil, but it can't hurt that there is still regular maritime trade between the port of Salvador and the West African nations of Nigeria and Benin.

The neo-African cults are not simply museum pieces. Like anything else that flourishes in new circumstances, they have survived by adaptation. There are religious groups that represent a blend of African and Roman Catholic belief (Macumba) and others featuring African and Amerindian elements

(Guarani and Caboclo). They reflect their mixed origins in their music. A good example is the first track of the Library of Congress record of Afro-Brazilian cult music, which I have mentioned, a Caboclo song to Santo Juremeiro, who sounds like Saint Jerome but is also the spirit of the *jurema* tree. Herskovits, who recorded the album, points out the influence of Catholic liturgy in the invocation, but there is also an obvious Portuguese sound to the later solo singing, while the choral singing is call-and-response. The same record, incidentally, has a fine example of the use of the lead drum in a Ketu rite for the god Oshossi. First, it calls the god with the correct pattern and then, as the "voice of the god," signals the proper movements to the possessed initiates.

The underlying structure of the *candomblé* cults of Brazil, voodoo in Haiti, and Abakwá, Lucumí, Arara, and other cults in Cuba is African, though each has taken in Christian elements to a greater or lesser degree. In Haiti, for instance, voodoo altars are decorated with richly colored pictures of various saints and angels that have become associated with the *orisha* or *loa*, usually because of some detail of appearance or clothes. The god of iron and war, Ogun, for example, is often represented by a picture of the Archangel Michael, usually shown in armor with a sword. In Port-au-Prince, the capital of Haiti, worshipers at a voodoo ceremony often go on at dawn to early Mass. At the same time, Saint Soleil ("Saint Sun") has also been welcomed into the voodoo pantheon.

The Bantu religio-philosophical outlook seems to have been especially prone to change. The Bantu cult groups consequently have often disappeared or altered beyond recognition. It was mostly Bantu cults that blended with Amerindian elements in the Brazilian Macumba, Caboclo, and so on. In Cuba, the Congo communities recently have tended to group and regroup. Similarly, as Cuban musicologist Argiliers Leon points out, Bantu musical instruments, instead of being preserved unaltered, acted as prototypes for new Afro-Cuban versions. The conga drums, found in Latin American groups of all sorts, came from Bantu originals. Bantu drums are still known as *ngoma* in Cuba, just as they often are in Brazil (or by other Bantu forms such as *ingome*).

Of course, there are also considerable differences between African and Afro-American cults. The Nigerian Yoruba cults closely follow family lines, which in the New World were broken by the anarchy of slavery. In Nigeria each cult is devoted to one *orisha*, whereas in Cuba, Brazil, and elsewhere, the cults lost their ethnic exclusiveness and, because numbers were smaller, brought devotees of various *orishas* together. As a result, in Africa usually only one worshiper is possessed, while in America many may be.

Haitian voodoo is a particularly rich faith, although (or perhaps because) it has grown away from West Africa more than the Brazilian has. Brazil maintained close contact with Africa; heads of commercial houses in Salvador received honorary distinctions from the government of Dahomey, and rich Brazilian Negroes even imported soap from Africa. The continuing ties between Brazil and Africa include one reported by Roger Bastide that is quite modern. One Martiano de Bomfin went to Nigeria to be initiated, and on his return he introduced a new Yoruba element that he had learned there into his cult house.

In both Brazil and Cuba, ties with Africa were maintained in a more grim fashion by the continuance of slave smuggling up to the end of the nineteenth century. Haiti, on the other hand, became independent in 1791–1793, and when the Haitian revolution brought an end to white rule it also cut Haiti off from Africa. Many in the country's mulatto middle class continued to take their fashions in music and other things from France. More paradoxically (because voodoo priests had played an important part in the independence struggle), the first three rulers of independent Haiti—Toussaint-L'Ouverture, Dessalines, and King Christophe—totally banned voodoo assemblies. Toussaint-L'Ouverture banned all sorts of African dancing as well. The result has been that Haitian voodoo has developed strongly non-African ingredients, though these are often African in character.

As the Haitian experience shows, the threat of the cults to slavery's "law and order" was real, hence they were much persecuted. After the slave revolt of 1760, Jamaican authorities banned *obeah*, a less highly structured form of neo-African worship that may get its name from one of a number of similar African words—one of which is Ibo for doctor, *obia* (a term also used by the Bush Negroes of Suriname). The leader of the revolt was a priest called Tacky, who is said to have been a Coromantee and a former chief in Guinea (a term used rather vaguely by the geography-challenged slave owners of the time). "Coromantee" refers to the Ghanaian port of Cormantyne; it is more likely that Tacky came from there, as the African elements in Jamaican culture are largely Fanti-Ashanti. In Jamaica, atypically, the ban was extremely effective. Obeah still exists semisecretly, but seems to have lost much of its West African roots.

The political potential of the cults, which acted as a powerful unifying force, was not the only reason why they were attacked. Most whites of the New World were entirely uncomprehending about African culture, but they did at times distinguish between forms, and of course they objected most to non-Christian religious practices. A good example of the distinction between sacred and secular came out in a discussion held at the end of the eighteenth century, as reported by Gilberto Freyre. Talking to the Minister of State, Martinho de Mello e Castro, about black dances in Brazil, the Count of Pevolide, a former governor of a captaincy, was of the opinion that such dances should not be considered more indecent than the fandangos of Castile and the *fofas* of Portugal and the *lunduns* of the whites and mulattoes of that country. The Negroes dance in tribal groups and with the instruments typical of each, whirling like harlequins and with diverse movements of the body. From these acceptable dances those should be separated which are deserving of complete reprobation like those danced by the Senegalese Negroes in the secrecy of their homes or in clearings, with a black mistress of ceremonies, an altar to idols, adoring live buck goats and other fetishes of clay, anointing their bodies with oils and cocks' blood, eating cakes of cornmeal after pronouncing heathen blessings on them, making the countryfolk believe that those cakes so blessed bring good luck, working love spells on men and women, and the credulity of certain persons is so great, even those one would not think so ignorant, such as friars and priests, who have been taken prisoner in the ring I threw around such houses, and to unmask whom I had to make confess their deception in the presence of the blacks of the house, and then turn them over to their authorities so they could be punished as they deserved, and I had the Negroes severely flogged and ordered their masters to sell them far away.

The notion that all whites were ignorant of and hostile to African survivals was as dubious as other stereotypes. In fact, the varying degrees of tolerance or hostility directed against neo-African cults (for reasons of fear, prejudice, or genuine religious belief) had a direct effect on the black music of the New World. The African elements in U.S. music are far more transmuted than those of other parts, and there is no surviving neo-African music such as is found in the Caribbean and parts of South America; even such new cultural practices as Kwanzaa are African-American, not African (as Kwanzaa's creator, Ron Karenga, stresses). One reason, no doubt, is that contact with Africa was broken earlier, and another is that—compared at least with some parts of the Caribbean—the black population in the United States is smaller. In addition, contrary to stereotypical images, many slaves worked domestically or on small farms, sometimes shoulder-to-shoulder with the farmer, and many in the nineteenth century were semi-independent craftsmen whose only practical burden was to pay a percentage of their earnings to their owner. These were not the conditions in which neo-African culture could survive, though many Africanisms did. Perhaps most important of all, it is probable that the main African musical influence on the United States came from a tradition that could blend relatively well with white styles, because many of the earliest slaves came from the Wolof and Mandingo groups with their preponderance of stringed instruments. But the banning of drums in many parts of the country was certainly a factor, especially in the disappearance of the African religious groups. The prohibition of the drums, where successful, was bound to have a fundamental effect on the cults, because when the drums were silent, the old gods came no more.

Nevertheless, elements of African religion survived even where the cults themselves vanished. They included the central role of dancing (as well as music) and possession states. Possession states came about when the gods were summoned and entered into certain members of the congregation, or "rode" them, as the cult members call it. These people then "became" the gods for a while, and each would dress and act like the god possessing him and dance under his impulsion. And speaking of survival: the drum most closely associated with Cuban music across the world, the conga ("Congolese" in Spanish) is simply the drum derived from the religious drums of the *palos;* another Cuban religious drum, the *batá,* is not as well known but is often used in hip New York salsa recordings of the more Afro-minded sort, as well as in religious music both during services and in concert.

It is not only the fully developed cults that have helped keep neo-African music alive, but also customs that are a memory of them. The Caribbean island of Carriacou, in the Grenadines, still preserves a "nation dance" that was originally Coromantee (Ashanti) but took in Ibo, Mending, Arada (Fon), and Congo elements—presumably because on such a small island there were not enough members of any one group to remain self-sustaining. African words are preserved in the dance, which is used in various rituals, including healing ceremonies. The name of Damballa, the Dahomeyan snake god, is preserved in the song "Caribo Damballa Bother Me."

Religion was only one way in which African music was preserved in the New World. Another was flight: a significant minority of Africans escaped their slavery by flight into the interior, when the interior was of a type that would allow for this. The best known of these groups are the Boni, Saramaka, and other so-called Bush Negroes or Maroons of the Guianas, who were largely protected by dense jungle, and the Maroons of Jamaica, who preserved their independence in good measure by arms. Both were, not surprisingly, repositories of neo-African musics.

The majority of slaves who did not escape, organize doomed rebellions, or commit suicide, found other ways besides religion to organize themselves collectively in a strange and hostile environment. Slaves often formed themselves into groupings that continued, either fairly exactly or in new forms, their old

Among several living Jamaican neo-African drumming traditions is *kumina*, whose origins are Congolese. Not only did *kumina* itself undergo a revival in Kingston, but it was a major influence on Rastafari drumming.

Photo by Kenneth Bilby

tribal ties. Slaves in the cities who themselves performed heavy labor, such as unloading ships or acting as porters of heavy loads, sometimes formed into groups of half a dozen or so men, led by a "captain," all of the same tribe. In the early days before the slaves willy-nilly picked up English, French, Spanish, or Portuguese, their purpose was to be able to talk with one another. By working and living together, these groups preserved elements of their culture, including musical elements. A visitor to Rio de Janeiro in 1838 wrote that the porters there ran through the streets behind the leader of each group, who, to the sound of a gourd rattle, paced the others in a kind of trot; they all sang.

At a deeper level, the slaves in the Americas found a way to preserve old ties and come together for mutual support in new circumstances by forming ethnic clubs. These clubs, remarkably widespread, played a great part in the preservation of neo-African music. They were known as "nations" and, in the Spanish areas, *cabildos*—named after the city governments in Spanish colonial administration. The "nations" and *cabildos* tended to preserve the names of African ethnic or regional groupings or to create new names to reflect new conditions in the Afro-American experience.

The "nations" were governed by a hierarchy and sometimes acted as intermediaries between their members and the slave owners. In Colombia, the *cabildos* included the Mandingo, the Caravali (Kalabari), the Congo, and the Mina (after the Gold Coast slaving port of Elmina), each with its "kings" and "princes." There were apparently *cabildos* in Venezuela among free blacks as well as slaves. In Peru there were Angolas, Caravalis, Mozambiques, Congos, Chalas, and Tierra Nuevas. Old writers from virtually all the other Spanish colonies report similar groups. An eighteenth-century Nigerian former slave, Equiano, described in memoirs what he saw in Jamaica:

> When I came to Kingston I was surprised to see the number of Africans who were assembled together on Sundays, particularly at a large commodious place called Spring Bath. There each different nation of Africa meet and dance after the nature of their own country. They still retain most of their native customs: they bury their dead and put victuals, pipes and tobacco, and other things in the grave with the corpse in the same manner as in Africa.

The "nations" and *cabildos* suffered various fates. Some were banned, like those in Colombia, because enmity among the groups reached the fighting stage, they were seen as a threat to order, or their dances did not suit the notions of "decency" or "civilization" of rulers and lawmakers. By contrast, Cuban slave owners, finding that slaves grouped by tribe worked better, encouraged them. Other "nations" moved from a social to a spiritual role, either merging with or developing into religious groupings, which preserved the faiths of various regions of West and Central Africa. Sometimes the division into "nations" continued in new settings. In the Brazilian army, for example, the black soldiers formed four battalions: Minas, Ardras, Angola, and "Creoles." Some of them acted as mutual-aid societies; all, with the abolition of slavery, gradually ceased to be strictly ethnic organizations. That is to say, though they kept African ethnic names and customs, their members in fact came from various backgrounds, and not always African ones. Harold Courlander tells of seeing six people initiated into the Abakwá secret society of Cuba (whose origin is Nigerian), all but one of them white. The French anthropologist Roger Bastide remarks that he knows "Daughters of the Saints" of French or Spanish origin who "are no doubt white of skin, but who are considered as Africans because they take part without any reservations in a culture brought from Africa."

An even more African form of organization that has occasionally acted as a cultural preservative in the New World is the secret society. In many West African groups, secret societies were not only in charge of such issues as puberty initiation rites, but acted as disciplinary forces (other tribes had no secret societies at all). The best known of these is the Cuban Abakwá, whose origin is in the Ibo of eastern Nigeria. Its secrecy is far from total these days, given that a Cuban anthropologist, Lydia Cabrera, filled an entire book with information given by initiates. But it preserves a strong neo-African voices-and-percussion music, used like that of the *griots* to present the group's legendary history.

Though organizations like the "nations" discontinued the ethnic divisions in which they were founded, like the Abakwá they did extremely important work in preserving strong cultural elements of Africa. It is doubtless partly thanks to them that the dances of Afro-America include so many that are either neo-African or, although developed in the New World, grew out of overwhelmingly or largely African elements. These go far beyond musical instruments and the way they are played.

Many descriptions of neo-African dances show a close relationship between dance and music, in which neither is subsidiary. The *bomba* of Puerto Rico certainly existed by around 1820, and seems to have developed in the slave-barracks. The daughter of a Puerto Rican *bomba* dancer from the days before it started dying out once told how her father would hold dances on Sundays, at which—just as in Africa—the spectators formed the chorus for call-and-response singing. The music was supplied by two drums, maracas, and two sticks tapped on a bench; this kind of ad hoc percussion instrument

The Nation Dance on the small island of Carriacou, in the Grenadines, ingeniously dove-tailed and combined traditions from widely separated African cultures.
Photo by Don Hill

was common in Cuban rumba, and a Folkways recording of Liberian music includes a track in which a singer is accompanied by a man tapping on a chair.

One oddity of the *bomba* is that the rhythm was set not by the drummers but by the lead dancer. The whole form of the *bomba* was like many African dances, in which the voices open unaccompanied, then the drums come in with dramatic effect. The dancer would often integrate his movement with the music still more by dancing up to the lead drum and beating out an improvised rhythm with his feet. The drummer would reply, and a competition would develop between dancer and drummer.

The *bomba* has many African elements: melodies of short phrases constantly repeated; varied, complicated rhythms; a collective dance form involving instruments, dancers, and spectators in which nobody is passive; and, in many cases, simple, much-repeated lyrics, often of no importance, as in many neo-African forms. (A group I recorded near Santo Domingo used virtually the same words for four different numbers.)

All these qualities are true of a large number of Afro-Caribbean dances. Nor do they all reach back to the early years. The most famous of all, the street-rumba of Cuba, is newer than the Puerto Rican *bomba*. As Peter Manuel points out in *Caribbean Currents,* the rumba in its various forms is derived from Congolese secular dances, but it is a distinctively Cuban creation that seems to have emerged in the late nineteenth century as entertainment music at parties, mostly in urban barrios. The basic instrumentation for rumba is two differently tuned congas, one with *palitos* playing on the side, and *claves* struck by the lead singer. The higher of the conga drums, the *quinto*, improvises throughout. But being newer than the *bomba*, the rumba's vocals are more of a mix of European and African styles than many older forms. The *guaguancó* in particular uses call-and-response in its second section, but its opening vocal is usually a fairly loose verse form of obvious European inspiration.

Different subbranches of rumba have somewhat different origins, but they all began life as strongly neo-African secular dances. Their percussion shows the common African feature of a lead drum improvising over constant rhythmic patterns from the supporting drummer(s). Besides these drums, spoons sometimes played a part rather like metal percussive instruments in some West African ensembles; the more recent *claves*, commonly used in dance band rumba groups at least until the 1940s, have a role much like the *gankogui* double bell in Ewe music, its equivalents in other West African music, or even the bottle tapped with a knife often found in African rural guitar music. The *claves* supplies an unvarying skeletal rhythmic pattern to which the other patterns are related and that acts as a regular base against which the rhythms of the other instruments are set off.

Another instrumental Africanism, taken over from the ritual styles of the Cuban Bantu ritual styles (collectively known as *palo*), is the use of rattles strapped to the *quinto* player's (*quinteador*) wrists. The instrumentation of the rumba group was not highly standardized, of course; the *cajones* (wooden boxes used as percussion) could be replaced by two barrel drums, a *tumbadora* and a *quinto*. Harold Courlander, in an article on Cuban musical instruments in the *Musical Quarterly*, mentioned a lineup consisting of a piano, two conga drums, *quinto*, maracas, piano, and *claves*, the last also used as sticks on the side of one of the conga drums, in neo-African style.

The dance form of the rumba was a part of the festival as a whole. Sometimes it was just one incident in the course of events, sometimes there would be several dances linked together under the general name of "rumba." Like many Afro-American and African dances, the dance tended to open with solo song. In the *Rumbas de Tiempo' España*, a form that seems to have disappeared, two solo singers would sing a short passage, and the call-and-response would begin. The first soloist would also set the rhythm with the *claves*, to be picked up first by the *tumbadora* and then by the *quinto*. The pattern is very similar to that of a number of African and neo-African dances discussed so far, although here the soloist marks the beat with a percussion instrument, whereas in others the drummer picks it up from the vocal. The dancing itself

Street rumba in Cuba shows the flexibility of Afro-American tradition. The dancer's clothes are strictly modern, but her use of a kerchief is far older than the rumba itself. Similarly, the Yoruba-derived double-headed *batá* drum played by the musician on the left is a deviation from the usual lineup.

Photo by Robin Moore

took the common African form of a couple (or solo) dance inside a ring of singer-watchers. In some rumba dances, like the *yambú*, there was—as in many African dances—a large element of mime, in the case of the *yambú* itself, imitating old age.

The traditional *guaguancó* is the form of rumba that most often surfaces in dance band forms and which is still being played by percussion groups such as Los Papines and Los Muñequitos de Matanzas (who have both brought innovations to the basic percussion tradition). The *guaguancó* begins with a long solo vocal passage in narrative form, often with a topical or personal subject, which has a fairly fluid melody line with held notes and a rhythm faster than the *yambú*. The dance was essentially an attraction-repulsion courting dance.

Another common form of rumba dance, this one for a single person, was the *columbia*, which made references (usually joking or satirical) to the Lucumí and Abakwá rituals. The soloist often gets into a rhythmic "argument" with the lead drummer of a sort we have met elsewhere. All these types continue the strong song-dance, visual-aural, performer-spectator continuum fundamental to African aesthetic concepts. Though versions are occasionally recorded, the *columbia* is closer to vanishing than the *guaguancó*.

Brazil was and remains particularly rich in neo-African dances. The general style loosely called samba (or *batuque*, a now-extinct specific dance that has come to mean any Afro-Brazilian percussion form) had a large number of forms. The urban samba that Americans became acquainted with in the 1940s was a twentieth-century creation, and some of the earlier forms were only partly African musically, but even the highly stylized *sambas enredo* of the Rio Carnival are still accompanied by percussion both entirely Brazilian in spirit and pretty much entirely African in origin. The *sambas da roda*, or ring dances, remain quite African, including features like the *umbrigada*, a belly-bounce that is a sure sign of Africanism in New World dances and that, incidentally, considerably upset white observers in the nineteenth century. The belly-bounce illustrates how Africanisms were present in countries where they tend not to be recognized; it turned up early in Mexico in a group of songs and dances called the *chuchumbe*, which drew a denunciation from the Inquisition in 1766. It was also a feature of the Afro-Colombian *cumbia* and other forms including the *mapalé*, a dance style thought to have grown out of the religious cults.

One type of samba described in Alvarenga's *Popular Music of Brazil* began much like the Puerto Rican *bomba*. A solo singer would open by improvising, then the chorus would come in. (This pattern of varied lead with set chorus extends to the *tamboritos* of Panama, the calypsos of Trinidad, and many others, and is a basic feature of much if not most African choral singing.) The drummer, playing the *bombo*—apparently a Portuguese, not an African name—would listen carefully until he heard that the singing was set, then would give a call-beat and launch into the rhythm of the song. On the call-beat the other drummers would enter and the dancing would begin. The lead drummer's main role was to direct the dancers. This is also a common form of opening in many areas of Africa.

Besides the sambas in particular and *batuques* in general, which now belong to the whole country, Brazil has had many less renowned dances. There was the *congada*, a dance-drama with strong African ingredients. The *mozambique* (not to be confused with the modern Cuban rhythm of the same name) was a war dance using only percussion instruments. The *cucumbí* used to be danced at Christmas and Carnivals. Because *cucumbí* was a local nickname for people of Congo origin, and because the songs had words of apparent African derivation, the dance is thought to have Bantu roots.

Most of these Brazilian dances—like their equivalents all over the area—were not "purely African," but many seem to have had very few Portuguese elements, if any. It is possible that, like much Afro-American drumming, the dances represented a fusion of different African elements to arrive at a style that was generically "African" rather than Ewe, Yoruba, Fon, or whatever. It is also possible that some of them existed in Africa but simply disappeared there, where art forms are fairly fluid, to be preserved only in the Americas. (Similarly, more of the melodies of British ballads have survived in the United States than in Britain.)

A great deal of work remains to be done on the relationship between African and Afro-American dances. In Brazil it is said that the word *samba* comes from an African word for the belly-bounce, *semba,* and that the word *batuque* is used in Congo-Angola as it is in Brazil, for a dance type rather than a specific dance. It is also said that Portuguese travelers in the past saw dances just like the original Brazilian *batuque* in Angola. But drawing linguistic parallels can be even trickier than speculating about musical ones. Colombia has a merengue, but its rhythm is very different from the Dominican merengue and very like what the Dominicans call a *mangulina*. On the other hand, if the word *samba* (and its cognates *semba/zamba/zambra*) come from an African word referring to a step rather than a rhythm, that might well explain how it ended up referring to very different dances in several Latin American countries. And a few of the derivations are provided by writers who seem unaware that there is no single language called "African" but rather an enormous number of specific tongues belonging to linguistic groups with pretty much no connection between them. This is an area where there are many probabilities but very few certainties.

Although the Spanish-speaking nations and Brazil are particularly rich in neo-African music, examples persist in every language group in the Caribbean, and several in Central and South America. Some genres were quite widespread, crossing even language barriers—particularly in the Caribbean, whose cultural links are far more complex than even the map. Almost every island was swapped back and forth between Spain, France, or Britain (sometimes all three). Inhabitants of British colonies like Dominica and Saint Lucia, geographically interspersed between the French *départements* of Martinique and Guadeloupe, in fact spoke French creole; Trinidad also had a French creole that was still widespread in the nineteenth century, as well as strong Venezuelan-Spanish cultural, and particularly musical, influences. On top of that, refugees from the Haitian revolution, including free blacks as well as mulattos and whites, strongly affected music in Cuba and even New Orleans.

As a result of all this, it is more confusing than surprising to find dances with the same names cropping up all over the Caribbean: the *bamboula* found in parts of the French- and English-speaking Caribbean and up to the nineteenth century in Louisiana and the Georgia/South Carolina Sea Islands; the juba (which in the United States went into early minstrelsy); and one of the most widespread, the *kalinda,* also known in Louisiana. A local form of the *kalinda* is still occasionally sung in Trinidad, where it used to accompany the stick-fighters at Carnival time. Incidentally, the *kalinda* and the juba (or *yuba*) crop up in a group of Puerto Rican *bomba* dances.

Along with these dance genres (or perhaps dance-titles), most if not all islands had their own neo-African forms of dance music. Many of these vanished, but others have been revived as symbols of black pride or nationalism or both. The *gwo ka* percussion style of Guadeloupe is a prime example. It is ironic that its last great traditional exponent, a drummer nicknamed Vélo, lived and died in poverty, but that thousands attended his funeral.

An interesting side issue is the way in which music is used in both Africa and the New World to accompany formalized athletics. Wrestling to the accompaniment of drums and praise songs in support of one or another combatant is not uncommon in West Africa. Trinidad once had a sport called stick-fighting (until it was banned), that was always accompanied by *kalinda* music, mainly praise songs to a percussion accompaniment. The Brazilian *capoeira,* a form of skilled fighting faintly reminiscent of karate, is accompanied by African-style lyres, called *berimbau,* playing melodies of an African cast. The fighting is closely linked to the music, which, far from incidental, acts as a motivating force. Alvarenga states that the *Capoeira de Angola* cannot take place without the *berimbau* lyres. The music consists of short melorhythmic phrases much like those played on African stringed instruments. The constant repetition of short phrases, often with a slight increase in tempo, acts here as a physical energizer, much as in cult music, where it serves in attaining the desired state of possession. Repetition of all kinds is a major positive feature of African-style singing, as a Panamanian woman affirmed: "The more you hear it the more harmony it has." A Jamaican interviewed by Helen Roberts remarked: "It don't make no matter how many time you sing it, you sing it till it get sour to your mouth." Westerners who use the word "monotonous" in criticizing black music are on the wrong cultural wavelength—and seem especially absurd coming from a culture whose greatest composers could spend twenty minutes saying "amen!"

Capoeira was the favorite sport of gangs of young blacks in Brazil (the *capoeiragem*) in the nineteenth century. The sport got a bad name when the *capoeiragem* used it effectively against police harassment, but the same *capoeiragem* also quelled a rebellion of European mercenary troops in 1828. The *capoeiragem* discovered something that has frequently been rediscovered since: If you are young, black, and poor, your activities are likely to strike the older, whiter, and richer power structure as subversive whatever they may be: *capoeira* in nineteenth-century Brazil, steel band in 1940s Trinidad, rocksteady and reggae in 1960s Jamaica, or rap in the contemporary United States.

Another neo-African form that has died out in most parts of the West is the work song. I shall be looking at the work songs of some areas in more detail later, but it is worth remembering that they were found in most places where people of African descent lived. Many work songs are highly African. In the Brazilian mining district of Minas Gerais, black diamond miners sang songs with the Bantu-sounding name *vissungo*. An unidentified author from long ago, cited by Oneyda Alvarenga, wrote: "At work, the blacks sang the whole day. They had special songs for the morning, midday and afternoon. As work began before sunrise they directed to the moon a song with an obviously religious theme." The texts of the *vissungo* mixed Portuguese words with others apparently from some corrupted African dialect. Like many African-derived or African-style songs, they were accompanied by sounds made with the working tools. In the mining area of Montijo, Panama, a black enclave in a largely Indian and white province, there was a song with the bitter line "Con los minerales vine, con los minerales voy" ("With the minerals I came, and with the minerals I am going"). Not all work songs are neo-African; Jamaican digging songs have strong English as well as African elements, and sea-chanteys, which may have strong U. S. African-American elements, are essentially multicultural. But on the whole the work songs of any country are among its more African styles.

Neo-Africanisms, where they occur, are a clear and impressive demonstration of the connection between the New World and Africa. But there are some less striking elements that are more widespread, including many aspects of singing technique. As shall be seen time and again throughout this book, African singing—in its use of call-and-response, varying vocal tone, endless variation on the part of the lead singer, and use of falsetto—is common to all the black areas of the New World, whether it dominates or not. Another component of African musical taste, an affinity for buzzing or rattling tones, was noticed by Lafcadio Hearn during a stay in the French West Indies in the 1870s. He found drums across which had been stretched a string with thin strips of bamboo or cut feather stems to give the tones what he described as "a certain vibration."

Neo-African forms often exist cheek by jowl with styles having strongly European ingredients. In some cases the neo-African survivals seem to result from a region's isolation, but by no means always. The highly African *congos del Espiritu Santo* of Villa Mella in the Dominican Republic are a famous feature of a town only a dozen miles from Santo Domingo. Their music, associated with an Afro-Christian sect, is highly African in its characteristics. The *congos* themselves are two drums, *el mayor,* the larger, and *el alcahuete,* the smaller, which plays the lead role. The rest of the accompaniment is carried by the *canoa,* a *claves*-like instrument, and by maracas. The most striking thing about the Villa Mella *congos* is the call-and-response singing, whose choral style could be taken for Congo-Angolan. The dancing is strongly Spanish, with no recognizable Africanization. The music of the Villa Mella *congos* serves equally for sacred and secular purposes: I first heard it at a wake, which involved dancing around a shrine by a young adept in a state of semipossession, but when I recorded it a few days later, people were performing secular dances with no significance other than enjoyment.

The Dominican Republic was relatively isolated for a long while, which no doubt helped music like the *congos* of Villa Mella not only to survive but to thrive. But there are other possible reasons. One is the religious significance of the *palos,* as the African drums and their music are called there. Villa Mella has a legend involving the miraculous arrival of the drums in the village. If popular belief is correct, the Dominican *palos* are a legacy from the period of the 1820s to the 1840s, when Santo Domingo was governed by Haiti. This belief is held by many Dominican scholars, though the music of the *palos* appears to be rather different from Haitian music. If it is true, the fact that it arrived in the Dominican Republic relatively recently would explain its survival. On the other hand the historical hostility to Haitians, which is still strong, would surely have prevented anything introduced during what is still referred to as the Haitian invasion from becoming so widespread and lasting so long. On the whole the belief in the *palos*'s Haitian origin seems mistaken.

Much of the neo-African music of Cuba and the Dominican Republic is well established. In other countries it may exist in isolated pockets, as in the case of a number of strongly African survivals in Jamaica. Though Jamaican culture as a whole was always regarded as Ashanti, strong Congolese elements were discovered about fifteen years ago. Most of them are to be found in Afro-Christian and neo-African sects, which preserve a number of Congolese words in their songs. A particularly important example is Kumina, a sect whose connection with the Congo is considerable and beyond dispute. Not only is the one Congo-Angolan ritual called Kumunu, but the Jamaican rites include a substantial number of words from the KiKongo language; the reason so much of the Kumina ritual has survived seems to be that it was not a legacy of slavery, but of contract workers from the Congo who arrived in the mid-nineteenth century.

Kumina's quite distinctive drumming moved to Kingston in the 1930s and became one of the roots of Rastafarian drumming, itself a new neo-African form belonging to a faith that goes back only to the 1930s and has strong roots in the Afro-Christian Revival groups, much as both sides would be indignant at the notion. A still more isolated example, already mentioned, is the Jamaican *tambo* drumming, which so far has been found only in the northern parish of Trelawney.

Similar examples continue to be discovered, and there is obviously much neo-African music known only to the people who make it. A couple of decades ago, the first known survivals in Jamaica of Yoruba were discovered in the form of a number of songs sung in a garbled dialect, some of whose words were clearly Yoruba, by an old man in the parish of Westmoreland.*

But neo-African music is not confined to forgotten or even surviving music from the early days. For a complex of social, musical, and political reasons, new neo-African styles have been evolving from older traditions. Nor are the reasons necessarily religious, like the development of Rastafarian drumming. The most famous example of all is Cuban *guaguancó* or street-rumba. But as Kenneth Bilby points out in a chapter of *Caribbean Currents*, the Guianas—Suriname, French Guiana, and Guyana—have more than one neo-African percussion style that has developed or been renewed in recent decades.

Surinamese *kawina* is a drum-based music of coastal Creoles, descendants of freed plantation slaves. According to Bilby, *kawina* is thought to have developed during the late nineteenth century, and *kawina* musicians used trumpets

---

* Two of the songs were issued on a record of the field recordings of Olive Lewin of the Jamaica School of Music, called *From the Grass Roots of Jamaica*.

Drummers of the western Afro-Jamaican tradition called Goombay Play. The square instrument played by the seated musician is a *goombay*, developed in Jamaica on African principles and re-exported to Africa in the early nineteenth century.
Photo by Kenneth Bilby

and other European instruments for a while during a creolizing period, but the music has recently reverted to an essentially neo-African idiom, percussion-based, with only the occasional addition of a small guitar called a *kwatro.*

An even newer Surinamese percussion music is *aleke,* which developed in Maroon communities in the 1970s out of a Njuka maroon drumming style, *lonsei,* which itself peaked in the 1960s. According to Bilby, *aleke* became pan-Maroon and quite eclectic during the 1980s and 1990s, and is now a mixed creole-Maroon idiom. But if it is new, it also is haunted by older African elements. The very fact that its central percussion is a trio of *aleke* drums echoes the three-drum organization of much West African music, and the close links between the past and the present are strongly symbolized by the fact that the *lonsei* rhythm is believed to have been passed from the other world during spirit possession.

A recording of a percussion music next door in French-speaking Guyane, *kassé kô,* seemingly illustrates a version of neo-African procedures perhaps more common in Africa itself than the New World: the apparently total Africanization of European material. Though *kassé kô* is classically neo-African with its African-derived drumming and call-and-response singing, most if not all of its major dances are thought to be reinterpretations of French originals. The *gragé* is a transmuted waltz; *les rôles* is a particularly Africanized version of that Caribbean favorite, the quadrille; and the *camougué* has been linked to the *bourrée* of Auvergne. Even the drumming, which sounds more African than most neo-African percussion to me, is explained in terms of adaptation from the European forms—which, if accurate, represents an extraordinarily complete makeover.

Surviving or revived, neo-African music is only part of the story, and only a small part of black music, though a crucial one. Moreover, many styles fall somewhere between the neo-African and the creolized, very often according to how one defines either term. If a music is all percussion, is it necessarily neo-African? Certainly not in the case of the drumming of the "East Indian" people of Trinidad, but many other contemporary styles, including Guadeloupe *gwo ka,* could quite reasonably be defined within either category.

While the slaves of the New World preserved a great deal of African culture, they were neither musically conservative or unenterprising, and in the Americas they came in contact with the music of various European countries. When that happened, the stage was set for what is thought of as New World black music today, in all its extraordinarily varied glory.

Cultural Blending
The First Afro-American Styles

Far from arriving in the New World without any cultural baggage, the Africans not only brought a great deal with them but planted it so well that it took root and grew profusely. But the Africans were not the only people who brought their culture with them. Nor, perhaps, did they alone cling to their culture as part of a memory of a lost home, even though they suffered the worst loss, with the least compensation and the least choice in the matter, of all the new arrivals.

In a natural revulsion against the old racist theory that black musicians, having nothing worthwhile of their own, created their superb music as if by magic entirely out of scraps taken from their white rulers and neighbors, it has sometimes been suggested that Africans in the New World fought against white musical influences, trying to keep the music of their past as pure as possible. But the evidence suggests something between the two possibilities. Dena Epstein, in her *Sinful Tunes and Spirituals*, cites a great deal of evidence from the French and English Antilles as well as the United States, showing that slaves clung to their own traditions (whether African or neo-African) well into the nineteenth century and that pockets of neo-African tradition remained even in isolated parts of the United States into the 1930s at least. But there is equal evidence that the slaves were playing and adapting European dances very early, not just when playing for whites but for use in their own parties. Some of the citations seem to indicate that there was a division between new arrivals and New-World-born slaves, who each did their own thing. But I believe that slaves in the New World began co-opting European and adapting

European music very early, while also holding onto and adapting African-derived music.

Here another element in history is important. Though the United States was far later than the British and French West Indies in ending slavery, the Royal Navy had effectively hampered large-scale slave-trading in the early nineteenth century. This meant that slaving from Africa thereafter was surreptitious. Examples cited by Epstein and others make it fairly clear that all over the New World it was the African-born who most actively preserved what really was their own music, while creole blacks (slave or free) tended to make use of more European-derived elements—sometimes at the same time and the same party. Epstein cites an example from 1808 New Orleans in which some of the slaves were dancing a *bamboula* and others a *contredanse*.

Africans continued to reach the Caribbean and Brazil for much longer than the United States, even if in small quantities: in Cuba and Brazil because slavery was not abolished until the 1890s, and in Trinidad and Jamaica because contract laborers from Africa were brought in during the 1850s. Moreover, the cotton gin—which made large-scale plantation slave labor viable in the southern United States—and the large-scale production of sugar were at their peak in the nineteenth century. In the United States in particular, this was too late for the resulting concentration of slaves living in barracks to act as much of a preservative of African music, though in some places it intensified neo-African survivals. And according to Morton Marks, more Yoruba slaves were smuggled to Cuba and Brazil after the 1820s than were involved in the entire slave trade of the early period.

African musicians and (to a weakening extent) those of African descent in the Americas, then, certainly preserved and developed their African heritage. But they also latched onto the new musical experiences they encountered, took from them whatever suited them, and blended both what they took and what they already had into something their own. Their attitude, in other words, was entirely positive, as indeed one would expect from highly creative people.

Francis Bebey quotes André Schaeffner to the effect that the African musician is "extremely gifted, sensitive to the smallest of influences, capable of assimilating them completely, always recognizable through what he has borrowed." John Ligon, "Gent," an apparently skillful amateur musician (whom I quoted in Chapter 1), provides an excellent example of the inquiring nature of the dedicated musician. We heard from Ligon how he came across a slave named Macow making a six-note xylophone. Having got over his surprise that the thing worked, he wrote, "I then shewed him the difference between flats and sharps, which he presently apprehended, as between *Fa* and *Mi:* and he would have cut two more billets to those tunes, but I had then no time to see it done, and so left him to his own enquiries." Macow, in other words, did not ignore the Gent. He took his chance to learn something new and to test its usefulness. Whether or not he decided that fa and mi suited his purpose after trying them out, he did not simply reject a new possibility as coming from a member of the slave-owning class, no doubt proffered with some condescension.

But granted that musically inclined slaves and free blacks—the manumitted slaves who began to form a growing minority quite early in South America and parts of the United States—might seize upon any chance to add to their musical range, how much chance did they have? Was there opportunity to hear European music, or were slaves kept too strictly out of contact with whites? The answer is that contact was usually plentiful, though the amount varied from area to area and from time to time. The evidence is that *musical* contact, too, was widespread and started early.

In the Spanish and Portuguese colonies, in fact, it was organized. The Portuguese and Spanish took a deep interest in the spiritual welfare of the slaves as they saw it, which entailed teaching them church music. In Brazil, the Jesuits had by the early seventeenth century set up a school for the musical instruction of slaves, which later became known as the Conservatorio dos Negros. Activity of that sort had to be confined to the towns, but there is evidence of some social and musical mixing even on the plantations.

Mixing seems to have been heaviest and come earliest in the Spanish areas, because the Spaniards did not subscribe to the apartheid notions common among the slave-owning classes of the Anglo-Saxon countries. The earliest written account of the *bomba* dance of Puerto Rico was published in 1798 by a French naturalist, André Pierre Ledru. Ledru refers to "a drum popularly called bomba by the workers of an estate, white, mulatto and black, as accompaniment to their dances." Elsewhere, describing a dance given at a country house for the birth of a child, he comments: "The amalgam of whites, mulattoes and Negroes formed a pleasing and agreeable group. . . . They danced in turn Negro and creole dances [creole here meant Spanish-Caribbean], to the sound of a guitar and of a drum commonly called the *bamboula*."

Ledru mentions two of the most widespread Afro-Caribbean dances (more precisely, the drums from which they took their names), and both in connection with multiracial parties. In fact it seems as if the dances Ledru saw may have been re-Africanized later, so to speak, a common enough happening, as we shall see. Certainly the *bomba* dances came under heavy Haitian influence through slaves brought by French settlers after the Haitian rebellion. Their mixed ancestry is particularly relevant to their history in Puerto Rico, where the *bomba* did not become a national dance but remained part of the black heritage there, mostly in the area of the sugar plantations. Some *bomba* lyrics preserve a large number of words of African origin, like this one:

> Aya, bombe, quinombo!
> Ohe, ohe mano Migue!
> Ayaya, sahu, caru!
> Che, Che, quinombo!

The contact of blacks with white music did not stop with partying. The historian Gilberto Freyre says that in Brazil "there were also plantations that had their black choir boys, their musicians, their grand pianos. As early as the sixteenth century a rich planter of Bahia had his orchestra of Negroes directed by a Frenchman from Marseilles." He also reports the surprise of a nineteenth-century traveler (a missionary from the United States) when he visited a plantation and heard an operatic overture and the Stabat Mater performed by a full orchestra and choir, all black.

Contact between white and black Americans varied in its nature, of course, as well as in degree. By no means was it always strictly a master-servant relationship. Frederick Olmstead, visiting the Southern states shortly before the Civil War, remarked: "I am struck with the close cohabitation and association of black and white." LeRoi Jones, quoting Olmstead in *Blues People*, observes that, apart from a growth in the mulatto population, "certainly the most significant result was the rapid acculturation of the African in this country." And in fact, except in some parts of the South, the average slave owner lorded it over an average of two or three blacks. Narratives by escaped slaves make it clear that they often worked on virtually equal terms with whites, especially on small farms.

In the cities, there was a growing number of free blacks and also of artisan-slaves, who in many instances, as Henry A. Kmen describes them in eighteenth-century New Orleans, "lived as though they were free, reporting periodically to their owners for the purpose only of making a stipulated money payment from their earnings. . . . In short, New Orleans was full of slaves who, for part or most of their time, were not too distinguishable from their legally free brethren." In 1806 a number of slave-owners complained to the U.S. governor of New Orleans because the police did not prevent their slaves from frequenting bars run by free men of color. The slaves, the owners said, "passed most of their nights in dancing and drinking," and their work suffered next day.

Most slaves may not have had as much freedom as the blacks in New Orleans, and conditions on many plantations (especially in the British West Indies) were bestial, but there still were plenty of opportunities for Africans and creole blacks to hear and, more important, to learn whatever they found valuable in the music of white Americans. And that was true of the North as well.

There is, however, a problem of language in sorting out this very complex situation. Epstein's sources were not uniformly contemptuous of even the neo-African music they heard. One, in fact, reported of a West Indian island that the blacks were far more musical than the whites. But even when the commentators were themselves musical, they used European terminology to describe what they heard. And that was even truer of commentaries on Afro-American dance. Especially in the early days, a large number of obviously African and neo-African social dances were called "jigs" by white writers even though they bore very little resemblance to the Irish and English jigs in footwork, which in Africa tend to be flat-footed, although they may be quite as fast as the very rapid Irish jig. However, there may have been a mixed Irish/African-American jig, as well. Marshall and Jean Stearns, in their *Jazz Dance,* quote an account of a great warren of a place in New York City where free blacks and recently arrived Irish cohabited cheek by jowl. Charles Dickens described a dancer there who was, the Stearns say, almost certainly "Master Juba"—William Henry Lane, a freeman probably born in Rhode Island, who was by all accounts the greatest dancer of his generation. All the descriptions make it clear that Lane danced an Africanized jig, full of cross-rhythms traceable back to African practice, but as far as one can tell from Dickens's quote, it was also based at least in part on Irish footwork (no mean feat; as the Stearns remark, good Irish jig dancers execute fifteen taps a second).

This close and equal contact between African-Americans and Irish peasants explains how African-Americans could encounter the jig and adapt it to their own purposes and their own dances (so much so that this Anglo-Irish word joined the long list of opprobrious nicknames for African-Americans, as in "Jigtown"). Thus a truly Afro-American dance idiom developed with strong elements from both Europe and Africa.

Similar contacts in New Orleans no doubt explain the adoption of songs like the Anglo-Irish "St. James's Infirmary." One common variant called "Gambler's Blues" has many added verses, but the original Anglo-Irish funeral-procession verses are still central to the song, although adapted. Even on the U.S. plantations, opportunities for this kind of crossover were not totally absent. Many slave owners actively encouraged music-making (except for the dreaded music of the drums), especially the playing of white or white-oriented music, often going so far as to supply fiddles and strings.

Of course, musical acculturation was a two-way process, a fact still too little emphasized on either side of this culturally artificial fence—blacks and whites influenced *each other* consistently and complexly. Indeed, the Inquisition in the Spanish parts of the Western Hemisphere spent a large part of its time taking futile legal action against manifestations of black influence on its white charges. St. Hilaire, a French scientist who visited Brazil in the nineteenth century, reported rather disapprovingly on a governor's ball at which a mulatto girl had danced a fandango, with much shaking of her hips, in an intermission between the quadrilles. There were complaints as early as 1691 in Puerto Rico that the dances for Noche Buena, which was celebrated in the cathedral, were becoming scandalous. Bishop Padilla wrote that mulattoes taking part "danced to the music of guitars; their movements were correct, but a voluptuous and sensual suppleness invaded the people watching."

It is no coincidence that so many examples of "contagion" occurred in the Portuguese and Spanish areas. As I noted earlier, the Iberian Peninsula—especially the south, from which most of the emigrants to the New World came—had musical and dance cultures influenced by eight centuries of Arab-Islamic rule. Two of the three largest groups of Africans taken to the Americas, especially Brazil, had themselves come under second-degree Maghreb Arab musical influence. Where African and European music have the most in common, in fact, is in the Islam-influenced areas of both continents, and it is the black-Latin regions of the New World where a most truly national music has been synthesized from the two sources.

But just because it is less obvious, it would be totally misleading to discount the effect on whites of black musicians, attendance at black dances, the close relationship of white children with black servants, and all the other ways in which whites picked up post-African music and dance, as well as the reverse. As always, stereotypes disguise the richness of the two-way contacts, but it has been convincingly shown that—just as blacks adopted Irish and English ballads and fiddle-tunes, and elements of Appalachian dance—so "white America" from speech to posture to hillbilly music to American modern dance are centrally and essentially "Afro-European."

At all events, for different reasons and in different degrees, Africans and black creoles quickly became involved in the musical activities of their areas—as early as the seventeenth century even in Mexico, which was obviously less affected by the black experience than many other countries. In places where there were few whites willing to take up the relatively low-status music professions, the pattern that soon developed had blacks playing to entertain whites.

Black musicians had to play music acceptable to whites, but when bending this music to match their enduring African or African-derived concepts of musicianship, they were also bound to Africanize white tastes.

In all the black regions of the New World, African-Americans made two contributions to the cultural pattern: the neo-African music they developed and maintained for their own private consumption; and the transformations they wrought in predominantly white music when they performed it. Black performance led to the creation of new black musical styles out of mixed elements, imparted African influences to white styles, and at the same time played a major part in the development of Afro-European national styles. The existence of both plantation slaves remote from white cultural influence, and house and urban slaves who not merely shared but heavily influenced a mainly white life, was mirrored in a wide variation in the extent of black musical experience and effect from one place to another.

The degree to which an Afro-European culture developed or a neo-African culture was retained depended on the relative geographical isolation of the areas involved and on their economic and social stagnation or development. Where the old single-crop plantations have survived—in much of Haiti, coastal Venezuela and Colombia, northeastern Brazil, and even parts of the U.S. South—change has been slow. It has always come fastest in any part of the world where different cultures have met and mingled most intimately.

Anthropologists have long recognized the differing degrees of African survival. Melville J. Herskovits devised a method of grading this survival on a scale from A to E in the categories of technology, economic life, social organization, institutions, religion, magic, art, folklore, masks, and language. The village of Toco in Trinidad scored A for technology (meaning a high African-derived content), while Port of Spain scored E. The Bush Negroes of Suriname rate consistently highly African, and northern U.S. urban blacks are consistently low. This sort of scale is a handy way to encapsulate findings, but it can be dangerously misleading. It would be absurd to claim that northern U.S. blacks no longer retain any part of an African heritage; it has simply transmuted into a rich African-American culture. Besides, the question of quantity is vague and to some extent irrelevant. What makes a curried chicken: the chicken or the spices? If one could measure it, would "5 percent African" or "7 percent Irish" be much or little? It might well be crucial in the development of a new culture.

The total impact of the various Afro-American cultures has been massive both in the New World and beyond it, and they have depended on the creative use of elements from several cultures. All these cultures have, in one way or another, preserved African characteristics, not just as decoration but as the major element distinguishing them from surrounding cultures. As will be seen, this is as true for the United States as for areas where far more overtly African music is preserved. Indeed, it may be more so: in countries where the neo-African music survives, the alternate music is often more a black-influenced national music than Afro-American music as such.

The mutual influences of different cultures in the New World were not all black-white, though these were dominant because of the numbers involved. I have already mentioned the Afro-Indian cults of Brazil. Another fascinating Afro-Indian mix is seen in the black Caribs of Honduras, the descendants of two shiploads of slaves who were wrecked on the coast of Saint Vincent in 1635. They were subjected by the Carib Indians among whom they fell to a gentle domestic form of slavery. Soon they, and other escaped slaves who had joined them, intermarried with Indian women and produced a people who look physically African and speak a Carib transmuted by African pronunciation. The black Caribs were deported to Honduras during one of the many Caribbean wars, and there they are to this day, partly descended from Nigerian Efik and Ibo, and partly Carib Indian.

As time went on, blacks who were excluded from all forms of political organization sometimes built up parallel structures, like the bodies in New Hampshire and Rhode Island set up to arrange Carnival displays. Some were new organizations, others grew out of the neo-African nations. They often set up, in what appears to have been a double entendre, governing hierarchies led by kings or governors, possibly to deride white institutions or possibly because West African secret societies were hierarchical. In Haiti, communal work groups set up for harvesting and other farm work had a quite complicated mock military and governmental framework. Such organizations, wherever they grew up, ostensibly adopted white forms but also seem to have kept many Africanisms (of course, there were parallels between the African and European power structures to begin with, particularly relating to monarchy/chiefdom).

By far the most important Afro-American organizations, of course, were the black churches. In the United States, and to some extent in the British Caribbean, these took the loose form natural for adherents of certain Protestant denominations (mainly Methodist and Baptist). In the Roman Catholic areas the black churches, springing up around a church that was much more rigidly hierarchical but also gave scope for far more kinds of official grouping, were more variegated but less fundamental to the central faith. They were also more upsetting to the majority church because of the strongly centralized nature of the Roman Catholic Church during much of its history, which extended its usual insistence on religious uniformity into areas

In much of South and Central America, the musical strands were threefold—African, Amerindian, and Spanish. African elements in fact color virtually all New World music, including that of people like this Uruguayan melon-seller, with no apparent African ancestry.
Photo courtesy of the United Nations

where an outsider might consider it entirely irrelevant, such as details of worship practice. In seventeenth-century Mexico, for example, there were complaints that Negroes were holding their own religious festivals, called *oratorios*, simultaneously with the official festivals to "ridicule" them. These *oratorios* were first reported by the Inquisition in 1669. They continued for a considerable time despite the Inquisition's persecution. There was a mass trial of people who took part in a similar function, called an *escapulario*, in Mexico City in 1682.

I really doubt whether the black *oratorios* were in fact mocking white activities. In view of how extremely tenacious they were in the face of persecution, it seems more likely that the *oratorios*, *escapularios*, and similar happenings were devout attempts at a reinterpretation of Christian festivals to suit African and African-inherited attitudes toward worship. Such a reinterpretation is occurring in twentieth-century Africa, where a large number of indigenous churches have sprung up because European worship styles do not adequately express African devotion. The Spanish Catholic hierarchy of the time being both powerful and rigid in attitude, it is not surprising that black attempts at freedom of Christian worship met persecution in the Spanish Americas, when similar attempts in the United States met little worse than disapproval or con-descending amusement.

The Mexican black Christians could not set up separate churches, but they did (in Guadalajara at least) have communities simulating the orders of Saint Dominic, Saint Francis, and others; they held regular offices, services with sermons, and so on. In the Week of Our Lady of Sorrows, a Dominican friar reported, these bodies held parades with trumpets and drums, "going round the wine shops," as he indignantly remarked.

As the Africans and their descendants moved toward the center of New World cultures, many of their customs also moved in the direction of Afro-Americanism. Thus, while preserving the neo-African cults, Afro-Americans developed all sorts of specifically Christian black traditions. In Venezuela, the feasts of San Juan and San Benito have their own music involving praise-songs in call-and-response style accompanied by drums. Afro-Christian traditions persist in a variety of burial customs found through most of the black Americas.

Africans attach great importance to funerals, believing that a dead man's send-off will affect his status on the other side. Venezuelan blacks hold partic-ularly elaborate wakes for small children who have died, as do those of the Dominican Republic and Puerto Rico. The gaiety of such occasions seems to reflect an African attitude, though it is rationalized in various ways. The Puerto Ricans hold a *baquiné*, a cheerful sung ceremony, on the ground that a child dies without sin and becomes an *angelito*. The Jamaicans hold that noth-ing sad must happen at a wake—locally called a "dinky" or a "nine-night."

A much-discussed U.S. phenomenon is the ring shout, a religious dance of considerable Africanism. It will be discussed in Chapter 5, but for the moment it should be included in the category of religious adaptation. Its possession states and its features were described by Courlander: "Postures and gestures, the manner of standing, the bent knees, the feet flat on the floor or ground, the way the arms are held out for balance or pressed against the sides, the move-ments of the shoulders, all are African in conception." Such traits are also fre-quent in Jamaican Revival Zion services, where a dipping and swaying of shoulders and a kind of marching on the spot are akin to dancing. Some orig-inally religious music and dances became secularized, usually in connection with Carnivals, like the Uruguayan *candombe*, a parade dance to devastating percussion only tenuously related to its ostensible origins in the "nations."

The Afro-American role in the growth of New World festivals and Carnivals is significant. The Carnival at Mardi Gras is an old European Roman Catholic habit; indeed, in France and Spain—and to a lesser degree Britain—saints' days have always been associated with jollity (and very often, to the distress of the authorities, "lewdness and offensiveness"). Anybody who has been in a small Spanish town on the local saint's day or on London's Hampstead Heath at Easter knows this. European fiestas include dancing and parades but do not accentuate them (except for maypole dancing, a relic of pre-Christian ritual). If anything sets the New World Carnivals apart, it is their highly African mix of music (usually heavily Afro-American music), dancing, and parades, in which costume is a most important element. Most Carnivals have focused on Mardi Gras, and most, from Brazil through Trinidad to New Orleans, are associated with Afro-American musical forms. These will be described in more detail in Chapters 3, 4, and 5 for each region; for the moment their African content is worth noting.

The history of the slaves' attempts to squeeze a little fun out of life in the face of the authorities is filled with accounts of black dances held in city squares. When they became loud and frequent enough to get on the nerves of white residents, they were either banned or confined to certain times and places. The celebrated dances in New Orleans's Congo Square are an example. Mexico City at the beginning of the seventeenth century allowed slaves to dance publicly only in the main square on festival days. Such actions may well have helped to bring about the Africanization of Carnivals.

The process of Afro-Americanization is reflected, at a more functional level, in the appearance of a variety of Afro-American musical instruments that are clearly African in inspiration but cannot be called neo-African. The best known, of course, is the banjo. Another is the Cuban *cajón*, a hollow box used as a rhythm instrument, developed from the African slit-drum. Harold Courlander surmises that the U.S. washtub bass (which I have also seen and recorded in Tortola, British Virgin Islands) was a descendant of the earthbow, described in Chapter 1 and found in Africa, Haiti, and occasionally the Dominican Republic. (A particularly esoteric equivalent of the earthbow recorded in Florida involved attaching a cord to the side of a house and essentially playing the house!) Courlander also mentions the use in the United States and Cuba of frying pans tuned a fourth apart, an obvious substitute for the two-tone bells or gongs found in many parts of West Africa.

The Cubans also used a door, hit with the hand, as an instrument in some forms of the rumba (some experts claimed the music was not the same without a good door part!). The use of the washboard is quite well known. U.S. bands also used a jug, blown across the opening to produce a bass note. This too was used in Cuba: It can be heard on records by the Septeto Habanero, an old band that made many fine recordings of *sones*. Various other homemade instruments were contrived to make bass sounds. Old Jamaican *mento* (country dance) bands sometimes used what was called a "wooden trumpet." I own one that is a straight length cut from a hollow branch of a trumpet tree. The man who

led two holes in the side near the end into which he blew and dec-
th faintly West African-looking doodles in red paint. It produces
ious notes, rather reminiscent of jug-blowing. All these instruments, when used, sound much like African friction drums, and it seems possible that they were developed as substitutes.

The New World *marimbula* falls between the categories of neo-African
and Afro-American. Though it is bigger, it is still similar in principle to its
African counterpart, the finger-piano. But its pitch and its function have
changed. In Africa the finger-piano normally supplies melorhythmic counterpoint, often to a singer; the Caribbean *marimbula* is used to provide a bass line.
It still often shows African details in its construction—most instruments of
more than five notes place their longest and deepest-sounding notes in the
middle, not at one end—but it usually plays the bass in popular dance styles
that are themselves a mixture of European and African ingredients.

It is relatively easy to spot instruments with a wholly or partly African
background, but, as the case of the *marimbula* shows, one is on trickier ground
when looking for the origins of playing techniques or the overall role of certain instruments. Some techniques—that of the *cata 'ticks* or the use of a heel
as a mute when drumming—are simple and obvious. But other possible elements are less so; Courlander suggests that the use of a double bass as a wholly
rhythmic instrument, never bowed (at least in the same piece), is an Afro-
Americanism. This seems plausible, but it is something one either believes or
does not.

Other basic Africanisms that writers have detected in jazz include other
aspects of the rhythm section. Composer Olly Wilson, as quoted by Ingrid
Monson in her study of jazz, *Saying Something,* argues that the jazz group's
basic division into separate melodic and rhythmic sections is a characteristic of
African music, and Monson herself observes argues that "this idea of one
limb carrying a solid, repeating rhythmic pattern that other rhythms are
played against has strong continuities with both West African drum ensembles
and the Caribbean Latin percussion sections they have influenced." She also
suggests plausibly enough that the function of the ride cymbal in bebop
drumming is analogous to that of the bell pattern played by the *gankogui* in
Ewe drum ensembles, and adds: "This repeating pattern is the reference point
against which the remaining percussion instruments orient their parts. The
timbales part, which is an elaboration of an underlying clave pattern not
always directly played, often fulfills this function in Afro-Cuban music." So,
more obviously, does the *cencerro* or cowbell.

It would be remarkable if African ideas of musical function, musical customs, and ideas of music's social role had *not* had an effect on Afro-American

Percussion in the making: male and female goatskins pegged out to dry in the Dominican Republic, ready for the construction of an archetypally Euro-African drum, the tambora.
Photo by John Storm Roberts

music. But many must remain a matter of belief. The Panamanian *tamboritos* appear to be exclusively a women's music, or at least to have been so in the past. Does this reflect the widespread African tendency to regard certain sorts of music (and even certain musical instruments) as being men's, and others as women's? I think so, but the idea is neither provable nor disprovable.

Of the strictly musical Africanisms that have endured to become fundamental Afro-Americanisms, one of the most obvious, though difficult to pin down, is an attitude to rhythm. In the words of Nestor Ortiz Oderigo, writing in the magazine *African Music*, "even in the countries where the melodic ground shows the impact of Occidental cultural patterns, the unmistakable Negro rhythm pulsates in full strength." The pervasiveness of neo-African rhythmic attitudes is hardly surprising, given the sophistication of African rhythmic techniques, but it is perhaps surprising that they persist even where the blacks themselves have either totally or largely disappeared, as in Chile and Argentina. Ortiz Oderigo reports that two of the most widespread Argentinean rural dances, the *chacarera* and the *gato*, make use of duple and triple rhythm played together, and that the *bombo* players beat alternately on the head and the rim of the drum, a practice that seems to be drawn from both Africa and Spain (and which is a feature of the drumming in the Colombian *porro*). Naturally, the use in Spanish music of triple and duple meter in the same piece of music, shared by many African groups, facilitated the adoption and retention of the African joint duple-triple polyrhythmic approach, but it is still a striking survival in what is considered "white" South America.

There used to be a good deal of argument, apparently designed to downplay the African rhythmic contribution, about possible Spanish roots of various Caribbean and South American rhythms. There is an extremely widespread rhythmic pattern in the black music of the Americas, whose most usual form is this:

This is the basic rhythm of the Cuban habanera, the Argentinean tango, the Dominican merengue, and many Trinidadian calypsos. Alvarenga says it is widely used in Brazilian music; it is also the rhythm of the Puerto Rican *danza*, which was widespread in the Caribbean in the nineteenth century and is still popular in places.

There are those who have pointed out that it is much the same rhythm as the *tango andaluz* of Spain, and have argued a Spanish origin from that. But there is growing evidence that the *tango andaluz* is in fact a Hispanicization of the Argentinean tango, carried by the very large number of Andalucian settlers who went back home to Spain during a recession at the turn of this century, when the tango was already developing in Argentina. The view that the tango had to come from Spain is not so much racist as culturist—part of the old European view that Americans of whatever hue couldn't really come up with much of anything culturally, let alone feed it back to Europe.

The case for an ultimate Spanish origin of this widespread little rhythmic figure, dubious even in the tango itself—most Argentinean scholars now believe it was a multiracial (that is, Afro-Italo-Spanish) development with an African-derived name—becomes much weaker when one considers how many songs from the folk stratum of the southern United States use versions of it, not, it is true, as the basic rhythm, but in melodic phrases that recur far too often for coincidence, and many of which are stressed not *with* the verbal stress of the lyric but *against* it. And it spread far beyond the folk, being an extremely common rhythm in the right hand of piano ragtime (set against a steady "oompah" in the left) in the form known as the "cakewalk figure." (I also believe it was strengthened by a strong influence from the Cuban habanera popular in the United States in the 1880s, but that is to date very far from proven). From ragtime, of course, it passed into jazz, where it is a common phrasing in front-line solos (an example is Jimmy Archey's trombone solo in "Edna," as a member of King Oliver's band).

The *tango andaluz* would be a small root to bear this huge flowering, even if there were any evidence that it yet existed at the time of the Cuban habanera's greatest popularity, which began in the 1830s and lasted half a century. A common rhythmic element in Spanish and Caribbean music, traceable back one way through West Africa and the other through Iberia, meeting in the Muslim Maghreb, is plausible. But when I see a widely differing European element and a common African element, in a field (rhythm) in which Africans excel, I see little reason to look further.

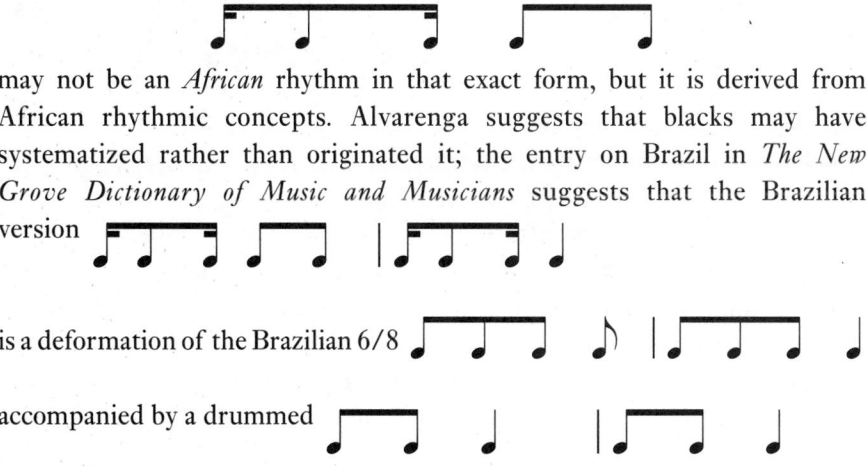

may not be an *African* rhythm in that exact form, but it is derived from African rhythmic concepts. Alvarenga suggests that blacks may have systematized rather than originated it; the entry on Brazil in *The New Grove Dictionary of Music and Musicians* suggests that the Brazilian version

is a deformation of the Brazilian 6/8

accompanied by a drummed

Either way, it represents a common cultural element spread through the black New World from Brazil to the United States.

African melody seems not to have survived in a pure form except in the neo-African forms, and even there the sung melodies usually show a strong European influence. Very few actual African melodies can be found in the United States, despite frankly implausible attempts to find a Zambian origin for "Swing Low, Sweet Chariot." On the other hand, African *attitudes* to music almost universally have parallels on the western side of the Atlantic, and so do certain techniques. One important instance is the universality of call-and-response singing in work songs.

Not only are the more neo-African work song forms cast in the call-and-response mold, but also work songs that in other respects show a good deal of non-African influence. It is true of U.S. work songs; of Jamaican work songs, which show strong elements of British folk and hymn harmonies; and of blended styles in Spanish-speaking areas too. On the island of Margarita, Venezuela, two women were recorded pounding corn and singing like this:

> *c:* Ay ay ay ay
> *r:* viva el sol y viva la luna
> *c:* Ay ay ay ay
> *r:* viva limata 'e limon
> *c:* Ay ay ay ay
> *r:* Ay que vivan mis amores con el joven Asunción

This is a beautiful example of an Euro-African blend, its lyric and melody in a highly Spanish mode with the repeated "ay ay ay ay" (thought to come from the Arabic device of a highly ornamented, long-drawn-out "ah-ah-ah" before a line), but split up by the African influence so that it is call-and-response instead of solo. This work song comes from the largely black province of Barlovento, where the call-and-response form in melodies showing both Spanish and African content—usually accompanied by drums in a rhythm much like the

I mentioned earlier—is quite common. The Dominican Republic has a range of *cantos de hacha* (axe songs) in which call-and-response is used to keep a group of men, or even two men, alternately chopping the same log, in time. These are remarkably varied: the response is often a two-note "ah-eh eh-ah," but the call lines vary from very African phrases to European-derived quatrains with the response at the end of each line.

Of course, many if not most sorts of work song are a natural form for call-and-response, and it might be said that the demands of communal work explain its widespread occurrence. But call-and-response is also found in music where its presence has no such logic. In the Cibao area of the Dominican Republic, for example, the most common forms of folk music are the religious *salve* and the secular *tonada,* sung unaccompanied, usually by groups of women. Both are of highly Spanish influence in music and words, and show absolutely no black characteristics, except that the *tonadas* are almost universally sung call-and-response (the *salves* use a more European lining-out technique, of two choruses singing against each other). A large number of the *tonadas* use the old ten-line Spanish *décima* verse, and breaking into this tight form with single-line group responses is in the highest degree illogical when there's no excuse for it like chopping wood. The practice is so ingrained that, when I asked one woman in a group I was recording for an example of a solo lullaby, the whole group came in massively with a "response" at the end of the first line! So there it is: *One* African feature in an otherwise totally un-African music—and a theoretically functionless (although beautiful) feature, at that.

Given the importance of dance in African culture, it is not surprising that a wide range of Afro-American dances developed out of a twin Afro-European tradition. Both the African and the European dances that met in America tended to consist of a series of linked sections, each with its own music. Sometimes a fundamentally European dance became partly or largely Africanized, either taken over by blacks or "Afro-Americanized" by the infusion of creole elements, many of which were African-derived.

Not all definitely or possibly African-influenced music was working class or peasant in origin. One European dance with a quite classy ancestry was the Spanish version of the *contradanza,* which reached broad areas of the Caribbean and was popular as a salon dance in the nineteenth century. It is thought to have started as an English "country dance" of the type that were at one time fashionable at the English court and spread to the courts of France and Spain. During the nineteenth century the *contradanza* was popular both at ballroom and folk levels, especially in Cuba and Puerto Rico. Its descendants are not black dances as such, but it seems unlikely that they could have become what they are without the black experience.

Venezuela has a dance that preserves the dual cultures quite neatly, the highly complex *tamanungue,* which has eight figures. The center four figures have pronounced black features, including a good deal of room for improvisation (unknown in analogous European dances). The outer four stem from

Clifton Chenier singing and playing a Louisiana *zydeco,* a blend of blues with the music of French-speaking white Cajuns of the region. Much of Louisiana's music is closer to Caribbean music than to that of the rest of the United States. The metal percussion instrument worn by one musicians is unique to zydeco.

Photo by Chris Strachwitz, courtesy of Arhoolie Records

creolized European dances, including the *contradanza.* The dance itself takes its name from the *tamanungo* drum, which is the core of its rhythm section.

Creole dances with European roots were extremely widespread in the Caribbean at least until the 1920s. Local forms of the quadrille were still remembered with affection by older country people in Jamaica when I was recording there in the early 1970s. The French islands of Martinique and Guadeloupe, as well as a large number of other islands (Latin and non-Latin), have adopted and adapted the Polish mazurka and Bohemian polka, along with creolized waltzes. Creolized waltzes are also found in the French-language black zydeco music of Louisiana, whose link with the Caribbean, via New Orleans, hasn't really been explored. A highly syncopated "Lafayette Waltz," played by the accordionist Clifton Chenier, is fairly typical. Such dances were played in a wide variety of styles. Some were only lightly creolized, like quadrilles I recorded in Jamaica, which still preserved recognizable Scots tunes and rhythms. Others, like a quadrille I recorded among English-speaking settlers in the Dominican Republic, had recognizable British antecedents, but the hot drumming and fife-playing showed a high degree of Africanization of European material.

The "mummies" of Saint Kitts and Nevis (and these Nevis settlers in the Dominican Republic) preserve a form of English medieval Christmas play accompanied by a highly Africanized version of fife-and-drum music probably derived from eighteenth-century British military bands. The costumes are a pastiche of European styles old and new, common in the New World.
Photo by John Storm Roberts

The flute-and-percussion bands are a subject in and of themselves. They are found throughout the anglophone and parts of the francophone Caribbean, playing all sorts of music. And they also had a parallel in the United States in the fife-and-drum bands of Mississippi musicians like Napoleon Strickland and Othar Turner, described at length in Alan Lomax's *The Land Where the Blues Began.* Some similarly sounding bands also exist in West Africa, notably on the coast of Ghana and Sierra Leone. This underlines the importance of not blindly attributing everything found both in Africa and in the Americas to an African root; both in Africa and the New World, these bands appear to have derived from the European and Revolutionary War fife-and-drum bands. They are in fact not direct African survivals but further examples of a re-Africanization of European material through inherited and African-derived attitudes to music (and dance, as Lomax's description makes clear).

It would, however, be equally as dangerous to assume that every African-like survival in the United States was a re-Africanization of European sources as to assume the reverse. I've already mentioned some of the music found in the Gullah culture of the Sea Islands. This was a very isolated area with a very

Blending traditions: a version—this one Dominican—of the almost ubiquitous Caribbean fife-and-drum music uses home-made drums Africanized from an old European military model, played with purely Afro-American intensity.
Photo by John Storm Roberts

small white population, and many of its special features are very clearly African or neo-African, including the large number of Bantu words in the Gullah dialect and everybody's childhood chum Brer Rabbit in the bargain, who is simply the hare found in Bantu folk tales all over sub-Saharan Africa.

The black modification of dances extended beyond the folk stratum. One Afro-Brazilian dance, the *lundú,* moved from the streets to the bourgeois salons during the nineteenth century (purged of most of its hip movements), and thence traveled with a talented mulatto composer to Lisbon, where it became the rage. Allusions to a salon dance called the *congo* in Cuba and Louisiana and to hybrid dances like the *congo-minuet* indicate the same process.

It is remarkably easy to sell short surviving Africanisms in a country or region where they have been thoroughly assimilated into the general culture. Marvin Harris, in a fascinating book entitled *Town and Country in Brazil,* states: "Throughout the area there are very few remnants of African culture patterns." Harris remarks that what there are have moved out into the non-African population. But he underestimates the African contribution to national culture when he points out (rightly) that the samba and allied forms are pan-Brazilian and ignores their neo-African sources. He then goes on to recount a wedding custom that incorporates a samba containing the African

A virtually unique nineteenth-century example of Afro-European blending was provided by New Orleans creole composer Louis Moreau Gottschalk, who worked in Cuba and Brazil among other places. In the 1870s he wrote several Brazilian- and Cuban-inspired works, including some remarkable piano solos like a Cuban rag 20 years early.
Courtesy of Special Collections Division, Tulane University Library

umbrigada, that is, the belly-bounce! The essential point is not, of course, that Africanisms are rare but that here, as in throughout the New World, they have become a fundamental part of everybody's inheritance. The New World black culture is at the heart of the American experience in many fields, including some not particularly associated with African-Americans. (I remember a striking lecture by Dr. Brenda Dixon-Gottschild in which she established, at least to my entire satisfaction, that all the elements distinguishing American modern [ballet] dance from European are Africanisms.)

Is there any logic in what died and what lived on? Were the survivals no more than lucky, passive survivors of an onslaught, whether of physical oppression or of cultural overlay? The British anthropologist Ernest Bornemann fifty years ago argued in *A Critic Looks at Jazz* that, from the start, all the songs and dances that filled no function in the new master-slave pattern died out; the surviving songs and dances were the ones that fitted into the new cultural and economic patterns: work songs, love songs, lullabies, play songs, and song games. Among the songs that died out, he contended, were those related to African social structures, such as initiation songs, legend songs, and genealogical songs.

There's no contesting this argument, if it is strictly limited to the songs and dances that have obviously survived unaltered or whose functions have not changed. But legend songs as a genre most certainly survived, even though with changed circumstances came changes in the legends. Both hero ballads like "John Henry" and badman ballads like "Stackolee" "and "Railroad Bill" are legend songs. Further, if legend songs are defined by function—giving the individual a sense of cohesion with his group, elaborating the way in which the group understands itself, and in general expressing the group's myths about itself—then the blues fit that definition, too. And even the historical and moralizing role of the *griot* seems echoed in some of the blues-ballads ("Frankie and Johnny" for example). It is important, however, not to ignore the body of white ballads, both brought over from the British borderlands like "Barbara Allen" and built of new circumstances like "The Wreck of the Old 97," or the great *corrido* tradition of the Spanish-speaking Southwest. Here, I think, we have the mutual fertilization of two or three traditions to create rich new versions in the United States.

The crux of the matter of Africanisms in the New World lies in what one means by "survival." Nothing, from an amoeba to a planet, can survive without adapting itself to new circumstances. Indeed, adaptation is a prime sign of life. Some people saw the arrival of the electric guitar as a sign that the blues were dead, when in fact it was a sign that the blues were living.

At one time anthropologists talked of survival and adaptation as if they were opposites. More to the point is what the French scholar Roger Bastide called "adaptive survival." In his book *Les Amériques Noires*, Bastide remarks that the African (or, as I have called them, neo-African) civilizations disappeared because the channels upward in the societies of the Americas demanded the acceptance of Christianity and Western values, and thus the rejection of African customs or beliefs. But in fact this rejection was never complete. And was it ever possible? Can any group of people really deny itself? That is what wholesale rejection of one's background (really the opposite of enriching it by taking in new ideas and concepts) would mean. If I am to assimilate new ideas, my conception of them must be affected by my background, and thus by the old ideas that I am consciously rejecting. If I am to borrow some new religious or social structures, they are not going to provide the close web of direction for the myriad choices of attitude I have to make every day. For these I have to fall back on what I learned from infancy onward.

The conscious adoption of a new culture, of course, is very different from acquiring new concepts by "infection," so to speak, by living cheek by jowl with new people in a new environment. This is not just possible but inevitable. Bastide remarks that a Brazilian black can participate in Brazilian political and economic life and at the same time be a member of an Afro-Brazilian cult without feeling any contradiction in this. And contemporary Kenyans will feel no contradiction in watching *Star Trek* while eating roast goat and drinking Scotch, because there *is* no real contradiction, only an apparent contradiction in a set of categories set up by somebody else for academic convenience.

Perhaps the best statement ever made about the ultimate meaning of music in *any* people's life was made by LeRoi Jones in *Blues People:*

> The most expressive Negro music of any given period will be an exact reflection of what the Negro himself is. It will be a portrait of the Negro in America at that particular time. Who he thinks he is, what he thinks America or the world to be, given the circumstances, prejudices, and delights of that particular America. Negro music and Negro life in America were always the result of a reaction to, and an adaptation of, whatever American Negroes were given or could secure for themselves.

Two related questions remain, presumably never to the totally answered. What survived, adapted or not? And further, given that there are many elements common to most African cultures, why did particular elements— Yoruba, Fanti-Ashanti, Congo-Angolan Bantu, Senegambian—dominate or die? Bastide sees the answer as chronological, with statistics showing that, in Brazil, the slave trade in the seventeenth century was mostly with Angola, and in the eighteenth and nineteenth centuries mainly with the more northerly area embracing the Yoruba, Fon, Ibo, and others. He points out that the latter elements dominate the Bantu in the Bahia area and concludes that the African cultural traits brought over in the seventeenth and eighteenth centuries were evidently lost, and that Afro-American civilizations stem from the influences at the end of the slave trade.

This may have a certain amount of validity, but is an oversimplification even for Brazil. Again the question of quantity versus quality arises. The *berimbau* musical bow (see Chapter 1) and its relatives almost certainly are Congo-Angolan in inspiration, if not direct origin, and they are hardly a marginal or obscure part of Afro-Brazilian culture, especially since their revival over the last twenty-five years. And if the chronological thesis is shaky for Brazil, it seems to be way off base elsewhere.

Paul Oliver, who discussed the question of Africanisms in the blues in the book *Savannah Syncopators*, argues convincingly that it was the Senegambian cultures (and allied cultures from the savanna belt) that provided the African

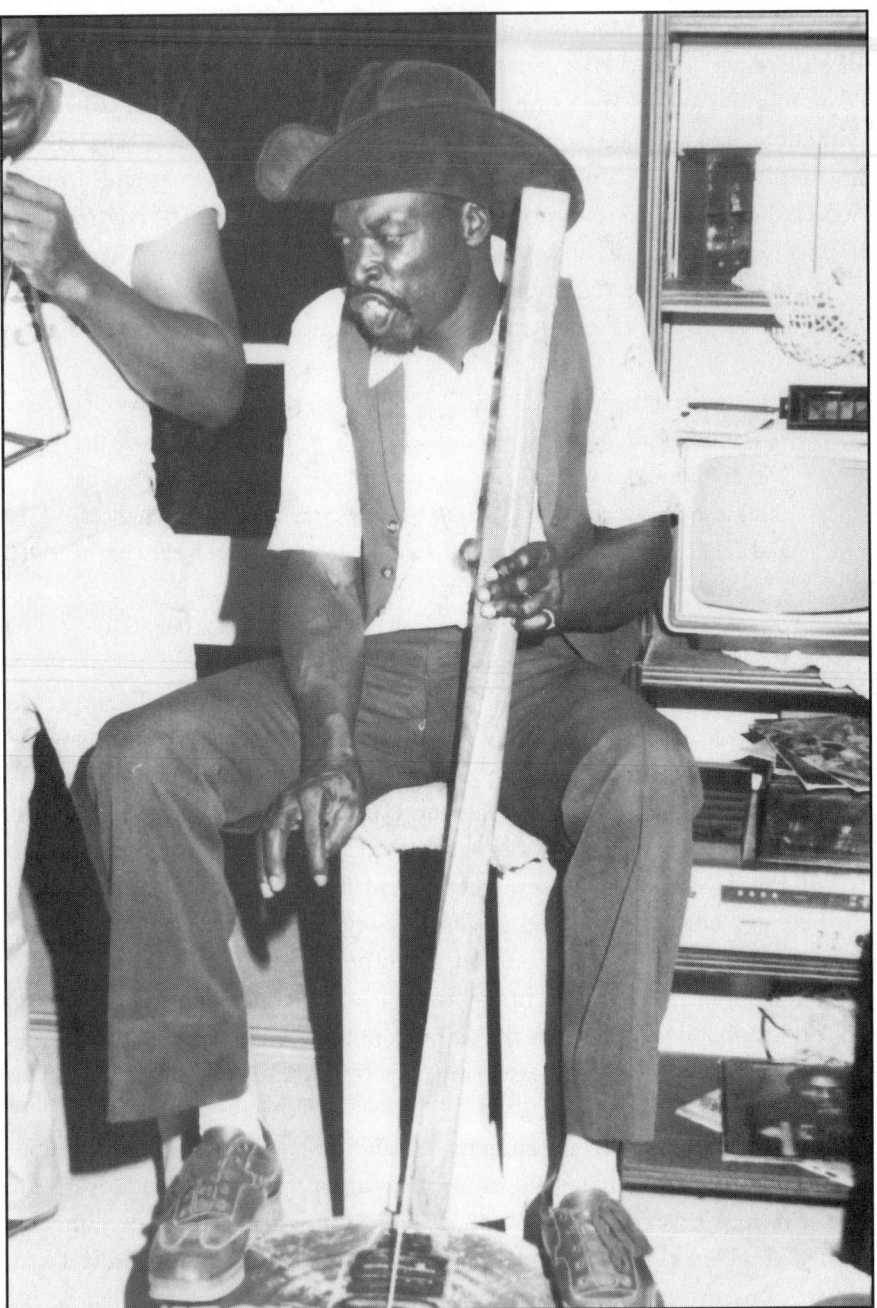

The washtub bass, whose inspiration is thought by some to be African, is found in the Caribbean as well as the United States: in this case in the Sparkplugs funji band of Tortola, BVI. The washtub bass, like the Haitian earthbow and the U.S. diddly bow and many African instruments, has one string. But the production of a large number of notes per string is a European concept.

Photo by Anne Needham

ingredient in the blues—and, according to the same logic, in a wide range of Afro-American breakdown and other dance music played on fiddle and banjo. Yet the Senegambian peoples were the earliest ethnic group in the United States to dominate statistically, and after the early days they never dominated again. This apparent anomaly is explainable, if one accepts that the early arrivals provided the basis for the enduring elements in many mainstream Afro-American forms, and the last arrivals the basis for the most African (least digested) forms. And in the case of the Senegambian presence in the blues, the issue was probably compatibility: the Wolof and Mandinka peoples played fiddles and other stringed instruments in small ensembles, and could adapt to Western equivalents without much effort. Therefore the early arrivals would have been likely to establish a precedent.

Of course, it is easy to make mistakes in deciding what Africanisms have survived. Moving into a wider field than music for a moment, various Africanisms survive in African-American English, although this is a highly speculative area with a lot of traps. (The mostly excellent book *The African Heritage of American English* ascribes the word "loll" to African sources, but Samuel Pepys used it in London when anglophone North America was in its infancy.) An area that sometimes intersects with music is Afro-American story telling. It is pretty widely recognized that the West African spider Anansi lives on in many Caribbean islands, lightly disguised as Anancy or Nancy. But far fewer people realize that Brer Rabbit's grandfather came from the Bantu peoples, whose Rabbit stories stretch all the way to East Africa; if you ever read a Swahili story about Sungura, that's him ("sungura" simply means rabbit).

Some survivals are too small or intimate for people to pay them much mind. An oral example is proverbs. "If snake bite you and you see lizard, you run" is a Jamaican version of a West African saying: "He whom a snake has bitten fears a slow-worm [a kind of lizard]." Such apparently unimportant traces are apt to be ignored, as are many intimate Africanisms in modern or recent Afro-American experience, from the naming of children after the day of the week on which they were born to ways of tying a head-cloth, carrying a baby straddled on the hip, or plaiting hair into what the Haitians call a "garden" of little braids (and some African names from before the post-1960 vogue for them, for example, trombonist Ed Cuffee was carrying the Ewe name "Kofi" under a different spelling).

Many survivals are somewhat special cases, like both language and customs associated with the Gullah of the Georgia Sea Islands. But African survivals are not necessarily obscure or rural. Both Africans and Jamaican farmers use big hoes or mattocks rather than spades to turn soil. When I had a house in Brooklyn in the 1970s, my tenant in the basement was a young

African-American musician from a Bronx middle-class background. Both being keen gardeners (he was a vegetable man, I wanted to plant flowers), we divided the back garden into zones of influence. Then I went out to buy a spade, Europe's sod-breaker, and he came back with a mattock of a type universal in Africa. (And no, he was not making a political statement.) Although he didn't sing while gardening, what he was doing was a one-man version of what rice-growing slaves in the Carolinas did, or the Jamaican peasants working their way in a line across a field with pickaxes singing a digging song, and what their ancestors had been doing in the fields of West Africa for centuries. How many other small, unnoticed differences of this kind are still alive at the center of American life?

At the other end of the scale, one would look for any fundamental attitude or group of attitudes—whether inherent or due to early social training—that might have some African background and that is shared by Afro-Americans as a whole, after allowing for individual differences. The political-cultural concept of "soul" certainly supposes that such an attitude exists. And John Miller Chernoff links the concept of "cool" with elements desirable in West African drumming and life. (This doesn't mean it is an exclusively African concept; the qualities defining a "man" in Kipling's poem "If" add up to a pretty cool dude.)

The Malawian scholar Dunduza Chisiza, writing on the question of an "African personality" in the *Journal of Modern African Studies* in 1963, contended that there are common features found in most African communities. He noted that Africans are not inclined to meditativeness like Eastern peoples, nor are they "inquisitive searchers" like Europeans, but primarily "penetrating observers, relying more on intuition than on the process of reasoning," and excelling in personal relations.

Chisiza also found them to be in pursuit of happiness rather than "truth" or "beauty." The ideal African way of life is communal, he wrote, based on strong and loving family relations shading into a general compassion (the Swahili expression for "my house" translates as "our house"). All activities, from hunting and harvesting to leisure pursuits, are communal; generosity and forgiveness are encouraged, malice and revenge abhorred. Moreover, Africans are renowned for their sense of humor and dislike of melancholy. Now, Chisiza is clearly accentuating the positive, and his profile could be said to have its drawbacks as well as its merits. But in my experience it is both true and highly significant in outline, and this pattern of qualities seems to be both preserved in Afro-American life (where circumstances permit) and relevant to musical developments, though mostly in ways not easily described.

One other remark made by Chisiza is, paradoxically, relevant to what I described as a highly conservative field, religion. Chisiza holds that African cultures have "a habitual desire for change, even in religion." This interesting thought bears upon the rise of black Christianity and upon syncretism, the blending of traditions, in general. It has often been said that Africans have traditionally had a respect for their conquerors' gods. African theology tends to explain the universe as being run according to a fate whose decrees can be changed by a supernatural being, if one can, by sacrifice or propitiation, persuade such a being to help out. Defeat in war suggests that the enemy has been enlisting gods with greater power than one's own, in which case it is only logical to do the same, but without deserting one's old gods, who may also have their strong points.

Something of the sort seems to have happened in many parts of Afro-America. I think it is safe to say that *all* black religious groups—from the largely African-derived cults like *candomblé* or Shango to the black Protestant churches of the United States—still contain Africanisms of either belief or liturgy and worshipping practice, or both. Some of these are quite striking. This is not to say, as some authors seem to suggest, that there is little substantive difference between the worship of Shango and the services of the Baptist churches of the United States. Worship is a conscious act, and people who say they are worshiping the God of the Bible are worshiping the God of the Bible, not a lightly worked-over Obatala figure.

On the one hand, West African religions survived and flourished in the New World, taking in Christian elements that suited them. On the other, black converts to Christianity worshiped in ways that expressed their devotion adequately, whether with rhythm, dancing, or ecstatic possession. In countries that followed the relatively rigid Roman Catholic liturgies, West African faiths flourished, whereas in the Protestant areas they did not. One reason, surely, is that it was entirely possible for black Protestants to integrate into Christian worship healing, speaking in tongues, dancing, handclapping, a variety of musical styles, chanted sermons, possession by the Holy Ghost—features they knew from Africa, none of which was alien to Biblical Christianity. The Roman Catholic tradition, meanwhile, was less able to shed its European cast.

Speaking of possession and trances, W. E. B. Du Bois commented that "many generations firmly believed that without this visible manifestation of the God there could be no true communion with the Invisible." Black Protestants saw no difficulty in integrating this central African belief with Christianity, because it already existed in the Christianity with which they had first come into contact. In fact, black Christians appear to have taken both African and white possession states and blended them. Possession is a major part of West African worship and, in an African form, in neo-African religions in the New World.

But possession was also common in the Methodist and Baptist "Great Revival," which spread from Britain to the United States and was responsible for the first large-scale conversions of slaves—in part because it was an integrated movement but also because it had many features in common with African worship practice (a quite different matter from theology).

White possession states are different in many respects from African, as Dr. Erika Bourguignon pointed out in an essay in *Afro-American Anthropology* on the difference between possession states in Haiti and those on the island of Saint Vincent. She showed that the Vincentian pattern of jerks, rocks, trembles, and talking in tongues is close to early British Methodist possession states, and that Haitian possession, which is much more specific to action, is African-based. Vincentians, unlike Haitians, do not interact with other people while in trance states. And most important of all, African and African-based trance states—whether in Benin, in a rural Haitian temple, or a storefront church in Brooklyn—are closely related to music and involve dance.

Based on Bourguignon's comparative analysis, possession states in black U.S. churches, and in at least some Caribbean ones, appear to result from a blend of African and English Methodist elements. I once witnessed a woman at a Jamaican Revival Zion meeting whose trance showed all the characteristics of the "English Methodist" forms: shudders, undirected swoops across the chapel, and "speaking in tongues" of a "white" variety. On the other hand, she played the tambourine and sang as part of the congregation and, while "speaking in tongues," certainly interrelated with another person after the service, shaking my hand and addressing me in glossolalia for what seemed like about five minutes. While trance states in United States Sanctified churches seem to have detached from the idea of possession by specific gods, Kenneth Bilby has told me that Afro-Christian worshipers in some West Indian churches believed themselves possessed by the archangels, a clear transference of West African possession by the gods.

Du Bois saw the conversion from African to Christian beliefs among slaves in the United States as a slow process. It was only in the early years of the nineteenth century that white Christians in any numbers showed much interest in ministering to the slaves, and these were mainly Baptists and Methodists, themselves hardly Establishment dignitaries. He believed that the link between Africa and the new black churches was the medicine man or priest: "He early appeared on the plantation and found his function as the healer of the sick, the interpreter of the Unknown, the comforter of the sorrowing, the supernatural avenger of wrong . . . thus, as bard, physician, judge and priest, rose the Negro preacher." Du Bois believed that Afro-American worship began as an "adaptation and mingling of heathen rites"—a *candomblé* or voodoo—which moved toward Christianity through time, contact with whites, and missionary effort.

Bastide cites the case of Jamaica to suggest that the old faiths broke into two parts, one united with Christianity and surviving through reinterpretation according to Christian beliefs (water rites blending into baptism, and possession by the gods becoming possession by the Holy Spirit), and the other losing most of its theological qualities and becoming mere magic. Most Jamaicans think of *obeah* as witchcraft, but in fact it has retained some religious elements, quite possibly Fanti-Ashanti, mostly to do with ancestor worship. It is, for one thing, connected like voodoo with the world of the spirits, although the sinister living dead, the *jumbis,* or the ghosts, the duppies, seem to play a more important part than do the zombies, whose role in Haitian folklore is rich but not very relevant to the basic concerns of voodoo. However, this is somewhat of an oversimplification. Both voodoo and Lucumí/Santería are products of New World blends, but their Roman Catholic elements are small though highly visible. In Santería they consist largely of gods/saints with dual identities, such as Shango/Saint Barbara.

In many African religions, the dead play a part in the affairs of the living that may be benevolent or malicious. When religion degenerated to magic, the dead on the whole turned sour. The special importance of the dead in black Christianity is not easy to define, though it is easy to recognize from the emphasis given funeral rites, wakes, and similar ceremonies in all parts of Afro-America. Possibly it has moved from the realm of belief to the realm of custom. Sometimes one catches a glimpse of something deeper, such as the belief that you could send a message by the dying to the already dead:

> If you see my mother
> Oh yes
> Won't you tell her for me
> Oh yes
> I'm a-riding my horse in the battlefield
> I want to see my Jesus in the morning.

The lavishness of black U.S. funerals (which are less directly related to the status of the deceased than the European equivalent) may reflect the African idea that the status of the shade in the other world is affected by the style of his going. One could perhaps make a case that the omnipresent funeral clubs of New Orleans were in themselves an echo of the *cabildos,* if not the socially oriented African secret societies. And it is quite possible that the famous New Orleans jazz funerals, with the dirge on the way to the cemetery and the upbeat pieces played on the way back, is of African origin. At least it has neo-African roots: Epstein cites a description from Jamaica in 1809 which describes exactly the same proceeding, though the rejoicing seems originally to have stemmed from the idea that the spirit of the departed had returned to Africa rather than the later concept (often, no doubt, overly charitable) that the deceased was now being greeted warmly by St. Peter.

Just as magic (European, African, or New World) is not necessarily malevolent, its aims are not necessarily grandiose. It can involve healing, or it can involve smaller practical matters. In much African and Afro-American magic, music is present. Sometimes the custom itself is not only African. Lydia Parrish, in her *Slave Songs of the Georgia Sea Islands*, mentions that "when a field needs to be burned over, a sail is flapping idly, or rice is to be fanned, you may hear a Negro 'calling the wind.' 'Co'win'! Co'win'! Co!, Co'!' A prolonged whistle follows. . . . A gramophone record of a Togoland rain invocation is astonishingly similar." There is no reason why in fact such a small, intimate, and yet deeply important practice as wind-summoning should not preserve an African form among people of African descent, even though the practice is European also.

Other social functions besides worship have acted as "adaptive preservers" of Africanisms in music. Charles Keil, in *Urban Blues*, makes a persuasive case for the ritual function of much black U.S. entertainment. Many forms of black music have performed an important function as a catalyst of group identity. The soul syndrome, wherein a variety of social, cultural, musical, and even culinary elements are conceived as one clearly recognizable but hardly definable whole, is in itself reminiscent of the African fusion of aspects that Europeans perceive as separate.

I have already said that the legend-role of African music, by no means lost in the Americas, is very much alive in the hero ballads and, in a less obvious but more pervasive way, in blues and soul. What more *universal* manifesto has there been than Aretha Franklin's "Freedom" and songs like it? What is "Say It Loud, I'm Black and Proud"? Much more, certainly, than a political statement, and meaning more to more people on a more profound level.

And if the blues and soul (and, in a less obvious way, gospel music, more totally black in creation and audience than either) perform a group function, this reinforces the Africanisms in the music. Self-definition for any black group, at the mythopoeic level on which music works, must come about by contrast to an idea of "whiteness." As a result, what are perceived as "black" elements are reemphasized. Perhaps this role has helped to reinforce continuously the Africanisms in a music that (like all American music) is in many respects deeply biracial. To quote Keil, black U.S. music "has become progressively more 'reactionary'—that is, more African in its essentials—primarily because the various blues and jazz styles are, at least in their initial phases, symbolic referents of in-group solidarity for the black masses and the more intellectual segments of the black bourgeoisie."

Albert Murray makes a similar point in *The Omni-Americans*:

> When the Negro musician or dancer swings the blues . . . he is making an affirmative and hence exemplary and heroic response to that which André Malraux describes as *la condition humaine*. . . . The blues idiom become[s] survival technique, esthetic equipment for living, and a central element in the dynamics of U.S. Negro life style. [Note the reference to "or dancer."]

The social role of music in Africa is, as we have seen, all-embracing and paramount. And it is not much less all-embracing in the Americas. Take the mutual-help societies, which help to ease life and guard against trouble ("'societies to care for the sick and bury the dead'—and these societies grow and flourish," Du Bois remarks). There is no inherent reason why such societies should be intimately connected with musical functions or social festivity, yet they are. Just as African, Haitian, and Trinidadian communal labor groups blended work and mutual help with a picnic atmosphere, music, and dance, so did the black lodges and societies of southern U.S. cities like New Orleans give endless picnics and take part in endless parades, supporting an extraordinary number of black musicians in the bargain.

The importance of musical parades is not new. Benjamin Latrobe, visiting New Orleans in 1819, was struck by the funeral parades, which he claimed were unique to the city, and described two, both black. In one, he said, there were more than two hundred people, mostly dressed in white (a probable Africanism). Militia band parades were popular among New Orleans whites, but they were standard European nineteenth-century activities anyway. What is important is the way they were adapted to communal social functions.

Musical parades, often associated with dancing (and often with Carnivals), are a feature of most of the black New World. The *rara* bands of Haiti, the highly danceable *marchas* of Brazil, the New Orleans marching bands, and the Trinidadian calendar groups seem to be a part of a loose tradition associating dance, music, religion, social function, and royalty (real or assumed), which I believe is to be traced to African origins in royal and religious ceremonial in such old kingdoms as the Ashanti, Yoruba, and Fon, and maintained right

This famous etching from a local magazine of the 1870s shows the world-famous Trinidadian Carnival or "mas" in its formative stages, when Afro-Trinidadians were taking it over. Under the street sign on the left is a man playing a local version of the African-derived banjo. By contrast the dance step shown is clearly English-derived.

Courtesy of Don Hill

through the colonial period. It is significant that parades and military-style paraphernalia seem to strike a responsive note in Africa as trappings of social dancing—as is evidenced by the Malawian *chiwoda* and the Ghanaian *konkomba*, both twentieth-century group dances that show strong parade influences, and the *beni ngoma* of the East African coast, which go back to the turn of the century and seem to mix elements of European military counter-marching with earlier local forms.

The Carnival, parade, and society supply symbolic group identification—and indeed a physical haven—for people who might otherwise be under threat, such as the nineteenth-century *capoeira* fighters and the Trinidadian stickmen, whose art was already akin to music and dancing. Parades and Carnivals must have allowed a larger amount of self-assertiveness with impunity and, indeed, provided an opportunity for people rarely allowed to assert themselves to do so in ways of their own choosing, the ways at which they were best.

The African concept of the total art form—music, dance, costume, and visual art combined—is by no means dead, of course. James Brown is adept at it, as is Sun Ra. Jones described a Sun Ra concert in *Black Music:*

> Sun Ra wants a music that will reflect a life-sense lost in the West, a music full of Africa. The band produces an environment, with their music most of all, but also with their dress (gold cloth of velvet, headbands and hats, shining tunics). The lights go out on some tunes, and the only lights are flashing off a band on Sun Ra's head.

Conscious efforts to achieve an effect may be less successful than the same effect achieved unconsciously, but the attempt seems to reflect something basic and enduring in Afro-American art.

The process of self-definition and group support in music has had some more direct factors, of course. Music of overt protest and resistance has not been common, but there are examples. One is a Brazilian dance called the *quilombo*. The original *quilombos* were independent hamlets of escaped slaves, the most famous of which, at Palmares, lasted from 1630 to 1697. Quilombo dances are danced in the State of Alagoas at Christmas or local festivals. There are few things more African than dances in praise of group heroes.

Politics has often formed part of a more wide-ranging element of social commentary. Perhaps the most famous example is Trinidadian calypso, which comments on anything and everything, as will be seen in Chapter 4. Paul Bowles, writing on calypso in *Modern Music* in 1940, argued, "There is no doubt that Calypso songs were used like our spirituals here, as a clandestine means of spreading illegal knowledge among the slaves." Bowles suggested that repression partly brought about by this function helped preserve Africanisms in calypso. As regards calypso itself, he is off the mark by a half-century (slavery ended in Jamaica fifty years before calypso developed), but calypso may contain such songs among its many roots.

The question of resistance spirituals is not so clear-cut. Perry Bradford says in his autobiography that "Steal Away to Jesus" meant "steal away from their bosses and beat it up north to the promised land." The choice of verb, which seems odd in a religious context, makes this plausible. On the other hand, there seems little justification for Janheinz Jahn's wholesale co-optation of the spirituals as disguised freedom songs. True, "Follow the Drinking Gourd"—the Big Dipper, which points to the North Star—appears to have been a sort of oral escape map, but it also was clearly written by somebody who thought in European poetic terms ("When the sun comes back and the first quail calls . . . Left foot, peg foot, traveling on"). Courlander says that, according to legend, the slaves learned it from a peg-leg sailor who wandered around telling people how to escape. Many spirituals, obviously, could be taken in a number of different ways without departing from the religious connotations, but there seems no doubt that the religious context was the original one.

A common social use of music in Africa is to satirize people who have broken social rules. This function has carried over to the New World. Courlander, in *Negro Folk Music USA,* writes that in the coastal area of Georgia the banjo was often used to accompany songs of ridicule directed at members of the community who had got out of line, a procedure known as "putting on the banjo." I shall be looking more closely at the various social-commentary uses of individual Afro-American styles (see Chapters 5 and 6). Fundamentally, they follow the charming description by the freed slave Equiano of his Nigerian society's songs:

> Each represents some interesting scene of real life, such as a great achievement, domestic employment, a pathetic story, some rural sport, and as the subject is generally founded on some recent event it is therefore ever new. This gives our dances a spirit and variety which I have scarcely seen elsewhere.

One of the most-quoted forms of Afro-American functional music is the work song, and it is true that work songs have retained many Africanisms. I have mentioned the quite remarkable similarity in sound between U.S. prison work songs and some African singing, even where some non-African harmonic strands are present. Work songs are particularly suitable for group manual labor, whether gang-hoeing in the fields, loading on the docks, tamping railroad track, or hauling up sails or anchors.

All these and many more activities had a rich body of song associated with them. Epstein, in *Sinful Tunes and Spirituals,* cites many examples of early work songs, including the renowned boatmen's songs of the Carolinas. The communal work songs seem to have been dying out for a long time under the impact of new methods of farming and mechanization in general, but they were widespread until recently. An author writing in the 1940s reported group work songs in a call-and-response style much like the U.S. versions as having been sung in Trinidad "within the last decade." As in African work song practice and its U.S. equivalents, the lead singer was frequently employed full time to lead the work by singing.

Rice-thrashing songs, rowing songs, a Louisiana creole song for sweeping floors, and even songs to accompany ironing have been recorded in the United States—not to mention a song to wake laborers on the railroad:

> Wake up buddy and sit on the rock,
> It ain't quite day but it's four o'clock.
> *Ratatat* (stick on the door).

In the Dominican Republic, work songs called *plenas* seem to have been used mainly to relieve the monotony of work rather than to pace it. Some Dominican *plenas* adopted a more European form than the U.S. versions: They often used a rhyming four-line verse, and the chorus sang a brief, often wordless phrase after each line or two. On the other hand, many chopping songs from the southern Dominican Republic are almost wholly African. Whatever their form, the work songs followed the pattern of other Afro-American music: They endured as long as they fulfilled a social role, and not necessarily a practical role.

Even ritual songs of a highly African nature, like initiation songs, have endured until relatively recently in various places—despite Bornemann's thesis quoted earlier. Edric Conor recorded examples of West Indian games for teaching rhythm and self-reliance; a mock-fight dance called "Mama Today Is Your Son's Funeral" (a *kalinda*) with Yoruba-sounding singing and percussion like Yoruba *apala* drumming; and even a quasi-Senegalese dance song performed by girls at a puberty ceremony with the cautionary lyric: "I send you to school and you bring back a belly for me." Besides the patently initiatory songs, black U.S. taunting songs like "The Dozens" arguably filled an initiatory function—teaching adolescents to keep their cool.

Finally, black children's songs and games in most parts of the Western Hemisphere show a clear mixture of European and African elements. The original song is frequently European. A classic example: the widespread "Sally Water," found in most Caribbean islands and the United States, stems from a northern English source, there called "Sally Walker." What seems to be consistent, and African in its source, is the way Afro-American children's songs tend to turn all play forms into dance, very often with the call-and-response form and lively or complex rhythmic patterns.

Function, then, appears to be the key to Afro-American survival-adaptation in the New World as a whole, and it has provided forms and elements that are in some degree common to the whole area. But Afro-American styles, despite much common background, are highly individual. Now, we will look at each of the main regions—South and Central America, the Caribbean, and the United States—separately.

South and Central America

Though there is a good deal of overlapping among its various regions, South America falls roughly into three zones of cultural influence: black, white, and Amerindian. "White" South America consists of Argentina, Chile, and Uruguay. "Indian" South America comprises Bolivia, Paraguay, Peru, and vast inland areas of Brazil, Ecuador, Colombia, Venezuela, and the Guianas. "Black" South America is a coastal strip running north from Uruguay and all the way around to Ecuador, the countries mostly concerned being Brazil, the Guianas, Venezuela, Colombia, the northern part of coastal Ecuador, and Panama, which, though in Central America, has strong musical connections with Colombia: it not only was part of the old Spanish colonial viceroyalty of New Granada (together with Venezuela, Colombia, and Ecuador) but was a province of Colombia until 1902.

Only certain areas of these countries can be considered "black South America." Brazil varies a great deal in the makeup of its population. In Bahia, blacks and mulattos constitute seven-tenths of the total population; in the southern part of Santa Catarina State, they represent only 5 percent. In the south virtually the only blacks are in the cities. In the northeast and the east they are concentrated in the coastal areas, where the plantations used to be.

This uneven distribution holds true for the rest of South America. According to Roger Bastide, blacks represent just under .5 percent of the Peruvian population, but on the coast they are almost 5 percent. In Colombia and Ecuador there are blacks on the coast and in the valleys of the interior—as well as in the valleys of Bolivia—but none in the Andes. In Venezuela, the black population is again concentrated on the coast, the area of the old slave plantations. And in all these countries there are areas with an almost entirely black population.

Of course, the term "black" itself, like any racial term, is vague and open to dispute. South American countries (like nineteenth-century New Orleans) generally divide people into several categories: white, mulatto (mixed black and white), black, Indian and mestizo (mixed Indian and white), and—in popular parlance—ever more absurd subdivisions. But in Brazil, mulattos and mestizos are lumped together as *pardos*. This causes problems when one tries to establish cultural links between groups. Nevertheless, the main patterns are clear.

Though in some respects the Guianas, and particularly Suriname, are more African, Brazil undoubtedly has the most impressive and most varied black music in South America. Like most of the music of Afro-America, Brazilian music grew out of a complicated intermingling of all sorts of musical styles, so that it is dangerous to be too dogmatic about who contributed what. Analysis is doubly hazardous in that all the main strains in Brazilian music—Iberian, West and Central African, and Amerindian—have a number of features in common. Characteristic elements of Brazilian Indian music are similar to basic elements in African styles: call-and-response singing, a wide variety of subject matter, a group of ritual dances, and the use of rattles in music. Nevertheless, it is thought that the Amerindian contribution to Brazilian music as a whole has been much smaller than the African contribution, largely because black and white were in constant contact with each other in wide areas of populated Brazil, whereas most Indians lived in areas isolated by forest.

The African contribution was certainly major. Oneyda Alvarenga, one of Brazil's leading musicologists, has described thirteen major Africanisms in Brazilian music. They include:

- the frequency of six-note scales with a flatted seventh-note, usually held to be a hallmark of Afro-American music and a feature of the "blues scale" of the United States;
- the origin, or at least the standardization, of the rhythmic phrase

  which, as has been shown, is common to virtually all Afro-American regions;

- call-and-response singing involving a single solo line, often improvised, followed by a short, unvarying chorus;
- the breaking-up of the neat melodic framework that European music tends to use;

◆ the *umbrigada,* or belly-bounce, in dancing;

◆ a large number of musical instruments, including the *berimbau* musical bow (see Chapter 1), the West African–derived double bell called an *agogô,* and the various big, single-headed conga-like drums known collectively as *atabaque;*

◆ the great importance of drums generally in Brazilian dances and their frequent function as organizers of the choreography;

◆ dramatic dances, not found as such in Portugal, though the Brazilian dances may have Portuguese components;

◆ a certain rather nasal tone of singing, which may be a cross between the rather open African tone (or the pinched Islamic-African sound) and the more harsh, high sound of Mideast/North African origin favored in Iberian music.

Alvarenga also suggests that the importance of wind instruments in Brazilian music reflects African practice, but that seems more likely to be a result of two traditions supporting each other. Africa makes use of rather more wind instruments than Portugal, but the *gaita,* a shawm descended from Morocco, is quite widespread in Portugal and common in Muslim West Africa; and bagpipes and various forms of flute are also used. The popularity of bowed string instruments again seems more probably a joint than a solely African tradition. The fiddle, under its Arab-derived name of *rebeca* or *rabeca,* came from Portugal. However, the enthusiasm with which New World blacks took to the fiddle, not only in Brazil but in the United States and Cuba as well, is surely related to the occurrence of fiddle-type instruments in parts of Africa. Portugal supplied virtually all of the nonrhythm instruments of Brazil and the chordal basis for the plucked or strummed instruments, mainly guitars of various sorts.

The harmonic base of Brazilian music as a whole is usually said to be European, but that is probably an oversimplification. Group singing in Brazil, when it is not in unison or the African form of near-unison called heterophony, most frequently uses parallel thirds, with one voice singing the same tune (or virtually the same tune) a third below the other. Parallel thirds are known in Portugal but do not constitute a major part of Portuguese folk music. On the other hand, they are widely used by certain African groups, including some that supplied slaves to Portugal. So it looks very much as if *vocal* harmonies, at least, owe a good deal to Africa, the Portuguese contribution being a reinforcing element, the sort that often determines which qualities become part of a permanent cultural blend.

The general quality of melodic lines in Brazilian music is mainly Portuguese. Even the gayest Portuguese melodies are found to have a certain underlying melancholy, and this applies as well to Brazilian tunes. Much of the decided difference between Portuguese and Brazilian melodic styles seems to stem from the Brazilian use of a frequently syncopated and more complex rhythmic approach with displaced accentuations and cross-rhythms against the percussion, all features of West and Central African technique.

The heavy Portuguese content in Brazilian melodies does not mean there are many tunes originally from Portugal that are now regarded as Brazilian. There must certainly be some, just as there are surely melodies in Spanish South America that came from Spain. But on the whole Latin American melodies appear to have developed in Latin America, either because people made new tunes in European styles or because melodies originally brought over were so changed as to be unrecognizable. A third, quite strong possibility is that at least some Latin American melodies are in fact ancient Iberian tunes that are forgotten in Spain and Portugal and preserved in Latin America (just as many British border ballads were preserved in the United States after being forgotten in Britain). Certainly not only verse forms like the *décima* but some actual lyrics survived in extremely Spanish forms in the New World. And even where lyrics did not remain unchanged, subjects whose interest had long faded in Europe sometimes endured. A Library of Congress record of folk music from Venezuela contains a *galerón* about an incident in the wars between the Moors and the Christians. On the same record is the "Corrido del Pajarillo," basically a famous fifteenth-century Spanish romance with an improvised beginning and end.

Portuguese is by far the most important European strand in Brazilian music, but not the only one. Others include Italian art music, which swept Spain and Portugal in the latter part of the eighteenth century and arrived in their colonies a little later, and children's songs from various countries, including that international favorite, "Sur le Pont d'Avignon." There is a fairly important Spanish admixture that arrived indirectly through the influence of various Spanish-American forms. The Argentinean tango and the Cuban habanera, both of which use forms of

were major components of the Brazilian *maxixe,* an urban popular dance that gained international popularity during World War I—in this case not surprisingly, since it was a mix of the *lundú* and Argentinean tango sometimes called a Brazilian tango (with enough similarities to the urban samba as to cause bickering over the attribution of certain individual songs). Cuban urban popular music has had a recurring influence on Brazil as in most other parts of

Afro-America, and cool or West Coast jazz, atypically, was a major root of bossa nova.

The dramatic dances of Brazil have few counterparts in Portugal but many in Africa, especially in mime dances, which are extremely common. Some Brazilian dances, like the *congos* and *congadas,* offer ample reason, in addition to the African roots of their names, for supposing that they have connections with the Bantu Congo-Angola region. A salient feature of the *congos* and *congadas* is the "embassy," a mock emissary-to-a-royal-court episode, which is thought to be a purely African element. One of these dances involves two characters named Prince Suena and Reina (Queen) Ginga. Prince Suena is probably a corruption of Suana Mulopo, the title of the immediate heir of leading or royal families of the Lunda empire. The real Reina Ginga (also called Zinga Nbangi in some versions of the dance) was an Angolan princess, Anna Nzinga, who fought the Portuguese at various times during the early seventeenth century and notably led a mission to them in 1622 that resulted in a peace treaty favorable to the Angolans. The Brazilian *congadas,* therefore, fairly clearly commemorate a woman who must rank as a leading figure in African resistance to colonial rule in the early days, if only for her tenacity and resourcefulness. (Jan Vansina's *Kingdoms of the Savanna* has an account of her activities.)

Most of Brazil's dramatic dances are clearly African-derived, but some are of highly obscure and debatable origin. One such is the *bumba meu boi,* about which there is frank disagreement. The dance drama involves the figure of an ox, which Brazilian authors seem to feel has some link with Africa. In this case I suspect the link is illusory. It is true that African mime dances quite often involve animal characters, but the ox is not an African animal. It seems far more likely that the *bumba meu boi* goes back via Portugal to some European ritual complex related to bullfighting (perhaps even to Mithraism, popular in Roman Iberia until Christianity replaced it). Other bull-mime dances are known elsewhere in Iberian America, including a *seis del toro* in Puerto Rico.

Of the nondramatic or "straight" dances, the best known outside of Brazil is the samba, the history of whose modern form is known down to individual names and dates. There are many different versions of the samba, from neo-African to polite salon varieties. The best known, of course, is the urban dance famous worldwide. This was a product of World War I Rio de Janeiro (the first song registered as a samba was "Pelo Telefone," recorded in 1917). Yet none of this invalidates the samba's African roots. The urban samba was generated partly by a large influx of people with strong African traditions, including religious worship, from Bahia. And Bahia had its own samba, or sambalike tradition, including a ring-dance version, *samba da roda,* of obviously African derivation.

The Carnival *samba de enredo* developed by the *escolas de samba* (samba schools) of Rio's slums, music of devastating polyrhythmic drive, provided much of the aural impact of the film *Black Orpheus,* whose soundtrack gives some impression of the sheer power of Afro-American drumming and dancing. It is an instructive irony that the samba schools themselves are a recent creation; the first, called Deija Falar, was founded in 1928. It is also ironic that modern *samba de enredo,* while maintaining its overwhelmingly Afro-Brazilian aura, has become so stylized as to verge on self-parody.

A basic Africanism in many forms of samba is the overriding importance and complexity of rhythm. Another—not striking in any individual case but important in the sum of its appearances all over the Afro-American world—is the common use of "nonmusical" instruments (from a white point of view, at least). In the 1930s, the samba writers of Rio used to meet in a certain cafe and sing each other their latest soon-to-be hits. None of them played instruments, so as accompaniment to their songs they used only the matchbox, which, according to Nestor R. Ortiz Oderigo, was often joined by the straw hat and a dish beaten with a knife. Ortiz Oderigo goes on to say, in an article in *African Music:*

> Moreover, in the streets of Sao Paulo, the writer has heard Negro shoeshine boys making rhythms and singing to the accompaniment of their wooden boxes and brushes played as if they were drums with their tin cans of shoe polish played as *agogos* or *adjas,* both of them similar to African instruments of the Candombles of Ewe-Yoruba origin.

The Bahian proto-samba at least, and perhaps other variants, stemmed among other sources from *candomblé* cult drumming. There is an example of a highly neo-African *samba da roda* on David Lewiston's Nonesuch recording *Black Music of South America.* Apart from the call-and-response singing typical of Bahian samba (led here by a woman in the center of the circle), the recording demonstrates how a neo-African rhythm (skeletal in this case—the instrumentation sounds like one drum and handclapping) gave rise to the characteristic samba beat. The singing shows the African trait of relatively unchanged choral responses to improvised (or at least embellished) lead phrases. The Bahian samba is not always accompanied by percussion alone; Alvarenga says its most typical instrumentation is a *pandeiro* (a form of tambourine), guitar, and rattle, sometimes with castanets and *berimbau.*

The *favelas* that cling to the mountains behind Rio de Janeiro are home to the samba schools at the heart of Rio's world-famous Carnival, and perhaps the most lively of contemporary neo-African forms.
UNICEF photo by Don Briggs

Robertinho Silva (right) with colleagues and a few of the phenomenal array of African-derived percussion typical of today's Afro-Brazilian music.
Photo by Wilton Montenegro, courtesy of Milestone Records

The transference from religious to secular music, incidentally, reflects a general tendency for forms to feed back and forth. Not only have ritual styles influenced the more neo-African sambas; they often filter into urban popular music—and not just as influences, but as actual melodies. There are two examples of transference in Folkways' *Songs and Dances of Brazil*, recorded on the island of Itaparica in the Bay of Salvador, Bahia. The group recorded is of a popular type consisting of a small, guitarlike four-stringed instrument called a *cavaquindo*, a guitar proper, and a tambourine. It presents a "Brazilian" rather than a "neo-African" style, but two of its numbers come from cult music. One is the samba "Pena Verde," which was on the popular market at the time as *macumba* music (a category that in itself is an indication of transference). Although it was credited to a popular composer, J. B. de Carvalho, it was originally sung only in the Indo-African rite *candomblé de caboclo*. Another samba, an instrumental, opens the second side of the record. Alvarenga says in the liner notes to the album that she once heard it also at a *candomblé de caboclo*. (The *candomblé de caboclo* seems to be the least "pure" of the rites, and the most open to nonreligious influences.)

Other black dances of Brazil included the *jongo*, described by Alvarenga as "a violent black dance" accompanied by drumming, which displays the repetitive and fragmentary lyrics typical of much neo-African music. The *lundú*, which we have met in Chapter 2, has a convoluted history apparently not uncommon for Afro-American dances of the nineteenth century. It began as a neo-African dance, and indeed some Brazilian musicologists claimed that it originated in Congo or Angola. It became entirely urbanized relatively early, turned into a bourgeois social dance, and in this form was taken to Portugal and Spain. One expert held that either the fandango or the bolero of Spain might be a descendant of the *lundú*. The *lundú* was the first African-derived music accepted by the Brazilian bourgeoisie, and it brought into middle-class musical customs both the flatted seventh and syncopation as a way of life.

One of the features of Brazilian music is a large variety of urban popular styles. In fact, though far from being an Africanism, this seems to be something of a feature of Afro-American music as well. Virtually all the urban *popular* music of the New World (as opposed to Tin Pan Alley music), from jazz through calypso to the sambas, are wholly or partly Afro-American, whereas most white American music is rural (as is, of course, a great deal of black music).

Town versions of the samba are the Brazilian urban music best known to the rest of the world, but many other forms grew up in the towns of Brazil before it, and had their influence on the world. Surprising as it might seem, Marvin Harris, in *Town and Country in Brazil*, argues that the Brazilians have in fact a largely urban mentality, however small the towns involved may be. Historically, the towns have been the centers of cultural communication, which was true of other regions, notably Puerto Rico and Cuba.

Perhaps the first Brazilian urban form to grow up was the *modinha*, which developed as a salon music in the second half of the eighteenth century and was widely popular in both Brazil and Portugal. Forgotten in Portugal, in Brazil the *modinha* spread and became a popular dance by the latter part of the nineteenth century but was always a fairly European style. Popular *modinhas* had a melody line full of decorated phrases and made much use of arpeggios and wide jumps of interval. Originally it was accompanied by piano, but more recently by guitar, a frequent development for dances that moved out of the salons into the streets.

The Rio urban samba stems from the slum dwellers who live on the hills (*morros*) around the city. It has produced two versions. One, still danced by the people of the *morros*, flourishes among the samba schools, societies of dancers that arrange Carnival parades, with a director who teaches and directs the singing and dancing. There is some argument about what is the "true" form of this sort of samba. One kind consists of a call-and-response technique in which the director sings a line which is repeated by the chorus. It often shows the highly African feature of an improvised, changing solo line and a more fixed choral line.

The other form involves a previously composed refrain sung by a well-drilled ensemble and a more improvised solo part. A characteristic of samba is a kind of back-to-front call-and-response, fairly common elsewhere in South America and parts of the Caribbean. Either there is a refrain first and then call-and-response passages, or a line-by-line call-and-response, but with the chorus providing the first part, or "call." Whether this is simply a variant on African call-and-response forms, or comes from a blend of African and European elements, I do not know. The opening section often follows an introduction with guitar, *cavaquinho* (small guitar), and tambourine, or a concertina and rhythm. The singing is backed by percussion only, consisting of two drums, a tambourine, and a friction drum.

The growth of the "downtown" samba is typical of the confused situation in which differing samba styles exert influence, and are influenced, in several different directions; popular music has this tendency, irritating to the tidy mind but very good for the music. It is related to the *maxixe*, which is itself a hybrid of Brazilian and non-Brazilian ingredients, and to the rhythmically simpler *marcha*. Alvarenga holds that the first stage in the *maxixe*'s development was a habanera-ized *lundú* which the Brazilians called a tango. The European polka gave the *maxixe* its movement, according to Alvarenga, the Cuban habanera its rhythm, Afro-Brazilian music added its syncopation. In reality, the *maxixe*'s major debt seems to have been to the Argentinean tango, and directly so. Like the tango, it was attacked as indecent, or at all events overly sensual, by the bourgeoisie, and became acceptable only in a toned-down version. Even so, it met with great hostility, as did most dances that grew out of Afro-American forms.

Modern urban sambas cheerfully go on taking in influences from all over in true popular style, including jazz drumming licks, guitar phrases, and (when appropriate) piano stylings. The bossa nova became a mass-popular form, but its origins were among musicians and intellectuals looking for something hip, and more or less strongly influenced by United States cool jazz. The core of the bossa nova was João Gilberto's extremely elliptic guitar style, and an equally cool vocal sound.

Another form connected with the samba and with even stronger Carnival connections is the *marcha*, which has little to do with the military but is ideal for the dance-parade of Carnival time. The *marcha*'s main feature is a fairly simple and very lively two-beat rhythm, and it tends to be a sing-along music. Modern Brazilian pop composers often use the *marcha* form, sometimes to contrast with a slower and more romantic style. An example is "Voce Passa eu

Dominguinhos is one of the enduring stars of the accordion-led forró of northeastern Brazil, an example of the riches of Afro-Brazilian music that is totally different from the percussion-heavy roots samba.
Photo by Ruy Mendes, courtesy of Luaka Bop Records

Acho Graca,"* which opens with a terrific Carnival-style jam session for percussion including friction drum and chorus, then distills out into a skeletal rhythm for a beautiful ballad-like solo song. The *marcha* has been open to all sorts of influences at various times, including the North American one-step.

Brazil also has a musical style often described as a parallel to jazz—not in the way it sounds, but in that it is instrumental and employs contrapuntal techniques somewhat as the early New Orleans jazz groups did. This is the *choro*, which originally referred to the band itself but is now applied to the music it plays. The *choro* groups have a woodwind front line—flute, clarinet, sax, and so on—that is, without the brass typical of jazz, an additional major difference, apart from all the stylistic differences. *Choro* involves quite a lot of improvisation, though usually only from the lead instrument, and a competitive edge symbolized by the *derrubada* ("drop"), the moment when the accompanists could no longer keep up with the soloists' flights of fancy. The *choro* goes back to the early nineteenth century, when military or semimilitary music, or at least groups vaguely based on the small German and French military

* On Odean MOFB 3549.

orchestras that oompahed away in the parks of Europe and the Americas, were popular. It was, in fact, a thoroughly creolized style, with roots that were quite similar to ragtime and jazz. But it was certainly no imitation of jazz, because its great days—when hundreds of *choro* groups roamed Rio looking for parties—were from the 1870s to around 1920, while the first published rag came in 1897; jazz only hit the international consciousness as *choro* was fading.

Choro music started out as a distinct instrumental form, but many of its most famous composers also wrote a wide range of other material including sambas, and *choro* itself began to include vocal pieces with samba connections. The typical *choro* vocals used fluid and leaping vocal lines derived from the clarinet solo lines they displaced. *Choro* music in fact often used the samba form more or less completely, in hybrids known as *samba-choro*. Indeed, at times it has seemed that *choro* itself had pretty much disappeared into the samba. But like so much apparently vanishing Afro-Latin music, it has undergone more than one resurrection. There was a *choro* revival in the 1940s, another retreat into apparent oblivion, and then another revival in the 1970s, this one helped on by the fine saxophonist Paulo Moura and keyboardist Hermeto Pascoal, known in the United States for his work with Airto Moreira and Flora Purim.

By now it should be clear that Brazilian music as a whole could not exist without either its African or its Portuguese components, and that in fact stereotypes about "European melody, African rhythm"—though they do, very inadequately, represent a very general musical tendency—are not the end of the matter. Even the question of rhythm in Portuguese music is not as simple as it might seem. We have seen that, in a very general way, the music of the Iberian Peninsula and the music of West Africa share a liking for brisk, pulsating, fairly dominant and complex rhythmic patterns.

The dominance of percussion in most popular Brazilian music is obviously related to African attitudes, but it should not simply be assumed to be totally African in its source. Many of the percussion instruments are of African origin, and the use of cross-rhythms is African, but the rhythms of Portuguese music themselves seem to be a blend of Iberian and African. In fact, the presence in Brazilian *national* music of so much percussion must derive from the fact that Portuguese music also quite regularly uses drums, tambourines, and triangles—a legacy, along with some of the rhythms, of the Arab period. Indeed the Brazilian name for the bass drum, *bombo,* is also used in Spain and Portugal, as is the general Brazilian word for the drums that figure in ritual ceremonies, *atabaque,* though the names of the individual cult drums are usually African. Because the music of Portugal, especially southern Portugal, was influenced by the Arab domination (though not as fundamentally as southern

Singer-songwriter Milton Nascimento—perhaps the best-known in the United States of Brazil's post–bossa nova "musica popular brasileira," or MPB as it is known for short—draws both on the traditions of his native Minas Gerais province and on a wide range of U.S. idioms, white and black.

Photo by Marcio Ferreira, courtesy of Luaka Bop Records

Spain), and because at least one of the African regions represented in Brazil was also musically influenced from North Africa through Islam, the potential for a high degree of blending was plainly there. It seems that in secular, generalized dance music, particularly that of areas other than Bahia, the typical Brazilian rhythms are as often Portuguese rhythms treated in an African fashion, as African rhythms. The same reinforcement may have occurred in harmony, because, like the music of many African groups, the folk music of Alemtejo often used parallel thirds, but never three-voice harmonies.

Brazilian music and the music of Spanish South America sound quite different because, despite an underlying connection, Spanish and Portuguese music differ considerably. One reason for this difference is that the Portuguese and Spanish languages have a totally different sound and rhythm, and the link between language and melody (sometimes acknowledged in passing but almost always underestimated) is extremely fundamental. Besides, the *national* musics of Spanish South America—even of the parts with the greatest African influence—tend to contain fewer Africanisms than Brazilian music. Within the Afro-Spanish area, similar general situations, together with regional variations, led to the growth of musical styles that were distinct but related and that modified each other mutually. The similarities were helped by the fact that the main Afro-Spanish countries—Venezuela, Colombia, Ecuador, and Panama—were cut off geographically from the rest of South America and were governed together for a good deal of their history.

The ties between Spanish music and the music of Spanish South America are, if anything, more obvious than those between Portuguese and Brazilian music, but this does not mean that South America has not developed highly original styles. Both Spanish and West and Central African music, in Bruno Nettl's words, "favored complicated driving rhythms with steady, pulsating patterns." This is true of the Spanish music best known to non-Spaniards, flamenco, and also much other Spanish folk music, especially from the south.

The similarity between Spanish and African approaches extended to the occurrence in much Spanish music of combinations of duple and triple rhythms, though not played simultaneously. Many Spanish rhythmic patterns are quite near enough to African patterns for African techniques (cross-rhythms, the overlaying of triple on duple rhythm, and so on) to fit them perfectly. And the rhythmic improvisation, which is such a feature of some African drumming—the approach of the lead drummer in many areas—is not alien to the Spanish. A magnificent collection of Spanish folk music, *Antología del Folclor Musical de España*, recorded on the Spanish label Hispavox contains examples of very complex percussion, including a stunning display from a girl singing to the accompaniment of her own tambourine, which incorporates long passages of fiery rhythmic improvisation.

Even the cross-rhythms of African music are not totally foreign to Spanish music, one of whose Moorish-derived features was the use of handclapping (another important element in African music) to provide rhythms cutting across the main pulse. Drums themselves are not at all unusual in Spanish folk music of some regions, though unlike the tambourines they usually play a skeletal beat. All in all, therefore, conditions were good for a high degree of merging between the two traditions. One difference between Spanish and Latin American music is an apparent greater importance of musical instruments in America. This becomes more significant when we realize that the same appears to be true of U.S. black music and of the music of some parts of the Caribbean, and when we remember the number and importance of instruments in Africa, as compared with Europe.

Nevertheless, the Africanisms remain obvious in many cases, especially in the music of the coastal areas of the countries with most black inhabitants, Venezuela, Colombia, Ecuador, and Panama. Panama and Colombia, in fact, share a number of musical forms, including the *cumbia*. Colombia is the fourth largest South American country, with a population of 21 million, of which nearly one-third are of Spanish descent, one-half mestizos, and the rest blacks or Indians. Colombian music as a whole contains much that is African, but it is most noticeable in the coastal music. The main "national" forms were, until recently, the *bambuco*, the *paseo*, and above all the *cumbia*.

The *cumbia*, the unofficial national music/dance of Colombia, comes in almost every conceivable form, including a polite salon version, but whose true home has been the streets. The general view of Colombian musicologists is that the *cumbia* combines Africa, Indoamerica, and Europe more clearly than any other Colombian rhythm, which gives it a certain symbolic resonance. But expert opinion is still sharply divided on whether its origin was African or Amerindian; one not altogether convincing explanation of the word itself is that it derives from the *cumbé*, a dance from Equatorial Guinea.

The *cumbia* has always been both music and dance. The music traditionally combined percussion and wind instruments and was originally nonvocal. The *cumbia* had developed on the Atlantic coast by the seventeenth or at the latest eighteenth century, when it was described as forming part of the festival of La Virgen de la Candelaria in Cartagena, and as blending African drums, *gaitas*, and cane flutes. The "traditional" *cumbia* instrumentation includes three drums of African origin. Two, the *llamador* and the *alegro*, are single-headed, the third—the *bombo* or *tambora*—double-headed. They back two *gaitas*, one of which carries the melody while the other plays two or three bass notes. These *gaitas* are often said to be Amerindian, but instrument and name alike are found in both Spain and West Africa, and they are much the same as reed instruments found almost everywhere in the Islamic world. My suspicion is that they were introduced by Spaniards, Africans, or possibly both, and that their survival is due partly to this bicultural reinforcement. In some areas traditional groups use cane flutes with four holes, which could be Amerindian, or local versions of an instrument familiar to all three cultures. The rattles that are often part of the ensemble could be Amerindian or Afro-Amerindian in origin. Contemporary versions of the "traditional" *cumbia* are still played with a lot of drive and a good deal of emphasis on percussion, including variations from the lead drummer and much use of cross-rhythms. The *gaitas* and flutes have not disappeared from the scene but tend to be increasingly the mark of revivalist groups. The lead is nowadays often played by fiddle or accordion.

All in all the *cumbia* still displays many Africanisms, and even its obvious Spanish elements are heavily Africanized. Contemporary sung versions have an intriguing vocal feature that may well be an adaptation of an African technique: a verse ending on a chord whose resolution comes only during the first line of the next verse, so that the tune seems to have no beginning or end. (A common African equivalent is a final beat of a drum pattern acting as first beat in the melody line.) This is not at all the same as the frequent European technique of launching again into the tune without a pause.

The dance, usually called *cumbiamba*, seems to have joint Spanish and African origins, with the woman's movements being more Spanish and the male's more African. It opens with a male dancer inviting a woman to dance by giving her a handful of candles, which she holds while dancing in a circle around the musicians and her partner, with much hip movement.

The *cumbia* had become a popular style with city bands by the 1940s, a time at which tours by top Cuban bands also popularized the main root of contemporary salsa. It has been caught up in the enormous changes of the 1970s–1990s, during which Colombia has become a major market for salsa, and contemporary bands like Grupo Niche and Joe Arroyo mix salsa with modernized *cumbia* (and in the case of Arroyo, *currulaos*) in their repertoire.

The *cumbia* has been called the "mother of Colombian rhythms," and a large range of them have been assigned *cumbia* origins, although—because nobody was paying much attention at the time most of them developed—this whole subject is inevitably speculative. By contrast, the *bambuco* has sometimes been claimed as the ancestor of the *cumbia*. It is also often described as heavily African, but in fact it is, as played, not strikingly so. (Various explanations link the name with an old kingdom in Mali.) The *bambuco*, it is true, mixes duple and triple beats, but they are not played together for the most part, so this could just as well be a Spanish trait as an African one. The fact that the *bambuco* tends to "European" types of lyric, with related narrative themes of unhappy love (a topic of minor interest in Africa), social injustice, and the faraway home, also suggests a heavy Spanish element.

The *paseo* is a relatively recent dance which seems to have links with both the Venezuelan *pasillo* and the waltz (which has become thoroughly acclimated in some parts of the New World); in fact it is really a sort of syncopated waltz with heavy first and last beats. Its main interest here—apart from showing what a mixture of Spanish and African techniques can do to a highly European form—is that the Venezuelan *pasillo* rhythm is an element in the Trinidadian calypso.

Perhaps the most characteristic Afro-Colombian music of the Pacific coast of Colombia—and the most overtly African of any—is the *currulao,* a fiery rhythm that is both a dance form and a background for songs of praise (*alabao*) for the festival of San Antonio. Lewiston's record *Black Music of South America* contains some examples of *currulao* from Guapi, an extremely isolated black community on the Pacific coast that has kept many Africanisms in its music, such as the marimba xylophone, whose name is widespread in Africa. Hugh Tracey, the African musicologist, theorizes that the marimba may actually have traveled to the New World from Mozambique, because the Shangaan people of Mozambique—a coastal group—call it *marimba,* and the first boatload of slaves was taken from the Shanga coast to South America as early as 1530.

The *currulao* songs have many African traits, including call-and-response singing of very oblique and fragmented texts. Lewiston recorded one song full of double entendre of a sort particularly enjoyed by West African audiences, who delight in songs that on one level are highly sexual and on another asexual, being sometimes instructional songs for children. The overall style of the lyrics of many of these songs is reminiscent of African songs using apparently unrelated proverbs, references known only to a particular group, and so on, to build up a whole that, as it were, glances sideways at the main topic.

In the valleys away from the coast of Colombia, where the population is divided among Indians, blacks, and mestizos, there is a good deal of mixing of African and Indian elements. An example is a piece played at a cowherds' festival with pipe-playing that is mainly Indian combined with plenty of improvisation in the drumming. Colombian Indian music goes in for a good deal of pipe-and-tabor styles; one of the popular types of Indian ensemble in the Cauca region is the *chirimia,* containing many Indianisms but named after a Spanish type of shawm.

As was true of everywhere in Latin America, the late nineteenth century brought a large number of changes to Colombian music. One of these was the creolizing process, by which music became increasingly local and increasingly less easy to separate out into its African and European roots. On another front, the old instrumentations came under enthusiastic threat from the accordion (popular almost everywhere else in Latin America), the clarinet, and various brass instruments, notably the alto horn. One result (inevitably classified as a *cumbia* offshoot) was the *porro,* which is intimately bound up with the clarinet. The *porro* has been described as halfway between a *cumbia* and a merengue, and in fact grew out of a section of the *cumbia* that used a contrasting beat. The first group recorded as playing clearly identifiable *porro,* in 1900, involved a Puerto Rican clarinetist, José de La Paz Montes, playing melodies previously played on fifes. *Porro* groups used clarinets, brass, and percussion. A major *porro* innovator whose recordings can still be found is clarinetist Lucho Bermúdez.

Truly Afro-Colombian music falls into two parts, that of the Atlantic coast and that of the Pacific (divided by the southern border of Panama). The Atlantic coast has the merengue, *cumbia* and related *cumbiamba, punto, porro, mejorana,* and rumba. The African and African-descended instruments found there include the marimba, the *quitiplas,* and the *merecure* (a drum). Colombia has also seen a particularly striking return to the *típico,* or down-home, in the last twenty years, with the rise to national (and to some extent international) popularity of so-called *vallenato* music. This comes from the fairly Afro-Colombian coastal regions, and is accordion-based. The accordion in Colombia was originally a middle-class instrument, but it climbed out of the drawing-room window and into the street; by the end of the nineteenth century, to the horror of the bourgeoisie, it was playing *cumbias* and all sorts of street music. In at least one town, in fact, separate parties of middle-class waltzers and servants dancing to *cumbias* would mingle at the end of the evening.

Soon the countryside became home to wandering troubadours such as Francisco "El Hombre" Moscote, who was said to have beaten the devil in an accordion contest. Nobody is sure when the first *vallenato* accordion trio was formed but the style really took off during the 1940s, basing a punchy, irresistible idiom on *cumbias, paseos,* and other familiar rhythms. Soon things became professionalized enough that composers, accordionists, and singers stuck to their own jobs; the last of the great downhome singer/accordionist/composers, the Afro-Colombian Alejandro Duran, died in the early 1990s.

Contemporary *vallenato* is a major pop phenomenon stretching from the village sound of Duran through the earthy/sophisticated Lizandro Meza to the gold-lamé-jacket pop of the duo Binomio de Oro. There is even a long-haired *nuevo vallenato* star, Tulio Zuloaga, who mixes reggae and a bit of rock into the accordion sound. But *vallenato* remains both highly varied and strongly national. The accordion groups proper also combined with the Colombian taste for clarinets and deep brass and gave birth to the *sonora vallenata* in the hands of the long-lasting talent-incubator Los Corraleros de Majagual. The sound of clarinet, baritone horn, and accordion, like some mad Cajun/jazz mix, is one of the wonders of the Latin music world.

As the existence of a large number of forms known collectively as *golpe* (beat) might suggest, Venezuelan music has a rhythmic basis heavily influenced by its more neo-African forms (and the neo-African forms themselves), and of course plenty of music whose background is largely Spanish.

The *golpe* is originally a drumming pattern, stemming from the basic pattern of the *tambor redondo,* the purest neo-African mode, and the basic pattern of the *tambor grande* or *merecure.* The neo-African drum dances of the Barlovento region were discussed in Chapter 2, with their call-and-response patterns for drums; their polyrhythms, the extra beat provided by a second player drumming on the side of the drum with a pair of sticks; and the call-and-response singing, which proceeds according to its own rhythmic structure (independently of the drums) and thus provides another polyrhythmic element. The *golpe,* in some forms, have become basic rhythms for a number of more generalized musical styles. The Venezuelan *pasillo,* incidentally, was a strong influence on early Trinidad calypso.

Black music in most Latin American countries shows a wealth of religious forms, often associated with elaborate wakes, an Africanism in the New World, and often accompanied by possession states similar to those in African and neo-African spirit cults. The wakes are socioreligious occasions, and much of what is played is whatever secular music may be popular at the time. The black areas of Venezuela, and many other countries, had an elaborate ceremony for the death of a child, the *mampulorio,* involving song-and-action rituals. The custom was dying out in the 1940s, having been outlawed, perhaps because the corpse of the baby, apparently, was often boiled.

Another religious ceremonial associated with black music in these countries, especially in Venezuela, is the *Velorio del Cruz,* celebrated in May. *Velorios* are celebrated in private houses, where an altar is set up with an image of the saint being honored. The music usually takes the form of praise songs, and in Barlovento it is broken up with competitive recitation of *décimas,* a basic Spanish poetic form, which died out in Europe but is still preserved in Spanish America. The *décimas* may be either religious or secular. The *velorios* are by no means exclusively a black phenomenon. In some parts of Venezuela the music is entirely Spanish in origin or often has strong Canary Islands influences. But the *fulias* sung at *velorios* in Barlovento show strong African qualities mixed with their fundamentally Spanish features, such as a long, highly decorated melody line. They are not always call-and-response, but when sung solo they may make use of a short refrain repeated after every line. The instrumentation for the *velorios* is usually *cuatro* (a small four-stringed guitar), six-stringed guitar, drums, and maracas.

Black Venezuelan music is often associated with religious festivals, like various types of black music elsewhere. The Maracaibo neighborhood has a form of Christmas song called *gaita,* in call-and-response style, with a good deal of percussion, much of it improvised. The *gaitas* used to be religious but have tended to develop into praise songs for the stores being serenaded in the hope of handouts (the praise song aimed at earning gratuities is a common phenomenon in many parts of West Africa, especially those having professional *griot* musicians). There is also a dance music in the Lake Maracaibo area associated with New Year's Eve, which features improvised call-and-response songs accompanied by clarinet and drums.

The most "national" styles of Venezuela, the *joropo* and *galerón*, are both dances of mixed ancestry, usually played by string orchestras. Not particularly "black" music, they nonetheless show clear African characteristics, such as the *galerón*'s frequent use of a call-and-response technique in the melody. The *galerón* forms part of the *Velorios del Cruz* on the coast, but on the plains it used to be danced. The old string-band dance form traveled to Trinidad, where Venezuelan music was one element in a highly complex mixture. The *galerón* does not use much percussion, and the rhythmic techniques of the guitar, *cuatro*, and mandolin seem to be largely Spanish and perhaps Canary Islands-derived, though undoubtedly the existence of black musical forms in Venezuela has influenced it, just as black U.S. music has influenced most of the styles thought of as most typical of white folk music.

"Joropo" is one of those words that, like "samba," mean all kinds of things; indeed, it is often used simply to mean "dance," as in "Voy a un joropo esta noche." On the whole it is a popular style, with composers who are known by name, but traditional *golpes* are often called *joropos*, especially when their origin is not known. In fact, the public will sometimes give the name *joropo* to a piece of music called something quite different by its composer.

Besides these examples, of course, Venezuela makes use of styles that started elsewhere, such as the merengue and the *cumbia*. Sometimes they may become naturalized and give rise to a new form. This seems to have happened with the *guasa*, a dance music that is said to be a development of the merengue.

Venezuela also has its share of dance-dramas, some of them reminiscent of European mumming plays, with a cast including a Doctor (or Sorcerer), a Snake who may represent the Devil, and various religious and magical symbolisms. These on the whole seem far less African than the Brazilian dance-dramas, though they have ritual elements that could well appeal to Indians and Africans and attract Indian and African musical traits. A Library of Congress recording, *Folk Music of Venezuela*, contains a "Snake-Killing Song" in this vein, and while much of it is in European-derived, acted mumming-play style, it contains songs with African elements of call-and-response, extreme repetition, and so on (and a tune in places remarkably like the old British West Indian song "Hold 'Im Joe").

On the whole, Central American music seems to have relatively little African content, though there is certainly some, notably in the area of Vera

Cruz on the Caribbean coast. But Indo-Spanish traditions dominate, even in the music of the Guatemalan and Mexican versions of that archetypal African instrument, the marimba. The exceptions tend to lie outside the dominant Spanish language, because many of the smaller Central American countries have black English-speaking minorities on their Caribbean coasts whose music belongs to the Caribbean tradition (see Chapter 4). The major exception to this rule is Panama, which is geographically Central American but culturally (and for most of its history politically) part of Colombia.

Panamanian music, though strongly connected with that of Colombia, has one notably African-derived form that is more or less exclusively Panamanian. This is the *tamborito,* essentially a women's music, accompanied by drums. I have already mentioned some of its African features in Chapter 2, including the lead drum's role in guiding the choreography and the way in which musicians, dancers, and spectators each have a role in a musical whole. The lyrics of most *tamboritos* show strong Africanisms. They tend to be couplets rhyming in European style but are endlessly repeated, often highly cryptic, or proverbial (or simply in the general form of a proverb). Narcisco Garay, in his *Tradiciones y Cantares de Panama,* says of one *tamborito:* "It says nothing, in two lines: it is a mere pretext for singing and dancing." An example of the proverbial quality of many *tamboritos* is this one, with its suggestion of several layers of serious and ribald meaning:

> Mi mama me dió un consejo,
> No comer conejo viejo.
> (My mother advised me,
> Don't eat old rabbit.)

There is an old tradition of political *tamboritos,* going back at least to 1830. One of these, from the beginning of the century, was a response to the action of General Davis, president of the commission of the Panama Canal, in establishing separate postal facilities:

> Los gringos son los que mandan, Panameños en la yaya
> Los gringos no mandan nada en la Zona de Canal.

Another mixes business and pleasure:

> Con mi morena voy a bailar
> Lunes y martes de Carnaval
> Chiari sera, Chiari sera

El Presidente de Panama.
(With my girl I'm going to dance
On Carnival Monday and Tuesday.
Chiari will be, Chiari will be
President of Panama.)

Some *tamboritos* show other Africanisms. "El Frijolar" has melody and words that in places do not coincide, in a fashion reminiscent of the music of the Ewe, who frequently treat the last beat of a drummed pattern as the opening beat of the vocal part. It is intriguing that, in North African dance music (especially Algerian), it is often difficult to tell where the music starts and finishes, and the rhythm of the melody is independent of that of the accompaniment, as is the case in many *tamboritos*. An example of this "free rhythm" singing can be heard in a *tamborito* called "Hojita de Limon," issued by Original Music, where it is backed by 2/4 clapping and fast drummed triplets. This is a feature of some Spanish music, and of much more West African music, so there is an apparent continuum in which coincidence seems more improbable than influence, though of course which way the influence ran is not clear. In the New World, the effect may be an Africanism, a Hispanicism, or more likely a phenomenon of mutual support.

Call-and-response is quite common in the *tamborito*, often with very short melodic phrases:

Y mueve la colita
Tio Cayman
Como una señorita
Tio Cayman.

In general the melody is quite African, with its two short phrases repeated many times. Together with the drumming, this repetition raises tension to a pitch at which musicians, dancers, and singers are whipped into a collective emotional and physical experience that provides a powerful sense of catharsis. The rhythmic buildup of constantly repeated phrases goes on until there is a sense almost of imminent explosion, when suddenly the lead drummer will signal a change from one rhythm to another, creating an extraordinary emotional discharge. As anyone who has danced to African or Afro-American drumming will know, this creates a slight dissociation like very mild hypnosis and is a highly refreshing phenomenon.

As Garay describes it, the drummers, as the point of maximum tension approaches, appear "possessed by a strange mysticism; their glances, their contortions and the movements of their heads remind one extraordinarily of the gestures of the oriental fakirs." The accumulation of nervous tension is reflected in the singing, the dancing, and the women's handclapping; then, "when everybody seems about to reach a point of paroxysm, the sudden change of rhythm, the transition from *corriente* to *norte* or from *norte* to *corriente* opens like a safety valve." *Norte* and *corriente* are common names for the two main drummed sections, one in 2/4 and the other in 6/8 time, though the names vary from region to region.

A more creolized Panamanian style (also found in Colombia) is the *mejorana*. The *mejorana* has two modes, one sung and the other for dancing. It is traditionally played on a small five-stringed guitar known as a *mejoranera*, with percussion. The *mejorana* has one very African quality, a blend of two meters—accompaniment in triple time and melody in duple—and frequently has a tune built up of short, much-repeated phrases reminiscent of a common African melodic technique. One form—the *mejorana-poncho*—makes some use of duple and triple rhythm played together. Also, the small fiddle, a very common instrument in danced *mejorana* (a three-stringed instrument with the originally Arab name of *rabel*), often plays a melodic line of a quite different rhythm from the accompaniment.

The effect of African music on the music of the other countries of South America is somewhat more vague and open to argument one way or the other, all too often on grounds of cultural chauvinism. There is little doubt that the music of Chile and Argentina in white South America and of Bolivia and Paraguay in the mainly Indian sector has been affected by black music, whether through the former presence of slaves who left the country (as when Rosas gave freedom and a passport to many thousands of slaves in Argentina), became absorbed into the population as a whole, or formed small minorities of African descent in these countries, or through the influence of the music of other countries.

Ortiz Oderigo claims that not only did the Amerindians adopt the African marimba, they also adopted African drumming techniques. In exchange, black musicians in some countries have borrowed the pre-Columbian *quena* flute. There are also a number of dances with names of apparent African origin, like the Argentinean *milonga* and *malambo*. (One can go too far in making these analogies, like Albert Friedenthal, who claimed that the Amerindian *yaravi* of Peru, Bolivia, and Ecuador was connected with the Arabic expression "Ya Rabi"—("Oh, Lord"!).

Some dances with African-style names presumably came from blacker neighbors, like the Argentinean *zamba*. Other influences in Argentina may have stemmed from the small coastal black population of Uruguay, though most of the musical currents flow the other way. On the other hand, there was at one time a definite neo-African culture in Argentina itself; many authors have reported the presence in the eighteenth and early nineteenth centuries of "nations" and cults. Much of the African musical practice presumably just stayed behind when the majority of the slaves left, to become progressively absorbed into the mainly Spanish-influenced mainstream. Incidentally, that absorption would be the more complete in that Argentina, along with Chile, is one of the few countries that preserved mostly northern Spanish traits—those that have least affinity with Islamic African music through North Africa.

One of the larger mysteries—if only because of the dance's importance—surrounds the Argentinean tango, which I discussed briefly with regard to Spanish and African origins in the Chapter 2. The tango is a prime example of the problems involved in pinning down styles that in their early days were assessed by the literate on an undesirability scale that ranged from "regrettable" to "outrageous." The tango is generally said to have stemmed from the mix of the *milonga,* an earlier Argentinean style that seems to have had largely Spanish roots, and the Cuban habanera, which certainly had African elements. Both very early and very recent accounts stress the tango's real or imagined African elements. But for very different reasons, both attributions could possibly be overstated. While one's own reaction against the old Europe-invented-everything myth can lead to overstating non-European elements, nineteenth-century sources often found it comforting to blame something rowdy and disreputable on nonwhites.

It is generally agreed that the tango grew up in the slum outskirts of Buenos Aires during the 1880s and 1890s. Its immediate ancestors were the habanera, brought in from Cuba by merchant seamen, and the *milonga,* a local development from an earlier form called the *payada,* an improvised song form described as based on verses of six, eight-syllable lines. In the late nineteenth century, the *payadas* were the province of wandering musicians called *payadores* who inevitably ended up in the bustling outskirts of Buenos Aires. There the *payada* gave birth to the *milonga,* a four-line variant of the *payada* with between-verse fills in 3/4 (some say 6/8) time, a description, incidentally, that sounds remarkably like the northern Spanish *jota.*

The most obvious influence on the tango, Spain aside (and perhaps even including Spain), was Italian. Italian migration to Buenos Aires at the time the tango was being born was enormous, and impoverished immigrants, gauchos-come-to-town, and blacks all lived together in slum neighborhoods. The Italian influence was not confined to the very obviously Italianate singing style, so different from almost anything else in Latin America, but included the classic accordion sound. Yet the attack of the classic tango *bandeoneón* accordion

As this 1879 etching of gauchos in a bar documents, Afro-Argentinians were a part of what is generally conceived as one of the most Eurocentric of Latin cultures—and gaucho music was one ingredient of the tango, along with more obviously African-derived urban elements.
Etching from Martin Fierro, *Buenos Aires, 1897.*

sound has a percussiveness that is most un–Italian. Is it an Africanism? It sounds to me more like the attack of Andalucian guitar-playing.

What goes for the music goes for the dance style, which has been described variously as a mix of *milonga* and mazurka and as a version of the Afro-Uruguayan *candombe*. Alien and creolized though it seemed to the politer elements of Euro-American society, I see little or nothing African in tango dancing, and a lot that might through oversimplification be symbolized as a waltz with flamenco touches—not in rhythm but in body posture and movement. But the tango has undergone so much tidying-up over the decades that the present form is not much in the way of evidence. Even in very early twentieth-century photos it was a couple dance performed in the customary European ballroom posture. But very early accounts of the proto-tango talk of Afro-Argentinean dancers. And one even claims that the *milonga* dance was a white bravos' parody of the Uruguayan *candombe* (a nice reversal of the cakewalk's

Manuel Donayre is a leading member of the recent Afro-Peruvian revival. As the guitarists make clear, the issue is not one of genes so much as of cultural survival.
Courtesy of Luaka Bop Records

parody of white dances). Certainly there seems no disputing an Afro-American root in the tango's immediate predecessors. Ortiz Oderigo pointed out years ago a cartoon in *La Ilustración Argentina* for November 30, 1882, captioned "The Tango" which showed a caricatured black couple dancing. And even the gaucho element in the tango may have had African-derived elements, because there were indeed black gauchos, as the 1879 engraving on page 97 shows.

Moreover, though the research into the African origins of American English are at times extremely sloppy, and the same is probably true of the Latin equivalents, current attempts to tie both "tango" and "milonga" linguistically to Africa are a lot more convincing than some such exercises. One early source attributed "milonga" to the KiMbundu language of Congo and Angola, and while there is no exact parallel—the nearest is perhaps "lunga," a drum, whose plural might well be "milunga"—the word certainly has the form of an extremely common Bantu plural. As for the word "tango," attempts to tie it to the Latin "I touch" strike me as plainly obtuse. Attempts to make a connection with "-tango," the root of the KiMbundu verb for talking or discussing, or "tantango," the generic Mandinka word for a drum, are very far from watertight, but not as loopy as trying to tie a working-class (or to be honest, pimping-class) Argentinean dance with a language 1500

Cuba in New York: The great *guarachera* Celia Cruz in full flight.
Photo by John Storm Roberts

years dead. If you are confused by now, you are beginning to get a grasp of the subject!

My own belief is that the *milonga-tango* started out as a Euro-African creole form, that absent a time-machine it will never be known which was the chicken and which the egg, and that its European elements were strengthened as it moved from the slums to the bordellos and then the cafés, thanks to a large and musical Italian migrant population. (Music of course has been a way out of the ghetto for all sorts of migrants, as well as African-Americans.) This is partially reinforced by the fact that so many of the great tango musicians have Italian names, even admitting that a lot of other Argentineans do so also (and that the greatest of tango singers, Carlos Gardel, was—just— French by birth).

At one time, it seemed that the specifically Afro-Latin musics of South America might gradually disappear into the creolized mainstream, or rather become part of a more national array of styles with both African and European elements, played by musicians of every conceivable melanin-count. To a large extent that seems to be happening, and while it is obviously a loss on some levels, it is also a side effect of the movement of Afro-Americans into the center of their various national lives. Afro-Brazilian music is very much alive, but it is no longer the perquisite of Afro-Brazilians alone, any more than grand opera or Mozart is the exclusive perquisite of whites. But some styles that were always marginal in their own countries have undergone a renaissance thanks to growing ethnic and cultural consciousness.

An example is Afro-Peruvian music, which was not a major part of Peruvian music taken as a whole and was also somewhat isolated. The grassroots forms included ritual music and an array of dances, many of them with vaguely familiar names. The oldest were the *landó, festejo, alcatraz,* and *ingá.* The major surviving dances are the *landó, alcatraz,* and *samba malato.* The archetypal small Afro-Peruvian combo combined a guitar with percussion consisting of a *cajón,* a *quijada* (ass's jawbone used as a shaker), and—much more unusual—a little box called a *cajita* whose lid is clacked in rhythm.

Since the 1950s, a conscious attempt to preserve and make over Afro-Peruvian music has brought it to the forefront of Peruvian consciousness in ways that bridge revivalist folklore and pop. In part this was the result of a "leftist" military dictatorship that encouraged nationalistic expression, and the revival was to some extent middle-class and self-conscious, driven by poets and musicologists rather than musicians out of the tradition (although people with more connection to the grassroots soon became involved). The major catalyst came in the 1970s with the group Peru Negro. Peru Negro's big hit was the song "Toro Mata," which in the Peruvian form had a classically African twelve-pulse rhythmic framework. "Toro Mata" was picked up and turned into an international hit by the great Cuban singer, Celia Cruz; her version lost a lot of the song's original flavor by giving it a Westernized, sixteen-pulse salsa frame.

The Caribbean

The music of the Caribbean, including the Guianas (essentially Caribbean cultures on the South American mainland) and English-speaking minorities in Nicaragua and Panama, is crucial to an understanding of how Africa and Europe gave birth to Afro-American music. The music of South America comes from African blending with two European elements, Spanish and Portuguese, that had a certain amount in common with it to begin with. By contrast, in the United States the blending process has gone so far that it is difficult to disentangle the strands involved. But the Caribbean contains music that embraces quite neo-African styles, styles that still preserve old European elements in a pure form, and every possible amalgam of European and African styles.

Moreover, the European ingredients present in the Caribbean—not just Spanish, British, and French, but also Dutch—are fairly different one from another. Hence, apparent Africanisms that are widespread are likely to have an African background, although extensive communication among various parts of the Caribbean carried certain elements of the music of one island to another. The interconnections were chiefly between islands speaking the same language, of course, but not entirely. Inter-island migration, as well as the ebb and flow of pop styles, has made of the islands a network of influences. Besides, Trinidad has been affected by Venezuelan music, and Louisiana under French and Spanish rule was culturally part of the Caribbean, so that elements of Caribbean music have had their effect on the United States.

Of the whole Caribbean, Cuban music is by far the richest and has had the most international influence, both within and outside the islands themselves. For both these reasons, it merits particularly detailed description. In the very early days, Cuba, along with Santo Domingo and Puerto Rico, was a neglected backwater of the Spanish Empire. Until the middle of the eighteenth century there were very few settlers of any kind in Cuba, and slaves formed a small minority. It was not until the 1760s (about 250 years later than Brazil and Central America) that Cuba became involved fully in the so-called South Atlantic System and developed a plantation sector worked largely by African slaves.

Once change started it was rapid. By 1800, Havana was the third largest city in the Americas after Mexico City and Lima (and a good deal bigger than any U.S. city). When the South American territories achieved independence from Spain during the 1820s, Cuba became the unofficial capital of the Spanish New World. In 1842, a visit from an Italian opera company started a rage for opera. By the 1880s the city was a major cultural center with a ballet company that toured the United States and a respected opera house. Havana, in fact, was part of a southern touring circuit for artists like Adelina Patti that included several U.S. cities—notably New Orleans—as well as Rio de Janeiro; the influence of romantic operetta on bolero singing in Cuba (later reinforced by the partially Italianate influence of tango singing) is still obvious. Cuba's interest in conservatory music drew New Orleans creole composer Louis Moreau Gottschalk there to work as a piano teacher—and to be inspired in turn by the local music, composing some brilliant small piano pieces on Cuban themes like a sort of Latin proto-ragtime.

Both the European and African influences in Cuba were very considerable. The island was a Spanish colony longer than any other country in the Americas, and even as a republic it received a major Hispanic influx in the persons of 300,000 legal and several thousand officially "illegal" Spanish immigrants. Another important immigration brought Canary Islanders in to help develop the cigar industry. Canarian music is akin to, but not the same as, Spanish, and one of the differences (including some ancient North African Berber elements) are probably relevant to blending with African styles. As just one example, whereas Spanish music tends to regular verse forms (though less rigidly than northwestern Europe), some of the main Canarian styles—especially the *folia*—go in for single lines separated from each other and building up a melodic pattern of phrases rather than verses.

One of the remarkable factors in Cuban music is the extraordinary breadth and richness of idioms for a country with a population in the low millions. Another is how many of these fed into the mainstream Cuban dance styles that were not only to spread all over the world, but to be the major root of the music eventually called salsa that moved from Cuba to New York and then spread to Colombia and other Latin American countries, taking in new local influences all the time.

The course of Cuban popular music was affected by a range of sometimes paradoxical social developments, including the desire of the Cuban elites just after independence to show that they were the equal of the "civilized" nations—equality in their minds meaning more opera houses and fewer Africanisms. In 1913, traditional Carnivals were banned, and the African cults were intermittently persecuted for years, mostly at the whim of the local police. At the same time, the purely African and neo-African elements in Cuban music were, as we saw in Chapter 2, among the strongest in the New World. The quintessential creole Cuban form—created largely by black and mulatto Cubans out of both Euro- and Afro-Cuban elements—was the *son*. This has also arguably been the single most internationally influential style of the twentieth century, as well as one of the most instantly and permanently beguiling.

To what extent the *son* came from black use of Spanish elements, or how much it was a general music with strong black content, there is no telling, though there is some evidence—as was usually the case with creole styles— that the early versions had stronger European influences than the later classic form, and that *son* always showed a dual influence even in the vocal. In the first part, these were normally strophic and strongly Spanish, while in the more improvised second section call-and-response took over and the percussion began to dominate. Nor is it clear how old the style is; the once-popular "Ma Teodora" theory, which traced it all the way back to two or three black musicians of the very early days of the colony, has recently been fairly convincingly debunked. But the *son* itself seems to have sprung from an earlier and simpler form, the *estribillo,* which had been around since the eighteenth century, accompanied in the early days by the guitar and a small guitar with a very distinctive sound called a *tres* (because its six strings were arranged in three double-courses).

At some time the bass came to be filled in by the *marimbula,* the big descendant of the African hand-piano, and the *botija,* a jug blown into to give a booming bass note (also used by many jook, spasm, and skiffle bands in the United States). The presence of these instruments, especially the *marimbula,* suggests a black origin for the *son,* which is not invalidated by the early use of the guitars; there is evidence that black Cubans took to the guitar much earlier than blacks in North America—which is hardly surprising, because the guitar is fundamental to Spanish music and not to white U.S. music. The bongos— the linked twin drums—and other small drums were used in *son* groups, as were the *güiro* and the *maracas* from time to time. The *estribillo* developed from the *décima*, the ten-line Spanish poetic form, but is said to have been adopted by black Cubans quite early. (Just to confuse the issue, the second section of the classic *son*, which was its more African-derived part and used call-and-response singing, was also called the *estribillo.*)

The classic *son* form was rich in African concepts, though its vocal tone, melodic elements, and guitar playing have always had strong Spanish elements. Most *sones* use call-and-response singing, and some show an African attitude by making the response the tune, for example, "Para Que No Pago" by the Cuarteto Machin. During the B tune, the solo vocalist was often dropped altogether, replaced by improvised phrases first from the trumpet and then from the guitar, a technique greatly amplified in later Cuban-based styles and highly idiosyncratic (in most musical cultures, instruments are used to reply to). The *son* groups were an important link between Cuban rural folk music and the urban popular groups of today's Hispanic music world. They bridged the gap in their instrumentation and in their growing complexity, but also in their remarkable ability to retain the feel of rural music in a professional music world. Nor is the style in any sense dead: both in New York and Cuba, younger bands are playing *sones* of considerable power and purity.

The *son* came to town from the country in the early part of the twentieth century; the date generally given is the 1920s (although W. C. Handy describes street groups in 1906 that sound awfully like the so-called *cuartetos*). The classic urban *son* groups took two forms. One was a strings-and-percussion group called a *cuarteto*, even though it very often ran to at least five instruments: guitar, *tres*, bongos, *marimbula*, and *claves*, whose tapping marked the basic beat. To the *cuartetos* was often added a single trumpet, to form groups known as *sextetos* or *septetos* which became the most popular format in the 1920s.

The *cuarteto* and *septeto* style remained enormously popular and influential until the 1940s, when the *septeto* transmogrified into the so-called *conjunto.* Moreover, it was the *son* that the Americans took up as the rumba and which enormously influenced African urban music. Among the best-known groups from the great days of the urban *son* (many of whose recordings have been reissued on CD) were the Sexteto Nacional, led by Ignacio Piñeiro; the Sexteto Habanero; the Trio Matamoros, whose leader, Miguel Matamoros, was responsible for a remarkable number of the style's most classic compositions; and an equally famous and popular group, the Guaracheros de Oriente.

One of these was the *guaguancó*, which has been discussed in its neo-African percussion form. Even more important was the *guaracha*, which—along with the *son*—was to form the basis for the dance band mambo. The *guaracha* was a natural for this kind of synthesis, bringing together Spanish

Arguably the most influential music of the twentieth century was the Cuban *son*. Recordings by the Sexteto Habanero among others were sold throughout Africa as well as in Latin America and the Caribbean.
Photo courtesy of Centro Odilio Urfé

and African vocal habits by using improvised solo quatrains answered by regular choral refrains. It too was a strongly mime-oriented dance form, beginning in the brothels in the nineteenth century and taken over by the popular theater. It tends to have satirical lyrics somewhat along the same lines as the Trinidad calypso. Some *guarachas* printed in the 1880s both began and ended with a solo verse, which is normally a strong African element.

The Cuban dance par excellence of the nineteenth century, the *contradanza*—not in its original Spanish form, a round dance which the Cubans found overly formal—was a modification of the French *contredanse*, a line dance introduced by the many thousands of refugees from the Haitian revolution. The Cuban *contradanza* was largely European in inspiration, and there is no proving whether its extra panache came from the more percussive attitudes of black music, the more percussive attitudes of southern Spanish dance music, or the kind of general New World oomph that pervaded the marches of Sousa. When it began to spread in the nineteenth century, it became known elsewhere as the *contradanza habanera* (Havana *contradanza*) or simply habanera, in which form it was highly influential internationally. Bizet's *Carmen* aside, the habanera rhythm was at the heart of the contemporary tango and also seems likely to have been a influence in proto-jazz and ragtime.

The various forms of *contradanza* were widespread in the Caribbean, together with many of the nineteenth-century European dances. The polka, the quadrille, the mazurka, and even the waltz have become acclimated in many parts of the Caribbean, and less familiar dances like the lancers were also localized in some islands.

The *contradanza* also gave birth to the *danzón*. This surfaced during the late 1870s and really developed from the 1880s on, thanks in particular to the compositions of Miguel Failde. As Peter Manuel wrote in his *Popular Musics of the Non-Western World*, "For some forty years hence the *danzón* became the single most popular Cuban dance genre. . . ." In fact, it survived in various hybrids for longer than forty years, and was still around in 1960s Latin New York.

To what extent the habanera and *danzón* owed their individuality to Afro-Cuban (and thus ultimately African-derived) elements is not entirely clear. Certainly, their late-nineteenth-century opponents thought so, denouncing them in depressingly predictable racist terms. These days, the same dances exude the pure essence of white gloves and potted palms, the tea dance, and the (by implication white) bourgeoisie.

The *charanga francesa* at times became extravagant and bourgeois, as can be heard in the recordings of the Orquesta Antonio Maria Romeu, which used florid piano, instruments that it would be coarse to call fiddles, and a suitably white-gloved rhythm section. Some of the Romeu orchestra's recorded pieces showed mainstream Cuban styles, but many take deep bows in the direction of Rudolf Friml and various other figures from overseas (and were not alone in that: one of the classic *danzones* is based on a theme from *The Barber of Seville*). But the *charanga* and the *danzón* were re-Africanized in the 1940s, when a group called Arcaño y sus Maravillas combined the elegant *danzón* with the driving Afro-Cuban mambo, ensuring its adaptation rather than disappearance. And it transmogrified once more, giving birth to the *chachachá* in the 1950s.

The two major types of group were not the only ones in Cuba, by a long way. The Afro-Cuban *sones* were paralleled by a Euro-Cuban tradition exemplified by the declamatory *punto cubano*, the Spanish-derived *décima*, the nostalgic *guajira*, and the *trova* ballad, known collectively as *guajiro* music (the *guajiros* being the peasant farmers of Cuba). Even though *guajiro* music had fewer African elements than the *sones*, it was in reality another creole form, often performed by Afro-Cubans like Joseito Hernandez, composer of "Guajira Guantanamera" (almost *too* well-known in the United States at one point as "Guantanamera"). Then there is the bolero, influenced by Mexican guitar techniques in the nineteenth century but whose present ultra-sentimental nature seems to have come from fashions for would-be romantic (but mostly merely sentimental) music among the Cuban middle class in the nineteenth century. The bolero rhythm was so emphatically guitar-based that it becomes bland in more percussion-oriented salsa groups; it became an essentially international style as performed by smooth duos and trios like the Trio Los Panchos.

A major feature of Cuban popular music in general is the importance of instrumental music. This has tended to follow two lines of development: Afro-Cuban on the one hand, and more white-oriented on the other (though both, of course, fed into each other). In fairly familiar terms, one might say, the first was represented by the mambo, and the second by the *chachachá*.

The Afro-Cuban strain grew out of various neo-African combinations— not only the rumba groups, but the *comparsa* Holy Week procession bands— using various combinations either of drums, rattles, and scrapers alone, or of drums, rattles, and scrapers with a guitar or two (or, in the case of the *comparsas*, trumpets) added. This line fed into the somewhat separate *septetos*, notably during the late 1930s when the addition of a piano, another trumpet, the conga drum, and more stylized arrangements, turned them into the *conjunto*. The more European form was represented in the late nineteenth century by Cuban versions of the sort of small military band that once gave concerts in the parks of Europe. These would typically consist of two clarinets, cornet, valve trombone, double bass, *güiro*, and a couple of small drums, at some point combined into the timbales just as U.S. marching drums were combined into the traps set or drumkit. How they sounded is uncertain, but the presence of the *güiro* makes it clear they had local elements. These groups attest to a level of formal musicianship in Cuba which most accounts tend to ignore. The rigorous *solfeggio* method, which involved a couple of years of thorough theoretical training before the student even selected an instrument, was common even in smaller towns. This level of classical training not only kept the island's symphony orchestras supplied with competent musicians, but meant that players moonlighting in the dance field maintained a high level of technical expertise.

The *orquestas típicas* (which have, alas, disappeared) had an equivalent more suited to playing indoors, the *charanga francesa* ("French orchestra"), which consisted of a flute lead backed by violins and (at its most classic) a cello, and a rhythm section that was also defined by the timbales. The *conjunto* and *charanga* singing styles were also different: the more African *conjunto* style continued the solo lead and call-and-response elements on the *septetos;* the *charanga* used a duet lead. Neither the distinction between the two types of group nor their "African" and "European" derivations should be taken too rigidly, however. Both were pure Cuban creole, and both mixed African and

European in proportions that varied within as well as between each type of band. And both were the purview of black, white, and mulatto musicians.

Just as jazz was influenced by Cuba, so Cuban music was influenced by the United States. From the 1920s on, the more upper-class nightclubs featured jazz bands, the local music being regarded as unhip if not vulgar. (Pianist/bandleader Don Azpiazu, who introduced "The Peanut Vendor" to the United States, is said by his son to have ruffled feathers by insisting on playing some Cuban numbers at the Havana Casino in the late 1920s.) Moreover, as Robin Moore has documented, earlier U.S. African-American forms (including nineteenth-century minstrelsy) had an influence that has been almost entirely ignored by Cuban musicologists.

The more polished urban dance bands of the 1920s developed relatively complex arrangements for the front-line instruments, especially U.S. techniques, which came in via books with titles like *Arranging in Five Easy Lessons* and with the many Cuban musicians who went to work in the United States for a while. These began to have an effect both on bands actually playing jazz, and on groups with American-style front lines playing Cuban music; these were called *orquestas,* a term which sometimes developed the more specialist sense of groups combining brass with *charanga* elements (a format preserved by several of Cuba's most innovative dance bands of the 1980s and 1990s).

The new techniques contrasted with the old way of arranging by giving each instrument a fairly simple riff pattern to stick to, which in a sense provided a melodic equivalent of the drum patterns. Other developments included the tendency for solo vocals to imitate the more complicated lines of the trumpets, especially in some *sones.* As time went on, like most dance band musicians, Cuban band members were able to play music of both types. As a result, such features as solo trumpet work with heavy jazz overtones and ensemble arrangements borrowing from big-band jazz became an integral part of a style that it would be artificial to call "black" or "white." Later, especially in the mambo (which grew from the rumba/*comparsa* Afro-Cuban styles), scat singing appeared, along with the use of disconnected syllables and words symbolized by the celebrated "grunt-break" in Damasiano Pérez Prado's recordings. This indirectly brought an African element, that of the cryptic vocal, back into Cuban pop music. It also heavily accented the rhythmic side as against the melodic. These elements had been present in other forms, but their systematic use came with the mambo, which was introduced to the *conjunto* and big-band style during the 1940s, and is often said to have come from the Congo-Angolan cults, along with the conga drum, introduced to the *conjunto* about the same time (the *canto de puyo,* of Congo-Bantu origin, used this type of cryptic vocal with interspersed cries, and the Cuban Bantu word for a song is *mambe* or *mambo*).

The *chachachá* swept the island in the early 1950s, bringing the *charanga* back into a vogue that led to a wide range of *charanga* styles: the fairly classic and elegant sound of the Orquesta Aragon and Enrique Jorrin's Orquesta America (often credited with the creation of the groups of the *chachachá* boom) and a much hotter sound with jazz influence in the solo fiddling exemplified by Sensación and in particular Melodías del 40.

The U.S. rumba craze of the 1930s, the mambo and *chachachá* of the 1950s, and the growth of U.S. salsa created a constant musical feedback between the United States and Cuba far too complex to deal with here. The embargo after Fidel Castro's takeover cut this direct link but provided the United States with many permanent residents who were Cuban musicians. At the same time, music in Cuba continued to develop at various levels. The Afro-Cuban *guaguancó* in its pure form was preserved and in some way revitalized by groups like Los Papines and Los Muñequitos de Matanzas. At the other end of the scale, Irakere combined avant-garde jazz with reworkings of *típico* music (and supplied the United States with several major Latin-jazz innovators through defection). And a great array of dance groups created new sounds such as Los Van Van's *songo,* the first Cuban idiom to have U.S.-style trap drums as an integral part of its rhythm section.

In its broad outlines, Puerto Rican music is fairly similar to Cuban, although it has fewer African-derived forms and characteristics except in specifically black modes like the *bomba,* discussed in Chapter 2, and in the island's major creole form, the *plena.* Like Cuba, Puerto Rico's level of musicianship during the nineteenth and early twentieth century was remarkable. Every provincial town tended to have a group of musicians—many of them from the same family—who played band music, dance music (including the elegant Puerto Rican *danza,* a local version of the *contradanza*), and classical music as the occasion demanded (Duke Ellington's famous valve trombonist, Juan Tizol, was but one member of the Tizol musical dynasty of San Juan). It is important to stress that while Puerto Rico did not have the extraordinary variety of styles of Cuba, Puerto Rican *musicians* of high caliber were important not only in the development of New York salsa but elsewhere in the New World (like the clarinetist who led Colombia's first *porro* band).

In its earliest form, the *plena* seems to have been accompanied by ad hoc groups using guitars and whatever percussion was around, or even percussion alone. But it soon settled down to a grouping that normally included the melodeon as a lead instrument, guitar, *cuatro, güiro,* and—an important element of the *plena* sound—the frame drums called *panderetas,* which resemble large tambourines without the rattles. The bongos, conga drums, and so forth, which are now used are another example of Cuban influence.

The vocal part of the classic *plena* consists of a four-line verse answered by a chorus, usually for two voices singing in parallel thirds, sixths, or unison with occasional octaves, a verse form a good deal more European than most of the Cuban styles. The lyrics tend to contain social comment or (often sharp) comment on girls and other subjects of general appeal. There is often a strong topical element:

> Cortaron a Elena
> Cortaron a Elena
> Cortaron a Elena
> Y la llevaron al hospital.
> (They wounded Elena
> And took her to the hospital.)
> Papeles son papeles
> Cartas son cartas
> Palabras de mujeres
> Todas son falsas.
> (Papers are papers
> Letters are letters
> Women's words
> Are all false.)

One of the earlier *plenas* still remembered, dating back to World War I, was called "German Submarine."

The overall quality of the *plenas* is faintly melancholy, though they are usually up-tempo. The touch of sadness remains even in highly "Cubanized" *plenas* played by Puerto Rican salsa groups on the island and in New York. Of course, the changes in the *plena* have given rise to complaints from musical conservatives, but most of them are in line with inevitable musical evolution. (No doubt there was much complaint when the early *plenas* began to use melodeons.)

Younger musicians have been apt to adopt the fast *güiro* pattern of the Dominican merengue, as well as Cuban drumming, and the harmonies are sometimes stretched to include flatted sevenths and other "atypical" chords. But the *plenas* are still instantly recognizable for what they are, quite distinct from Cuban music. Moreover, there is still a large body of *plenas* played with the old melodeon-led lineup, besides the groups using trumpet or saxophone.

A typical rural merengue trio with metal scraper (just visible on the left), accordion, and tambora drum. Here the drummer is using his hands—evidence that a *mangulina* rather than a merengue is being played.

Photo by John Storm Roberts

It is interesting that even the most Cubanized groups tend to use a large number of old *plenas*, like "Cortaron a Elena" or the beautiful and much-quoted "Santa Maria." The *guaracha* is also found in Puerto Rico, usually close to the *plena*, though it tends to have much simpler forms. It is, in fact, an earlier import from Cuba.

A feature of Puerto Rican music was the number of creolized European dance forms played by the same groups as play the older style of *plena*, which were still popular in the 1950s. These also are often accompanied by melodeon, guitars, and *güiro* and are frequently nonvocal. The mazurka and polka (still found elsewhere, as will be shown) had pretty much died out; but there are recorded accordion-led versions of the Puerto Rican *danza*, the *contradanza*, and splendid local examples of *vals criollo*, which was slower than the common European variety, with its beats more percussively marked, and very frequently used as backings to nostalgic or romantic lyrics.

In Puerto Rico as everywhere in the New World, African elements have formed part of styles that are not particularly associated with black populations. The various forms that make up what is known as *jíbaro* music (*jíbaros* being the peasant farmers of the island) are predominately Spanish in origin, but are still given part of their individual nature by African-derived elements. The archetypal *jíbaro* dance form is the *seis*, whose many types often show African traits in their rhythms and their call-and-response techniques, but whose dominant content is Spanish. And there is sometimes early evidence of black roots in forms considered generalized, or even white. As everywhere in the Spanish New World, religious festivals were important in black Puerto Rican music. *Aguinaldos* are a rough traditional equivalent of Christmas carols, though their subject matter ranges far beyond carols into moralizing tales and social comment of various kinds. For many Puerto Ricans the archetype of *jíbaro* music, the *aguinaldos*, were the songs of groups called *parrandas* that went from house to house singing, rather like the waits of a British Christmas. And though the association has been lost, there seems to have been a black element in them, because bands of black Puerto Ricans going around with drum groups singing *aguinaldos* for alms were described by a visitor of the late eighteenth century.

All in all, in fact, although Puerto Rico's black citizens have—or had—their own musical style (the *bomba*), for the most part they have influenced national popular forms rather than creating a separate musical tradition. The *bomba* has almost vanished as a purely un-self-conscious folk dance, though it is preserved by folkloric ensembles and had a period as part of the repertoire of Cuban-influenced salsa through the work of Afro-Rican percussionist Rafael Cortijo; on the other hand, the *plena* has remained as the symbol of Puerto

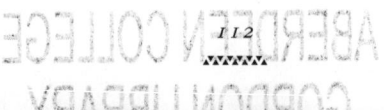

Rican music for most Puerto Ricans themselves, to the extent that there were several revivalist *plena* groups in both Puerto Rico and New York City. And the *plena* is Afro-Rican and Hispa-Rican in perhaps equal proportions.

If Cuba has a host of national forms, and Puerto Rico has the *plena* and to the lesser extent the *jíbaro* tradition, the Dominican Republic has produced one dance that is overwhelmingly the unofficial national music, a musical flag for Dominicans both on the island and in New York City. This is the merengue, which seems to have appeared in a fairly complete form around 1850. One old account of the first dancing of the merengue places it in 1844, during the war between Haiti and Santo Domingo. According to a Dominican writer, Rafael Vidal, a certain standard-bearer abandoned his post during a temporary setback, and the Dominicans, having finally won the battle, sang and danced a new song satirizing the deserter:

> Toma' juyó con la bandera,
> Toma' juyó con la bandera;
> Si juera yo, yo no juyera,
> Toma' juyó con la bandera.
> (Tomas fled with the flag,
> Tomas fled with the flag;
> If it had been me, I should not have fled,
> Tomas fled with the flag.)

Whether or not there is any merit in this story (Paul Austerlitz considers it apocryphal), the word "merengue" was being used in Dominican songs of the merengue form by about 1850. Austerlitz suggests that the word came from the Haitian version to the Dominican. If so, this would weaken the theory that the word is probably cognate with "maringa," a name given to a range of dances in coastal regions of West Africa, because the Haitian creole word "mereng" is clearly further from "maringa" than "merengue" with the final *e* pronounced. As to the origin of the dance itself, dances called merengues are also found in Cuba, Colombia, and Venezuela; but the differences are sufficient that this may be a case (as with the cognates *samba/semba/zamba*) of a linguistic rather than a musical tie.

In any event, like so many popular styles in the Caribbean, the merengue is dance music par excellence. Its basic rhythm is sharply distinct from Cuban-style, African-derived rhythms, being as much like a polka as anything but with a version of the *cinqillo* overlaid, usually in the form of a very rapid drum pulse that kicks the band from the fourth beat of one measure into the first beat of the next—a possible echo of a common West African drummers' practice. In fact, despite the indignant denials of a largely white Dominican elite, the merengue, like most Caribbean music, seems to owe much of its characteristic rhythm to the black element in the Afro-Spanish equation, even though its African elements are not so strong and obvious as many Cuban forms. This is one of those styles in which the African influence and the Spanish have blended over a long time and become largely indistinguishable in detail.

There is a description written in 1810 by an English visitor, William Walton, which points to an Afro-American rather than neo-African music at an earlier stage of development:

> The lower order of the Spanish people of color accompany their grotesque dances with yells and music created out of slips of hard-sounding wood, a furrowed calabash scraped gently with a thin bone, the banjo, rattles made by putting pebbles into a calabash, the teeth fixed in the jaw-bone of a horse, scraped with rapid motion, and the drum.

Walton's use of the phrase "Spanish people of color" suggests that the players of this music were not slaves, nor were they the most African of the island's people, whom travelers of that time almost always described as African or Negro. "Of color" normally implied people of mixed blood.

The modern merengue form was established around the end of World War I. It has three parts: a short introduction (often in practice left out); and two main sections, one of sixteen bars, which may have been the original form and whose length is likely to be a European influence; and another of a more African-derived type, which consists of two, two-bar phrases repeated many times with variations. The effect somewhat resembles what happens in many Afro-Cuban numbers, such as the *guaguancó,* which has a fairly "melodic" first part, in the European sense, and a second part using more chopped-up phrasing during which the percussion goes to town. The latter section is often instrumental, but when it is vocal the singing becomes much more fragmented and rhythm-oriented, improvisation reigns, and everything cooks. The typical merengue is fast of rhythm and funny of lyrics. The vocals are often call-and-response, and even some of the solo vocals have a form that suggests they may once have been call-and-response. The vocals in the final section, when there is one, are quite often call-and-response. A simpler version of the merengue, called the *pambiche,* consists of the last section only. A dance somewhat similar to the merengue is the *mangulina,* which comes from the south of the Dominican Republic.

The instrumentation of the merengue varies, but in the rural form generally associated with the northern province of the Cibao (and often called *merengue cibaeño*), the classic line up is melodeon (which virtually drove out the guitar during the late nineteenth century), *güiro*, and the *tambora* drum. To these may be added a *marimbula* or a bass guitar depending on the archaism or commercialism of the group. You can still hear *merengue cibaeño* played all over the Dominican Republic in a version that has many earmarks of the folk style unaffected by "art" or cabaret styles: a high, hard vocal tone that varies very little according to the subjects of the songs; a liking for repetition with slight variations; an absence of such musical effects as contrast; and a complete lack of such conscious stylistic tricks as holding certain notes to underline emotion or to dramatize, slowing up for the final notes of the song, and so on.

Though the archetypal lead instrument in rural merengues is the melodeon, a solo saxophone began to be used in a rural and small-town form often called *perico ripiao*, which has an interesting mix of traditional and non-traditional elements. The saxophone began to be used by some rural and *barrio* musicians before World War I, and as time went on (as Austerlitz has documented at length in his groundbreaking study of the merengue), merengue saxophone playing developed strong though extremely well-integrated jazz influences that came into it from more urban styles. The end result of the fast 2/4 merengue beat, the throb of the *tambora*, rapid accordion riffs, and a saxophone style that can reach positively manic enthusiasm is a style that can verge on the hallucinatory. The rural accordion style was regarded as corny when I was recording in the Dominican Republic in the early 1970s. Happily, a new generation of players has revived it, sometimes in even more manic forms—the playing of the woman accordionist Fefita La Grande has been compared with Don Cherry, yet she essentially plays a hard-core merengue style.

The merengue in general and the urban dance band style in particular was given a lift by the dictator Rafael Trujillo, who used it as a stick to beat the old-style Dominican elite who looked down on it. The first big hit of the dance band style, according to Austerlitz, was the 1937 "El Compadre Pedro Juan" by Luis Alberti's Orquesta Presidente Trujillo. The elite groups of the time, particularly in the 1940s, used swing-influenced brass sections and mambolike interplay, though Alberti also sometimes included *güiro*, *tambora*, and accordion.

In the 1950s and particularly the 1960s, the urban or *salsa-merengue* developed into a punchy salsa analog in the hands of several musicians with an understanding of jazz and Cuban music, notably Félix del Rosario and Johnny Ventura. Ventura in particular reduced the big merengue band to something more the size of a *conjunto* and is said to have added the conga drum to the lineup, producing a new sound that was somewhat Cuban influenced, but probably prevented Cuban forms from ousting the merengue from the realms of the hip.

Beginning in the late 1970s, the dance-band merengue underwent an extraordinary success in the hands of a generation of young players, of whom the most important by far was Wilfrido Vargas, a musician of great talent and wit. Aside from launching or encouraging pretty much every successful musician of the era, Vargas broadened the style's canvas, playing Haitian and *zouk* numbers and scoring his first really major hit with a song that had begun life as a Mexican *ranchera,* "El Jardinero." A band sound developed (notably in the Orquesta Liberación) that set creamy trombone slurs against the wriggling saxophones.

By the end of the 1980s it looked as though merengue might oust salsa even in New York City, thanks to being easy to dance, manic, and of course new (to New Yorkers). It was also helped by the ever-growing community of New York Dominicans, who soon produced the first United States-based, pop-merengue group to take the island by storm, Millie, Jocelyn y Los Vecinos. There was a heartthrob wing led by Fernandito Villalona, and Juan Luis Guerra with his vocal group 440 produced a polished version of both merengue and other Dominican forms, influenced by Manhattan Transfer but also with excellent lyrics and arrangements.

So far from being some kind of dilution, the recent foreign influences on the merengue, whether they be from Haiti, Guadeloupe, or Manhattan, are absolutely at the center of Caribbean musical history. The merengue itself is related in ways that are still topics of hot argument to the Haitian *méringue* or *mereng.* And both supplanted a dance called the *tumba,* which in varying forms was popular in both the French and Spanish halves of the island and could until recently still be heard occasionally in the mountains of the Dominican Republic. Just before the merengue became popular, there was a vogue for a dance called the *upa,* which had been introduced by Cuban regimental bands stationed in Puerto Rico. As an example of how complex Caribbean musical history can be, in Puerto Rico, the *upa* offended the authorities and was banned on moral grounds in 1848. As a result, new steps adapted from the *contradanza* were put to it, and the new dance was sometimes known as the merengue. Whether the dance went to Santo Domingo from there, or whether the one name was attached to different but similar dances, is not clear.

Though the merengue (in its generalized and multiple local variants) is overwhelmingly the Dominican national dance, plenty of others exist. One is the *mangulina,* a 6/8 rhythm often played as a contrast by rural merengue groups (for a *mangulina* the tambora player abandons his drumstick and plays the drum with his hands like a conga). Other dances show various blends of the Spanish and African-derived traditions. The *sarandunga,* a dance confined to the town of Baní, is very like the fast tap dance known in Spain as *zapateado,* but in the Dominican Republic it has acquired a far more African section during which only the percussion elements play, often the African-style drums known as *palos.* And instead of a tap dance for one couple, a whole group of dancers do a shuffle-step. Like the *mangulina* it was usually accompanied by accordion, *güiro,* and *tambora* played with the hands only.

Like Cuba with its rumbas and *comparsas* and Puerto Rico with its *bomba,* the Dominican Republic also has music that is more specifically black and uses neo-African drums in groups of two or three, the *palos* or *congos.* The country, in fact, illustrates the great richness and diversity of music in areas touched by the Afro-American experience. Within a country of four million people, the styles found range from the almost pure Africanism (language and musical implications aside) of some of the *palos* drum music and *cantos de hacha* (ax songs) of the black, sugar-producing south, to the almost pure, ancient Spanish *salves* and *tonadas* of the Cibao around Santiago de los Caballeros in the north of the island. And together with these extremes exist the country dance forms, the merengue and *mangulina* and others, which have combined Euro-Dominican and Afro-Dominican elements into a music belonging to everybody.

The music of the *palos,* the *cantos de hacha,* and the other Afro-Dominican forms belonging to the black Dominicans contain Spanish elements, particularly in the solo "call" melodies; but the choral response as well as the drumming (in the music of the *palos*) are extremely African in melodic and harmonic quality. So are a number of other features, including the lesser importance of lyrics in many cases. The *congos* of Villa Mella, whom I mentioned in Chapter 2, sang roughly the same set of lyrics to a *criolla,* a *calunga,* and two other songs. The *tonadas* and *salves* of the Cibao, on the other hand, display no Africanisms at all except for their call-and-response pattern. Their melodic qualities are very similar to ancient Castilian vocal forms, and many of their lyrics clearly came from Spain many years ago.

The example of the Dominican Republic illustrates that the question of Afro-American or Euro-American culture is not necessarily one of skin color. While it is true that the southern provinces have a high percentage of black inhabitants, the people in and around Santiago who sang old *salves* and *tonadas* to me included black, brown, and Spanish-looking women in the same groups.

On the whole, the most African-inspired styles are sung and played by black Dominicans, but the reverse is by no means automatically true of the Spanish-derived styles, and these extreme musical types are not the only music in which their performers participate. Everybody shares the merengue, the *mangulina*, and similar dances.

The Spanish-speaking West Indies form a relatively cohesive picture: three fairly large islands with a clear pattern of similarities and differences. The English-speaking West Indies are far more confusing. Jamaica and Trinidad are large enough to contain a number of fair-sized towns and several different types of rural areas. On the other hand, they are at opposite ends of a long chain of islands, and Jamaica is further separated from the other formerly British territories by Hispaniola and Puerto Rico. The smaller islands are divided into the Leeward and Windward Islands. Each of these small islands has some element of geography or history to make it unique. Nevis and Saint Kitts, originally settled by British convicts, have preserved full versions of medieval mumming plays, such as "St. George and the Turkish Knight"; these have become so much a part of their heritage that settlers from these islands who migrated to the Dominican Republic still perform "the mummies" in the streets of San Pedro de Macoris. The music of Barbados, like its history, is firmly connected with Britain. Saint Lucia and Grenada, on the other hand, have folk styles that are largely Afro-French. The Commonwealth of the Bahamas, though its political links have been with Britain, has (like the U.S. Virgin Islands) come under heavy U.S. musical influence. The Cayman Islands have a fiddle tradition that stems almost equally from Scots and U.S. rural elements, and a "polka drumming" style that is astonishingly like the drumming in records of southern English folk dance bands of the early twentieth century (a technique that sounds almost like a derisive parody of military drumming, but I suspect of being quite ancient). The Virgin Islands (both U.S. and British) have dance groups called scratch or *funji* bands, combining strings and percussion and playing local forms calypsolike forms and older dances. And both in Tortola and Grand Cayman I came across sea chanteys in Anglo-American style that reflected the seafaring tradition of the small islands. I have mentioned the neo-African "nation dance" of Carriacou; the island also preserves a strong quadrille tradition and related fiddle style.

Not themselves islanders, but with similar traditions, are the anglophone minorities on the coast of various central American countries. On the Caribbean coasts of Nicaragua and Costa Rica, and in Belize (formerly British Honduras), there are English-speaking black populations who play versions of calypso and scratch music. Besides the strongly neo-African inland *punta*,

The Afro-English end of Caribbean music: the Cayman Islands polka drum is played like southern English traditional drumming, and one of the fiddler's showpieces, "The Devil and the Tailor," is a Scots classic.
Photo by John Storm Roberts

Belize has accordion quartets (as does anglophone Nicaragua) and scratch bands known locally as boom and chime, along with a vaguely calypsolike idiom called *brekdon* (breakdown) that grew up in the logging camps. Panama's Anglo-Panamanians are mostly famous for providing a surprising number of jazzmen among immigrants to the United States. But Colon was also a major port, and the old man in Grand Cayman from whom I recorded old (and in part previously unknown) sea-chanteys and fo'csle songs had learnt them in Colon as a young seaman. All this Anglo-Central-American music has been sorely neglected, though there exist a CD of Afro-Limonese calypso from Costa Rica and a small handful of good recordings of Belizean music.

Before the arrival on the world scene of reggae, the best-known music of the English-speaking Caribbean was calypso. There is a basic problem determining whether its association with Trinidad also reflects its origin. In other words, is it a Trinidadian style that spread to other islands or an interisland style of which the Trinidadian version is simply the best known? As so often with issues capable of raising a lot of heat, the whole question is ultimately one of definition. Other islands certainly had forms similar to calypso, whether called calypso, *kaiso* (a word sometimes also used in Trinidad), or

Seminal 1920s calypso recording artist Sam Manning. "My
Little West Indian Girl" was one of his early hits.
Courtesy of Don Hill

something like it. But these styles were influenced by Trinidadian calypso, both because of the usual interaction of musical elements and because a certain businessman who had most of the Trinidad calypsonians under contract also owned a chain of record stores in many of the other islands, through which he pushed the Trinidadian records. Because the Trinidadian style of calypso was popular, the music of the other islands was sometimes played in a "calypsofied" way, and musicians from the other islands sang calypsos.

The definition issue haunts even discussions of Trinidad calypso itself. Though rural calypso bands existed, the Trinidadian calypso itself is and seems always to have been essentially a town music. The calypso singer Atilla the Hun (Raymond Quevedo), who edited a collection of calypso lyrics in the 1940s, claimed that the earliest calypso was this "definitely captivating chant . . . sung in African":

> Ja ja romy aye
> Ja romy Shango
> Ja ja romy meta buri
> Ja romy Shango.

But this song bears no apparent relation to the calypso form as it grew up in the nineteenth and twentieth centuries. Quevedo suggested that its meaning was "I'm coming to the god's dance" and that Ja Ja was a god. Shango is the Yoruba god of thunder, and there is a much smaller Shango cult in Trinidad which, according to Peter Manuel, is not a relic of slavery—which ended in the British Caribbean before the period of Yoruba slavery—but of contract workers hired during the mid-1800s. It seems likely that the song quoted by Quevedo is connected with that cult. His attempt to link it closely with the origins of calypso seems to be pan-Africanist romanticism.

Quevedo also asserted that the calypso was "undoubtedly African" and that the earliest version developed during *gayap*, a form of organized communal work that does in fact have African parallels. After the day's work was done, the work song leader, according to Quevedo, would improvise praise songs for his own team and songs of derision about the others. There certainly were songs of this type in Trinidad's past; in fact, work songs associated with *gayap* still exist there and on other islands where the same custom is maintained under various names. But it seems unlikely that satirical songs sung after work in the country can really be considered the first examples of a music that grew up almost entirely in the capital city of Port of Spain. It is much more probable they were only one of a number of styles that helped feed the calypso at various times.

Another possible source of the calypso is mentioned by Daniel Crowley in an article in *Ethnomusicology.* There is a legend that, during the French rule over the island, a certain Pierre Begorat appointed a slave called Gros Jean as "Mait' Caiso" on his Diego Martin estate. At that time, it is said, songs were usually improvised, with laudatory or satirical subjects, and frequently constituted wars of words between singers (a tradition that still lives, as will be seen). The early calypsos are sometimes said to have been sung in French patois. A singer called Norman (or, according to another version, Cedric) Le Blanc claimed in 1898 to have been the first to sing calypso in English. But while Trinidad's French-creole tradition was strong, it seems to me that direct ancestry (as opposed to partial contribution) is unlikely—and if it existed, did so at an extremely early stage.

The English-language calypso was without a doubt fairly well known locally under its present name, or a version of it, in 1859. That was the year a luckless U.S. ornithologist, William Moore, was unwise enough to claim that calypso was nothing but variations on British ballads (an unlikely claim if it was being sung in French creole). Moore immediately experienced a full-blooded Africanism—the use of song for public and embarrassing rebuke—when a singer called Surisima (or Sirisima) the Carib turned up outside his hotel with a large, vociferous crowd and serenaded him in call-and-response fashion, the spectators in African style providing the responses:

> *Surisima:* Moore, you monkey from America,
> *Crowd:* Tell we what you know about we cariso!

Another Africanism, the dynamic use of repetition, also came into play, and a lengthy good time was had by all but one until the police finally broke up the party.

By the 1870s calypsos were regularly sung in English in something like their present form. Charles Espinet and Harry Pitts, in *Land of the Calypso,* claimed that the earliest known calypso *tune* was "Jour Ouvert," composed in 1876. (Jour Ouvert is the first day of Carnival, and the peak of calypso in any year is the tent competitions during Carnival time, when the king calypsonian is chosen.) But some *lyrics* survive from before that. A famous calypso singer of that time was a woman called Bodicea. Calypso at that period was very much a music of the Port of Spain underworld, and many of the singers and subjects of the songs, like many of the people responsible for the blues, were pimps, prostitutes, and *obeahmen.* The singers were "deeply involved in *obeah,* and most died violent deaths." Then as now, calypso throve on gossip, current events, and personalities. When Hannibal the Mulatto died in 1873, his grave robbed, and his head stolen for *obeah*, Bodicea was inspired. Tearing off her dress, she led a rowdy crowd around Port of Spain waving it as a flag and singing:

> Congo Jack steal Hannibal head
> You steal from the dead
> Look bacchanal.

(Congo Jack was another singer of the day. "Bacchanal" is still a Trinidadian word for any riotous occasion, from party on up.)

A rival calypsonian, either because he was shocked or far more probably because he was a friend of Congo Jack, was moved to reply to Bodicea in what is known as the "oration" form of calypso, which used fine phrases and a declamatory tune mostly on one note, an indication that calypso was fully developed by the 1870s:

> It was shocking, it was shameful and bad to see
> Carnival in the cemetery.
> It couldn't happen in Grenada,
> Saint Kitts, Martinique or Antigua.
> When such lawlessness can prevail,
> Tell me what's the use of the Royal Jail?
> Bodicea the jamette [prostitute] whom we all know
> Is a real disgrace to we cariso.
> I really can't understand
> Why she didn't take the training of the Englishman.
> Cat and dog passing they mouth on she
> Is better she die or lock up in jail,
> She disgrace every woman in Port of Spain.

There is nothing African or neo-African about this lyric except the rebuking of social misbehavior, but call-and-response and other elements are frequently present in calypso, to say nothing of the whole concept of a satirical and topical "news sheet" music. The original instruments which accompanied calypso included drums, a scraper called a *vira*, rattles, and a bottle and spoon used like a West African gong. Early calypsos often used short call-and-response verses. When guitars and the smaller *cuatros* began to be used, Venezuelan-derived dance tunes, particularly the *pasillo* and *castillan*, already played by the people of Spanish and Venezuelan descent on the island, were adapted to two- and four-line English lyrics. Espinet says the Venezuelan influence is recent, though "Jour Ouvert" is clearly Spanish in style, and suggests that there were two separate Spanish influences in calypso, one on the developing form, from the Spanish rule in the island, and the other Venezuelan, from the radio and other sources during this century.

Certainly calypso is a highly eclectic music. It has drawn heavily from various sources within Trinidad itself, including sources of a higher African content than calypso itself. It also shows the effect of Spanish, British, and French music. Some individual calypsos have even taken elements from the East Indians, who form the largest minority on the island. Similarly, though most calypsonians were black and uneducated, Lord Executor had a high-school education, Le Blanc was in fact white, Sirisima may or may not have been a Carib, Hannibal was a mulatto, and, to judge from photographs and his name, Atilla the Hun was at least part Venezuelan, Spanish, or Portuguese.

At various times calypso backings have favored Venezuelan music, jazz, Cuban touches, and rhythm and blues. But like any strongly based and original music, calypso has benefited from, rather than being swamped by, these outside influences. Similarly, it has been under fairly steady attack ever since at least the late 1930s for having "gone commercial." It seems that the latest but one generation of calypsonians is always the last true one.

The music of calypso is impossible to pinpoint, because it was so varied. The rhythm was Afro-Spanish, at times more black and at others more Hispanic. Call-and-response was used quite often but is probably not the majority form. Perhaps the most striking Africanism lay in the nature and function of the lyrics. Like much folk and semifolk music, calypso tunes did not vary much. There is a floating pool of about fifty that are used and reused, altered and re-altered, but the words must be fresh. Part of the nature of calypso is tied to its connection with Carnival, whether it is in fact a Carnival music or merely, as Espinet claimed, linked to Carnival by a "marriage of convenience." The famous calypso tents have long been tourist attractions, but it is still there that the kings are crowned, in front of an expert audience. The calypsonians themselves possibly fulfill a group-identification ritual role. They are extremely dashing and must be surrounded by women and admiration. One calypsonian, who had taken a job in a fit of absent mindedness, never appeared in the tent again. The flamboyant names—Lord Beginner, Atilla the Hun, the Mighty Sparrow, Edward the Confessor, the Lion, Black Stalin, the Mighty Chalkdust (a teacher by profession)—are part of this function. It is in part at least a stereotype, the idle rascal who contrives to live without actual criminality, one shared by the blues singer and, in many African societies, by the professional *griot* musicians. In the New World as in Africa, the cap may fit some individuals, but the image is often encouraged for professional reasons.

The social role of calypso is strong but difficult to assess. It has always served as a vehicle of social and even political comment. Sir Patrick Renison, a former Colonial Secretary of Trinidad, once stated that the colonial government did in fact "take cognizance" of political calypsos. In 1990, when a Muslim militant called Abu Bakr launched an unsuccessful coup, almost his first decree was the founding of an all-calypso radio station. Sometimes calypsos would exhort the public to civic duty, like Sparrow's "You Got to Pay Tax." But much more common is the sort of current-affairs approach of Growler's comment on the 1943 meat shortage:

> I think I got to make a firm determination
> To stop eating beef in this meat depression.
> For we can't get cattle and we can't get hog
> And me mind only telling me I'm eating dog;
> Beef and pork was always me line,
> So them wolf-hound wouldn't eat out me intestine.

The twisting of words to make rhymes of excruciating ingenuity was a particular feature of the calypsos of the 1940s and 1950s. It was not simply a trick of prosody; it formed part of a battery of devices for producing a wide range of rhythmic effects in the vocal line. Another device was the use of lines of greatly varying length, which gave something of the effect of the drummer who enlivens a piece by contrasting patterns of few beats with bursts of many beats. The rhythmic effect often would be enhanced by the insertion of short phrases or cries between the lines of the verses themselves. Such a cry would produce a feeling of drive and gaiety, like the Spanish *olé*, but it also supplied offbeat rhythmic accents.

A popular aspect of the tent competitions were the wars of words, or *piccong*, an exercise in institutionalized abuse like the U.S. "dozens." The *piccong*, or *mepri*, the only form of calypso in which much improvisation is used nowadays, preserves the calypso flavor in phrases that are often fairly standard:

> . . . why you standing there,
> You smelling like Pointe-à-Pierre.

(Pointe-à-Pierre is an oil refinery.)

Calypso has been used for social comment, and also in its time—so rumor persistently has it—for blackmail. ("Pay me or I'll write a song about you.") The calypsonians' moral judgments are often subtle. One old lady who exposed a juicy sexual scandal was disconcerted to find not the sinners but herself the target for calypsonian outrage at the meddling of the elderly. Perhaps the most common single subject for calypso is sex. Invader's "You Don't Need Glasses to See," Lord Kitchener's "Kitch," and Bedasse's "Night Food" all feature the naïve, uncomprehending male and the increasing ire of the woman scorned. But anything may surface. One of the finest calypsos ever was the Mighty Sparrow's little-known 1959 "Simpson," a hilarious epic about the results of a false rumor of his death and its effect on "Simpson the Funeral Agency Man" along with sundry women and competitors.

Though the calypso's melodic ancestry is mixed, it has a fairly high European admixture, including English, Spanish, and French. Basically the various forms of calypso corresponded to certain root types. The so-called double-tone calypso had fairly long melody lines. The single-tone calypso had a higher proportion of elements of African or probable African origin: a shorter melody line in call-and-response form, and generally more improvisation and rhythmic interest. Another variant was the *leggo*, described by Espinet as consisting of the choruses of the calypso, "stripped of all the humor and other commentary trimmings." The novelist/composer Paul Bowles, in a quite insightful article in *Modern Music*, stated that, besides greater simplicity, the percussive strain was more prominent in the *leggo*. The opening procedures of the *leggo* as described by Bowles suggest an African background:

> The soloist announces phrase number one, and then phrase number two, the chorus responds with phrase number one, which henceforth is to be its private property uttered with unchanging uniformity throughout the song. After two or three responses a police whistle is blown, the signal for the entrance of the battery of percussion.

Like any music of course, calypso changed from the 1930s through the 1950s. During the 1950s, three major talents replaced the older generation: Lord Kitchener, Lord Melody, and above all the Mighty Sparrow. All three continued pretty much in the main line of calypso tradition, but all three renewed it simply by the brilliance of their lyrical and melodic sense. On a more negative note, the accompaniments that in the 1930s had included loose rhythms and improvised clarinet, trumpet, and piano, had been abandoned in favor of punchy but dull head arrangements for trumpet and saxophone, mostly in unison.

But the major change in calypso came during the 1970s, when a dance-oriented style emerged with a lot of U.S. soul influence called soca, apparently an abbreviation of "soul calypso." The first soca number was claimed by Lord

Latest round in the constant mutual feedback within the black diaspora is rapso, a Trinidadian blend of calypso and rap, one of whose major stars is Brother Resistance.
Photo by Mark Lydersay, courtesy of Rituals Ltd, Port of Spain

Shorty, who has said be was deliberately mixing calypso with rhythms from the music of the Trinidadians of Indo-Pakistani descent (colloquially called chutney in Trinidad). Naturally the old guard disapproved of soca, and when Lord Kitchener in 1978 mixed soca elements into his "Sugar Bum Bum" there was a huge uproar. Ever since, there has been a running argument about what is soca, what is calypso, and every conceivable variant, most of which is largely semantic. Soca and the more recent calypso are far more heavily rhythmic than old calypso (even if the horn sections are just as dull, though brasher). Some soca singers largely sing sexually oriented songs; but Mighty Chalkdust and Black Stalin frequently record political or social comment (and occasionally let a horn player loose to solo). And given that Sparrow won king of Carnival every year until he retired to let others have a chance, it is hard to see soca as a total break from tradition. Whether or not soca had a Trinidad-Indian element, as Lord Shorty claimed, it certainly fed back to younger Indo-Trinidadians in an intriguing Afro-Indo-creole mix. Not only are there mainstream soca singers of Indian descent like Dhrupati, there is also a style called chutney soca, whose main stars are the duo of Babla and Kanchan, and Sundar Popo that uses Indian elements like the rhythms of the Punjabi dholak drum and certain singing techniques. And most recently, predictably enough, the impact of United States rap has been felt in a new blend known as rapso, whose texts tend to combine the editorializing of calypso and the rhetoric of rap, notably in the work of Brother Resistance.

A final factor in soca as it sounds today is one that has been pretty much ignored. That is the fact that almost all of it is recorded in Brooklyn, and involves only three or four record companies and producers. This certainly in part contributes to the similarity in soca backings, whoever the singer; in fact, it's surprising soca bands aren't even more like each other than they are. Moreover, the horn sections often contain non-Trinidadians; jazz trombonist Clifton Anderson, for example, recorded behind Sparrow and Nelson in the late 1970s and the '80s. All this may account for the general over-reliance on prewritten charts and the freshness of the occasional recording that allows a soloist to break loose.

Calypso was never the only Trinidadian music associated with Carnival. To judge from an indignant report in the *Port of Spain Gazette* in the 1830s, some of the earlier modes were strongly African:

> We will not dwell on the disgusting and indecent scenes that were enacted in our streets—we will not say how many we saw in a state so nearly approaching nudity as to outrage decency and shock modesty—we will not particularly describe the African custom of carrying a stuffed figure of a woman on a pole, which was followed by hundreds of Negroes yelling out a savage Guinea [song] . . . we regret to say that nine-tenths of those people were creoles.

The *Gazette*'s fulminations were not caused by culture shock alone. The Carnival had been a grand white affair during the time of slavery but was taken over by the street people after Emancipation, and like calypso it flourished on a mixture of fine music and low life. One of the features of Carnival in those days was *canboulay* (*cannes brûlées*), a torchlight procession with "stickmen" singing *kalindas* and performing stick fights. Otherwise known as *bois*, the stick fights may have derived from a blend of African war-training dances and European single-stick fighting. The sticks themselves were "mounted" with spells to help their owners. The *kalinda* was used to pace the game itself, like the Brazilian *capoeira* music, and was a music for drums and assorted percussion. A *chantwell* (solo singer) often accompanied the band to praise one fighter and deride his opponent in two-line songs in creole or English, with the band singing responses. Besides the *kalinda* instruments, marchers used bamboo stamping sticks called *tamboo bamboo*, rather like the Haitian *ganbo* but longer, as percussion. They were dropped on the ground or beaten together. Unfortunately, they were also brought down on the

Steel drums or pans in marching band configuration, held in a frame with wheels. What started (typically) as a street idiom of dubious reputation has become a major tourist attraction; but away from the tourist centers, the more modest and authentic version lives on.
Photo by Don Hill

heads of opponents and were eventually banned, along with *canboulay* and *kalinda* fights.

After the calypso, the Caribbean music best known overseas is the steel band. Most islands have their steel bands these days, but they began in Trinidad. Ironically, for a style that has been plugged to death by the tourist boards, it started out with as many strikes against it as most other twentieth century urban popular forms. Crowley put it this way: "Here is a complex art form created by lower-class, ill-educated, underprivileged adolescents against the will of their parents, the ruling class, and the police." It is often claimed that steel band is in some way descended from African drumming. Handed-down Africanisms of rhythm and form added to a percussive instrument obviously offer some parallels, but in fact the steel drums have a range and sound rather nearer to African xylophones than to African drums. And even here, any parallels would be due to a generalized web of musical Africanisms rather than more specific "folk memories." The music, it is said, developed as a reaction to the banning of the *tamboo bamboo*. The basic instruments, called pans, are made out of large oil drums. The head of the drum is cut off, leaving six inches to a foot of the body. A series of bumps, each giving a musical note, is produced on the surface by heating and hammering. The pans range from instruments with many notes, to carry the melody, to bass pans of three or four notes. Their sound is resonant and rather sweet. Indeed, by the early 1970s the trouble with steel-band music was that it was often too sweet and too eclectic.

The steel bands playing in the Carnival contests are enormous (they are officially restricted to 120 members!), and musicians refuse to be daunted by anything, playing Tchaikovsky as enthusiastically as the latest winning road march song. But the pans are arguably best suited to Trinidadian music and to techniques like the call-and-response passage in the Trinidad All Stars' "Diana," where the call function is taken over by a pan with voices supplying the response (as Cuban musicians often do with trumpet and voices). This fact is implicitly recognized in a style of pan that developed in the early 1980s, in which a pan player is one element in a small group including guitar and rhythm, playing jazz-influenced calypso and soca.

The tradition of waking the dead is (or was) common all over the Caribbean. In the English-speaking islands, the ceremonies could stretch over many evenings; the Jamaican name for the wakes, "nine-nights," was at one time not metaphorical. In Jamaica and elsewhere, "setups," the first night—occurring before the actual funeral—featured hymns and religious songs, but after the funeral all sorts of songs and games were the custom. Some traveled from island to island, like the "Guavaberry Song" that I recorded in Tortola, versions of which have cropped up in Jamaica and elsewhere. Its reference to "young massa" could mean it goes back to slavery, but may simply be a reference to a plantation head in post-slavery days.

A dual function—at least in European terms—is reflected in many of the older musical forms of the islands. Often they reflect characteristically West African social or spiritual attitudes, in their function if not in their music. The Tobagan reel dance for solo singer, tambourines, and other percussion is a dance music, but at the same time it is used for the invocation of spirits before weddings and in cases of sickness. Its composite role suggests a reinterpretation of a healing dance. The small island of Carriacou has two dances with obvious African ancestry in both music and function. Earlier I mentioned the "big drum" dance in connection with the "nations" (see Chapter 1). It is music for a family or neighborhood ceremony to ensure the favor of the ancestors, accompanied by offerings of food. The *reel engagé* is a social dance music used for reels, quadrilles, and so forth at family dances, again connected with offerings for the ancestors. These musics contain Africanisms of performance as well as of instrumentation or form. A common one is the use of falsetto, as in Carriacou, when a singer will begin a dance song in falsetto and turn to normal voice when the drums come in.

Trinidad also has a minority population with strong links with Venezuela (a connection reflected in some of the earliest commercial recordings, for string band). In the past these people preserved Venezuelan customs, including the *veiquoix* (from *Velorio del Cruz*), which in Trinidad involved *piccong* (insult song) competitions as well as the recited competitive *décimas* common in Venezuela. The instruments used in Trinidad as well as in Venezuela were *tiple, cuatro, bandol* (mandolin), guitar, and *chac-chac*. Unlike Venezuela, drums were not usually used. After the *veiquoix* came the *fandang*, a dance at which a string band would play Venezuelan *joropos, galerónes, castillans*, and so forth. The people who play this music live in a region called Grand Curucaye and are of Venezuelan descent. The *veiquoix* and the *fandang* groups nowadays are small, but in the past they were larger and grander.

A fine recording of the Venezuelan string music of Trinidad was made by Beryl McBurnie years ago.* It contains *joropos, galerónes*, a so-called *parang, veiquoix* music, and an *aguinaldo*. The *parang* and the *aguinaldo* are in fact much the same thing: Strictly speaking, *aguinaldos* were sung at *parangs*, though now English and German carols have crept in. A Tobagan parallel is the *quesh*, which involves the singing of French carols. These styles did not operate in total isolation from each other, of course, and the calypso also drew on many of them, at one time or another, until it became so codified that it could no longer easily take in folk influences.

A religious music of a different sort is that of the Spiritual Baptists of Trinidad, popularly known as Shouters. The Shouters practice a form of Christianity in which many African elements remain, reinterpreted to suit a new theology. Among them are the use of an inner priestly sanctum called a "sacred chamber," where certain rituals are carried out, and the division of priestly functions into a number of offices, some of which have no mainstream Christian equivalent: shepherd, prophet, healer, interpreter, pointer, diver, prover, nurse, and matron. Shouter ceremonies involve possession by the Holy Spirit, and sometimes by one or another of the Shango powers, with "tongues." Music is extremely important, but (unlike similar sects in Jamaica) the drum is frowned on. The rhythmic base is provided by hand clapping and foot tapping, as it was in older black chapels in the United States. Baptism is important, of course, and pouring rites similar to ones used in the Shango cult sometimes take place. Worshipers occasionally dance; birds are sacrificed from time to time; and, more significant (having no sort of Biblical sanction), food is sometimes offered to the spirits. Shouter music is clearly European Christian in origin, and the sermons are similar to black U.S. sermons.

* Issued in the United States on the Road Runner label.

Calypso forms are found in various other islands, whether they originated in Trinidad or developed separately. In the Virgin Islands there was the *careso* composed by the Queen of a *bamboula* dance in the nineteenth century. The *careso* was a two-line topical song. Saint Lucia has *caliso* topical songs resembling some old *bamboula* songs, but many of them seem to come from Trinidad. This is obviously the case with some calypsos recorded on the Colombian English-speaking island of San Andres (issued on Folkways).

The Trinidad calypso has been circulating throughout the Caribbean for so long that it is tough to unscramble the older styles. I recorded a scratch band in Tortola, one of whose songs, "Sunday Morning Well," was a local calypso about emancipation on the island. Its individual elements were largely due to the instrumentation which was unlike Trinidad calypso bands. But the same group backed an older singer in a range of Tortolan songs, including one called "Ella Gift" (about a woman smuggling rum to the U.S. Virgin Islands in her "pantalettes" during Prohibition), that have the social comment element of calypso but a quite different rhythmic and melodic approach, rather nearer to nineteenth-century country dances.

The same thing is true of a number of songs I recorded in Cayman, which tend to be full of *very* local anecdotes like "Munzie's Boat on the Sand," "Beef in the Cane Piece," and "Sammy Beatin' Suzanna," about all of which incidents the singers could name people, places, and rough dates. And what is true of Cayman and Tortola is true of most Caribbean islands. Even heavily touristed areas like Saint Croix keep a scratch band tradition going, in part by playing it for the tourists if the younger locals haven't the sense to hang on to what they've got. An excellent example of a contemporary Crucian scratch band (with a fine example of Antillean saxophone playing) is preserved on the Rounder CD *Blinky and the Roadmasters,* with excellent notes by Mary Jane Soule.

If Trinidad calypso was the most famous Anglo-Caribbean music for decades, it has of course been totally displaced by Jamaican reggae in the past couple of decades. But there is a lot more to Jamaica than reggae. It is the largest of the English-speaking West Indian territories. Despite 200 years of Spanish rule, it was not subject to the variety of influences that history brought to some of the others, especially Trinidad, and the types of British who worked there were not particularly cultured, so that while Jamaica has quite a large number of English folk survivals, nobody ever dreamed of building and staffing an opera house in Kingston as they did in Havana. But the broad sweep of Caribbean history affected Jamaica as it did the other islands.

A noticeable feature of Jamaican music is the high degree of British content that goes along with its plentiful Africanisms. Both are evident in this early praise song, sung by some black Kingstonians to welcome a British captain who had fought off French ships in one of the numerous eighteenth-century wars in the Caribbean:

> Capy Crow da come again
> But em always fight and lost some mans.
> But we glad for see em now and then;
> Wit em hearty joyful gay,
> Wit em hearty joyful gay,
> Wit em tink, tink, tink, tink, tink, tinkara
> Wit em tink, tink, tink, tink, tink, tinkara.

This is clearly akin to eighteenth- and early-nineteenth-century English songs, including many soldiers' songs (likely to have traveled to Jamaica with British garrisons), in that it begins with a couplet that changes from verse to verse, then goes into a nonsense formulation designed to express merriment: "With a two row, row, row, row, row, row," and so forth. The praise-song form itself is African; ballads about the deeds of an individual did exist in the British music of the time, but they were far more narrative and tended to concentrate on official heroes of higher rank than captain, or else on folk heroes who more often than not were far out of favor with the Establishment.

It is possible that the word "da" in the first line is "is" in the Ghanaian Twi language, because the form "de" for "is" was common in Jamaica until recently. It may, of course, be the equivalent of the North American black usage "done"; but "done," as in "my man done gone," may itself enshrine a reinterpreted version of "da" or "de" attached to a phonetically similar English word. It may also echo another African construction, found in the Swahili *amekwisha kwenda*—"he has finished going," that is, he has just gone.

Neo-African music such as *tambo* drumming and the Yoruba songs recently found in the parish of Westmoreland still exists in Jamaica, though it is dying out (only a few elderly people maintain it in a living form), partly because it is a century and a half since the last Africans came to Jamaica, and partly, perhaps, because it has lost its original function. Where it has not, or where it has found new functions, as with the Congolese ingredients in the religious sects, it is stronger.

The most consistent body of mainly African survival in Jamaica is perhaps the Anancy stories. Significantly, the Anancy stories are highly eclectic. In Ghana, *anansi* is a spider, a rough analogy of the Bantu hare who became Brer Rabbit in the United States. (Another wily Jamaican animal figure is the crow, who turns up as "John Crow" as well as plain "crow" in many old songs, and occasionally crosses swords with Anancy himself.) In Jamaica, too, Anancy is a spider, though he has acquired cosmopolitan and humanoid traits (and conversely, the big spiders apt to hang above one in Jamaican rural outhouses are also called anancy). The Anancy stories often preserve the old device (almost universal in Africa and occasionally found in Europe) of introducing a snatch of song at crucial moments (for example, "Rumpelstiltskin"). A detailed collection of Anancy stories and Jamaican music was made by Walter Jekyll at the turn of the century. Even allowing for the collector's probable tendency to reinterpret elements he did not understand in the direction of European models, it is still the best and certainly the most thorough collection there is. The eclecticism of Anancy is well illustrated by the names of three princesses in one of Jekyll's tales: Yung Cyum Pyung, the Ghanaian *Accompong;* Margaret-Powell-Alone, which looks like a reworking of two characters in English children's game songs, Margaret-All-Alone and Eggie-Law.

This eclecticism is furthered by the very nature of oral folk tales when they do not have a function—such as the perpetuation of oral history—that demands consistency. Storytellers weave their favorite features from other tales into whatever story they are telling. This was strikingly illustrated for me when I listened to two quite different Anancy stories, one told by Aubrey Davis, a man in his seventies in a village near Kingston and the other by Valerie Walker, a girl of nineteen from the parish of Clarendon. Both included in their tales an incident in which Anancy makes one egg look like 100 by lifting it out of a barrel 100 times. Both tales showed the survival power even of vestigial Africanisms: Davis used several words of African origin, such as "nyam" ("to eat") and Walker interspersed her story with snippets of song in African style, while adding something of her own generation to the tradition with the introduction of occasional recent slang expressions.

The musical themes of the Anancy stories are varied. One of those in Jekyll's collection consists of a snatch of a very old ballad known in Britain as (among other titles) "The Bonny Broom" and in the southern U.S. Appalachians as "The Devil's Nine Questions." The Jamaican tune differs from these but is clearly a reworked border ballad. The riddle formula is almost identical, though all three versions have different refrains. The Jamaican version uses one of the answers to the Devil's questions (What is louder than a horn? What is deeper than the sea? What is meaner than womankind?—and so forth):

> The devil roguer than a womankind,
> The devil roguer than a womankind, oh
> Fair and gandelow steel.

There are several other examples of reworked bits and pieces from the English folk stock in Jekyll's collection: "Man Crow" is the tune of a widespread English children's game often called "A Finger and a Thumb Keep Moving"; another song uses the international children's tune whose original version is the French "Ah, que dirai-je vous maman?" but which has also gone into English infant lore; a line is taken from "The Three Little Pigs" ("I'll huff and I'll puff"); one song is very much like the Anglo-American "Paper of Pins," with a tune often associated with British ballads; and there are many other examples.

But, prominent though the English influence is in the collection, there is plenty that is quite foreign to English practice. One example is a form of call-and-response. I have italicized the response element and also corrected an obvious misunderstanding of Jekyll's: he transcribed it as "commando," which makes no conceivable sense:

> None a we, none a we, *come an' go.*
> Sairey gone home, *come an' go.*
> Yahka yahky yak, *come an' go.*
> Suck your mother bone, *come an' go.*

The call-and-response form of this song is typical of what seems to be a particularly Jamaican style in that the response is a short semichant of two or three syllables, often on one note.

Another version, from the Anancy canon, is:

> Timmolimmo, *man dere*
> Timmolimmo, *man dere*
> Come down make we battle, *man dere.*

In the case of "Come An' Go," the rhythmic pattern of verse and refrain are the same, but in "Timmolimmo" the verse consists of eighth-notes and the refrain of two quarter-notes, which gives a definite total shape reminiscent of a drummed dance pattern common in Caribbean music, including some *kalinda:*

This contrast of long-note and short-note phrases is so widespread as to be a major feature of Jamaican folk music. It has rather the same effect as the Trinidadian custom of varying the rhythm with long and short verse lines. Not all the examples are like the ones I have quoted: "Matilda," a popular

Jamaican digging songs are a classic cultural fusion: the call-and-response of their main body is largely or entirely African in inspiration, but the free "bobbin" that is sung before work begins often draws from Anglican hymn harmonies.
Photo by John Storm Roberts

song that originated in the Anancy story "Devil's Honey-Dram," opens with two long-note phrases, "Wheel-o, wheel-o," and then comes the name Matilda in the shorter-note rhythm, which is maintained for the rest of the verse.

There is an obvious connection between this form of Anancy song and the digging songs that are an important part of Jamaican vocal music, as Jekyll's description makes clear:

> One man starts or "raises" the tune and the others come in with the "bobbin," the short refrain of one or two words which does duty for chorus. The chief singer is usually the wag of the party, and his improvised sallies are greeted with laughter and an occasional "hi," which begins on a falsetto note and slides downwards, expressing amusement and delight very plainly.

The call-and-response form; the singer chosen not for his singing but for his wit; the improvised lead and set chorus; the unscheduled "audience" participation by an audience that is also the chorus; the use of falsetto in a "shout for joy," often used by much more modern Jamaican popular singers—all are from Africa. The choice of a wit as leader is paralleled in Haiti, incidentally, where the song-leader (*simidor* or *saniba*) of a *combite* communal work gang provides allusively witty comment on the workers and the passing scene.

Jamaican digging songs (unlike the work songs recorded on U.S. prison farms, unsurprisingly) tend to be cheerful. They are attended by a good deal of merriment, with cries of "quarter-master" when the rum or water bottle is wanted, and so forth. For Jamaicans, communal work is a good opportunity for gaiety as well as mutual help. The communal nature was strongly underlined in the case of some digging songs I collected in the village of Maryland. They were preceded by a very slow, richly harmonized passage, which the diggers called a "bobbin" (they called Jekyll's "bobbin" a "chorus") and sang all standing together before work began, almost like an invocational hymn. Then the leader would break into the faster lead of the main body of the song itself, the picks would flash up, and work would begin.

Jekyll quotes digging songs with the typical short two- or three-note refrain. Here are just two:

> (1) Tell Mister Bell me go, *plant coco*
> Tell Mister Bell me go, *plant coco*
> Tell Mister Bell me go, *plant coco*
> Fuppence a quart for flour!
> Flour, flour, flour, flour,
> Fuppence a quart for flour.
> (2) Bad homan oh, bad homan oh, *nyam and cry*
> Me coco no ripe, *nyam and cry*
> Me hafoo no ripe, *nyam and cry.*

The repeated "flour, flour" in the first one is comparable to the opening phrases of "Matilda," except that it is a rising and not a falling call. The rhythmic effect is much the same. "Nyam and Cry" is about a lazy woman who does nothing but eat and complain. "Nyam" ("to eat") is almost certainly related to the Twi "enam" and perhaps to the Bantu form "nyama."

Digging songs cover a wide range of topics. Some in Jekyll's anthology seem to have come from English sailors' songs, like "Miss Nancy Ray," which opens:

> Oh Miss Nancy Ray, *oh hurrah, boys.*
> Oh Miss Nancy Ray, *oh hurrah boys.*

The words and the tune of this were clearly picked up from contact with English sailors, perhaps by somebody working on the Kingston docks for a while, though by the end the song has become pretty thoroughly Jamaicanized. Some work songs offer personal comment faintly reminiscent of the blues: "The one shirt I have, ratta cut ahm." Others may be carried across from other sorts of music, like "Kisander," which I recorded in Maryland. This was obviously at one time a play-party song and may have come originally from an Anancy story. The chorus "Kisander" is the name of a cat who appears in some old stories. The song itself sounds as though it began as a word game in which participants had to find new adjectives for the phrases:

> Show me your true name, *Kisander;*
> Come and show me your secret name, *Kisander;*
> Won't you tell me your first name, *Kisander;*
> Oh, tell me your funny name, *Kisander;*

and so on.

Digging songs in their turn may become dance tunes. Among those quoted by Jekyll is one that became famous much later, under the name of "Hold 'Im Joe." The old version starts: "Me donkey want water, rub him down Joe, rub him down Joe, rub him down Joe," and the long bobbin is repeated after a series of short phrases describing the donkey: "Me donkey like a peeny, Me donkey full of capers," and so forth. The modern versions are similar, and both forms allow for a great deal of improvised bawdy lyrics, as do other donkey songs, like "Donkey City," whose usual versions do not get onto commercial records.

In the past, digging songs were sometimes accompanied by instruments, including fiddlers whom Jekyll describes condescendingly but revealingly: "Holding it not up to the chin but resting it on the biceps, they rub a short bow backwards and forwards across the strings. If one of these is tuned it is considered quite satisfactory, and the rest make a sort of mild bagpipe accompaniment." This playing stance—Jekyll's amusement apart—is usual alike for players of the numerous African one- and two-string fiddles and for British folk fiddlers. In fact, the British fiddler often uses his lower strings as a drone, or what Jekyll terms a "mild bagpipe accompaniment," and some groups in West Africa use their fiddles to somewhat similar effect. This looks like an excellent example of two traditions coming together and reinforcing each other in the New World.

An important traditional Jamaican form, widespread in the Americas and usually showing mixed Afro-European components, is the ring game, or ring play, a large complex of games played in a circle. It is just as popular among adults as among children and is still a flourishing part of Jamaican life, especially in the country. The games used to be played on all kinds of festive occasions, but these days they are most often found at setups and nine-nights, the beginning and end of a mourning period. Some ring plays, like "Sally Water" (also found in the United States), are of unmistakable English derivation (although in England she is Sally Walker):

> Little Sally Water, sprinkle in the saucer,
> Rise Sally rise, and wipe your weeping eyes.

Others have African words, repeated bobbins, and other national traits:

> Where me lover de? *See mya, see mya.*
> Me lover gonna sea? *See mya, see mya.*

"De," we have seen, is an African word; "see mya" is "see him here."

But whether of English or African source or influence, Jamaican ring plays are truly Jamaican. And many, of course, were born on the island; one such is the very popular "Emmanuel Road," or "Mandeville Road," as it is sometimes called. This has been played as a band number, but it is basically a ring play. I saw it played after a digging session, when the men sat in a circle passing around stones that had been loosened by their picks. The object of the game is to pass the stones on rapidly without injury, or, as the song says, "finger mash no cry!"

Children's songs are in some ways more traditional but in others more volatile than adult music, and Jamaican children's songs are no exception. They include many games like "Emmanuel Road" and "Sally Water," but I also collected versions of "Humpty Dumpty" and other nursery rhymes sung in a style that owes a great deal to the local reggae style and, through reggae, to rhythm and blues. Children also make up their own songs reflecting immediate concerns, including one that I recorded, with the immortal line: "ABC is a bloody botheration!"

Definite Africanisms are difficult to pin down in both ring games and children's songs, because even call-and-response is not uncommon in English children's games. The tendency of Jamaican ring games to turn into dances is a probable African trait. The freer and more complex rhythms of the songs or, in the case of English-derived songs, of their performance is another. Jekyll noticed this rhythmic approach in a song called "Ring-a-Diamond": "In many bars it is almost impossible to distinguish whether the tune is triple or duple." It is tempting to see this as a variation of the African use of duple on triple time. Some Jamaican children's games are, as we have seen, reminiscent of

African games designed to teach skills. I mentioned earlier the stick-fighting game collected in Jamaica in the 1940s; the fact that Jekyll also collected it at least forty years earlier is an indication of the strength of tradition.

Digging songs, traditional tales, ring plays, and to some extent children's games all tend to change slowly and to be remembered from generation to generation. Dance music naturally changes more quickly, but Jekyll's description of a country dance band is not so very different from what could still occasionally be found in remote areas today:

> The music consists of three "flutes" [fifes], two tambourines and a big drum. This is the professional element, which is reinforced by amateurs. One brings a cassava-grater, looking like a bread-grater; this, rubbed with the handle of a spoon, makes a very efficient crackling accompaniment. Another produces the jawbone of a horse, the teeth of which rattle when it is shaken. A third has detached from its leather one of his stirrup-irons, and is hanging it on a string to do duty as a triangle. The top of the music is not always supplied by fifes. Sometimes there will be two fiddles, sometimes a concertina.

Besides its general similarity to groups found in most other parts of black America, the rhythm section described here corresponds closely to West African popular bands. There are the drums, including tambourines, which play something of the same role as the Ewe frame drum. There are scrapers and rattles. And the stirrup is a successful substitute for the Ewe *gankogui*. The European or rural Jamaican instruments that augment the vocalists sit on top of a highly African rhythm section. At the same time, the popular country dances played by these groups were creolized European, just as many were in the other islands. The main dances at the turn of the century were the waltz, the polka, the schottische, and quadrilles in five figures or six, of which the fifth was the most popular and tended to become separated from the rest. Jekyll reports that a version of the old Jamaican song "Linstead Market" was used as the fifth figure of a quadrille.

This type of country band has virtually disappeared from Jamaican life, killed off by Jamaica's equivalent of the juke box, the sound system. In some cases, death came as late as the early 1970s. At that time, I was lucky enough to find a group that had given up the unequal struggle only a few years earlier, some of whose members reformed to record old *mento* numbers, quadrilles, mazurkas, and polkas. The group consisted of harmonica, grater, bass-trumpet, and various ad hoc instruments, such as bottles tapped together. Other groups soldiered on, like the Manchioneal Village Band in

Like many Caribbean traditions, Jamaica's mento country dance bands combine pan-Caribbean elements and strong local characteristics: in the case of the dance from which they get their name, a back-beat that traveled into early reggae and thus around the world.
Photo by John Storm Roberts

Portland, associated with a youth club with a strong sense of the need to preserve Jamaican traditions. Yet others remain only in the memories of older men, like our host in the village of Chatham, Saint James, who had played the guitar and mandolin for country dance groups until the mid-1920s and remembered with nostalgia the days when there were dances almost every night and when every parish had its own way of dancing the Lancers and polkas. In Chatham and its environs, he told me, bands would often comprise a guitar, a flute, and an accordion, without graters. "I used to love dances, I used to love the quadrilles," he remarked wistfully. And a handful have survived into the 1990s by entertaining tourists, such as the Jolly Boys, who preserved the banjo lead of 1950s *mento-calypso* stars like Count Lasher (and Lasher's immortal double-entendre song "Water the Garden"). A rarer fiddle-led *mento* style barely survived in the repertoire of the Lititz Mento band, whose recording for the German Wergo label included a quadrille as well as old *mento* favorites like "Linstead Market."

The dance tunes came from a number of sources. Jekyll bewailed the tendency to depart from the "Jamaican type of melody" and to adopt, spread, and modify popular songs brought into port by sailors. But adoptions from English and other sources do not mean that Jamaican music is derivative, any more than any other Afro-American music. Songs borrowed from elsewhere were well and truly worked over, in line with the African approaches to music-making that were common everywhere in the Caribbean. The older examples are transcribed by the collector, and the mere act of writing them down strips them of most of their characteristic quality. In the hands of an amateur like Jekyll, with no knowledge of the background out of which Jamaican music sprang, the undoubted English element is likely to be overemphasized. Later examples, preserved on tape and occasionally on records, show what Jekyll left out. The Jamaican rhythms are faster and less flowing than Trinidadian calypso, perhaps because they had far less Spanish influence and retained the more four-square quadrille sections. But some also have a percussive quality that suggests a higher proportion of African influence in the rhythmic mix. Others reflect British dance music, brisk and gay, though neither as rhythmically pulsating nor as complex as Spanish, let alone African.

Though the major ingredients in Jamaican music—apart from Jamaican talent—are African and British, other influences are also present; after all, Jamaica was Spanish for 200 years, even if rather precariously so. The resulting Spanish streak that must undoubtedly be there has hardly been studied, but then Spanish dominion ended a long time ago. A notable infusion that still continues comes from the United States. North American influence can be heard everywhere, especially in the newer folk music being created by younger people. It is present in Jamaican religious music, including many of the Revival Zion "choruses," as well as the songs of the Pentecostal churches, which have been making many converts recently. The gospel influence on Jamaican religious singing, strangely enough, seems to be mainly white, principally because the recorded services of Billy Graham and Oral Roberts are popular. But U.S. influence is also present in many secular songs, including some of the newer play-party songs; they too are sometimes drawn from gospel tunes.

In the 1950s and 1960s, a phenomenon hit Jamaica that was eventually to sweep the world. A succession of styles, one leading directly to another, emerged. The first, called bluebeat, did not attract a lot of attention, being essentially a Jamaican version of U.S. (and particularly New Orleans) rhythm and blues. But soon, a series of distinctive rhythms began underpinning the rhythm and blues melodies, which themselves started to become distinctively Jamaican, without losing their rhythm and blues flavor. Thus was born ska, with its flaring fourth beat emphasis; then the slower rocksteady; and finally, reggae itself, which started as a new substyle but was soon being used as a generic term. Reggae itself gave birth to substyles such as dub, raggamuffin or ragga, and "dancehall." Like calypso and steel-band music in their early days, these genres were the music of the disapproved young; the Rude Boys of Kingston, or Rudies as they called themselves, proclaimed in different ways in a number of rocksteady songs: "Rudies is tough, boy, rudies is tough."

Ska and its descendants at first came under the usual heavy attack from all quarters; typical comments were: reggae encouraged or, alternatively, was the product of delinquency; it was a feeble imitation of foreign styles; it used electronic instruments; it was loud, uncouth, and generally obnoxious. However, because reggae has become an international success (a development foreshadowed very early by Millie Small's 1962 international pop-ska hit, "My Boy Lollipop"), spawning almost as many versions overseas as Cuban music did in its time, the Jamaican hierarchy has changed its tune. After its stint as a version of "devil's music," reggae has emphatically come into the sun and has, at the hands of many non-Jamaican writers, been weighted down by a sometimes absurd weight of "significance." But for all its current internationalism, reggae in all its forms has always been very closely tied to Jamaican tradition. For one thing, the basic rhythms often differ little from earlier Jamaican dance meters. They sound different, because they are apportioned in new ways between electric and bass guitars, being influenced to some extent by rhythm-and-blues and soul bass-guitar techniques.

Ska/reggae seems to have been born when the youth of the streets got fed up with calypso, which was too popular among their elders. Black North America being somewhat of a trendsetter (particularly records shipped straight from New Orleans to Kingston), various artists—notably, in the very early days of bluebeat, Prince Buster—cut records imitating such black ballad singers as Johnny Ace or duos like Shirley and Lee or Gene and Eunice. But because people unconsciously tend to follow traditions they know, however consciously in revolt against them, the older rhythms of Jamaica crept back in, sufficiently heavy, electrified, and ungenteel to upset older people quite satisfactorily.

The *mento* link was very plain for all to see in the late 1960s, when all sorts of *mento* songs were recorded in ska style, including the semi-classic "Penny Reel." And as Kenneth Bilby points out, the song usually identified as the first reggae recording—the 1967 "Nanny Goat" by Larry Marshall and Alvin Leslie—was also *mento*-based, and had some links to the older "Back to Back." Nor was *mento* the only older influence. Clancy Eccles recorded a song called "Feel the Rhythm," which included large chunks of a much older calypso called "So Them Bad-Minded."

Reggae has gone through so many changes, and many of the stages of its development have been so chaotic, that tracing trends is impossible—a situation made even more difficult by the near-deification by American critics of the Rastafarian strain of reggae, and neglect of such earthier but (in Jamaica) more popular strains as dancehall, with its often highly raunchy content. There was a fashion for sentimental strings, and another for effective but rather lugubrious slow trombone riffs over the mid- to up-tempo rhythm. There have been Jimmy Smith organs and James Brown vocals, but however many fads and enthusiasms rule the scene temporarily, the sound goes on being obstinately Jamaican.

"My Boy Lollipop" aside, reggae became a feature on the international pop scene beginning in the 1960s, although at first only a minor one: most notably, Desmond Dekker twice made the British hit parade. For a while, there were predictable divisions within reggae: the pop-oriented records of musicians like Dekker and Byron Lee, appreciated by the Jamaican middle class as well as foreigners; the groups that recorded for the little record companies on Orange Street, Kingston; performers who rarely made it onto an LP; singers who recorded titles with Rastafarian or, occasionally, Black Power messages; and artists whose songs were now and again banned by the Jamaican Broadcasting Company.

Many pop reggae numbers were excellent—Dekker's "A It Mek," for example, or Eric Donaldson's splendid single, "Cherry Oh Baby"—but they were often too tame. Orange Street, or "underground" reggae, was often badly recorded, but it is always interesting, because it was a "people's music." Not coincidentally, it showed a high incidence of African-derived features, including a large degree of creative repetitiveness, an emphasis on rhythm, and a lack of interest in harmony. Rocksteady was to some extent the music of the "Rude Boys," West Kingston's underprivileged teenagers, in and out of trouble with the law. Earlier reggae and rocksteady expressed unruly teenagers' feelings rather well, from the general joy in breakup of "Bangarang"—"Bangarang crash, everything smash!"—to the Heptones' "Be a Man," with its Black Power overtones, via the defiant "Rudies Is Tough."

Then, as had happened with so many styles before, the disapproved became the touchstone. In the case of reggae, notably, two aspects of a very complex idiom came to stand in foreigners' eyes for the whole ball of wax. One was the Rastafari-linked branch; the other was the rather unquantifiable substyle called dub, and its anti-twin, toasting. The word "dub" means many different things, but refers most commonly to a minimalist, heavily rhythmic style dependent on slow bass and drums, and is associated with the instrumental "versions" that were taking up the B side of singles by the early 1970s. These in turn were produced because the deejays who ran the fiercely competitive "sound system" dances (a prototype of American disco) had taken to spoken improvisations over recordings. During the period 1968–1972, "toasters" like

U Roy, I Roy, and King Tubby became stars in their own right, and the starker instrumentals were developed in part to suit their needs. Their work was not only important as a significant strain in reggae, but as one of the main roots of U.S. Afro-American rap.

The instrumental minimalism that dub introduced after the riotously varied early days combined with the huge success of three artists working in the Rastafari-influenced branch, Bob Marley, Peter Tosh, and Bunny Livingston. For a while, they created a kind of dub orthodoxy that arguably dampened some of the style's creativity—though there is no disputing the three men's brilliance (in my view, Tosh's sinister "Steppin' Razor" has a claim to be reggae's finest single recording, along with Donaldson's very different "Cherry Oh Baby"). Rastafarian or Rasta-oriented reggae by no means started with Marley, Tosh, and Livingston. About the time Marley was making his first recordings, the Ethiopians recorded a number called "Selah," and the Abyssinians made the great "Satta Amasa Gana," whose lyrics begin: "There is a land, far, far away, Where there's no night, there's only day." This refers, with true African allusiveness, to Ethiopia and its "King of King and Lord of Lords," Haile Selassie. Much more explicit is Maxie and Glen's "Jordan River," which opens: "I saw Selassie I [a misunderstanding of the Roman numeral one] stretch forth his hand to take I across Jordan River." Its chorus goes, "Zion oh, Rastafari." And while it is impossible to know how Rastafarian reggae would have fared without the talent of its Big Three, my bet is that it would always have been with us.

Nor is Rastafari the only Afro-Jamaican faith to have fed into reggae, though it is the only one recognized by outsiders. The various Afro-Protestant sects generally known in Jamaica as *pocomania* or *pukkumina* have lent their distinctive drumming and singing styles to the work of several artists, including a personal favorite, Lloyd Lovindeer's 1989 *One Day Christian*. And more generally, Jamaican revivalism is often the true root of what is otherwise perceived as soul or U.S. gospel influence in the work of groups like Toots and the Maytals.

Perhaps in reaction to the increasingly judgmental tone of Rasta-oriented reggae, the continuing dancehall tradition became increasingly raunchy, and around the mid-1980s gave birth to a substyle somewhat reminiscent of the old "rude boys" strain of rocksteady. This was raggamuffin or ragga, which made a point of "slackness" (obscenity), drug references, sexual braggadocio, and all the other elements that around the same time were causing so much sniping at rap. Ragga started out arguably not so much as a style but as a state of mind, but Bilby argues that (ironically) much of the musical element in ragga was drawn from *pocomania* and other traditional elements, and that in the hands of artists like Shabba Ranks and Buju Banton, a new electronic ragga drawing from neo-African Jamaican music has moved away from any real association with reggae toward what dub poet Linton Kwesi Johnson has called an "extreme minimalism."

Reggae at its best has always been a chaotic music, the product of a chaotic music business. Production methods have often been eccentric, not to say piratical. In the early days, one large British company found to its embarrassment that a reggae record whose British rights it had bought owed its fine backing to the unrecompensed (and quite unconscious) cooperation of the world's highest-paid string orchestra. And some reggae producers have proceeded past payola to the more cost-effective method of straight threats in their attempts to acquire good airplay for some extremely famous musicians. But out of this continuing chaos has sprung a new and very vital music, almost certainly the Caribbean's only entirely new musical form in this century.

Trinidad and Jamaica have tended to dominate the other English-speaking islands in the popular field. The Bahamas has its own tradition of church music, strongly influenced by antebellum African-American spirituals, and a local gospel style whose best known exponent is singer-guitarist Joseph Spence. But Bahamian calypso singers like Blind Blake (not the U.S. blues singer), and most of the Caribbean's steel bands, are pale versions of the originals, oriented principally toward a tourist market. For a different major group of creole traditions, based on different sources and with a different development, one must turn to the French-speaking islands: principally Haiti, Martinique, and Guadeloupe, and to a lesser degree the small French-creole speaking Dominica and Saint Lucia.

Haiti's "national" creole style from the nineteenth century until at least the 1950s was the *méringue* ("mereng" in Creole), whose name is virtually the same as the merengue of the Dominican Republic, on the other side of the hills. The *méringue*'s beginning is not entirely clear, but it certainly goes back to the first half of the nineteenth century. Like so many Afro-American dances, the *méringue* developed into two forms, one for the salon and one for the streets.

The salon *méringue* was frequently piano music, though it was also played on every sort of ensemble; early European travelers commented on slave musicians' skill at the violin, clarinet, and French horn. In the nineteenth century, the ability to dance it was a sign of breeding, and a host of *merengs* was written by Haitian conservatory musicians at the highest level of Haitian society. One of the most famous, Occide Jeanty's "Maria," was composed for the official band of the presidential palace. There are very few recordings of this salon *méringue,* but one on the Folkways label by member Fabre Duoseau, a Haitian family famous for its classical musicians, showed an idiom with Chopinesque moments and delicate decorations. Aside from its charm, at certain moments this nineteenth-century, bourgeois, Afro-Parisian music is distinctly akin to U.S. ragtime piano and to certain Puerto Rican dances that make use of the same running patterns of syncopated triplets and of rhythmic patterns that were also common in the habanera (the influence here was probably from Haiti to Cuba, given that the Cuban *contradanza* was adopted from Haitian refugees in preference to the more formal Spanish version).

The street *méringue* of the guitar-based *twoubadou* (troubadour) groups comes in various forms, all of which have met with complaints of foreign influence and general corruption. It is said, for example, that there is no Haitian guitar tradition and that love songs accompanied by guitar are foreign (of course, if you go far enough back, almost everybody's music came from somewhere else). The earlier style of rather sentimental, gentle solo *méringues,* such as "Nous Allons Dodo" on a Folkways record, certainly owes something to French music. So does most Haitian music, leaving out some of the most neo-African. The Orchestre Jazz Corondo, which I recorded in the early 1970s, certainly showed strong Cuban influence in the use of an improvised instrumental section with heightened rhythm, and according to Gage Averill a Cuban element is at the heart of *twoubadou* music. But it takes some perversity to see the music of the wonderful banjo-and-guitar band of Althiery Dorival, for example, as un-Haitian. And the *twoubadou* style gave birth to at least one very major Haitian star with some international following, Coupé Cloué (born Jean-Gesner Henry). What informs much of the older *twoubadou* music is precisely this blend of the rather gentle and at the same time straightforward French styles with the more ebullient Cuban approach and African material. (Jazz Corondo performed several pieces with rhythms associated with voodoo ceremonies, in *twoubadou* style.) The results are quite different from the music of the other part of Hispaniola, the Dominican Republic, let alone other parts of the Caribbean.

Dance bands like the Jazz Majestic Orchestra of the early 1950s consisted of saxophone, guitar, banjo, drum kit, conga drum, and iron percussion. Their music was patently related to other modern Caribbean forms and possibly had jazz touches, but it was also unmistakably Haitian in its gentleness. The saxophone player used a style that recalls the Dominican merengue style, the work of some New Orleans creole reed players (especially Sidney Bechet), the Martinican *biguine,* and to music recorded in the dance halls of French Guiana. Except for the Dominican Republic, all these places had cultural links with France, and the French are (or were, in the nineteenth century) famous for their clarinet technique, so this saxophone and clarinet style may well be part of the French legacy.

By the 1950s, a transitional dance band style had developed, which included but was by no means confined to the *méringue*. *Mascarons* and nineteenth-century dances like the quadrille—especially in the form of the Lancers—have been updated by such groups as the rival orchestras of Nemours Jean-Baptiste and Webert Sicot, who at the same time modernized their sound with Latin influences, including both Haitian merengue and Cuban and New York mambo, as well as developed a more driving version of the rhythm. Nemours Jean-Baptiste's early records, include a number of *contredanses* complete with promenade sections played by a group incorporating saxophone and accordion, backed by rhythm. On a later Nemours album issued by Cook Records, a *guaguancó*-style B section has been added to many of the tracks. The accordion is still there, in a lineup including two trumpets, alto and tenor saxophones, and a very light rhythm section of bass and conga-type drum. The basic style is similar to that of Nemours's older recordings, with gentle, "Frenchish" tunes, but Nemours's frequent use of unison trumpet shakes is taken over from the mambo bands and modified to suit the group. The effect is not of a copy but of yet another set of influences taken over and in the process of absorption.

Nemours and Sicot may sound somewhat quaint now, but they were extremely important in the recent history of all French creole music. Nemours's harder rhythm was, in Averill's view, heavily influenced by the Dominican *merengue cibaeño*, whose major proponent at the time, Angel Viloria's Tipica Cibaeña, was very popular in Haiti in the mid-1950s. Nemours built out of merengue influences a new and very popular rhythm, which he called *konpa direk* ("direct beat"), and built an accordion into the sound of his big band. In 1958, Sicot fired back by introducing a version of the new rhythm he called *cadence rampa*. Partly because the semiartificial rivalry of the two bands made for powerful publicity, the *konpa* edged the *méringue* out of the popular forum.

Another strain in Haitian music was what Averill identifies as voodoo–jazz, which had strong nationalist elements. The music of bands like Jazz des Jeunes drew on rural Afro-Haitian tradition, heavily reinterpreted, by incorporating *vaccines* into its rhythm section. At the same time, many of its tracks enthusiastically adopted a sentimentality that owed some debt to Cuban boleros, and perhaps even more to Parisian versions of Cuban boleros. The nationalist and roots strain in Haitian music has continued to the present day, notably in the work of the band Boukman Eksperyens (Boukman was a voodoo

Like its contemporary African equivalents, Haitian mini-jazz is essentially guitar based. But many bands also use small horn sections like Bossa Combo's trumpet and sax, seen here.
Photo by Gage Averill

priest and hero of the Haitian liberation). It is, to a greater extent than the publicity departments let on, a non-working-class movement, but the results are certainly generally popular.

A new sound (or group of sounds) grew out of *konpa* in the 1960s when a new generation of young musicians founded more or less rock-influenced bands playing a style they called mini-jazz ("mini" after the skirt). Most of the best-known Haitian bands of today stemmed from this period, when every neighborhood or even block had its mini-jazz band. The first to be commercially popular was Shleu Shleu; the internationally best known of all, Tabou Combo, was formed in 1968. Mini-jazz was as much a movement and a period as a style. The groups all had different instrumentations and sounds. Tabou Combo used an accordion; bands involving the Frères Dejean preferred a trumpet and saxophone sound; the less known but wonderful Difficiles de Pétionville was an all-guitar band. Like soca, most of the recordings by the top mini-jazz bands have been done in Brooklyn and overseen by a very small number of producers. But presumably because soca's stress is on the singer, not the band, the Haitian groups have remained far more individual. Averill has summed up two lines of *konpa*. One, represented by Shleu Shleu, Volo Volo, Djet-X, and other horn bands, features vocallike saxophone and throaty, romantic vocals. The other—Tabou Combo, DP Express (formerly Les

Difficiles de Pétionville), and the Magnum Band—are more guitar- and rock-oriented (according to Averill, Robert Martino of DP Express was influenced by Eric Clapton and Jimmy Page).

The political situation in Haiti also led to a strong strain of political music, both among exiles and, once things began to open up, in Haiti. The expatriate singer Farah Juste began a solo career in 1970s with a group called Soley Leve ("sunrise"), but the earliest protest singers to record (1978–1979) were Manno Charlemagne and Marco Jeanty. The texts of these songs were, of course, political; their musical styles, ranging from mini-jazz and voodoo-jazz to acoustic guitar, were apparently influenced by the Cuban *nueva trova* movement. And, as always, foreign influences have helped to shape new sounds in Haitian music. During the 1980s, some bands and singers (among them the Paris-based Toto Bissainthe) were experimenting with elements of avant-garde jazz, and most recently reggae and rap have made themselves felt.

Martinique and Guadeloupe, two islands that politically form part of France (each is a *département*), might appear to have had little opportunity to develop music of their own. In fact, however, both not only developed the usual variations on common Caribbean themes, but created styles that have had major international impact, Martinique from the 1920s and 1930s with the *biguine* (beguine), and Guadeloupe in the 1980s with *zouk*.

The Martinican *biguine* these days survives on collector-reissue CDs, but it was one of the great sounds of the early twentieth century. The classic *biguine* featured groups with a clarinet and trombone lead, playing in a jazzlike polyphony. It was influenced by both jazz and Cuban *sones*, for example, during the 1930s, *biguine* rhythm sections would often throw passages of offbeat, "straight" 4/4 to allow for jazz-oriented soloing. The greatest of all *biguine* musicians was Stellio, who recorded during the 1920s and 1930s; much of the recording and playing was done in France, where the *biguine* musicians frequently worked with Cuban musicians on the active Parisian Cuban club scene and more than a few U.S. jazz musicians, including New Orleans clarinetist Horace Eubanks in the 1920s, and trumpeter Harry Cooper (who survived World War II in Paris!). The classic *biguine* basically faded during the 1950s, the last of the great bands being that of a protégé of Stellio, Alphonso, though growing cultural nationalism in the 1980s has recently led to something of a revival.

Of the older local idioms, a style that hung on at least until the mid-twentieth century was the mazurka, yet another nineteenth-century European dance that was taken in and made over in many Caribbean islands; in Martinique, it was played by most of the *biguine* bands. Martinican mazurkas tend to be slower and more staid than *biguines,* but not much. According to some, the Martinique mazurka is simply the European mazurka superimposed on a *biguine* beat. That may be so; no one yet has seriously studied the various European dance forms and how they developed in the Caribbean. A somewhat similar history lies behind the Guadeloupian waltz, which was basically similar to other creole waltzes. A certain tension was set up between the waltz rhythm and the beat of the *maracas* or *güiro,* as they tried to mold an alien rhythm onto a relatively rigid form. When the performance was good, the tension was not unlike that of African drummers superimposing different meters. Martinique's Carnival music is the *vidée,* a street march related to the styles found in Brazil, Trinidad, and beyond.

Latin music was as well established in Martinique and Guadeloupe as elsewhere in the non-Latin Caribbean. The tango was present thanks to the link with Paris, always tango's second city. The international popularity of the samba in the 1940s and mambo and *chachachá* in the 1950s affected the islands, and were consolidated by tours by Puerto Rican bands in the 1960s, Dominican merengue groups in the late 1970s, and Cuban bands in the 1980s. This only intensified the Cuban influences on musicians working in the Paris, which went back to the 1920s. And the Parisian link also meant that by the 1970s, *soukous* and francophone African pop was also popular in the two islands. And jazz remained highly influential on musicians, more than either French or (until the 1980s) American pop.

But above all during the 1970s, Haitian *compas direct* and *cadence rampa*—both called *plain cadence* (*kadans* in creole) in Martinique and Guadeloupe—pretty much overwhelmed dance music in Martinique and Guadeloupe, along with a dual salsa influence via *kadans* and *direct*. Local bands basically imitated the Haitian sound and a musical inferiority complex. The first stirrings of a reaction, oddly, came not from Guadeloupian or Martinican groups but from a bilingual Dominican band working in Guadeloupe. Exile One introduced a mix of cadence and Trinidad calypso called *cadence-lypso* that helped introduce soca into all four islands. *Cadence-lypso* also drew on the traditional, mostly accordion-led Dominican music called *jing ping,* which was used for quadrilles, mazurkas, and other older dances. *Cadence-lypso* transferred some of *jing ping*'s accordion style to organ and synth, while the trap drummer and bass guitarist parceled out elements of the traditional small percussion (there is an example of *jing ping* on the Nonesuch CD *West Indies: An Island Carnival*).

A mix of soca and cadence that was a logical development of cadence-lypso was the basis of *zouk,* the music that put Guadeloupe and to a lesser extent Martinique on the international map in the 1980s, though early *zouk* also drew on more local traditions, including *biguine, gwo ka, belé,* and quadrille. To an extent unusual in popular music, the best known of *zouk* bands, Kassav, was also the creative leader; the leadership stemmed ultimately from bassist Pierre-Edouard Decimus, who was unhappy with Guadeloupe's reliance on foreign music. From the start, the aim was somewhat contradictory: a mix of cultural identity and a technical professionalism which meant the group had to record in Paris. Kassav's music was to be technically flawless, combine modern and traditional elements, and be sung in creole. This was one of the very few examples when such a calculated agenda produced a really successful popular music.

Kassav's early recordings, the 1979 *Love and Ka Dans* and 1980's *Lague Moin,* were cultural landmarks, with an extensive use of *gwo ka* which the band later abandoned. But Kassav really broke though in 1984 with the song "Zouk-la Sé sèl médikamen nou ni" and with a ten-day engagement at the major Parisian concert hall Le Zénith. Its success aside, Kassav was also important as a mixed Guadeloupe/Martinique band, given the long rivalry between the two islands. And as it became more successful, it became more international, taking on board musicians who were either African or had played with Camerounian Manu Dibango's Paris-based band. By 1989, the end of the band's greatest period, it had recorded twenty-eight albums.

Zouk was by no means confined to Kassav, though many of the other groups and singers were either spinoffs or had worked with Kassav. As time went on, two styles of *zouk* developed: the up-tempo *zouk hard* and the more romantic and pop-oriented *zouk love.* Nor was *zouk* the only musical flower of a growing cultural nationalism in Guadeloupe and Martinique, which took over from a political nationalism which never gained much support in either island. Economically, independence made relatively little sense, and a continued existence as French *départements* was to many people less galling than the French refusal to recognize the existence of a distinctive creole culture. For a while, separatists had refused to recognize the distinctive mix of French and African in the islands and recognized only the neo-African musics such as *gwo ka* and Martinican *ka* (*belé*), while rejecting *biguine* and other creole music—a form of elite "noble savagism" about as sensible as rejecting jazz because of its partially European background. So *zouk* was both culturally nationalist and a reaction against a nationalist reductio ad absurdum.

But if the separatist attitude was one-sided, it did rescue several older styles, neglected as being not only black but peasant or working-class musics. In Martinique, the singer Francisco adopted *tanbou belé* in the late 1960s, and (in the mid-1970s) a jazz group called Falfret used traditional *tibwa* for the first time with mainstream instruments. The movement gathered steam in the 1980s, in parallel with *zouk*. Dédé St. Prix modernized the country dance form called *chouval bwa* with his group, Pakatak, which consisted of flute, *ka, tibwa*, and two bass guitars. Eugène Mona brought back the local bamboo flute and a local drum, *tanbou dibas*, besides reinterpreting traditional tunes. And the percussion group Marcé & Toumpak integrated *belé* rhythms into new material.

As part of a similar movement in Guadeloupe, singer Guy Conquette (now Konkèt) promoted *gwo ka* in the late 1960s, and by the late 1970s, several all or mostly percussion neo-*gwo ka* musicians like Eric Cosaque, Ti-Celeste, and the band Anzala were playing the local clubs. As an ironic result, the homeless and marginal traditional *gwo ka* player Vélo, ignored during his lifetime, had thousands at his funeral. While *zouk* and the neo-African styles were developing, Martinique also saw the revival of the *biguine* and, most notably, of a version of the island's old string-band tradition in the form of the group Malavoi, whose early recordings mixed Martinican strings and influences from Cuban *charanga*.

Most recently, several new influences have begun to change *zouk* and other Antillean music once more. Congolese *soukous* and Camerounian *makossa* both drew from and contributed to it, and reggae also lent a rhythm or two. So did rap, in a vein less dour than the U.S. African-American version tends to be. A notably cheerful example is a CD by a teenager known as Ti Ken, which mixes hipped-up mixes of traditional material, *zouk*, rap, rhythm and blues/jazz tenor saxophone, French pop, and reggae, with a personnel who included the neotraditional banjoist Kali (who dodged stereotype by also doing most of the synth programming). The effect is as battily varied and jaunty as the work of Hispanic rappers like El General.

For obvious reasons, the Afro-English, Afro-French, and Afro-Spanish Caribbean loom very large. But the Dutch islands of Aruba, Curaçao, and Bonaire also have their own styles, ranging from the neo-African (including a musical bow unknown in the rest of the Caribbean) to rural creole groups called *tipikó*, and a nineteenth-century mechanical organ called the *ka'i* that plays huge metal discs with holes punched in them. These originated in Central Europe, but as far as I know they are only currently manufactured in Cuba, the only other Caribbean island where they are found. Just as the Dutch Antillean creole, Papiamento, draws from more languages than, say, Haitian creole, so Dutch Antillean music is heavily affected from outside. One major influence is Venezuela, but there are contributions from all over the islands. A dance said to be native to the Dutch Antilles is the *tumba*, although whether it is really local or a descendant of the Haitian or the Dominican *tumba* is not

Surinamese *kaseko* is typical of many modern New World idioms that preserve their strong Afro-American percussion roots while adding electric guitars and other instruments.
Photo by Essboom, courtesy of Kenneth Bilby

certain. Curaçao also has a creolized waltz form that was still extant though regarded as old-fashioned twenty years ago.

The Guianas are a special case, not only because they form an essentially Caribbean culture on the South American mainland, but because the close proximity of Dutch, French, and English elements next to fairly unified African ones (not to mention such special elements as the Indonesian music of former Javanese contract workers in Suriname) has led to an extraordinarily complex web of relationships. The major contemporary creole music of Suriname is *kaseko,* a name perhaps derived from the Guianan percussion music *kassé ko* (*cassez cou,* "break-neck"). *Kaseko* surfaced after World War II and is a riot of local influence—including an Indian-derived music from former British Guyana, *badji*—along with calypso, *biguine, zouk* (introduced via French Guiana), soca, reggae, and others (one well-known artist, William Souvenir, even plays a number with obvious Alpine/oompah-band elements in its arrangement!). *Kaseko* bands tend to fall into the general scratch-band category, though there are recordings of *kaseko* brass bands that sound like semi-Dixieland.

The Guianas are very far from being the only region where influences have crossed language barriers, of course. Aside from influences in the formative period, the twentieth century saw not only calypso's sway throughout the anglophone Caribbean but a Cuban influence in the muted trumpet and probably the clarinet of 1930s calypsos, not to mention all the other Cuban elements in other music. And the process has continued in the 1980s and 1990s. In the 1980s, Belizean *punta* rock, a local development of a neo-African form called *punta,* fed into the Spanish-language pop *punta* of Honduran bands like Los Roland's and Los Silver Star. This, like the Guianas, might be claimed as a special case: Belize used to be British Honduras, and indeed is claimed by its larger neighbor. But Honduran *punta* also drew on Guadeloupian *zouk*—as did the Svengali of 1980s merengue, Wilfrido Vargas, whose music was neither marginal nor in any pejorative sense derivative. There has even been even feedback from Africa, whose modern urban music (as will be discussed in Chapter 7) was born in large part of New World influences. Not only was a Congolese band, Ryco Jazz, resident and highly influential in the Caribbean for some years, but Paris-based *zouk* was—inevitably—influenced by Congolese *soukous,* and through both Ryco Jazz and *soukous,* so were many other styles.

The Caribbean, in fact, is a staggeringly rich musical area, not just as a unit but in detail. On any island one can find music that is essentially African and music both influenced by and influencing international show business.

There is what must surely be the largest reservoir (with the exception of the European conservatory tradition) of living forms from a previous century to be played anywhere. Everywhere, both Europe and Africa (even some Asian islands) have left their marks: in religious rites; in vocal and instrumental styles; in instruments themselves; and in the approaches to form, to material, and to function. But Africa has proved to be the catalyst—has molded and reworked European material until the music of the whole area, despite its several languages and myriad islands, is recognizably related.

North American Strains
From Spirituals to Blues

In both South America and the Caribbean, the existence of substantial African roots in the music of the black population is unarguable. A sizable body of music is either untouched or only lightly touched by non-African influences. In addition to the music of the black regions, the national styles (in the sense of styles belonging to everybody) owe their existence to both Africa and Europe. That is to say, *everybody's* music has an African as well as a European element, and in most if not all cases (the tango is arguably an exception) it is the African element that is the catalyst. Nor did the African elements work their effects long ago and then melt into history. They are still visibly present and important, and—particularly given developments in the last quarter of the twentieth century—new developments are as likely to spring from currents traceable ultimately to Africa as from European strains.

Is the same true of the United States? Certainly it used not to be thought so. Although what Melville J. Herskovits called "the myth of the Negro past"—that is to say, the myth that New World Negroes did not have a past—is fairly well exploded now, people often are not too clear about what, if anything, is African in black U.S. music and what was taken from European sources. Nor are they certain what the white folk and popular styles owe to black music. In fact, the histories of black and white musics in the United States are inextricably intertwined. There is black music, and there is white music, but they are brothers, or perhaps cousins.

The place and time where one would expect to find the most African music in the United States is the countryside in the nineteenth century, and it is true that various sorts of music found in the countryside have a large number of obvious Africanisms. This is largely a matter of function, because the strongest elements of African music are retained when the music continues to serve the same sort of purpose as it did in Africa. One purpose is to make work, especially communal work, go easier; hence, various work songs have preserved heavy African content in North America, just as they have in other parts of the hemisphere.

Naturally, work songs take on the qualities of the work they accompany. In Africa, for example, collective work songs are not all that common in the rain forest belt, which includes the Yoruba, Ewe, Ibo, and other tribes and corresponds roughly to the main drumming area. Forest crops generally need less communal labor than field crops. As a result, the more open savanna belt of West Africa has more group work songs than do the forests. But even in the savannas work songs often are supplied by professionals who play music to encourage, rather than direct, the labor. These musicians or singers do not take part in the work—or, rather, their part in the work is their music. Work songs sung by workers themselves tend to be fairly casual. There is an example on a Folkways record of music from Liberia, sung by men cutting back bush land preparatory to burning it off to take the new rice crop. They sing in an intermittent fashion, breaking off for conversation or a joke, their machetes providing percussion for their song.

Work songs in the United States do not share all the qualities of African ones, but they unmistakably share enough to place them among the most Africanized of surviving forms. A fundamental Africanism is the very attitude that song is so necessary to work. Harold Courlander quotes a number of remarks made to him that underline this. An African told him, "Without a song the bush-knife is dull" (this is in fact a West African proverb), and an Alabama track-liner said: "Man, singing just naturally makes the work go easier. If you didn't have singing you wouldn't get hardly anything out of these men."

The heyday of the collective work song in the United States was the period of slavery, and not only because more people were nearer to their African background. Another reason was the nature of plantation work, which was frequently team work. Though it is very far from true, as LeRoi Jones claimed in *Blues People,* that all the different forms of labor common to Africans in Africa were reduced to plantation farming in the United States, it is true that various forms of labor on the plantation had parallels with certain forms of labor known in Africa, which supplied soil in which Africanisms could flourish.

Some types of work song in particular survived until quite recently—not usually in free society but in the Southern prison systems, which made use of a convict-lease system in many cases and preserved methods of manual labor long after mechanization had been introduced into free farming. The prison work songs that were recorded in large numbers in various parts of the South from the 1930s to the 1960s provide a great body of music that to some extent represents an older stratum in black styles. To some extent only, of course, because convicts are simply people who have been locked up, and thus bring musical developments from outside into the prison-song tradition. The body of prison work songs is so magnificent musically that there is a temptation to write about it at length. But its flavor—of superb musicality in most cases, but also of human bitterness, humor, and courage in adversity—can better be caught by listening to the recorded examples listed in the discography.

The degree of direct Africanism in the work songs is a matter for argument. Pete Seeger, in his introduction to a collection of prison work songs on Folkways, says that one song, "Long John," has been traced to a West African source. Remembering that one optimist once traced "Swing Low, Sweet Chariot" to a canoe-burial ceremony in the Victoria Falls region, one has to be careful about such attributions. On the other hand, many work songs, like many other old black songs, may in fact have African antecedents. If "Stewball" can be traced with certainty to an eighteenth-century English source while African attributions are less certain, this is because eighteenth-century songs in England were written down and their African contemporaries were not. Even if no existing U.S. tune could be matched with an African one, this would not in itself disprove survival. Though African tunes are longer-lived than African lyrics, they seem to be replaced by new ones quite rapidly. Nor are work songs the most durable of forms, having nothing like a religious sanction to enforce their perpetuation.

Certainly nineteenth-century black work songs were of many types. The British actress Fanny Kemble, in a much-quoted paragraph from her letters, described in the nineteenth century how she had changed her earlier view that the black songs she heard were adaptations of Scots and Irish airs. She wrote about a series of rowing songs she had heard:

> I have been quite at a loss to discover any such foundation for many that I have heard lately, and which have appeared to me extraordinarily wild and unaccountable. The way in which the chorus strikes in with the burden, between each phrase of the melody chanted by a single

voice, is very curious and effective, especially with the rhythm of the rowlocks for accompaniment.

The description gives one reason to wonder if she may not have been listening to an African song like one that appears on a striking (although, alas, not generally available) record in the archives of the British Broadcasting Corporation, with the rhythm of the oarlocks substituting for the swish of the paddles that accompanies the Nupe fishermen on the Niger River.

At times difficult to analyze, but unmistakable, is the link between the group singing of many U.S. work songs, especially the earlier ones, and of examples from a wide range of tribes in West and Central Africa. Some work songs use a form of near-unison (heterophony) in which minute variations produce a distinct and unmistakable sound very like the singing in Yoruba traditional music. Ulli Beier, writing in *African Music,* described the effect this way: "Yoruba singing knows no harmony in the European sense. Yet the singers are never in perfect unison either. Very small intervals between the different voices seem to give a kind of 'colour' or 'texture' to the sound." Other American work songs, using fourths, octaves, and occasional fifths, have harmonies almost identical to certain Congolese recordings.

A minor but significant Africanism, mentioned by Courlander in *Negro Folk Music U.S.A.,* is a form of "dedication" in some work songs, which, like some African praise and chronicle songs, makes reference at the outset to all people of importance within earshot. Courlander quotes:

> I say I'm ringing in the bottom,
> I say I'm ringing for the captain,
> I say I'm ringing for the steerer,
> I believe we ring for everybody.

The formalities completed, the singer can proceed to another African favorite, the satirical song, with less fear of reprisal.

A large number of work songs have a structure that is definitely African, because it is common in African music and not used in Europe. They consist of a long litany with a group response after every line, often forming the second half of the "tune," in a version of call-and-response singing. The litany lines are often unrhymed; they achieve their aesthetic effect with striking imagery (balancing traditional formulations and fresh use of known images) and repetition, as does African poetry. "Hammer Ring," for example, is a series of single lines, each repeated and followed by the refrain "hammer ring." The key lines of the verse run:

Won't you ring old hammer? (Hammer ring.)
Broke the handle in my hammer. (Hammer ring.)
Got to hammering in the Bible. (Hammer ring.)
Gotta talk about Norah [Noah]. (Hammer ring.)
Well, God told Norah (Hammer ring.)
You is a–going in the timber. (Hammer ring.)

Noah here takes the role of a hero-figure who is invoked to inspire and encourage the listeners to emulate his deeds. The song, in fact, is not religious despite its use of a religious story.

The British blues expert Paul Oliver suggests that much U.S. black music may in fact stem not from the rain forest areas, as is usually assumed, but from the music of the savannas. In this context, it is extremely interesting that many U.S. work songs use a form of call-and-response slightly different from the common improvised-call, fixed-response formula. The chorus picks up variations in the lead melody and, as it were, tosses them back, so that there is a constant variation in which a number of melodic themes are worked in.

This is found in much savanna music, including most strikingly a long piece of ritual music recorded privately in northern Nigeria by Dr. Anthony King of the School of Oriental and African Studies, London. The woman lead singer is followed without a fault through a series of complex variations. Something similar is frequent in Yoruba *apala* music, which, although the Yoruba are of the rain forest drumming belt, is a result of Muslim influence, especially perhaps in the vocal parts. "Long John," as sung on a Library of Congress record of work songs, is a fine example of this style.

Work songs cover a huge range of subjects. Perhaps the most recurrent, natural in the prison songs, are women, the length of the sentence, escape, and harsh jailers. A most chilling example was recorded in Texas in 1933 by John and Alan Lomax. Called "Ain't No More Cane on This Brazos," two of its verses run:

You ought to come on the river in nineteen four
You could find a dead man on ever' turn row.

Little boy, what'd you do for to get so long?
Said, "I killed my rider in the high sheriff's arms."

An important feature of African music is the indirect allusion, the use of oblique or cryptic references. Naturally, prison conditions encourage such a tendency, and "Long John" is an excellent illustration. It is about a legendary man who outran police, sheriff, deputies, and dogs on his way to freedom. The first verse is clearly about the escape:

> It's a long John,
> He's a long gone,
> Like a turkey through the corn,
> Through the long corn.

The nickname is oblique in itself; the image is vivid, but bound to a very humble, everyday country context (incidentally, don't forget that animal similes of all sorts are extremely common in African song). The repetition of the word "long" is a highly poetic device that is closer to an African than to any of the European traditions likely to have affected the singer.

The next verse veers sideways, and John becomes the Evangelist:

> Well, my John said,
> In the ten chap ten [tenth chapter, tenth verse]
> "If a man die
> He will live again."
> Well, they crucified Jesus,
> And they nailed him to the cross;
> Sister Mary cried,
> My Child is lost!

The clear, though indirect, linking with the escaped convict of John the Evangelist and then, in an apparently irrelevant aside, of the crucified Jesus is evidence of major metaphorical subtlety. It is also typical of a tangential approach common in African music. Praise songs, for instance, may laud a man by mentioning all manner of revered figures and associations without ever drawing an analogy or otherwise connecting them to their subject. Similarly, the singer of this version of "Long John," known only as Lightning, makes no direct link between the Biblical characters and his protagonist, other than their appearing in the same song.

The allusive poetic style is not solely a matter of secrecy, though prison life naturally gives added force to the enduring African feeling that, the world being the way it is, too much frankness is foolhardy. The use of poetic images without attribution is a general principle of African verse. The difference from European poetry emerges in a comparison of examples. Shelley, in "The Moon," creates a long and striking image for the moon, "like a dying lady lean and pale," but in the fifth line he names the subject: "The moon arose up in the murky east." "Old Hannah," on the other hand, is only named, never explained:

> Go down, old Hannah,
> Won't you rise no more?

and, in the next verse,

> Lord, if you rise,
> Bring judgment on.

From the context, the listener may be able to deduce that Old Hannah is the sun, but he is not told so, nor does he learn why the sun is called Old Hannah. Like African singers, Iron Head and Clear Rock, who are singers of this version of "Old Hannah," are singing only for those who know or who feel.

Prison work songs represent perhaps the most cohesive body of recorded labor music in the U.S. black experience, because the old group hand labor continued longer on the prison farms than in the free world. Naturally, not all songs are sung in the same way, even in the same prison. There was what Alan Lomax called the Mississippi style, "distinguished by the rough voice timbre used, the savagery of the singing, the overlapping of leader and chorus." The first and last of those qualities are very African, and it is undoubtedly significant that parts of Mississippi have traditionally had a very high majority of black residents, because on the whole Africanisms survive at their most obvious in such conditions.

Not only did prison work songs endure longer than most others because conditions changed faster on the outside, but they perhaps reached a greater artistic peak because there was a good deal (to put it mildly) of the continuity essential to a group form. The prison songs are so superlative aesthetically that it is easy to forget the wide range of other work songs that were developed in the United States. Some were very simple, and some would seem at first sight to have little to do with Africa. The laying of railroad track, for example, was not a technique brought with the slaves, but the use of song for an extremely restricted purpose—instructing track-layers in what to do next—is indeed African. Europeans sing absentmindedly, as it were, or as a pastime while working (with the two exceptions of obscure music like Sicilian mule songs and the possibly black-influenced sea-chanteys). They do not pay heed to a man who stands by doing nothing but telling them in song, or in chant at least, how to unload and stack rails:

Walk to the car, steady yourself.
Head high!
Throw it away!
That's just right!
Go back and get another one.
You got the wrong one that time. . . .
Walk humble and don't you stumble,
And don't you hurt nobody.
Walk to the car and steady yourself.

The functionality of work songs (as opposed to the universal custom of singing while one works) is basic to African cultures and relatively peripheral though not nonexistent in Western European ones. Indeed, the curious, ambiguous status of this sort of form defies European categorization. Is it a song? Not really. Is it a call, musicalized? In a sense.

John W. Work, in his *American Negro Songs and Spirituals*, mentions a different category of work song:

> The men sang another type of song when they were not engaged in group efforts, but were working at individual tasks. This song was a solo affair whose melody had little significance. It was little more than intonation, though the two lines possessed a semi-cadence and cadence as well as a climax note. The song . . . was the singer's soliloquy on the trivialities of life as they directly affected him. Its verse was subjective, just as that of the blues, though probably not so poignant.

It was called the holler, a form of uncertain derivation for which much has been claimed, including parentage of the blues. Hollers consist usually of a long, wavering one- or two-line call, often using falsetto and in other respects suggesting African parallels. Lomax once wrote:

> The lonely Negro workers piling up dirt on the levees, plowing in the cotton fields, at work in the lonely mist of the river bottoms . . . have poured their feelings into songs like these. The songs are addressed to the sun and the choking dust, to the stubborn mules, to the faithless woman of the night before, to the hard-driving captain; and they concern the essential loneliness of man on the earth. . . . The listener will notice the same use of falsetto stops, the same drop of the voice at the end of lines, that characterize the blues.

And characterize, as has been shown, much West African music also. Moreover, there is a powerful signaling element in the hollers. Courlander speculates that early hollers, which, he says, "undoubtedly were in African dialects, insofar as actual words were used," may have been used for signaling. This is done in Africa; when it is, the signaler often imitates not speech tones but the sound of a horn imitating speech tones.

Some hollers strongly convey a personal and almost ruminative note: "Mmmmmmmm. Boys, I've got a boychild in Texas, he ought to be 'bout grown." Others were still used for signaling within living memory. Samuel Brooks, who recorded some hollers for the Library of Congress in 1939, commented: "They usually sing it on a plantation. . . . If one man starts, well, across maybe another field close by, why they sing that same tune back to him. . . .

> Oooooooooh,
> I won't be here long.
> Oooooooooh,
> Oh, dark gonna catch me here,
> Dark gonna catch me here,
> Ooooooh.

Clearly, many hollers shade into short songs. In 1959, Lomax recorded a beautiful holler, "Wild Ox Moan" by Vera Hall, which is quite remarkably like another intensely personal piece of music from the Central African Republic—a lullaby sung by an Isongo woman, available on an Ocora record. "Wild Ox Moan" is slower, and the singer's voice less hard. But both pieces have the same ruminative, sung-for-oneself quality. Most important, the same entirely un-European use of falsetto or yodeled notes as part of the main melody line occurs. European yodeling, when it is part of a song, is almost always a separate entity, whether a chorus or interpolated nonsense syllables. It does not happen on certain notes of a word. Vera Hall's "Wild Ox Moan" is still a holler, not a song, insofar as the two can be differentiated. A much longer version called "Black Woman," on the Folkways record *Negro Folk Music of Alabama,* is free-form but unmistakable blues. The distinction is often subtle. But it would be nonsensical to suggest, as some writers have, that the holler represented some sort of inchoate welling-up of a new-formed musical sense. It was a legacy from Africa of a particular kind.

The question of early black songs in the United States is complex. Quite early on, the slaves there, as elsewhere, began to make use (as highly creative people, why would they do otherwise?) of the white styles they heard around them to supplement the African forms they were continuing and transmuting. We saw in the case of Jamaica that children's games did just that (see Chapter 4), and, before going on to more complex forms, it is worth examining the same genre in the United States. Not only did U.S. blacks take to English children's games like the Jamaicans, but in at least one case they adopted the same game. Here is part of an American version, as recorded by Courlander:

> Li'l Sally Walker
> Sittin' in a saucer
> Cryin' for the old man
> To come for the dollar.

Naturally, African-Americans did not get the *idea* of children's games from the white population. African children's games are highly sophisticated aids to learning. When Afro-American children adopted elements of the white kids' songs, they reinterpreted them in many of the ways that adults reinterpreted white song and dance forms. For one thing, in North America as in Jamaica, a large number of black children's games were really an excuse for dancing, so what mattered was individual dancing rather than the development of the story content.

Besides, white-originated games like "Sally's in the Skiff" had plenty of black counterparts with African features. This one is in call-and-response form and has a rhythm quite beyond most white children in their present state of musical culture:

> *c:* If I live
> *r:* Chool-dy, chool-dy
> *c:* To see next fall
> *r:* Chool-dy, chool-dy
> *c:* I ain' gon' raise
> *r:* Chool-dy, chool-dy
> *c:* No cabbage at all
> *r:* Chool-dy, chool-dy.

Children—black, white, brown, and yellow—sing out of not only their own but their parents' experiences, and even their grandparents'. The old English nursery rhyme "Ring a Ring of Roses" is a grim historical allusion to the bubonic plague of 1665. The roses were a characteristic rash, posies the pathetic prophylactic of medicinal herbs carried in the pocket, and "a-tishoo" the pneumonic sneezing before we all fall down—dead. Alan Lomax recorded a group of children singing of a happier but just as traumatic a moment, Emancipation, when the plantation bell fell silent:

> Ring, ring the big bell
> Ain' gonna ring no more;
> Fill me a pocket before I go,
> It ain' gonna ring no more.

The well-known "Shortening Bread" tells a truer and grimmer story in one version than is usually heard:

> Two little babies layin' in bed.
> One play sick and the other'n play dead.
> I do love shortening bread.

Harold Courlander tells of places in the starvation lands of Alabama where he was a guest at tables that never saw anything but shortening bread and molasses. This sort of staggering poverty, incidentally, is responsible for allusions that have tended to baffle blues enthusiasts. When Bessie Smith, in "Empty Bed Blues," used the phrase "he boiled my first cabbage" as a sexual metaphor, the effect seemed to outsiders less than ecstatic. But in the areas whose bitter experience produced "Shortening Bread," areas where greens were a luxury, the metaphor would naturally make more sense.

In the nineteenth-century frontier lands, play songs and games were not only for children, either white or black, and accounts of the period make it clear that black and white could learn from each other. A play-party song called "Rosey" shows very clearly one strain in the developing black styles that were to lead to the various forms of music we know today:

> Grab you a partner and promenade round
> Hah–a Rosey
> Pin my true love by my side
> Hah–a Rosey
> You do that now, you do that again,
> Hah–a Rosey.

This was clearly the kind of barn dance that had a caller telling the steps, in the old English and Scots tradition transported to the United States. But a call-and-response pattern had been added, and the chanting and response "swung" not in the extroverted, gay but relatively simple white fashion, but so that an apparent on-beat clapping accompaniment served as a base for a series of minutely displaced vocal accents by a singer using passing falsetto and semiyodeling notes in the African style.

The evidence of early absorption of white music elements by black musicians is incontrovertible. The ways in which blacks learned white music and the types they learned were, of course, myriad. Henry A. Kmen's study of nineteenth-century New Orleans music reports the surprise of visitors to the city at hearing blacks in the street whistle operatic arias. Of course, not everywhere was there an opera house or a segregated gallery accessible to black citizens, and many influences came from quite different sources. Lydia Parrish, in her *Slave Songs of the Georgia Sea Islands,* reproduces a spiritual ("O the Robe") with a "Celtic lilt" and explains it by the presence of Irish hands imported to work alongside the local black labor, repairing the rice-field dikes of Glynn County and digging a canal between Brunswick and the Altamaha River in 1838–1839. Parrish did not attribute European origins to black music lightly; if anything, she rather strained after African explanations.

Because survival of Africanisms in the New World and the degree of adoption of new material depended partly on the strength of the traditions to be kept or acquired, it is not surprising that a whole field of black narrative song grew up with major white elements. Narrative song, in the form of both ballads and shorter numbers, is an important part of British folk music, whereas, except for historical epics (such as the Mali epic of Sundiata), it was rarer in African culture. U.S. black singers did not take over white ballads whole. The process was complex and piecemeal. Sometimes they used whatever images out of British ballads appealed to them. Thus, Lead Belly suddenly interpolates into the Negro ballad "John Henry" lines almost identical to an old Scottish ballad:

> Tell me who's going to shoe your little foot,
> Tell me who's going to glove your hand.
> Tell me who's going to kiss your sweet little lips,
> And who's going to be your man.

The ballad "John Henry" itself and a host of other "epic" ballads—most but not all featuring badmen—show interesting developments. Their fuller versions are clearly modeled on British ballad forms in their narrative progression, sometimes in their verse form, and in their fondness of dialogue verses between two protagonists. But even on paper, leaving aside any consideration of performing technique, there are differences. Within the narrative frame, allusiveness creeps in. Who, for instance, are those women dressed in red who recur time and time again, sometimes mourning and sometimes joyful at death?

When a British ballad is taken over by black singers, it often comes out unrecognizable except for isolated motifs. Perhaps the most famous traveling song is "St. James Infirmary," which went from Ireland to England probably in the eighteenth century; became a broadside ballad, "The Unfortunate Rake," about a man who dies of venereal disease; and split into myriad versions, all with certain common verses and much the same tune. Here is a version from southern England containing verses that have cropped up in two American songs:

> And when I am dead to the churchyard they'll bear me,
> Six jolly fellows to carry me on,
> And in each of their hands a bunch of green laurel
> So they'll not smell me as they're walking along.
> So rattle your drums and play your fife over me,
> So rattle your drums as we march along.
> Then return to your home and think on that young girl,
> "Oh there goes a young girl cut down in her prime."

During the nineteenth century, some version of this song took root in the seaport of Liverpool, became a seamen's song under the name of "St. James's Hospital," and set sail for the States. There it split. The tune and many elements of the lyric, including the drum and fife and the laurel (changed to roses), became the cowboy song "Streets of Laredo." The title, slightly changed, and the image of the pallbearers were taken over by black singers. Their versions told of the plight of a gambler cut down in his prime—it is sometimes called "Gambler's Blues"—and of course it played hell with the rhythm:

> When I die I want six crap shooters to be my pallbearers,
> Three pretty women to sing a song;
> Put a jazz band on my hearse wagon,
> And raise hell as we ride along.

It would be a mistake to overemphasize the amount of British balladry in black song of the nineteenth century, transmuted or not. The amount preserved even in what is usually considered the great ballad area, the southern Appalachians, has been exaggerated. Whereas seventy-three British border ballads from the massive Child collection were collected by five people in two northern states, Vermont and Maine, only sixty-nine were found in the whole of the South by an army of collectors. What did happen was the adoption of appropriate images and of the general ballad form, which was then altered and used for new creations.

Besides the few songs that have been transformed wholesale, British balladry seems to have influenced black forms and imagery enduringly. The structure of the blues song "Two White Horses," with its first line repeated three times (not two, as in most of the blues), is quite common in both black and white music of the South. Many of the images could be out of old British ballads. At the same time, the direct question in the third to last verse is most unlike British ballads, and very like the person-to-person blues forms. The questions in verses three and four are rather different; they sound like "dialogue" verses in a song with other verses omitted (a favorite black way of creating a subtle, allusive form out of the European narrative songs). In addition, the singer in each verse lets his guitar carry some of what were originally lyrics, a device reportedly to be found in the savanna regions of Africa, as well as being widespread in the United States:

> Now two white horses standing in a line,
> Now two white horses standing in a (guitar)
> Now two white horses standing in a (guitar)
> Gonna take me to my burying ground.
>
> Did you ever hear that coffin sound? (guitar)
> Did you ever hear that coffin? (guitar)
> Did you ever hear a coffin (guitar)
> You know now poor boy's in the ground.
>
> Please dig my grave with a silver spade
> Please dig my grave with a silver (guitar)
> Please dig my grave with a (guitar)
> You can let me down with a golden chain.
>
> It's one kind favor I'll ask of you
> It's one kind favor I'll ask of (guitar)
> It's one kind favor I'll ask of (guitar)
> Take pains see my grave be kept clean.
>
> Did you ever hear that church bell tone?
> Did you ever hear that church bell (guitar)
> Did you ever hear that church bell (guitar)

You know now poor boy's dead and gone.
Now two white horses standing in a line,
(continues as verse one)

Did you ever hear a coffin sound?
(continues as verse two)

The white horses might be an image from either tradition, though I suspect a thorough working over of an old ballad image. The silver spade and golden chain are originally British, in various forms. "Poor boy dead and gone" in different versions is a favorite wandering verse in the blues. The theme as a whole fits well with the inherited African concern for a rightful death and burial. The singing style and guitar are a country blues, as far as could be from British or Anglo-American singing.

In the black ballads and balladlike forms, therefore, there is no simple imitation. There is acquisition and reworking for a new purpose. The result is at times something between a ballad without the verse form and the blues without the blues form.

Another difference between white and black treatments of the same subject stems fairly directly from the respective African and British traditions. A black ballad about the death of Railroad Bill records the historical though trivial fact that he died with a cracker and cheese in his hand. This fixing of a scene by an everyday detail is part of a mundaneness common in African and Afro-American music of many types. White ballads on the death of an evil-doer almost invariably draw a moral. This tendency was the inheritance of the British broadside ballads rather than the old folk ballads, and it was exaggerated by market-minded songwriters. The Dixon Brothers' "Wreck on the Highway" is an extreme example of the tendency: "I saw the wreck on the highway, but I didn't hear nobody pray." It is true that "Frankie and Johnny" in some black versions has a payoff of a sort, but the tone is quite different:

This story has no moral, this story has no end,
This story only goes to show that there ain't
no good in men.

Interestingly, when black singers point a moral they frequently show a far greater awareness of the Biblical injunctions about judging one's neighbor. Olive Woolley Burts, in her *American Murder Ballads,* tells of collecting a song on the Lindbergh kidnapping virtually as it was being improvised in a free, archaic blues-ballad form:

> Oh who would steal a baby out from his little bed?
> The world is full of trouble, trouble,
> Oh Lord have mercy on us folks!

The finger-pointing of many white ballads is missing altogether from this lament for original sin.

The sources of black song are widely varied. The creole music of Louisiana had strong affinities with the French *patois* songs of the Caribbean and almost none with the rest of black music, except for zydeco, the music of the blacks in the bayou regions settled by the Cajuns, descendants of French Canadian refugees. The very form of these French-influenced songs set them apart. Call-and-response passages come out more like the bobbin of Jamaican song, as in "Zamours Marianne," which uses an interpolated "Michie'-la" or "Marianne" rather than the longer response phrases of the rest of the southern states.

But the Caribbean influence on Louisiana creole music (which is significant for the development of certain elements in jazz) is most striking in the dances. Louisiana knew the universal Caribbean dance, the *kalinda*. In Louisiana, according to Mina Monroe's *Bayou Ballads*, it took the form of a stick-fight dance, as in Trinidad and elsewhere, with the added complication that the opponents had to balance a full bottle of water on their heads, and the first to spill a drop was the loser. A white Cajun version, the colinda, can be heard on an Arhoolie recording of Cajun music. The *kalinda* was said to be the dance observed in New Orleans's Congo Square by early witnesses. Of the other dances described in New Orleans, most were Caribbean also: the juba, the *bamboula,* the *babouille* (*baboule* in Haiti), and others. The words taken down in various locations suggest that the U.S. juba was essentially a called reel:

> Juba jump, Juba sing,
> Juba cut that pigeon wing.

A version from the Sea Islands is reported by Parrish. It appears to have been known in Georgia and the Carolinas, as well as Louisiana, and to have become a children's game song:

> Juba this and juba that,
> And Juba kill the yellow cat.

The buzzard lope, highly African in inspiration, had a very common animal-mimicry basis. One dancer lies down in the center of a ring and plays a dead cow, while the other moves around him impersonating a buzzard. Its accompaniment seems originally to have been patted and clapped.

The neo-African dances of the Congo Square have been described by Benjamin LaTrobe (see Chapter 2), and there is every reason to suppose that their equivalents could be found wherever there were enough Africans to preserve them and hand them down. But the neo-African dances soon existed alongside music that made use of European instruments. As early as 1799, fifes and fiddles were used in Congo Square, and banjos, triangles, jew's harps, and tambourines also appeared. It seems significant to me that all these European instruments were counterparts of African types—especially, as Oliver pointed out in *Savannah Syncopators*, from the savanna regions. Hausa *griots*, among others, frequently played in groups consisting of *kukuma* or *goge* fiddles with drums or frame drums and some sort of metallic percussion instrument. As Oliver put it: "The skills of the players of *kukuma* or *goge* would soon have been adapted to the European fiddle under active encouragement. And encouragement was certainly there."

It certainly was. Though the drums (which could be used to signal revolt and by all indications were so used, not only in Haiti and Jamaica but at times in the United States) were banned in many states, many slave owners took the view that after hours their property could make as much racket as it liked—at a suitable distance from the house. Some, whether out of kindness or enlightened self-interest, not only permitted music but even bought fiddles and other instruments for their more musical slaves and encouraged Saturday night dances. The newspapers of the Southern states during slavery days were full of advertisements that explode two stereotypes at once: the happy slave and the African who rejects all he can of white culture. Paper after paper announced the flight of some slave "very skilled on the French horn" or one who "took with him his fiddle." There can be no doubt at all that the two black instruments of the nineteenth century were the banjo and the fiddle. One was African, the other European, but each represented a more complex version of an instrument known in Africa.

The blending of African and European styles was encouraged by contact between the races. As LeRoi Jones points out, it was after Emancipation that, with bitter irony, "Negroes became actually isolated from the mainstream of American society. . . . The newly activated Jim Crow laws (Virginia's were not passed until 1901) and other social repressions served to separate the Negro more effectively from his former master than ever before." The isolation was not actually complete. The father of Mance Lipscomb, the Texas songster, was a full-time fiddler who after Emancipation played for dances in the Scots-Irish, Bohemian, and Negro settlements of the Brazos bottoms in Texas. For each he must have produced the appropriate music, and it is inconceivable that he did not retain elements of all—music simply does not work that way.

Jones's thesis that, during the more repressive post-Reconstruction period, black music lost many of the more superficial forms it had borrowed from the white man might be rephrased: Black musicians were then in the process of integrating what had been, on the one hand, definitely African survivals and, on the other, relatively undigested borrowings. The synthesis was being completed. A music that was truly Afro-American, in which African-derived musical techniques and concepts fundamentally made over elements from white America, was coming to maturity. The white elements endured, of course, even in the blues, alleged to be the blackest of black music (not with total justification, perhaps). The blues of Sonny Terry, for instance, still shows signs of the old reels and jigs that went into country breakdown music. And breakdown music itself is a paradigm for the new black music that was slowly growing throughout the nineteenth century but was caused to explode when Emancipation caused profound social and economic changes. As Jones noted: "The entrance of Negroes into the more complicated social situation of self-reliance posed multitudes of social and cultural problems that they never had to deal with as slaves. The music of the Negro began to reflect these social and cultural complexities and change."

Meanwhile, country music of all kinds continued. Small dance groups used whatever instruments came to hand: fiddles, mouth harps, and guitars, but also washtub basses, kazoos, and various improvised percussion instruments. Having in the early days drawn much of their inspiration from Africanized white styles—reels and the like—they now moved on farther toward the newer musical styles. Ad hoc music took all sorts of forms. A nineteenth-century visitor to New Orleans made it clear that even brushing a customer in a barber's shop became a rhythmic art:

> With what facility he moves his supple wrist and makes the down-driving broom play over your back the most complicated tunes . . . beating time the while with his foot. . . . How often does the double and triple and common time put you in mind of the castanets of the Castillian maid, and rub-a-dub-dub of the drummer at tattoo or reveille!

This author could hardly be expected to know the real sources of this rhythmic genius, but his observations were sound enough. There is a track on an Arhoolie record in which a barber stropping a razor provides the accompaniment for a guitarist.

So far I have been discussing what might be described as "folk forms." However, during the slave period and, at a quickening pace, after Emancipation, major music was brewing, music that went far beyond the folkloric. Simply for analytical convenience, I am going to divide this into the mainly vocal and the mainly instrumental. In both cases the word "mainly" is important. It must be understood that all styles fed each other, just as they were fed by, and in turn fed, the folk music.

The first black music to catch the serious attention of white America was religious. Negro spirituals began to filter into the general American consciousness just before Emancipation, and its progress was highlighted by a spectacularly successful U.S. and European tour of the Fisk Jubilee Singers in the early 1870s. The Fisk Jubilee Singers undoubtedly presented something of the richness of what must surely be one of the world's greatest complexes of religious styles. Their music, though novel to white America, was not in fact new. Moreover, they appear not to have presented black religious music as it really was. That was not the aim of George L. White, the musical director of the original Fisk Jubilee Singers, as a contemporary described it: "Finish, precision and sincerity were demanded by this leader. While the program featured the spirituals, variety was given it by the use of numbers of classical standard." Something of the style of the Fisk Jubilee Singers can be heard on recordings of later versions of the group. The sound of these, together with the description of White's aims, make it obvious that the group's repertoire represented an art re-creation in a line that continued through the Eurocentric concert performances of Paul Robeson and Marian Anderson—music that had little to do with the worship of the black Christians who originated the spirituals.

The early history of the spirituals is uncertain. The Reverend Samuel Davies, in 1750, calculated that only 1,000 Negroes out of 120,000 in Virginia had been converted and baptized, and presumably that approximated the average for the colonies. In the mid-eighteenth century, therefore, slave religion was presumably African. Even in the absence of evidence, analogy with both the importance of religion in African life and what happened in other parts of the New World makes this a fair assumption. By the late eighteenth century some clergymen were quite active in pastoral work among the slaves. The Reverend John Davies of Virginia, in a letter to John Wesley, told of giving some of his converts copies of Watt's popular hymnal:

> The Negroes, above all of the human species I ever knew, have the
> nicest ear for music. They have a kind of ecstatic delight in psalmody;
> nor are there any books they so soon learn, or take so much pleasure in,

> as those used in that heavenly part of divine worship. . . . Sundry of
> them lodged all night in my kitchen; and sometimes when I have
> awaked at two or three in the morning, a torrent of sacred psalmody
> has poured into my chamber.

"An ecstatic delight in psalmody" might still serve as the best description for the superlative religious music of African-Americans. In the early nineteenth century, Fanny Kemble heard her boatmen singing what she called "an extremely spirited war-song, beginning, 'the trumpets blow, the bugles blow— Oh, stand your ground.'" This was almost certainly not a war song but a spiritual; military metaphor is common enough in Christian music, as witness "Onward, Christian Soldiers" and "I'm a Soldier in the Army of the Lord."

The term "spiritual" has come to cover a wide range of religious music. In fact, black religious songs include staid versions of white Protestant hymns; shouting songs that accompany the nearest thing possible to African dancing in a church that regards dancing as sinful; so-called long-meter songs, very highly decorated, which can be traced back to early white American religious styles (made over, of course, into something distinctive) and past them to seventeenth-century Britain; duet prayer song and solo street-evangelists' songs that musically are virtually blues; and chanted, almost sung, sermons.

John W. Work divided spirituals into three groups: the call-and-response chant; the slow, sustained, long-phrase melody; and the syncopated, segmented melody, the tempo of which is usually fast and "stimulates bodily movement" (gospel singers call these jubilees). The form of pre-Emancipation spiritual that caught visitors' attention most often was the so-called shout. The shout—whose name the black linguist Lorenzo Turner traced back to a Wolof word, "saut" ("to dance before the tabernacle")—was the most obviously African of the religious forms of the black United States. It was a call-and-response form and, besides, a religious dance, fundamental to African worship, but—except for certain parts of the Spanish Roman Catholic Church—unknown in Christianity.

There are several descriptions of shouts, or ring-shouts, as they were also called, in magazines of the 1860s. Essentially, they consisted of a circle of people moving single file around its center to singing, accompanied by stamping and heel-clicking. According to Lydia Parrish, the people of one Sea Island parish used broom handles to beat on the floor, a version of the Dahomeyan *dikgambo*, the Haitian *ganbo*, the Trinidadian *tamboo bamboo*, and instruments found in Jamaica and elsewhere. The tempo of a ring-shout may build up gradually. The excitement certainly does, until possession by the Holy Spirit takes place (or, where possession is not formalized, possessionlike states).

James Weldon Johnson described the moment:

> The music, starting perhaps with a Spiritual, becomes a wild, monotonous chant. The same musical phrase is repeated over and over one, two, three, four, five hours. The words become a repetition of an incoherent cry. The very monotony of sound and motion produces an ecstatic state. Women, screaming, drop out of the shout. But the ring closes up and moves around and around.

Johnson says that the shout was, in his experience, "looked upon as a very questionable form of worship. . . . The more educated ministers and members, as fast as they were able to brave the primitive element in the churches, placed a ban on the 'ring shout.'" He also makes the point that the shout was not, as far as he could discover, geographically universal.

The shout was clearly an attempt at preserving traditional forms of worship in a new context. The ban on dancing was circumvented, because the participants in a ring-shout never crossed their feet. Physical action, dance as well as music, was an integral, basic feature of African worship, brought in with the slaves and kept alive. And in the United States, wherever ring-shouts were not practiced, marching round the church often was—not in a European processional, but as a semidancing march to an intensely rhythmic spiritual. This was reported by Work as late as 1940, and various forms of dancing are part of worship in churches in many parts of the United States today, not only in the southern countryside, but also, and perhaps even more, in the ghettos of big cities like New York, Chicago, and Detroit.

The ring-shout was by no means the only way in which black Christians managed to reinterpret the use of dance in worship. A mid-nineteenth-century visitor to New Orleans described a service there:

> The congregation sang; I think everyone joined, even the children, and the collective sound was wonderful. The voices of one or two women rose above the rest, and one of these soon began to introduce variations. . . . Many of the singers kept time with their feet, balancing themselves on each alternately and swinging their bodies accordingly.

Soon the preacher "raised his own voice above all, clapped his hands, and commenced to dance." The implication of this testimony is that dancing was at one time more common in black churches than today. Beyond that, the mention of a "swinging" rhythm is interesting in the light of Work's remark that, "in all authentic American Negro music, the rhythms may be divided roughly into two classes—rhythms based on the swinging of head and body and rhythms based on the patting of hands and feet. Again, speaking roughly, the rhythms of the spirituals fall in the first class, and the rhythms of secular music in the second class."

This may well have been true of the early performance of many of the spirituals, though other styles of black religious music are based on patting, not swinging. Other qualities in the old spirituals, as described by those who heard them, are of obvious African derivation (most are precisely the elements European notation cannot express, which is why writing down spirituals, or any black music, is travesty). Work tells how a black musician plays around with the fundamental beat, a reinterpretation of West African rhythmic attitudes, applied to European or European-influenced measured time:

> He will, as it were, take the fundamental beat and pound it out with his left hand, almost monotonously; while with his right hand he juggles it. . . . Even in the swaying of head and body the head marks the surge off in shorter waves than does the body. . . . It is often tantalizing and even exciting to watch a minute fraction of a beat balancing for a slight instant on the bar between two measures, and, when it seems almost too late, drop back into its own proper compartment.

Work, like so many other writers, mentions the "turns and quavers and the intentional striking of certain notes just off-key." The use of sliding up to and down from a note is common in African singing; I have noted too that the "tempered" scale, in fact, belongs only to European art music.

Gilbert Chase's *America's Music* describes the distinctive choral sound of black congregations in much the same terms as Ulli Beier used of Yoruba music: "The manner of Negro singing cannot be accurately described in terms either of 'unison' or 'harmony.' It is more complex than that. . . . A clue to the style is contained in Emily Hallowell's remark that the 'harmonies seem to arise from each singer holding to their own version of the melodies.'" The concert-solo approach to the old spirituals has tended to obscure the fact that many of them were in call-and-response form. Here are two, both fairly well known:

> They crucified my Lord,
> And He never said a mumbling word.
> They crucified my Lord,
> And He never said a mumbling word.
> Not a word, not a word, not a word.

I know moon-rise, I know star-rise,
I lay this body down.
I walk in the moonlight, I walk in the starlight,
To lay this body down.

At one time, some scholars tried to show that the Negro spirituals were simply copies of white forms. And, more generally, the theory has been raised that it was natural for black Christianity to follow white models more closely than black secular music. Actually, however, much the same complex of influences seems to have operated in religious and secular music alike. It has been shown beyond a doubt that many Negro spirituals were adapted from white hymns. But music is not simply markings on a page, and black music is far more than that.

It is certain that black and white Christians worshiped together in the Great Awakening of the early nineteenth century, and trustworthy accounts written at the time attest that slave converts were most taken with the psalm books of white Baptist and Methodist preachers. The reasons for the great preponderance of Baptists among black Christians have been repeated many times: The Baptist preachers were willing not just to preach to the slaves but also to sit down and eat with them; the importance of water ceremonies in many West African religions, including water initiation ceremonies, found a parallel in the Baptist emphasis on immersion; and the organization of the Baptist churches was democratic, giving each church considerable autonomy and allowing it to supply the blacks with something they could seldom find elsewhere.

To cite Phyl Garland, in a reference to the modern Baptist and independent churches: "It was the sole arena where a chauffeur or a handyman, reduced to facelessness and namelessness by his employers and often mute within his own home, might speak with some seldom exercised authority as a deacon of the congregation." Equally important, though perhaps not at the conscious level, the Baptist insistence on personal experience of Christ, combined with fervent expressions of conviction regarding personal salvation, offered a rough parallel with the African custom of possession by the gods. In simpler terms, the Baptist tradition allowed Africans and their descendants to behave in what to them were the proper ways of expressing worship.

Many aspects that tend to be considered exclusively part of black religion were once shared by black and white. The phrase "to get happy," describing a powerful emotional conversion experience that sometimes borders on possession states, as in the lines, "I went to the valley and I didn't go to pray,/But my soul got happy, and I stayed all day," has been regarded by both blacks and whites as a purely black expression, implicitly of a black experience. Actually, the expression was common in camp meetings. McCurry's collection of revival hymns, *Social Harp*, has a version of a popular hymn, "Jesus, My All, to Heaven Is Gone," with the refrain "Happy, oh happy" added:

> We'll cross the river of Jordan,
> Happy, oh happy,
> We'll cross the river of Jordan,
> Happy in the Lord.

And an even more obvious white example occurs in a camp-meeting chorus:

> I want to get happy as I well can be,
> Lord, send salvation down.

The word "spiritual" itself is usually used to mean black religious music, but it seems to have originated in English evangelical circles as "spiritual songs" (in *America's Music,* Chase in fact accepts this derivation as definite). There is, however, room for doubt that either term was adopted outright from white religion. There is no such doubt in the case of the slow, ornamented "surge" style, discussed later in this chapter. The "happy, oh happy" chorus quoted above may well have served originally as the answer in a call-and-response formula. Because it is known that black Christians attended camp meetings in large numbers and that in fact black preachers at times preached to white and black together, it is perfectly plausible that the addition was actually an Africanization adopted by black and white alike. Again, one must emphasize that this was not a case of some untutored enthusiasts latching onto something totally alien and imitating it.

The "surge" style of Mahalia Jackson, Cleophus Robinson, and many others is undoubtedly seventeenth-century British in its broad conception and even, to some extent, in detail. And while the decoration of single notes called melisma is a feature of Afro-Islamic music, it also seems to have formed part of the ancient British folk hymnody that so upset educated musicians like Cotton Mather. And a particular stylistic trick, lining-out—where the leader calls a line and the congregation sings the same line in response—certainly stems from the days when many English rural churchgoers were illiterate.

If you copied down the notes of the female gospel quartet in the Caravans' version of "Jesus Saves," you would find it very similar to the old white version quoted by Chase. Some Jamaican hymn-singing occupies a position halfway between the British and black U.S. styles. However, a host of differences are there all the same: vocal tone, fractions of timing, backing—a whole developing tradition. Also, much Muslim African singing makes equally striking use of long, highly decorated notes. In other words, the surge style and melisma are probably instances of a feature taken over because it corresponded with something already familiar, and lining out was a British tradition that melded well with African call-and-response.

By no means were all Negro spirituals reworkings of white hymns or based on them. Chase cites Richard Waterman's report on an unpublished study by M. Kolinski showing that:

1. Thirty-six spirituals are either identical or closely related in scale and mode to West African songs. One, "Cyan Ride," is almost exactly the same as a Nigerian song, and "No More Auction Block" echoes an Ashanti song.
2. A wide range of technical musical elements are shared—too many for coincidence.
3. The opening rhythms of thirty-four spirituals are almost exactly like those of several Ghanaian and Dahomeyan songs.
4. The overlapping of call-and-response patterns produced identical polyphonic patterns in many spirituals and African songs. Fifty spirituals were found to have the same formal structure as some West African songs.

Kolinski concluded that many spirituals, though patterned after European models, were either bent to conform to West African musical practice or chosen because they suited it.

All in all, when early black Christian music used existing white material, this material was immediately subjected to a molding process, bringing it in line with established musical practices developed from African sources: call-and-response; increased rhythmic flexibility; the use of hand-clapping for percussion (which can lay claim to being the *major* African percussive practice, and which was reported in black U.S. religious music by the eighteenth century); and the emphasis on possession states as a form of worship and a sign that the spirit was present.

The African provenance of possession states has been disputed on the grounds that religious possession affected both blacks and whites at the camp meetings and had been known in Europe. But European possession was passive and never expressed itself in dancing (at least not in areas which could have affected the United States), and the white manifestations either died out after a few years or remained only in isolated cases. Possession is a *major* feature of many different types of black church in all types of community. Possession seems to be associated largely with certain kinds of music, or at any rate such music greatly increases its likelihood. On the subject of Africa, M. J. Field writes in an essay in *Spirit Possession in Africa:*

> Drumming, singing, clapping and the rhythmic beating of gong-gongs and rattles, alone or all together, are the most common inducers of possession. The drumming is exciting, the clanging iron is a harsh monotony from which consciousness readily recoils. More possessed people are likely to be seen at a well-orchestrated dance than on any other occasion.

Many of the elements described here are present in black church services, if one substitutes for the judgmental word "monotony" the more accurate concept of repetition. The ring-shouts, as we have seen, could continue for up to five hours; the singing in churches today—the congregational singing, not the music of the small, trained gospel groups—swells on and on in great waves whose result, conscious or not, is exactly that of the repetitive drumming of the cults of Africa, Brazil, or Trinidad.

A lesser similarity is the fact that the trances are in some cases controllable. Field says: "Most possessed persons appear to have some control over the duration of their trances and to come out of them conveniently at dinnertime or just before the passenger-lorry departs. This has been wrongly taken as evidence of faked possession, but it merely adds another similarity between trance and sleep." It does not always happen of course, but it is a feature in black U.S. Christian rituals as well as in Africa. A change from song to sermon or sermon to song will often suffice to end a trance. On a recording by Herbert Pepper of services in two Harlem churches, a woman who had been emitting frequent possession cries can be heard to tail off within minutes, at most, after a change of tempo in the service.

A tendency of the postulant on whom the hand of God has descended to go off and roam at night in the bush or the countryside is amply documented in Africa and referred to in a line from a spiritual: "My head was wet with the midnight dew." Whether the tendency of new converts in U.S. rural areas to go off into the woods was an unconscious reflection of the period of seclusion at initiation in African and neo-African cults or the "mourning" period in such sects as Revival Zion in Jamaica and the Spiritual Baptists in Trinidad is, for the present, a matter of conjecture.

The fact that many spirituals were written down early has created the impression that they were a fixed form. Nothing could be farther from the truth. Weldon Johnson makes the point that the creators of religious songs were rarer than those who could recall and lead them. Ma White, one of the latter, made it her task to "sing down" a long-winded or uninteresting speaker, or even to cut too long a prayer short. "Singing" Johnson, on the other hand, made his own songs, traveling from church to church and teaching new songs to the congregations.

The spirituals were essentially the congregational singing of the churches of the nineteenth century, and in that sense they still exist. Certain spirituals became codified simply because outsiders put them on paper. "Swing Low, Sweet Chariot" was a well-known spiritual in call-and-response form. Everybody knows it today, but only in one version that a collector happened to pin down. Lydia Parrish collected a radically different version:

> Oh swing low, oh swing low,
> Oh swing low sweet chariot, swing low.
> Oh swing low, oh swing low,
> Oh swing low sweet chariot, swing low.
> It must be Jesus passing by;
> Oh swing low sweet chariot, swing low.
> Swing low in the east,
> Swing low.
> Swing low in the east,
> Swing low.
> Swing low in the east,
> Swing low.
> Swing low sweet chariot, swing low.

We have no record of how this was sung, but its call-and-response form and its repetition of exhortatory formulations such as are basic to the success of West African rituals reflect something much nearer to Africa than to Europe or Euro-America.

A form of religious music quite common from at least the 1920s (and presumably in fact much earlier) was that of the wandering street evangelist, usually a member of the working-class black Sanctified churches. Singing solo or in twos or threes, usually accompanied by guitar, their music often had strong connections with the blues, though most would have hotly resented the association with "sinful" music. Many of these singers were recorded, but the

Sallie Martin, seen here in the middle of her Singers of Joy (in their earliest incarnation the first female gospel group ever), was one of the creators of modern gospel music, at least as a clearly defined entity. Along with Thomas Dorsey (formerly the blues singer Georgia Tom), she founded the Gospel Singers Convention.
Courtesy of Specialty Records

records of most are now rare. Blind Willie Johnson was perhaps the greatest of those who have survived on disc. Johnson accompanied himself on guitar singing songs with religious themes in a deep, deliberately gravelly voice that has been said to resemble the possession voices of priests in some African cults. Whether there is a direct link is unsure, but the adoption of strained and "unnatural" voices is widespread in Africa, particularly in ritual songs, and more generally in countries with Muslim influence. Other street gospel singers, like the Gospel Keys, used guitar and tambourine and a two-voice style that continued into the 1940s with the excellent gospel singers Sister Rosetta Tharpe and Marie Knight. It is still sometimes heard today: a 1960s recording of "Sweet Home" features Brother Cleophus Robinson and Sister Josephine James in a magnificent example. And inside the storefronts, Sanctified musicians—of whom the finest examples on record are by Arizona Dranes—often played the piano. (Nina Simone once remarked that her mother banned boogie-woogie at home and then played in church Sunday morning.)

This brings out an important point about black religious music: its many styles may perhaps be arranged chronologically according to which began first, but all are still sung today and are widely popular. Gospel music, said to have gotten its name from the former blues singer Georgia Tom Dorsey, who was converted and turned to religious music (he wrote the famous "Precious Lord"), dates from the 1920s. Dorsey's conversion is said to have taken place at the National Baptist Convention of 1921, though he was certainly playing secular music after that. Gospel music has been defined as music "addressed to the people as an expression of personal testimony. Its purpose is to direct the mind inward to one's own experience and needs; to warn each of us of the consequences of sin and give the promise of spiritual release. The gospel song is light in character and expresses a spirit of reverence." Ordinarily, gospel music is presented by a trained group. Some, like the Dixie Hummingbirds and the Original Five Blind Boys, are based on the old barber shop close-harmony technique, but with a soaring, improvised lead vocalist. It is tempting, and I believe valid, to see this style as a logical extension of call-and-response singing. As we have seen, African singing styles often increasingly overlap the lead and the response. Many black religious songs consist essentially of "response" phrases from the group, with the leader improvising above them as if the overlapping had become complete.

Another black religious style that grew up early and is still powerful today is what has been called the "surge" style, in which the slower spirituals were probably sung. This is highly decorated, majestic, of soaring power. Most gospel singers use it from time to time. Perhaps the exponent most famous outside the black community was Mahalia Jackson, whose early records were superb examples. It is typical of the complex story of American music that the surge technique is the one that can be most surely traced back to white origins. It is, in fact, a preservation of the very old British long-meter folk psalmody popular in the seventeenth century, which became equally popular in eighteenth-century America (to the disgust of the "trained" musicians in both lands). It became the patrimony of black and white Christians alike through such joint religious occasions as the camp meetings of the Great Awakening.

Mahalia Jackson, the greatest twentieth-century exponent of one of the oldest mainstream forms of African-American religious music, the spiritual.
Courtesy of Columbia Records Library

White versions of this decorated style can still be heard on recordings of Southern white folk singers, but it is rarer in white religious music. The white style is a rustic survival, but black Christians took the old Anglo-American form and really developed it. The white-derived decorations (something almost totally alien to African music, with the exception of strongly Arab-influenced styles) were made richer by the subtle displacement of rhythmic accents and by the addition of a clapped or patted rhythm, which simplified but retained something of the cross-rhythms of African music. To this was added a variation and contrast of vocal tone, which European singers mostly avoided in favor of a high, deadpan delivery. Black singers had made use of the dual heritage to create something essentially new.

Gospel music is varied and constantly changing. Early descriptions of church services make it clear that very rough tone was used in congregational singing in the nineteenth century, usually by the leader, but not always. This rough tone survives, often intensified, employed by Marion Williams with the Clara Ward Singers in "How Many Miles?" and by the Mighty Clouds of Joy in richly rhythmic numbers—their use of electric guitars and bass reflecting rhythm and blues—that are descendants of ring-shout singing, a rare example of which is preserved on the Library of Congress recording "Run, Old Jeremiah."

There has always been a close relationship between black U.S. religious and secular music. Even allowing for a proreligious bias in the earliest, usually abolitionist collectors, it does seem that a large proportion of nineteenth-century black song used religious themes. A report on a tobacco factory in Richmond, Virginia, quotes its manager, commenting on the workers' singing: "Their tunes are all psalm tunes, and the words are from hymn books; their taste is exclusively for sacred music; they will sing nothing else." Even songs of protest seem usually to have been adapted spirituals (which may account for the notion that spirituals as a class were disguised songs of protest). An example, which makes a direct reference to Emancipation, is:

> Done with driver's driving (three times),
> Roll, Jordan, roll.

The obvious modern example of the close relationship between sacred and secular music is soul-singing. Not only is it rooted largely in the churches, but most of its best singers began in choirs or gospel groups. But the connection between the two is much older than that, and has always been two-way. Rosetta Tharpe was a former blues singer, and her guitar playing owes much to secular hoedown styles. Thomas Dorsey's gospel songs, as well as those of Blind Willie Johnson, are "bluesy" in nature. There has never been a clear-cut division between "sacred" and "secular" musical instruments, either. Though the guitar was regarded by W. C. Handy's father as the "devil's box" (a role earlier reserved for the fiddle), it has backed many hundreds of sacred verses. During the period (still continuing, in some measure) when piano and organ were the favorite instruments to support gospel singers, the barrelhouse blues qualities in the piano style were often quite plain. (Trombones were common at one time, and Elder Beck of Buffalo played swinging vibes.) None of this is surprising. Junior Parker once claimed that the blues singers' stories of church background were often exaggerated, but there is no doubt that many blues and jazz musicians ended in the churches as singers, musicians, or preachers.

The stylistic elements of black religious music are, as can be seen, quite mixed. Many, but not by any means all, of the oldest spirituals came from white sources. A recording trip in Alabama, Louisiana, and Mississippi found many older people still singing hymns from the hymnal known generally as "Doctor Watts," which had an American edition in 1820. But just as clearly, the music was much changed. Later songs were composed by blacks in the various Afro-American or "re-Africanized" styles, using hand-clapping, falsetto singing, and a wide range of vocal tone, call-and-response, rhythmic complexity, and cross-rhythms through vocal syncopation and contrasting

Sam Cooke was among the first and finest crossovers from gospel to soul, one of the great gospel voices, and a creator of the gospel-influenced soul sound.
Courtesy of Fantasy Inc.

hand and feet rhythms, all of African descent, though sometimes considerably transmuted in the New World.

The very importance of song in black worship is an Africanism hard to overestimate. Possession by the Holy Spirit is the outward sign of worship and faith, and in Africa "the spirit will not descend without song." But the ubiquity of song is not the end of it. Religion is bound into everyday life in a way that ought to be true of all Christians but is not. Besides, God, Jesus, and other Biblical figures are extremely close to black Christians, just as African spirits and gods are felt to be very close. I do not believe it is a coincidence that the oldest spirituals did what only intellectual liturgy-experimenters do in the white churches: express Biblical stories and even the words of Jesus in what really was the singers' own languages. Courlander quotes two fine instances:

> Old Job said, good Lord,
> Whilst I'm feeling bad, good Lord,
> I can't sleep at night, good Lord,
> I can't eat a bite, good Lord,
> And the woman I love, good Lord,
> Don't treat me right, good Lord.

The second example comes from an account of Jesus's encounter with the Samaritan woman at the well:

> He said woman, where is your husband?
> She said that I don't have one.
> He said woman you done had five,
> And the one you got now ain't yours.

In *America's Music*, Gilbert Chase analyzes the song "Michael Row the Boat Ashore" and brings out a similar point: the bending of religious themes to suit the mundane activities at hand, in this case rowing.

Themes and subjects of religious songs vary immensely, of course. Some seem to belong to certain periods and not others. Some scholars have claimed that the doings of Old Testament prophets, which featured very prominently in slavery spirituals, have not been popular since. But because old songs are still used alongside new ones, this suggestion should be treated with some caution. Some themes are simply modernized. A Sea Island spiritual used the image of a horse as the way to salvation:

> Loose horse in the valley.
> Aye.
> Who's going to ride him?

Over the last five decades, the analogy of the train became well known, with a great range of versions. One of the most famous is:

> This train is bound for glory,
> If you ride it you got to be holy.

Similarly, in both songs and sermons there are extended metaphors involving the "Christian automobile," which runs on the word of God, and Courlander reports songs that update the theme by using an airplane.

Like the blues, black religious music covers the whole range of human experience and the whole range of artistic expression, including bathos. And even the bathetic sometimes is expressive. John Work was scornful of the improvised couplet:

> Wait till I get upon the mountain top,
> Goin' make my wings go flippety flop.

But it seems to me fairly expressive of the clumsiness an apprentice saint might expect to experience.

There is a tendency to say that modern gospel songs are exclusively concerned with personal testimony of salvation and exhortation; but though many are, like Sister Rosetta Tharpe and Marie Knight's superlative "Up Above My Head, I Hear Music in the Air," others may tell a Biblical story, like the same singers' "Two Little Fishes and Five Loaves of Bread," or may have a strong theological content, like the "salvation through works" theme of the Consolers' "May the Work I've Done Speak for Me." Gospel singers have lately tended to assume a more consciously social role, as have churches in general. In a concert in June 1970, Marion Williams sang the song for which she is perhaps best known—"He's Got the Whole World in His Hand"—and improvised verses about peace in Vietnam, Cambodia, and the United States. And Dorothy Love Coates of the Birmingham group the Gospel Harmonettes said in an interview: "I know who I'm singing to. Men who can't get jobs, deserted mothers, boys heading to the army. My people need a message."

The sermon is an important component of black religious services. While of course many black clergymen preach in styles indistinguishable from "mainstream" white sermons, the improvised or part-improvised "spiritual" sermon is regarded by most blacks themselves as a distinctive contribution to the service of the Word. The "spiritual" sermon normally begins in a conversational tone, differentiated from white sermons only by the responses of the congregation, reminiscent of the old African belief that it is discourteous to listen dumbly, without response, or of the interjections made during the *griot*'s telling of traditional tales. Gradually, the preacher's manner becomes more rhythmic. Soon he is chanting. Preacher and congregation begin to build up a complex pattern of call-and-response, not in song but in chant; very often certain preachers will begin to use the "holy laugh," a sharp exhaled "Hah!" between lines, which acts as an extra rhythmic element and is similar in sound (though not in usage) to the hoarse, rasping, rhythmic breathing that is part of Jamaican Revival Zion music. The congregation cries back, in agreement, in sympathy. The piano, organ, or whatever instruments are available may play a part. The tension rises until a point of maximum effect when the preacher, or sometimes the choir, will transform the chant into a song.

The origins of this style are not certain. White preachers in the South use a version of it, but a more hysterical and less integrated form. As Francis Bebey points out in *African Music: A People's Art,* there are African parallels. I have heard recorded sermons in Yoruba, from the Nigerian Church of the Cherubim and Seraphim, of almost exactly the same character. The emotional sermons of the Great Awakening are patently one point of origin. But, though it can never be proved, the presence in the chanted sermons (black and white) of certain Africanisms and the fact that the white style is vestigial and limited, whereas black chanting preachers may be rural or urban, peasant or middle-class (added to the presence of similar techniques in Africa itself), suggest that the transference was from black to white.

The mode in Africa is not confined to indigenous Christian denominations. Recordings of non-Christian rites sometimes give examples of something similar, and I myself attended a healing dance on the East African coast that involved an element of sermonlike exhortation. There, too, the officiant (in this case an *mganga*) built up to a strained-voice, rhythmic style culminating in full-scale music. The chanted sermons are not simply a southern rural or impoverished urban proletarian phenomenon in the United States. Nor do all sermons present the same sort of free-association evocation of Biblical and salvation motifs. Many show profound theological insight, the relation of topical subjects to religious interpretations of universal currents, and moral teaching of considerable sophistication. The notion of the "hellfire" preacher, as applied to these pastors, is a grossly false stereotype. Their sermons are a major aesthetic experience. They are certainly, taking their range as a whole, quite as pastorally and theologically excellent as the written and read homilies of the "mainstream."

How much of African belief, as opposed to practice, was carried over into black religion in the United States has been the subject of argument. First, it is obvious that, just as blacks come of all sorts of American backgrounds, so they hold to all sorts of styles of churchmanship and belief. But apart from old beliefs near enough to the new to be rationalized easily, certain elements of African religions have been preserved. One, missed by most early commentators but discussed fully by Herskovits, was the attitude to Satan revealed in many black Christian songs, whereby he resembles the trickster god of the Yoruba more closely than the mighty potentate of Christian belief. One should not go as far as Janheinz Jahn in *Geschichte der Neoafrikanischen Literatur,* who at times makes it seem as if black Christianity were the thinnest veneer for the old African faiths. However, Jahn's observations that African religion is not contemplative but evocative—and that in Africa, as well as in the Negro spiritual, faith is expressed through invocation, whereas in white Christianity it is expressed by adoration—contain some truth (though again he exaggerates somewhat a division which in reality is not easily separable).

Jahn also points out that the role of the spirituals as invocation is closer to African practice than to the European, where hymns almost always state theological truths (in fact serving as a major school of theology for the ordinary man). On the other hand, many gospel songs are declarations of faith, not invocations. If they have an African content, it is in the use of specific social comment:

> I got a home where the gambler can't go,
> I got a home where the gambler can't go.
> Oh, Jesus lord have mercy.
> I got a home where the gambler can't go.

To take "Jesus lord have mercy" as an African invocation, because it is sung, would entail the Africanization of the *Kyrie Eleison,* which is pushing matters altogether too far.

An especially interesting kind of survival—though one that does not receive much attention—is the continuation of belief in evil spirits, which exist in the Bible but seem to be insisted on by black members of some sects to a degree that suggests a link with West African belief. This insistence is not confined to obscure parts of the countryside. On Radio WADO in New York on February 21, 1971, I heard a preacher remark: "Yes, these evil spirits must go!"

Gospel music's variety, I think, indicates one reason for its popularity. Along with its relevance to a living and widespread faith, it provides a complete religious substitute for sinful secular music—fast, dancelike tunes, ballads, blues, barrelhouse piano, guitar, rhythm and blues, and even FM rock. In black gospel music, of all religious music, the Devil does not have all the best tunes—but, by the reckoning of the more devout he has most of the best-known ones. The blues was—and to many people still is—"sinful" music. Yet, as much as the spirituals or gospel music, it sprang from deep within a people's experiences to become one of the world's great musics.

Nobody knows when the blues began, partly because few people can agree exactly where other forms—the holler, in particular—end and the blues begins. When a worker on the levee sang,

> O-o-o-o-ah,
> Going down the river before long,

he was hollering. But when he developed the musical line a little and sang,

> Going down the river before long,
> Going down the river before long,
> Going down the river before long,

was this a complex holler or the birth of the blues? Does it matter? The man who sang those verses was singing in a tradition still full of African elements: allusive lyrics; presumably (given the lack of development of the words) interest in the music; and repetition as both a musical and a poetic form.

This man didn't call it the blues. The word, applied to music, began creeping into use around the first decade of the twentieth century. It seems to have been about that time that the music began to be codified into a number of forms, of which the most common was the twelve-bar blues, its verse consisting of a couplet with the first line repeated. But this form seems to have developed when blues began to be played by more than one man. A musician singing to the accompaniment of his own guitar or without any instrument at all can please himself whether he allows a verse twelve bars, eight, or eleven and a half, and many early blues songs were in fact that flexible. A good example on record is "Poor Boy Blues" by an obscure Texas singer called Rambling Thomas. His verses are irregular, and the whole piece is plainly close to the field holler, extended and with guitar accompaniment. Of course, blues singers did not sit down at a table and form a Committee on the Standardization of the Blues. Most blues numbers, once the style was developed, were

Texas bluesman Lightnin' Hopkins. Undoubtedly the major African-American secular music of the twentieth century, the blues is a typical mix of African-derived rhythmic approaches and vocal habits, along with melody lines that seem to mix African and British elements. Add lyrics that may quote a Scots ballad but consistently resemble the African bards' topical songs, and the result is a classic creole form that could not exist without either its African or European elements but has remade them into something totally original.

Photo by Chris Strachwitz, courtesy of Arhoolie Records

twelve-bar. But the great woman blues singer Bessie Smith probably sang more songs that were not twelve-bar than ones that were. What is true is that the blues *tends* toward a twelve- or an eight-bar form (a couplet without repetition of the first line).

The blues has a very complex history spanning seventy or eighty years, and our concern here is not to try to condense it, but to learn what we can about where the blues came from. At first blush, there does not seem to be the

Bessie Smith, the greatest of the "classic" women blues singers, was little known to white America, but she both fulfilled and transcended the musical idiom in which she worked.
Courtesy of Columbia Records

same African quality in blues forms as there clearly is in much Caribbean music. The blues is sung in English, accompanied usually by guitar (with or without rhythm section) or, at various times, by small jazz groups. It has, in its mature twentieth-century form, a harmonic structure apparently based on European theory. It also follows a rhyming verse structure.

One misleading factor is that the extensive recording of the blues began in the 1920s, by which time the form (as it was played in and around towns, at any rate) had become fairly structured. People are apt to base their impression of blues on the commercial records, and most of the earliest blues records were made by women singers in Chicago, accompanied by piano and sometimes small jazz groups. These women—of whom Bessie Smith was undoubtedly the greatest, along with Ida Cox and the slightly older Ma Rainey—were professional entertainers. Some of them had roots deep in the country but nevertheless were affected by the conditions of both the city and their own sector of show business. A great many of their songs were not blues but vaudeville songs, though by sheer artistry these singers made blues of them.

Still, the basic structure of the blues sung by the "classic" singers was rooted in the folk blues, and for good reason. Blues was an improvised music in which singers created either their own songs or new versions of old songs by impromptu imagination, free association, and the use of what the folklorists call "floating" verses (lines that crop up time and again in a wide variety of songs), for example: "I'm a poor boy, long ways from home"; "Laughing just to keep from crying"; and "I got a woman, she's six foot tall/Sleeps in the kitchen with her head in the hall." Other verses or phrases are borrowed because they are so expressive. In the 1940s, Hot Lips Page, in "Uncle Sam's Blues," sang: "Uncle Sam ain't no woman, but he sure can get your man." The same line turns up in Snooks Eaglin's "I Got My Questionnaire" in the 1950s. But it may well have originated long before Page put it on record. Borrowings may be direct quotes or more allusive, as when B. B. King picks up from "Make Me a Pallet on the Floor" in his own "Country Girl," with a reference to a "pallet laying on the floor."

Improvisation is a complex creative procedure, and an improvising musician—or poet—is greatly helped if he can use a framework that is both simple and flexible. The blues, whether of eight or twelve bars, supplies just that. Besides, the blues is not as neat as descriptions of the twelve-bar pattern might suggest, and many of the apparent raggedness turns out on inspection to be not incompetence within a European frame but Africanisms. In folk blues, for example, the last syllable of a line often coincides with the first beat of what is thought of as a separate section, the four-bar instrumental "answer." Significantly, call-and-response in earlier black American forms tends toward overlapping, and this is also a frequent trait in African choral singing. Even more relevant to the source of certain relationships between voice and instrument in the blues, in voice-and-percussion music the last beat of the vocal rhythmic pattern may often fall on the first beat of a drum pattern—exactly what happens in the blues, as well as in quite a lot of non-U.S. black music too. The principle was clearly important enough in African and

Toumani Diabate's contemporary version of the traditional Manding small group (*top*) is remarkably reminiscent of twentieth-century African-American blues trios like that of Sonny Boy Williamson (*bottom*), with its two-stringed instruments—a *kora* and the *kontingo* (*ngoni* in other languages) that is probably one of the ancestors of the banjo—and a *balafon* to stand in for the keyboard. Other similarities aside, in both idioms rhythm and melody have equal status. And while of course European music is full of trios, small mixed groups backing vocalists were rare to nonexistent in the areas of Europe that affected the New World.

Diabate photo courtesy of Hannibal/Rykodisc Records; Williamson photo: Chris Strachwitz, courtesy of Arhoolie Records

African-derived music to be preserved in U.S. vocal forms and then reapplied to the relationship between voice and instrument when the opportunity arose.

The question of call-and-response in the blues raises a basic problem of interpretation. Just as there have been scholars who have violated all sense in an attempt to prove the essential whiteness of black music, so there have been others who have too hastily ascribed an African origin to virtually all its features. One dictum is that the twelve-bar pattern—two-bar vocal, two-bar instrumental, two-bar vocal (first line repeated), two-bar instrumental, third line of vocal, two-bar instrumental—is a call-and-response pattern and thus a major Africanism. Now there are good reasons for accepting this in principle, but not without recognizing the considerable differences between classic African vocal call-and-response and this blues pattern. The first difference is that the response in Africa is indeed vocal, not instrumental. The second is that, on the whole, African tunes are defined by the *response*. I think it would take a fanatic to claim that "St. Louis Blues" was defined by trumpeter Louis Armstrong's obbligatos, not Bessie Smith's singing of the vocal! The third difference is that, while the solo lead, or call, in much West African singing is improvised, the response tends to be fixed; if it is not fixed, it reproduces the call line. The mere device of filling in gaps in a vocal form is obviously not African in itself, of course. European and Anglo-American folk music sometimes has instrumental bridges between the verses. It must be said that this is rare, however, and most Anglo-American singing was unaccompanied until so late that a black influence could be postulated. Church and conservatory music, of course, has always used instruments to bridge gaps between vocal passages.

This said, I believe that the case for the blues as a development of a call-and-response form—or at least as profoundly influenced by it—is overwhelming, provided one accepts that cultural survival is not the antonym of change but depends on it, and provided one does not assume all blues accompaniments take the call-and-response form. Many blues singers, especially country blues singer-guitarists from certain parts of the South, made little use of the call-and-response pattern. But for most, the two-bar instrumental sections were *clearly* used not as a bridge to lead to the next vocal line, as a European musician might use them, but as an answer to the previous one. The examples are endless. Some keep the form of solo/chorus, as when Ma Rainey in her magnificent "Stormy Sea Blues" is answered by Kid Henderson on cornet and Lucien Brown on alto. Others are duetlike, but still with an instrumental answer to a vocal statement, as in Armstrong's replies to Bessie Smith in "Reckless Blues," which bring the instrumental role onto an equal footing with the vocal so that it is part of a discussion rather than a chorus of assent. The call-and-response pattern has become as varied as the blues itself, but the

twelve-bar blues structure is as if designed for it, with its equal segments allot-
ted for the instrumental replies, so that in formal terms the instrument has as
great a role as the voice.

What else is African in the blues? In much country blues, the guitar is
used in ways reminiscent of the music of the West African savanna belt. A
notable feature of West African stringed-instrument technique is its relationship with singing. Bebey remarks: "The single-string bow-harp is often mag-
nificently used not only for accompaniment . . . but at the same time as a
percussion instrument, the musician plucking the string and knocking alternately on the resonator." This particular technique is not common in the
blues, but the joint "accompanying" and percussive function of the guitar in
much country blues is so powerful that the concepts "rhythm" and "melody"
can hardly be disentangled (as they never can in African music, in quite the
same sense as in European).

Another vocal-instrumental relationship common in African accompanying techniques is the repetition of a short phrase by the instrument or instruments (usually varied, though not greatly) while the singer uses a longer
melody, also repeated with improvised variations. This is also a frequent
means for accompanying fairly fast blues on the guitar, as witness Robert
Johnson in "Dust my Broom" or Elmore James's version of the same bass in
tracks like "Held My Baby." In fact, it is the foundation of most blues piano of
the style that became known as barrelhouse, especially in the specialized form
called boogie-woogie. A third accompanying style for guitar does not exactly
answer the vocal line but performs the function given to stringed instruments
in Ghana, which "*fill in the breaks* with accompanying figures." Perhaps most
striking of all is a possible link between West Africa and Mississippi bluesmen
such as John Lee Hooker. While many blues moved through a three-chord
pattern, some of Hooker's songs are set to an ostinato that never changes
chordally, or at most moves between two chords in an endless cycle typical of
the "open-ended" approach of much African music, and most specifically of
the ostinatos used by West African string players.

The parallels between African musical custom and blues techniques, many
still used by blues singers as well as the joint blues and gospel-formed soul
singers, are considerable. So endless, in fact, that one has to be careful not to
fall into the trap of forgetting that the blues has strong European strands also,
and calling it an "African music," as one or two people have done recently.
LeRoi Jones, in *Black Music*, brought out a fundamental Africanism almost in
passing, when he remarked: "Even beautiful R&B blues, or the uses made of
these forms by our contemporary mainstream, are repetitious, though not
necessarily boringly so—this music accepts repetition as an already accepted

fact of life." In fact, African and Afro-American dance music do not merely *accept* repetition. Repetition is a major functional element—in ritual as an aid to possession, in social situations as an aid to dancing without fatigue. And we must not forget, as people too often do, that the blues, like most black music, is closely linked to the dance. Mack McCormick, describing first-generation blues singers like Mance Lipscomb, made this point:

> These men did not think of themselves as blues singers. They were singers whose employment was often to provide music for dancers and thus they thought of its rhythms, not its poetic structure. Thus, to Mance, the ballad "Ella Speed" is a breakdown; the work song "Alabama Bound" is a cakewalk; the bawdy "Bout a Spoonful" is a slow drag. For the most part he thinks of "blues" as a particular slow-tempoed dance that became fashionable around World War I.

A most interesting subdivision of country blues is the music of the country blues bands, which tends to shade into the instrumental dance music we shall be discussing in Chapter 6. The typical lineup of many Caribbean and South American dance groups, with their iron gongs, scrapers, drums, and voices, corresponds to the West African rain forest's characteristic ensemble. The early blues bands, by contrast, consisted very often of fiddle, guitars, and sometimes homemade percussion, which would easily accommodate techniques learned in the savanna groups with their bowed *goge*, lutes, and rattles.

Paul Oliver draws attention to parallels with African savanna music:

> To the ear attuned to the blues it is the manner of playing that impresses, with the moaned and wailing notes of the bowed instruments, the rapid fingering of the lutes and harps, and the combined interweaving of the melodic-rhythmic lines when two or more musicians play together.

The analogy is especially striking when one listens to records with a strong Muslim element, such as the Ocora disc *Niger: La Musique des Griots*, in which, according to Alan Merriam,

> the vocal line tends to be more straightforward than that of the bowed lute, which elaborates and ornaments the melody fairly extensively, though the two are obviously the same basic line. . . . Other outstanding items include the long, cascading, downward-moving, orna-mented, arhythmic Arabic melodic lines.

Oliver points out that: "the blues uses stringed instruments in a melodic-rhythmic manner with a fairly complex finger-picking" and associates this with earlier black instrumental techniques: "The sliding notes and glissandi of the fiddle were matched upon the guitar strings. . . . The percussive 'thump and strum' of the banjo was carried on the bass strings."

The parallels between African savanna-belt string playing and the techniques of many blues guitarists are remarkable. The big *kora* of Senegal and Guinea are played in a melorhythmic style that uses constantly changing rhythms, often providing a ground bass overlaid with complex treble patterns, while the vocal supplies a third rhythmic layer. Similar techniques can be found in hundreds of blues records. In parts of "Let's Go to Town," Memphis Minnie sets up a complex pattern with the use of arpeggios whose rhythms cross with those of a fast dance beat. Fred McDowell's version of the Sleepy John Estes song "Drop Down Mama" uses very complex strummed guitar rhythms, far advanced from the basic "common time" four-to-the-bar stereotype of the blues. In a different vein, Robert Johnson's "Come On in My Kitchen" uses guitar in unison with his voice, a technique not unknown in European folk music but common also in West Africa, a case, perhaps, of twin-culture reinforcement. Rambling Thomas's "Poor Boy" is another instance of the same technique.

The rhythmic sources of the blues, as of black U.S. music in general, present more problems than the rhythmic elements of other parts of the black world. Certain specific ingredients can be isolated. One is "playing around the beat" or "singing around the beat," the displacement of accents so as to set up cross-rhythms—not between drums and various forms of percussion, as in Africa, but between voice and instrument in the guitar blues. Another fundamental feature of West African music-making, also widespread in Afro-America, is the tendency to use triple and duple rhythms at the same time, which is arguably the reason for the extensive use of triplets in both blues and jazz.

Blues are usually said to be in duple time, but the white rock-blues musician Al Wilson, of Canned Heat, once expressed the reality of blues rhythms far more accurately in an interview with Pete Welding in *Rolling Stone:* "There's really not a rhythmic definition because nothing in blues rhythm is anywhere near ubiquitous. Really, totally modally organized blues conforming to the basic model appears in even duple meter, in more or less metronomic triple patterns . . . and in loosened-up, jazz-influenced triplet patterns." The use of triplets against a basically 4/4 beat to create the duple-triple tension so fundamental to wide areas of African music, though perhaps more common in jazz, is frequent in music stretching from the Blind Lemon Jefferson recordings of the 1920s through the up-tempo "New Orleans" rhythm and blues style of people like Fats Domino, right up to the generation of Bobby Bland and beyond. It is also a major feature of the piano accompaniment to much gospel music. A good blues example is the opening to Howling Wolf's "How Many More Years."

Satisfaction with rhythmic interest and subtlety as sufficient in themselves, which has been emphasized as an aspect of African attitudes to music by Dr. J. H. Kwabena Nketia and others, is less obvious and more intermittent in the United States, but it is a recurring phenomenon in the blues and similar musics. The most obvious ingredients separating soul from the blues are the very strong gospel-song influence in the singing, and the general abandonment of the twelve-bar pattern. But just as important though less noticed were the progressive moves toward a music of "pure rhythm" on the part of several singers, most notably James Brown.

Besides stressing the interplay of bass and drums, Brown's cries and the jabbing sax interpolations build up a polyrhythmic structure that, however modified by contact with European measured time and the use of European instruments, owes its existence principally to Africa. For all that one may decry the loss of rhythmic subtlety and what used to be called swing in the thump and crash of so many rap accompaniments (whose frequent clunkiness is usually due to the inflexibility of synthesized percussion), it is difficult to make a case whereby they are not an intensification of elements prized in the work of James Brown, and for that matter in the interlocking ostinatos of much 1930s boogie-woogie playing.

The rhythm of blues verses themselves—though they have tended to become more regular as time went on—operates according to a metric system different from the European. In essence it is like, though less extreme than, the calypso verses, which allow for great rhythmic subtlety by using irregular numbers of syllables in between the main verbal or poetic stresses; the result is often a series of cross-rhythms over the (normally) more steady beat of the accompanying instrument. The importance of this factor is obscured somewhat by the overpowering early position of the "classic" women blues singers who dominated the first year or two of the blues recording industry. A large number of the songs these women sang were not blues in form, though they used blues vocal techniques in singing them. In fact, some of the classic blues singers constituted a separate substratum, with sometimes tenuous relationships with country blues on one side and jazz on the other, especially in the matter of rhythm.

Sippie Wallace's "Jack o' Diamonds," Chippie Hill's "Pratt City Blues," and even Bessie Smith's "Reckless Blues" simply do not swing in the jazz sense. Nor do they have what Paul Oliver calls the "'slow and easy' slow drag of the country blues band." But if some examples do plod, hampered by leaden tubas, others have a "sway," a reminder of Weldon Johnson's remark quoted earlier about the swaying and the patting rhythm. The classic blues often ceased to be dance music. When country techniques came to town, introducing various complex guitar- and piano-based rhythms, they revolutionized city blues in more ways than are always recognized. Incidentally, the use of a wide range of different *types* of beat-complex (not simply of time-signatures) is typical of African but not (except in Spain) of European music. This range of rhythmic complexity can be traced right through the blues and allied forms, through rhythm and blues, and into soul, where the "big beat" concept still exists. Singers like Martha and the Vandellas, in "Dancing in the Street," employ as rhythmically sophisticated a complex of displaced beats as do any of their more solemnly studied elders.

African-derived approaches to rhythm, of course, have long since been built into black music. In 1972 I wrote that any change in this trend is as likely to involve an increase as a decrease, and rap/hip-hop backings certainly seem to bear me out. The search for new sounds has never necessarily meant an adoption of Euro-American Tin Pan Alley methods. When the 1970s group Sly and the Family Stone began to work away from the gospel call-and-response techniques, they in fact developed a greater rhythmic subtlety with complicated scat and sung dialogues and a general breaking up of what was left of the European-style formal structure of their choruses. Insofar as many rap backings seem to have lost the rhythmic subtlety of previous African-American music, the reason may be that their line of development traces back not so much through sung forms as through earlier oral literature: through the Last Poets to jazz poetry, back through the Dozens and various signifying performances, including not only jazzmen's parodies of African-American sermons but some of those sermons themselves.

Much as most people over thirty-five (and maybe rap addicts dedicated to being cutting-edge) may long to deny it, in fact, rap is part of a strong and enduring African-American tradition, call it music, poetry, or spoken word. One direct ancestor is the Jamaican dub toasting of deejays like U Roy (hardly a surprise since U.S. rapping also began with deejays in the Bronx and Brooklyn). A quick glance through Steven Stancell's *Rap Whoz Who* will turn up several important rappers born in the West Indies—including the seminally creative Kool DJ Herc (Clive Campbell), both a Jamaican and creator of breakbeat deejaying, and there are others with parents or friends from the islands. But Jamaica is just one source: rap also continues a long U.S. tradition. Despite some irrelevancies, many tracks on the Yazoo CD *The Roots of Rap* document its roots not only in blues performers like Frankie "Half Pint"

Jaxon but Sanctified street singers like Blind Willie Johnson. While the trail leaves a large gap between late-twentieth-century Afro-America and Africa, I don't think it is unreasonable to remember that many of the *griots* of western Africa also chant their verses to fairly unvarying ostinato accompaniments, even if those ostinatos are a lot lighter-handed than hiphop's digitalia.

One of the oldest battlegrounds for the wars between jazzologists and bluesologists is the existence or nonexistence of a blues scale. Those who do not deny its existence (and they are few these days) say it consists basically of a diatonic scale but with certain "blue notes," that is, with the third note flatted irregularly (in the key of C, a blues pianist may use an E natural, an E flat, or, indeed, both together, and a singer or a player of an instrument capable of it will produce something between the two), and a flatted seventh note. It has been claimed that, since the development of bop in the 1940s, the flatted fifth has also become a blue note, but Gunther Schuller asserts that flatted fifths have been used since the 1920s. The question of scale is more complex than the existence (or not) of a "blues scale." Harold Courlander was once told by an Alabama blues singer that he "played with the notes" just as he "played with the beats," which suggests not the vagueness about pitch that some earlier authors have attributed to black singers, but a high degree of tonal sophistication.

An extremely interesting contribution to the argument about tone and scale was made by Al Wilson, quoted by Ingrid Monson. Of the relation between speech and song in the blues, which is so much nearer to African than European usage, Wilson said: "This is the thing about words, why they are important in singing the blues melodies using those four or five notes in the standard blues mode. . . . You pattern the words to rise and fall in a way similar to the way that you would speak them, and construct the words not just any way but so they flow naturally with the flow of the melody."

The intimate connection between speech and melody in African music, which arises partly from the fact that so many African languages are tonal, has been discussed in Chapter 1. The existence of a similar rapport in the blues is not coincidental. Much work needs to be done on the tonal values of black U.S. speech, incidentally. Could it actually preserve West African intonations, as does, for instance, the Haitian French *patois*? The possibility of a connection between speech tone and blues scales has not yet received enough attention.

Much of the dispute about the so-called blues scale seems to be a matter of definition. The basic question has not been whether "blue notes" exist (which is obvious), nor whether all or most of the blues use pentatonic scales consisting of either the top or the bottom half of the diatonic blues scale. The point of the argument has been whether, given that these things exist, they indicate an African ancestry for the blues. Alas, the blues scale is one of the least satisfactory of all areas for dogmatism about African roots in African-American music. It is true that a certain vagueness around the third and seventh intervals exists in some West African music. But it is also true that West African scales not only show differences with the European tempered scale—a relative novelty in European music, be it remembered, and relevant only to "art" or customarily written forms—but vary greatly among themselves. And as regards the blue notes themselves, English musicologist A. L. Lloyd points out in his book *Folk Song in England* that the vagueness about thirds is a prominent feature of English folk songs and, indeed, seems to be a major feature of the music of wide areas of the world. Moreover, pentatonic scales and some form of diatonic scale are now generally accepted as characteristics that African and European music have in common. The provenance of the blues scale seems likely to remain a topic for argument rather than resolution.

Though several authors have referred to the use of flatted sevenths in English country singing, it may still be true to say that while an ambiguous third is common to the music of all three continents, the flatted seventh seems more common in Africa, including at least one region that supplied cultural traits to the United States. Kwabena Nketia, in *African Music in Ghana,* says, "The flatted seventh is frequent and well-established in Akan vocal music." Al Wilson suggests that both the blues and soul music use basically five-note scales, but different ones. He allots the scale C, D, E, G, A, C to gospel music and soul, and C, E-flat, F, G, B-flat, C to the blues. If Wilson is right, it would certainly be one reason why the blues element in much soul music, though it is certainly there, is far less obvious than the gospel.

A large number of vocal and instrumental techniques are found both in some parts of Africa and in some blues. An example is the frequent tendency of a singer to drop the last word or two of a line and leave the guitar playing solo. Harold Courlander once asked a singer who had just done this whether he was tired or had forgotten the lyrics. The singer replied: "No, I just step aside and let the guitar say it." One instance occurs in the lyric "Two White Horses," quoted earlier in this chapter. Fred McDowell's "Baby, Please Don't Go" and Lightnin' Hopkins's "Black Cat" are other examples. Big Bill Broonzy does the same thing to great effect in a version of "John Henry":

> Well, he died with his hammer in his—
> (guitar finishes the phrase)
> Yes, he died with his hammer in his hand.

Behind this musical technique lie vestiges of two widespread aspects of musical instruments in Africa: (1) a "talking" function that goes far beyond the well-known use of talking drums, flutes, xylophones, and so forth; and (2) the semipersonification of instruments, which are considered to have some form of soul. Musical instruments figure prominently in many African creation myths, of course, and certain drums used in worship are treated as sacred, but personification goes far deeper than that. Francis Bebey tells of offering to buy a drum from a man, who coldly remarked that he came to market to play music, not to sell slaves.

A somewhat similar technique among country blues singers, incidentally, is to sing only a few words at the beginning of a line and then to hum, or even fall silent, so that the guitar carries not just the end of the line but the main burden. Many singers have used this style, from the gospel blues singer Rev. Gary Davis (who used to exhort his guitar to "talk to me" during an instrumental break) and 1930s urban blues singer and pianist Leroy Carr to John Lee Hooker and Howlin' Wolf. It is also common in some forms of African vocal-and-string music, and in both cases it indicates an attitude to the relationship between instrument and voice that is common to Africa and black America but alien to Europe.

In general, the great range of vocal tone used by blues singers—not just the differences among singers, but the contrasts of tone used by the same individual—appears to be part of the African legacy of the blues. The President of Senegal, Léopold Senghor, a noted poet, once wrote of African singers: "Negro voices, because they have not been domesticated by training, follow every shade of feeling or imagination; drawing freely from the infinite dictionary of nature, they borrow its tonal expressions, from the light songs of the birds to the solemn roll of the thunder." A striking example of vocal intensity, harshness, and rough tone is to be found on an Ocora record of music from Upper Volta (now Burkina Faso), in a track recorded by three Bousance praise-singers.

Though the rough tone in traditional western African music is mostly associated with a fairly high-pitched voice, rather than the deeper tone of blues singers like Bukka White, deeper voices are not unknown in Africa either, as a track on the Folkways album *Africa South of the Sahara* shows. This presents a Bakwiri singer with a deep voice, a fast vibrato, and a thick tone. Blues voices range from the highest of near-falsetto to the deep, gravelly quality of Blind Willie Johnson or Bukka White. The use of falsetto and the use of a passing hocket or one-note yodel in the middle of a sentence seem to some extent to fluctuate according to fashion. The yodel in midline was popular in the urban blues of Chicago musicians like Scrapper Blackwell in the

1960s soul singers such as Aretha Franklin recombined various forms of black music in a synthesis that brought many enduring Africanisms powerfully to the fore.
Photo courtesy of Atlantic Records

mid-1930s. A memorable instance was Casey Bill Weldon's "WPA Blues," though Robert Johnson also used it in "Walking Blues." It also occurred in a more rural setting, most strikingly in John Dudley's "Cool Water Blues," recorded by Alan Lomax on a field trip in 1959, and in "Lonesome Katy Blues" on the Arhoolie album *Mississippi Blues.*

The hocket and the full falsetto are extremely common techniques in African and Afro-American music. We have seen both in more folkloric settings in the Caribbean and South America (see Chapter 4). As individual notes (but not quite a yodel), it is an effective part of Red Nelson's "Sweetest Thing Ever Born"; Robert Johnson uses it in "Kindhearted Woman Blues"; so does Aretha Franklin in "The Thrill Is Gone." And gospel-singer-turned-soul-man-turned-gospel-singer Al Green made a specialty of it (incidentally, falsetto in both Africa and Afro-America more usually symbolized passion than lack of masculinity). In fact, if anything it came back with renewed force in the soul styles, which draw part of their inspiration from the falsetto lead singers, as well as the tearing, growling tones, that are an essential part of the hard-gospel style. Examples of falsetto singing from Africa are to be found on the Folkways album *Music of the Cameroons* in a song about a sanitary inspector and a funeral song, among others.

Blues vocal styles did not all stem from African models, of course. The shouting Kansas City style, of which Joe Turner and Jimmy Rushing were perhaps the most famous early exponents, was born, in part at least, of the need to dominate noisy bars and large bands. But the intensity and the tearing quality in many blues singers' voices have many counterparts in Africa and none either in Western Europe or in white American styles, and the same holds for the great variety of tone heard within one blues song. Euro-American folk music tends strongly toward a high, harsh, deadpan tone.

Charles Keil sets forth in *Urban Blues* a certain formula that he feels is at the heart of modern black music; he says it can be described in several different ways:

> "Constant repetition coupled with small but striking deviations"; "similar wails and cries linked to various tumbling strains and descending figures"; or simply "statements and counterstatements"— all of which equal "soul." It is a pattern that a Negro child in the rural South or the urban ghetto learns by heart, normally in a church context, and it is as old as the oral traditions and call-response patterns of West African poetry and music.

In strictly musical terms, this supplies quite a good definition of some of the major factors—generalized from a number of varying but in some respects interrelated African patterns—that go into Afro-American music, including blues of all sorts and church music, as well as the music that derives much of its manner from both sources—soul.

With soul music, the infusion of gospel elements into a popular music that until then had been developing from the blues on one side and white pop ballad styles on the other became so strong that most of the best soul and other gospel-tinged singers came from the churches—Aretha Franklin, Ray Charles, Wilson Pickett, Nina Simone, O. V. Wright, and many others—like the many before them who went into the fields of jazz, the blues, and popular music.

Of course, all the black styles, whether blues, country music, gospel, jazz, soul, or rhythm and blues, have drawn from each other continuously—though more at some times than others. Like any popular music, the blues has been subject to rapid change, and the Africanisms favored have changed along with everything else. "Dirty" tone, which was strong in the Mississippi-come-to-Chicago Blues of John Lee Hooker and Muddy Waters, has been rejected by some blues fans in favor of the lighter style of B. B. King. One interviewee told Keil, "B. B.'s cleaned up the blues; they've refined it, so it's smooth and easy—no harps, moaning, or shit like that. Those guys have brought the blues up to date." This is a reaction less against Africanisms in the blues than against the emphasis of some of them to the point almost of self-parody. African music itself is, however complex, "smooth and easy."

Many Afro-American songs continue the African use of song as a vehicle of social comment of all sorts, including praise songs and songs of derision. The blues maintains this tradition strongly, though with somewhat less emphasis on current affairs than, say, calypso. But social comment has always been there, from the 1930s "WPA Blues" through Leon Thomas on rent control in the 1960s:

> New York City without rent control would be like
>   a thief stealing from the blind.
> These leases and those rent increases would drive
>   a poor man out of his mind.
> So welcome to New York, brother,
>   it's a city full of fun,
> They got plenty of rats and roaches,
>   welfare for everyone.

Juke Boy Bonner's "I'm going back to the country where they don't burn the buildings down" is in the same spirit, and of course social commentary, frequently of a sort that aggravates outsiders, is an important part of rap.

A feature of blues themes that is most un-African is the large number of songs concerned with love. But even here, non-European attitudes to the use of song creep in. Some, but very few, blues songs express love for somebody and are addressed to that somebody. Most are in other categories, such as the boasting songs (an important African category with overtones of sympathetic magic):

> If your man ain't treating you right,
> Come up and see your Dan.
> I rock 'em, roll 'em, all night long,
> I'm a sixty minute man.

The blues appears to lack any counterpart to the African praise song, but as has been shown, the hero and the bad man change places in a hostile or indifferent society (a phenomenon extremely common in white U.S. folklore as well as black). The opposite of the praise song, the put-down, or song of derision, is certainly present in the blues, especially in the form of the old

Though thought of as a rock and roll figure, Little Richard's style was pure rhythm and blues, with an African-derived focus on rhythm allied with a New World boisterousness.
Courtesy of Specialty Records

game "The Dozens," a particularly in-your-face equivalent of the Trinidadian *parang* and Latin *controversia* that has been seen as a training ground for teenagers to learn grace and cool under fire. And a kind of sexual praise song, at least, has long existed—for what else is that old favorite, "My Daddy Rocks Me with One Steady Roll"? Here again, many of the themes of contemporary rap, from the sexual braggadocio to the badman-blues-ballad/gangsta parallels, suggest a more tightly woven continuum than many of us are prepared to admit.

The largely market-driven segmentation of music tends to obscure the interrelatedness among African-American vocal styles and of these styles with jazz. Bluesmen, soul arrangers, singers, gospel shouters, and jazzmen have all been learning from each other from the start. As Phyl Garland remarked in the early 1970s, much of the increasing complexity of soul arrangements was indirectly thanks to jazz, and in the 1990s the saxophone has begun creeping back into rock, soul, and even rap. Black styles were never totally separate, and they are not now. Nor are they protected from the effects of the mainstream record market, and have not been since the mainstream success of soul. In the mid-1960s LeRoi Jones, in an article reprinted in *Black Music*, remarked that "funk (groove, soul) has become as formal and clichéd as cool or swing, and opportunities for imaginative expression within that form have dwindled almost to nothing." He might have added that it had become part of mainstream commercial pop, especially when black producers began to get their hands on large budgets and multitrack recording and produce polished but producer-oriented supermarket soul.

But the doomsayers are rarely altogether right. The decline of one style has almost always led to the rise of another. It is no coincidence that hiphop and rap began emerging in the ghettos in the mid-1970s, any more than it was a coincidence that Natalie Cole's first big hit was one of the simplest arrangements on the album and a glance back to the brilliantly joyous simplicities of Aretha Franklin. Or that the Mighty Clouds of Joy "crossed over" in the mid-1970s with the classic gospel sound of "Mighty High" rather than the dreary number on the same album that the producers were clearly aiming at the disco market. And, of course, despite the intermittent headlines pronouncing it dead, jazz did not simply live on in the soul arrangements. The link between African-American vocal and instrumental idioms has been close from the beginning, and yet they have always had their own histories.

6

U.S. Black Dance Music
"People" Music Becomes "Classical"

Jazz is the best-known U.S. black instrumental music (and perhaps the most important individual style complex of the twentieth century), but of course African-American dance music far predated jazz, going back to the earliest days of the black experience in the United States. Early reports make it clear that black Americans were using European instruments, as well as European tunes, by early in the nineteenth century. The most common black instruments of that century were fiddle and banjo, together with percussion of various sorts; it is an ironic symbol of U.S. music's complexity that one of the main nineteenth-century African-American instruments was African-derived and the other hailed from Europe—and that both became the archetypal instruments of roots twentieth-century white country music!

Henry A. Kmen's book *Music in New Orleans: The Formative Years* quotes various pieces of evidence as to what black musicians were playing in that city, mostly culled from court reports and newspaper accounts of police action. In one raid, three slaves were arrested and charged with playing the violin and dancing with white persons; banjos are mentioned in a report of another raid. A reporter gave details of a somewhat grander affair, which was broken up at 2:30 A.M. one Sunday:

> In one part of the room a cotillion was going on, and in a corner a fellow was giving a regular old Virginia "breakdown." . . . The music consisted of a clarinet, three fiddles, two tambourines, and a bass drum. The dances played were galopades, cotillions, and others heard

also at white balls. In the refreshment room an old man was playing "Jim Along Josey" on a banjo.

A later description, quoted by Gilbert Chase from Lafcadio Hearn's "Levee Life," gives a vivid account of a working-class dance of the late nineteenth century, which seems to have been in itself a short lesson on the re-Africanization of part-European music and dance:

> A well-dressed, neatly-built mulatto picked the banjo, and a somewhat lighter colored musician led the music with a fiddle, which he played remarkably well and with great spirit. A short, stout negress, illy dressed . . . played the bass viol, and that with no inexperienced hand. . . .
>
> Then the music changed to an old Virginia reel, and the dancing changing likewise, presented the most grotesque spectacle imaginable. The dancing became wild; men patted juba and shouted, the negro women danced with the most fantastic grace, their bodies describing almost incredible curves forward and backward; limbs intertwined rapidly in a wrestle with each other and with the music; the room presented a tide of swaying bodies and tossing arms, and flying hair. The white female dancers seemed heavy, cumbersome, ungainly by contrast with their dark companions; the spirit of the music was not upon them; they were abnormal to the life about them.
>
> Once more the music changed—to some popular Negro air, with the chorus—
>
> Don't get weary,
> I'm going home.
>
> The musicians began to sing; the dancers joined in; and the dance terminated with a roar of song, stamping of foot, "patting juba," shouting, laughing, reeling. Even the curious spectators involuntarily kept time with their feet; it was the very drunkenness of music, the intoxication of the dance.

This happened to be an urban dance, but it could have been a country dance up to at least the 1930s, and—with a change in instrumentation—could have taken place last week. Well into the twentieth century, and to some extent until today, fiddles were used with guitar, which took over from the banjo; mouth harp (harmonica); and various forms of home-made instrument such as kazoo (a version of an instrument widely found in Africa), washboard, washtub bass, and whatever else was available to play for country dances in the jook and skiffle bands.

The origins of this music lay partly in the cotillions. In the country, much of the dances were probably picked up from Scots and other white neighbors, though instrumentally most of the influence was from Africa. Nor was it a southern phenomenon alone. There is an account, quoted by Marshall and Jean Stearns in *Jazz Dance*, of a dancer in a mid-nineteenth-century tenement shared pretty much equally by free blacks and new Irish immigrants; this black dancer was quite probably the great Henry Lane (known as Juba), who lived there. This suggests quite strongly that a major element of juba dancing was an Africanization of the Irish jig, to percussion (or largely percussion) music.

Black musicians in fact began to acquire elements of European music very early. The documentation varies. An escaped-slave notice comments sourly that the escapee was a skilled musician and would no doubt soon be able to afford new clothes. A 1690s local legal suit talks of a slave fiddler playing for white dancers in Virginia. And by the 1820s, U.S. commentators were talking of African music (by which they presumably also meant neo-African music) as a thing of the past. This was certainly an oversimplification—one writer describes a musical bow that he saw in Grenada, Mississippi, in 1858. And as we have seen, formerly French Louisiana and New Orleans in particular was witnessing fairly large-scale neo-African music in the 1820s. (And as to what was done privately or—in the case of African-derived religious practice—secretly, there is no knowing.)

But while it remained closely interwoven with its Anglo-American hoedown cousin well into the twentieth century, African-American string-band music soon moved away from its origins in ways that have to do with the African sources of black musical concepts. The relationship between blues practices and practices common in such savanna areas of Africa as northern Nigeria, where fiddle-type instruments are used with plucked strings and percussion, holds equally true for black American country breakdown dance music, with its "alley" fiddle style, as much rhythmic as melodic, its loose and constantly changing rhythms, and its persistent repetition. An Arhoolie record of music by Blind James Campbell's Nashville Street Band contains very good examples of this feature in the fiddle playing by Beauford Clay. Clay's breakdown is particularly fine.

Specific Africanisms in this music are similar to those found in the blues: variation of tone on fiddle or mouth harp; and long, blending and swooping notes similar to the Islam-influenced styles of much of West Africa. In early forms, an absence of harmony in the European sense is also common. In black country dance music, as in the blues, a more African technique was employed. It still can be heard in the way in which Alec Stewart on guitar backs up Sonny Terry's harmonica in a number of his Washboard Band recordings, for example. Rather than going through a harmonically conceived structural pattern of chords, Stewart will shift his chord at the end of a verse, thus using chord change without harmonic intention, but as a lute pattern will change under an African vocal to produce the effect of slight change in an apparently repetitive overall form. The result is not as formally integrated as much African music but creates a progression based on similar musical concepts. Of course, this is not the only formal structure used in country breakdown and rags, and in fact European-based three-chord progressions are more common. But one-chord accompaniment and chord changes that do not correspond to melodic changes but supply a second layer of musical interest under them are characteristic of the style.

Some of the rhythmic complexity of West African music is also present in music of the jook and jug bands, in the especially African form of an interplay of rhythms from different instruments, no one of which is necessarily complex in itself. A role rather similar to that of the lead drum in rain-forest music is sometimes taken by the guitar or, especially, the banjo, whose melodic function is often little more than that of an African tension drum.

The basic musical procedure is the use of short, melorhythmic phrases to provide a pattern or series of patterns. Sometimes the American banjoist will stick to an ostinato role, like many African xylophone or lute parts; sometimes he will improvise more freely, like a lead drummer. Sometimes, of course, he will carry a melody in a fairly European style, but even then the melody is almost always bent in the direction of African-derived techniques and is usually selected in the first place for its amenability to such techniques (like the European hymns used as a basis for spirituals; see Chapter 5).* The jug bands, especially, often used the kazoo as a melorhythmic instrument, repeating rhythmic patterns whose overall contribution was quite African and akin to the riff technique of the later jazz bands.

Like their descendants, black country dance modes were informal, largely improvised, and "people's" rather than "specialists'" music. But at the end of the nineteenth century a style of black music that was quite the opposite developed: ragtime. Ragtime in its "classic" form was a composed piano music, written down and intended—as one of the great ragtime composers,

---

* Examples of most of these elements can be heard on tracks from the Blues Classic album *The Jug, Jook and Washboard Bands,* on the Rounder *Altamont* CD, and on the Yazoo CD devoted to Gus Cannon, a banjoist who began playing in the nineteenth century.

Scott Joplin, writer of "Maple Leaf Rag" and of many other famous tunes, insisted—to be played as written.

Some authors have described piano ragtime as the music in which African components were weakest and most etiolated, and others have treated it as a straight transfer of "African" plantation banjo patterns to the piano. Both characterizations are overstated. Ragtime in its original form was the work of musicians who were well aware of "European" musical features and used them, just as early black dancers danced, among other things, the cotillion. Most true rags have a form comprising several contrasting strains based on the march form which had been an influence in both Brazilian and Cuban music (see Chapters 3 and 4), and which was an important ingredient in jazz. In fact, many early rags were called marches, like Joplin's "Combination March."

It is no coincidence that ragtime developed in the Midwest, where, as Gunther Schuller points out in *Early Jazz*, march bands have always been popular. The formal structure of piano rags, therefore, was extremely European and quite un-African, which allied them indirectly with such nineteenth-century Caribbean manifestations as the *danzas* and other dances taken over from European models and "Africanized," first rhythmically and then by gradually dropping the formal divisions into different strains. Indeed, the same thing happened to ragtime as time went on.

But ragtime also had strong connections with other black music. In particular, the dance called the cakewalk, which began as a slaves' parody of white "society" ways, became an important part of minstrel music and was popular during the growth of ragtime—which, remember, was a product of parts of the United States where blacks and whites mingled, if not on equal terms, at least a great deal. Many minstrel tunes, including "Old Zip Coon" and "Old Dan Tucker," use a syncopated figure that became a standard cakewalk figure; it is the first part of a pattern we have met before:

The novelist Rupert Hughes, in 1899, made a connection between more popular dance styles and formal ragtime when he wrote in the Boston *Musical Record:* "Negroes call their clog dancing 'ragging' and the dance a 'rag,' a dance largely shuffling. . . . Banjo figuration is very noticeable in ragtime music and division of one of the beats into two short notes is traceable to the hand clapping."

There is even more to ragtime than this, however, even if one accepts the reductionist concept of "classic" piano ragtime by which most of what was originally called "ragtime" is cast into outer darkness. I have found increasing evidence that the Cuban danza habanera may be a direct influence on ragtime's odd parallels with Latin music. A decade before the first rag was published, New Orleans was full of habaneras introduced by a large Mexican military band, the star of the 1883–1884 Cotton Expo in New Orleans. St. Louis, a heartland of ragtime, was a regular stopping point for Mississippi sternwheelers out of New Orleans, at least one of which featured a Mexican octet for many years.

One of the most common types of right-hand pattern in piano ragtime was the same one we have met from Brazil, right through the Caribbean, and into the blues. Many rags, including those by Joplin, have substantial passages over which the ghost of the habanera seems to hover. Another classic rag with an apparent Latin influence is Henry Lodge's "Temptation Rag," whose popularity William J. Schafer and Johannes Riedel, in their *The Art of Ragtime*, specifically attribute to a "persistent habanera-like rhythmic pattern developed through distinctive themes." And New York African-American composers such as William H. Tyers, Ford Dabney, James Reese Europe, and James Timothy Brymn, as well as the great stride pianist Luckey Roberts, wrote many works with a habanera bass, some of them long before the tango became fashionable. The most striking is the original score of Tyers's 1908 jazz classic, "Panama," but by 1896, just before the first published rag, Tyers had written a piece called "La Trocha"—and the examples stretch on.

It is generally held that ragtime's right-hand syncopation, which uses rhythmic patterns basic to black music from virtually every part of the New World, came from the banjo rhythms of less sophisticated musicians (in the European sense, that is). This is certainly true of much of it, which does not fit the habanera's rhythmic pattern. But it seems probable to me that an overlooked Cuban influence (apparently mostly imported via Mexico, whose music was popular in the United States in the 1880s) was also an important strand, with a considerable African component, in ragtime and its descendant, Harlem stride piano. Just as some of Joplin's compositions carry heavy hints of the habanera, so do many of James P. Johnson's have a strong whiff of the tango, which was at its height in New York when he began playing there professionally. And the earthier guitar ragtime—which Paul Oliver considered a parallel development (and from which the pianists may even have borrowed)—also included a rhythm called the "Spanish flangdang," a misnomer for the Spanish fandango.

Cuban influence or not, the history of ragtime repeated a standard pattern in Afro-American music, the blending of African and European ingredients. Like so much else, it loosened up and became more subtle as it went along. From the beginning it supplied crossed rhythms, right hand against left. But even in the hands of fine players, early piano ragtime was a little stiff.

Moreover, the march-derived four-strain form, with its codified formal repetitions, seems to have militated against improvisation. Guy Waterman remarked in an essay in Martin Williams's *The Art of Jazz*, "In ragtime there are four equal themes; each is as important as the others. Such a structure is not suitable for improvisation. Which melody shall be used as the base-point?" As a result, one theme tended to dominate.

Scott Joplin insisted that his music be played as written, but the recent attempt to rewrite ragtime as a "classical" music (as if it needed this tag to be taken seriously) has confined research to a relatively limited (though admittedly wonderful) field, writing out of the canon anything that smelt of the popular. Ragtime became infinitely more subtle in rhythm as time went on. Jelly Roll Morton above all demonstrated this: Compare his recording of "Frog-i-More Rag" with the way it looks on paper, or his version of "Maple Leaf Rag" with Joplin's own rendition, which has been put onto a record from a piano roll. Even allowing for the inflexibility of pianolas, whose rolls are the only examples we have of Joplin's playing, Morton's and Joplin's versions are clearly products of a different attitude to music. This is no criticism of Joplin's interpretations, of course; but ragtime was not a wholly suitable vehicle for African-derived musical Afro-Americanisms.

Even in the hands of Joplin, however, ragtime was not as purely European as the externals might suggest. Besides the basic rhythmic element, another African feature was the construction of melody from short, repeated rhythmic phrases; or repetition with variations. Almost all rags by black composers show this characteristic, though it is to some degree disguised by the use of European-style chord changes. Even in band ragtime the formal elements limited the musicians considerably, as is evident in a delightful ragtime-style version of Joplin's "The Entertainer" by Bunk Johnson. Consequently, the early concept was soon modified. On one hand it was taken over by white America, where a simple version of ragtime held sway until a simple version of jazz took over from it. In its piano form, ragtime developed until it merged into piano forms of jazz. How this happened, both at the piano and orchestrally, was illustrated by Jelly Roll Morton in a recording for the Library of Congress.

Morton's style was firmly rooted in ragtime, as many of his compositions and solos in band recordings show. But he was also one of the last jazz pianists to take ragtime's use of contrasting sections seriously (just as, on recordings at least, King Oliver's Creole Jazz Band was the last small ensemble to do so with any consistency). Morton developed a left-hand technique that was freed from the oompah bass and, by using syncopation, held notes, and misplaced accents, created a much more complex polyrhythmic structure. Morton, then, was a bridge figure, a jazz pianist with strong ragtime links. His approach to freeing the left hand was based on a jazz element. As his biographer, Alan Lomax, has brought out, many of his bass lines stem from trombone techniques (Morton's father was a trombonist). Besides, the greatest ragtime composers were themselves aware of the limitations of the straight march beat. Joplin's later rags began to take on a more melodic cast and to seek more flexibility generally. Pianists like Morton were roaming the country and introducing new ideas, however, by the time "Rose Leaf Rag" appeared in 1907; so Joplin's new flexibility may have been a jazz influence rather than an internal ragtime development.

Sedalia, where Joplin worked, was perhaps ragtime's birthplace, but St. Louis itself was the center for piano ragtime. Other cities witnessed significant moments in the growth of "rag" bands, basically small outfits of the brass-band type that played ensemble versions of rags. These groups were widespread, and their existence was an important source of early jazz. New Orleans was important in ragtime, as well as in the growth of jazz proper, because it offered so many employment opportunities for small groups, and because ragtime pianists (not jazz groups, as legend had it) were in demand in the brothels of the red-light district, Storyville.

It is important to remember the existence of small brass-and-wind groups playing ragtime in many parts of the country. The postulate that jazz was born exclusively in New Orleans has recently come under powerful attacks, but much of what is now held up as early non–New Orleans jazz was probably in fact ragtime, an element in jazz, but not jazz itself, which is a music of many elements. Similarly, claims about northeastern jazz piano styles at the end of the nineteenth century seem to refer to late ragtime, in which even the initiators were loosening up their left-hand rhythms. Eubie Blake learned ragtime from one Jesse Pickett, who played at various times in Philadelphia and New York. And Pickett's *pièce de résistance* was a composition called "The Dream" that combined the preblues slow drag with a habanera bass (that old strain again!; Blake recorded "The Dream" a couple of times in what he said was Pickett's version).

By the time of World War I, two widely differing types of black piano-playing had grown up. One, with strong ragtime derivations, is represented by the "stride" piano of musicians like James P. Johnson, Luckey Roberts, Eubie Blake, and Willie "the Lion" Smith. This tended to be a northern style, and many of its practitioners had some formal musical training; for example, Johnson, born in New Brunswick, New Jersey, was taught piano by his mother.

Fats Waller was perhaps the most famous inheritor of the "stride piano" legacy. It developed into a complex of styles that embraced those of musicians as disparate as Earl Hines and Art Tatum. The rather vague term "jazz piano" probably covers as well as any other the varying styles of this type, which drew not only from ragtime but from blues, band jazz, and you name it, but were nonetheless products of a broadly similar attitude to the piano. Like ragtime, the Africa-sprung factors in jazz piano were not immediately obvious but were fundamental. The most striking were perhaps the constant crossing rhythms between the two hands and the tendency to build triplets against duple time, which I have suggested is a reinterpretation of West African polymetric techniques.

Piano blues was another matter. Various styles have been distinguished, but basically barrelhouse blues—whether used as a solo style or to back the pianist's own vocal—contained a high degree of Africanism in its general concepts. This is most clearly shown by boogie-woogie, a spinoff of barrelhouse blues whose basis is the repetition of short, rhythmic phrases by both hands that continually cross each other rhythmically. Boogie-woogie must surely represent the purest U.S. example of how various African strands in a culturally mixed music can come together to produce music that, though nonexistent in Africa, is non-African only in that it is played on a piano and usually makes a nod in the direction of three-chord harmonies. Incidentally, one interesting though speculative explanation of the name itself is that it stems from one or other African word for dance or movement. Whether or not that is valid, the word "jook" (as in "jook joint" and "jook box") has a fairly strong claim to Sahelian origins.

There used to be a theory that the growth of boogie-woogie was due to lack of pianistic skill on the part of self-taught musicians, who were compelled to keep their left hand in one position and to repeat the same figure constantly. This is a classic example of the absurdities that can be advanced in the attempt to avoid looking Africa in the eye. Aside from the fact that playing these ostinato basses is very far from easy, boogie-woogie is only one form of barrelhouse piano, and the other forms do not in fact use such "restricted" basses. Certainly barrelhouse pianists did not have a very wide range by Eurocentric standards, but Eurocentric standards are irrelevant here. They acquired the technique needed to do what they wanted to do.

Paul Oliver tentatively points out the remarkable similarities between barrelhouse piano and West African xylophone techniques, where short, rhythmic, contrasting patterns are set off against each other, patterns that use a restricted number of pitches and of which it would be meaningless to try to categorize as "melodic" or "rhythmic." In fact, the analogy with xylophone music, though it must surely be indirect, is extraordinarily close. Hugh Tracey has recorded a Congolese piece with a xylophone introduction that is exactly the same as a fairly common boogie left-hand figure! Though such coincidences are not central (and coincidences they remain), they do illustrate that the basic techniques of boogie are very close to specific African examples.

William Russell once suggested that the piano enabled Americans to approximate the patterns of the drum orchestra. Indeed, barrelhouse piano *is* percussive; so, for that matter, is all African instrumental music, and boogie-woogie's melodic range on the whole is nearer to that of the xylophones than the drums. True, the left hand could be seen as substituting for the underlying drum patterns and the right as in some way duplicating the master-drum role; but that would be too simplistic. The point about boogie-woogie is that for a brief spell it brought together a number of Africanisms, all of which had been present in the United States in more diffused forms, and thus produced an eerie doppelgänger of African music.

Barrelhouse piano as a whole, and boogie-woogie especially, use the short, ostinato rhythmic phrases; cross-rhythms; lack of melody in a European sense; repetition with gradual development; and, in the very heavy use of right-hand triplets, the three-on-two rhythms of African music in a startlingly pure form. A perfect example is Meade Lux Lewis's "Honky Tonk Train Blues"; in the second and third choruses, triplets and eight-to-the-bar patterns are breathtakingly crossed. "Six-Wheel Chaser," by the same pianist, has virtually no "melody" at all. Its interest lies, as J. H. Kwabena Nketia said of Ghanaian music, in the relationship of rhythmic patterns.

Boogie-woogie is a special case, though not so much of a freak as some writers have made out. In most barrelhouse piano, the right hand plays a part that approximates a missing vocal line. Barrelhouse also tends to a looser left hand, in which walking basses and other figures—in boogie repeated with a remorseless build-up of tension—are mingled with passing melodic phrases and generally varied in a way that strongly reflects certain styles of blues guitar accompaniment. Blues piano and one version of "country ragtime" met, incidentally, in a piano style sometimes called western rag, a rough and ready, heavily blues-tinged ragtime typified by Will Ezell's "West Coast Rag" and Dink Johnson's "Las Vegas Stomp." Barrelhouse piano and boogie-woogie, both strongly formulaic musics, nonetheless do not restrict the development of individual styles. From Lewis's powerhouse approach, through Pinetop Smith's delicate drive, to Jimmy Yancey's strongly tango-influenced lyricism, blues piano—like the blues as a whole—shows the value of a simple but fairly flexible framework for the improvising musician.

The African legacy is an essential part, whether "major" or "minor," of all styles produced by black Americans. But detailed analysis of Africanisms in some modes is made difficult by the fact that many individual features are the result of musical reinforcement by compatible elements in both European and African music. The situation as regards band jazz is especially complicated. For one thing, the word "jazz" covers many different periods and styles, from Freddy Keppard to Sun Ra. For another, jazz and Tin Pan Alley—not to mention commercial dance music—often shade into each other. Would Ella Fitzgerald be a jazz singer while performing "Singing in the Rain"? If Dinah Shore sang "Beale Street Blues," would she become a jazz or blues singer? What about Peggy Lee?

The first apparent stumbling block for those who hold jazz to be African is its almost universal two-four or four-four beat. Early jazz came from a number of sources, including march music, ragtime, and the blues, with perhaps lesser contributions from spirituals and other sources—and *all* of these have a seemingly solid duple-time rhythm. The only exception among the elements that went into jazz was the creole tinge inherited from New Orleans's past position as an honorary Caribbean outpost. Attempts have been made to rationalize the apparently entirely European content of the basic jazz beat by analogies with African drum corps, polyrhythms, polymeter, and so forth. But listening to a wide range of early jazz will show that the *rhythm section* of virtually all the early groups was far removed from the superimposed rhythms of different time-signatures characteristic of the only African music the jazz writers seem to be aware of: that of the drum-oriented rain forest area.

Phyl Garland, in *The Sound of Soul,* quotes the musician Noble Sissle as follows: "Who created this beat? The answer is, the American Negro, because none of the other immigrants brought it with them." Yet actually the basic *beat* of jazz, in the sense of the basic time, was indeed European in origin, stemming from march music, Protestant hymns, and a number of other minor sources. But this is not to say that the rhythm was European. What *did* stem from Africa, not necessarily linked with the drum-corps music of a restricted region, was an attitude to various musical elements shared in differing degrees by most of the African groups that came to the United States. This African-sprung attitude was crucial: without *either* the European-derived common-time beat, *or* the African-derived rhythmic approach that transformed it, jazz would not exist. This is hard to prove from purely internal evidence. If anybody chooses to doubt that jazz drum phrasing springs from an Africanization of European marching band drumming, nothing within jazz can convince him. It was particularly exciting for me to find corroboration in a non-U.S. music: the drumming that accompanies a black version of a medieval British mumming play preserved by Nevis immigrants in the Dominican Republic. The black drummers turned the medieval-*cum*-military British origins of their music into something full of jazz-style phrasing.

Often assumed to be African, the fife-and-drum playing of older Mississippi musicians like Other Turner and Napoleon Strickland is almost certainly derived in part from Revolution-era military playing. But the fife phrases have become more fragmented like many African equivalents, and the percussion "hotter."
Photo by Robin Hough

One of the fundamental facts about most jazz (with the exception of some of the 1960s–1970s free jazz and some of the more heavy-handed soul-jazz) is that it "swings." Anybody with a feel for jazz knows what this means, but to define it is a very different matter. Barry Ulanov, in his *History of Jazz in America,* quotes the attempts of a number of musicians to define the concept of swing. The results are enlightening in their lack of enlightenment. The three best definitions of swing were from Frankie Froeba, Louis Armstrong, and Ella Fitzgerald, in the following order:

"A steady tempo, causing lightness and relaxation and a feeling of floating."

"My idea of how a tune should go."

"Why, er—swing is—well, you sort of feel—uh—uh—I don't know—you just swing!"

Schuller—in a chapter of *Early Jazz,* one of the first books to attempt to draw the relationship between jazz and African music—suggests that jazz has two elements that do not normally occur in academic music. One is a certain sort of accentuation and inflection, and the other is the way in which notes are linked in what he ponderously calls a "forward-propelling directionality."

Jazz is commonly described as "syncopated," meaning that what would "normally" be weak beats are accentuated. But among the least swinging of bands are precisely those Dixieland groups whose drummer consistently wallops the second and fourth beats, a technique used by many bands of the 1920s and 1930s for a special effect, particularly to ride out a final chorus when nobody had any better ideas. It can be an exciting effect, but only when used sparingly. What jazz musicians in fact do with the basic two-four or four-four beat is much more subtle, and more in line with African practices: they play *around* it, anticipating it, laying back on it, or creating a sort of reverse syncopation from it by cutting across a rocking rhythm with a series of notes of exactly equal value.

Basically, the good jazz musician plays melorhythmic patterns that intermarry; to this extent there is a resemblance with the drum corps, but only insofar as the drum corps is a special application of a more general principle. The effect of syncopation is caused by the use in jazz of an African-descended technique in a context that contains European material—measured meter, bars, and so forth. A fine example of polyrhythmic play between a lead instrument and the rhythm section is Henry "Red" Allen's solo in "Stingaree Blues," with King Oliver.

Paul Oliver has pointed out that the drum groups of the Ewe or the Yoruba do not swing in the jazz sense, that their procedures are built upon quite different principles. But this is not the whole story. Though Yoruba drumming does not use syncopation, the total effect of the music is similar to certain types of jazz's rhythmic effects. Moreover, what is true of the Yoruba and Ewe is not true of all the musical styles that influenced Afro-America. There is much music of the Congo-Angola region, especially music for groups including drums and xylophones, that does, in fact, swing like crazy.

Many of the African elements found in the New World, including North America, are also present in jazz, either in a pure form or, more often, as modifying or modified by European elements. The highly sophisticated syncopation jazz musicians use is a workable compromise of the desire for crossed rhythms with the European monometric framework. Baby Dodds's work in the second and third choruses of "Ain't Misbehavin'" with Sidney Bechet, on the RCA Vintage series *Blue Bechet* album, is a direct example. Dodds cuts loose from the basic, easy swing of the four-four beat and produces a series of patterns, vaguely reminiscent of brass-band drumming, that produce effective cross-rhythms, as well as melorhythmic patterns analogous to the sort of drum tune used by African drummers. Examples of the way in which jazz musicians employ polyrhythms in what is ostensibly a monorhythmic context are legion. The music of Charlie Christian, the guitarist who influenced the bop musicians of the early 1940s, was full of what Al Avakian and Bob Prince have called "metric denials." Bop rhythm sections made a conscious effort to go back to a more polyrhythmic style after the swing period's solid four-four, epitomized by Count Basie's rock-firm four-to-the-bar.

Yet even the swing bands did not really abandon polyrhythmic approaches, though some of the larger black bands of the 1920s, in reaction against what they saw as the stereotypes of "hot" jazz, came near to doing so. Most good swing bands—and even more the small groups of the 1930s and 1940s drawn from the ranks of the big bands—used the steady four-to-the-bar rhythm section as a floor off which to bounce a complex of front-line cross-rhythms and conflicting accents. Not always, of course: from the start, jazz has been a music of many different movements, and at times certain individuals or groups would opt for an on-the-beat approach in order to explore some other aspect of their style. But these other aspects in their turn were likely to prove to contain the same subtle indices of African-derived attitudes to music-making. I have mentioned my belief that the consistent use of triplets over a basically duple beat to be a reinterpretation of the three-on-two metrical phenomenon of West African music. An example of a reinterpreted binary-tertiary consonance comes in Lionel Hampton's recording of "Short of Breath," in the band breaks and also in a break in the middle of the piano solo, which makes use of the theme usually called "Snag 'Em."

Much of the misapprehension about polyrhythmicality in jazz stems from a tendency to concentrate on the rhythm section rather than to consider the rhythmic interplay of the group as a whole, and from a tendency to forget that jazz musicians vary greatly in stature. For example, Ross Russell writes, in an article on bop:

> One must listen carefully to the best records of Armstrong or Roy Eldridge, of Bechet or [Coleman] Hawkins, to find rhythmic accents as rich as those in Dizzy Gillespie's line on "Congo Blues" or [Charlie] Parker's on "Koko." Baby Dodds and Jo Jones are two of the greatest drummers of jazz, but the patterns of Kenny Clarke and Max Roach are more complex, and swing as freely.

Quite true—but then, one would expect only the best musicians to measure up to the best musicians! An interesting point might be made about the drumming: certainly the role of New Orleans drummers seems to have been less

The jazz funerals of New Orleans are just the best known of an array of New World funerary musical traditions with strong African elements—in this case not so much the music as the ways in which it is used.

Photo by Steve Franz, courtesy of New Orleans Metropolitan Convention and Visitor's Bureau

subtle than that of more modern musicians, though there is a good deal of conflicting evidence on this point. But rhythm is not the exclusive prerogative of drummers, nor are polyrhythms. Besides, early jazz *was* early. It is significant that, as jazz musicians became more at ease in their music, they re-Africanized it.

Speaking of bop drummers, it is interesting that Kenny Clarke is on record as saying that his style owed nothing to African music (he meant directly), but that he felt he had ended up close to the African style. Naturally enough, given the strong African content in all black music, this is not too rare a phenomenon. It happened especially with boogie-woogie, when a concentration on certain African-sprung factors in Afro-American music "coincidentally" produced a highly African (or, more accurately, neo-African) effect. Of course, the results may be a long way from Africa even when the procedures are similar, as in the case of the pianist Cecil Taylor. In an interview with LeRoi Jones reprinted in *Black Music,* Archie Shepp said of Taylor, "Cecil plays the piano like a drum, he gets rhythms out of it like a drum, rhythm, and melody. . . . In a way it's more of a throwback rather than a projection into some weird future. A throwback in the direction of the African influences on the music." Apart from the customary obsession with the drum, and the fact that "throwbacks" have been happening all the time, this is a fairly good assessment.

One last point about rhythm, jazz, and Africanisms. Jazz, like virtually all Afro-American music, has been a dance music for much of its existence. Like most Afro-American music, the rapport among dancer, spectator, and band is similar to the African totality. Here is Malcolm X, on the Roseland Ballroom in Boston:

> "Showtime!" people would start hollering about the last hour of the dance. Then a couple of dozen really wild couples would stay on the floor, the girls changing to low white sneakers. The band now would be really blasting, and all the other dancers would form a clapping, shouting circle to watch that wild competition as it began, covering only a quarter or so of the ballroom floor.

What was true of Roseland was equally true of the Savoy Ballroom in the time of the lindy hoppers, of the Puerto Rican *bomba* dances, or of social dances anywhere in Africa or Afro-America.

Structurally, the most obvious link between jazz and African music— descended through the music of the nineteenth century and the blues—is the call-and-response technique, instrumentalized. This was at its most obvious in big-band music like Count Basie's, where it was a favorite arranger's trick to have an ensemble riff answer a couple of bars of solo, or the brass section answer the saxophone section, or any number of similar possibilities. Perhaps nobody made more subtle and continued use of it than Duke Ellington.

Instrumental call-and-response existed in a number of forms before the big-band era. Sometimes it was a repetition of a phrase, the obvious example being opening bars of "Basin Street Blues," where the first line is first played by a solo instrument and then repeated by the full band. Another version occurs in many renderings of "Memphis Blues" and in Clarence Williams's "Milk Cow Blues," in which the call is the first half of the melodic phrase (often taken by trombone), and the answer the second half, taken by the ensemble. Sometimes there are longish calls and answers, and sometimes very short, as when Victoria Spivey's "moans" in "Moaning the Blues" are answered by the band. The call-and-response effect between soloist and ensemble is too common to need more comment.

An important development of call-and-response, which we touched on while discussing gospel music in Chapter 5, is the riff (representing the response) over which is played a free solo. Basie's "John's Idea" is an excellent example, but the style was already common fifteen years earlier in the so-called stomp pattern. This was a very highly rhythmic and repetitive tune, longer than a riff—which is a phrase, whereas a stomp pattern is more like a line of melody—over which a solo was also often played. King Oliver's Creole Jazz Band made extensive use of this pattern, notably in "Canal Street Blues," under Johnny Dodds's clarinet solo. I consider this style an extension of call-and-response arising partly from the demands for greater liberty posed by an instrument with wide melodic possibilities and partly from the common over-lapping of call-and-response found in both Africa and Afro-America.

The call-and-response structure of the riff gave rise to another melodic form that was extremely, though rather indirectly, African. The riff alone, used repeatedly to build a tune (Charlie Christian was an adept at this), is quite like the technique of short-phrase tunes used in Africa. Another jazz phenomenon that may descend from call-and-response, in this case evolving into the form of a dialogue, is the "fours," in which two or more musicians will trade passages of four bars apiece to construct a single, logical solo line. It has been claimed that the alternation of solo and chorus in jazz is an Africanism. Such a claim, however, is part of the Africa-or-bust syndrome. If anything, African music uses this pattern less than most. Besides, to term a thirty-two-bar chorus a "call" seems extreme; this practice clearly derives from European verse-and-chorus style.

There is, however, another way in which the chorus pattern of jazz does reflect African practice, and this has been pointed out (as far as I know, for the first time) by Gunther Schuller. He reminds us that the series of "choruses" conceived of as variants within accepted limits of the preceding choruses is the basic structure of at least the music of the Ewe studied by A. M. Jones. Each of seven dances analyzed by Jones comprises a certain number of "master patterns." Within each pattern some variation may occur. But more important, each "master pattern" is conceived as a variant of the previous pattern. Allowing for syncretism with European forms, this is very much what happens in jazz structure: The chorus is not simply repeated, as in simple dance styles in Europe, nor is the form one of contrasting sections, as in more developed European music, especially dance music.

When European-style tunes are played, jazz tends progressively to drop all but what is perceived as the main chorus. This is not universally true: the older jazz forms stick to the march form when playing numbers that originated as marches. But for the most part the chorus as a series of master patterns repeated with variants dominates, unless a composer's hand is at work or the jazz is in such an archaic state that the European contributions in it have not been re-Africanized. The recourse to the West African master-pattern formula is, of course, reinforced by the fact that it makes improvisation easier.

The bands that were supposed to be miracles of collective improvisation working their way through complex contrasting sections—notably King Oliver's Creole Jazz Band—have been shown, on the contrary, to have rehearsed very tightly, at least for recording.

I have already looked at the question of the blues scale (see Chapter 5). Whatever its origin, "blue tonality" permeates jazz. So does something else, which would tend to support Paul Oliver's positing of a savanna-land basis for many of the Africanisms in U.S. music: the frequent bending of notes, reminiscent of Islamic African music, but occurring among coastal peoples (except under Islamic influence) mainly in the relatively simple form of rising to the first note of a phrase and falling from the last. The bending of notes is, as we have seen, of major importance in vocal blues, producing quarter-tones especially at the third, fifth, and seventh steps of the scale. It has continued throughout jazz history, principally as a carryover from the blues; it is present in jazz descended from ragtime and march music, but less frequent. It has been most common, of course, among singers. Billie Holiday used it with the greatest variety perhaps, not only in the blues but in popular songs as well. As sung by her, a note may (in the words of Glenn Coutter) begin "slightly under pitch, absolutely without vibrato, and gradually be forced up to dead center from where the vibrato shakes free, or it may trail off mournfully; or at final cadences, the note is a whole step above the written one and must be pressed slowly down to where it belongs." Coincidence or not, all these features are found in Islamic African music and hardly at all in other styles.

A most fundamental feature of jazz style is the use of a variety of tonal or timbral techniques instead of the "pure" tone of the European classical ideal. The use of a wide range of tonal qualities—sharp, smooth, and piercing—of varied vibratos, and of special effects like growls, shakes, and dirty notes of all sorts is a noticeable part of jazz, to which the use of mutes with brass instruments for special effects is related. Legend has it that the New Orleans trumpeter Mutt Carey was the originator of the varied muted style of which King Oliver made such use. Trumpet-muting reached an apogee with the growl trumpet of Ellington's trumpeters, Bubber Miley and his successors, and was never again employed to such an extent. But it was jazz that created the array of cup, wah-wah, and other mutes from which a brass player can now select. Gone are the days when the trumpeter's only choice was a sort of metal pear.

The special effects, the growls and spitting tones, were only a part, usually a small part, of a wider concept of instrumental tone that is much more common in jazz than in Africa. As Nketia points out, the use of tone *contrasts* in African musical instruments is unusual, though tonguing and trilling are sometimes featured. More to the point is the type of tone chosen. African musicians in most areas have a great liking for burred or buzzing tones. There is no doubt at all that this is a matter of choice, not accident. In the Folkways record *Africa South of the Sahara*, there is a recording of a Hororo flute player using a burred tone, who very firmly said that this tone was "to my will." I have cited plenty of other examples from various African styles (see Chapter 1).

The fondness for a burred tone is equally present in jazz, though as a music of mixed origins jazz takes the opportunity to use it in contrast with "purer" tone. Here, too, the possibility that accident or incompetence has contributed can be ruled out. For one thing, a reasonably smooth tone is not difficult to acquire when learning a wind instrument, easier in fact than a growl. For another, examples abound of burred or rough tones used by musicians of the very highest skill, as well as the stylists of an earlier generation who sometimes come under attack from Eurocentric critics. Ben Webster, for instance, was unquestionably one of the five or six greatest tenor saxophone players. In "Jive at Six," he uses a heavily burred but not blurred tone; in fact, it has a sharp edge.

Sandy Williams, a fine trombonist of 1930s small-band swing vintage, specialized in a tone so hoarse that one note could identify him. Ellington, a composer of recognized genius, for many years incorporated growl techniques in his greatest works, and not simply because of Miley's specialty. Jabbo Smith sat in for Miley on one take of "Black and Tan Fantasy," and the main concern when Cootie Williams took over Miley's chair was whether he would be able to learn the growling plunger-mute techniques (he was).

Less outstanding examples of varied tonal quality can be cited by the hundred. However, like the contrasts, they are merely manifestations of a fundamental principle: the styles of playing instruments in jazz are based on the human voice, and an instrumental solo bears a singularly close relationship not only to song but even to speech. I have looked at the extremely intimate relationship of speech, song, and instrumental music in Africa (see Chapter 1). Some of the rationale behind it has been lost in the United States, but it remains operative in remarkable detail at times. Most African languages are tonal; that is, the pitch of a syllable can determine its meaning, so that a spoken sentence in some languages is sung on two, three, or four notes. Actually, there is no single middle note from which the ups go up and the downs down; different languages tend to have different overall sentence shapes (like a rising or falling melody), and the ups and downs are relative to those varying tone centers.

One of the most striking things about jazz instrumentalists of whatever style is their highly individual "tones of voice." I once had a Nigerian friend who, unlike most Africans, really knew jazz, historically and stylistically. He

Louis Armstrong and his Hot Five, 1926: As jazz developed, its African-derived elements became stronger, not so much overtly as in attitudes and techniques permeating an apparently European-based music. At the time of the Hot Five, the re-Africanization process was audible but it was to go a lot further. Meanwhile this music remained one of the pinnacles of African-American achievement regardless of the mix of ingredients.

Photo by Don Hunstein, Columbia Records

possessed the most remarkable gift for recognizing musicians after a few bars—not just soloists, but the bassist on some obscure and ill-recorded old disc. I asked him how he managed it. "Well," he answered, surprised, "you can recognize your friends' voices, can't you?" The components of a jazzman's instrumental tone of voice may vary, but it is always highly expressive and highly personal. Louis Armstrong, in his heyday, played the trumpet just as he sang, uncannily so. Other musicians simply let instruments talk for them. Listen to the incredibly varied voices of Bechet, Charlie Parker, and Lester Young, and individual performances like Rex Stewart's solo in "Finesse," or the bluffness of Jim Robinson's trombone. Every time a movement in jazz turns away from the instrument as human voice, there is a turn back again. Leon Thomas said in the early 1970s what Jelly Roll Morton had said another way forty years before: "The most proficient horns are those which do not play the regular phrases and come close to the human voice and screeching and crying and shouting." Morton was not a man for screeching and crying and shouting, but Thomas is saying what every black Christian touched by the spirit, every good blues singer, has always known and proved. And my mention of Christianity is not random. Marshall Stearns tells how Gillespie explained vibes player Milt Jackson's sense of rhythm (a vital element in powerful song and speech): "Why, man, he's sanctified!" All in all, the examples of "dirty" or "human" tone are so omnipresent in jazz, from King Oliver to the screams of free jazz saxophonists and beyond.

It is significant, by the way, that the role of the individual in jazz has been of such overriding importance. Virtually all the major changes in jazz have been associated with a few individuals (though clearly they could not have wrought the changes single-handedly): Buddy Bolden, who appears to have provided a bridge between band marches and ragtime to band jazz; Morton, in somewhat the same position; Armstrong, who introduced the era of jazz as a music for soloists; Hawkins and Young, who helped turn jazz from a trumpeter's to a saxophonist's music; Parker and Gillespie; Ornette Coleman and Taylor; and perhaps Archie Shepp.

If the African musician is, as is said, usually a communal craftsman; if the idea of the "personality" has come to Africa only recently, under European impact; and if the intense individuality of jazz speaking/singing/playing tone is not European—where does it come from? I think the answer is both simple and unprovable. African musicians spoke as secure members of a secure society. Black American musicians speak for a people whose major group experience has been a denial not so much of humanity as of individuality. For all their presence at the heart of the American experience, for all the plausibility of Albert Murray's claim that black Americans are *the* Americans (or, as he persuasively calls them, the Omni-Americans), black Americans have constantly suffered the indignity of being "they." Are the jazzmen not, each in his individual tone, saying "I am I!"? Certainly, just as black America is not Africa, black American music is not going to resemble black African music at every dot of a quarter-note. And the individuality of tone of voice does stem naturally from what *is* an Africanism, the speech/song/instrument continuum.

The same can be said of improvisation, another major element of jazz. There are differences between the contexts in which improvisation occurs in the United States and in Africa. African musical groups do not go in for "collective improvisation." They employ differing mixtures of improvisation within defined limits—usually, in the rain forest region, specific drum patterns over which the master drummer improvises more freely but also with limitations. And what happens in jazz, or, at any event, what did happen until the advent of Ornette Coleman and his followers? Exactly the same improvisation within limits: of a melody, chorus pattern, or chord progression.

In King Oliver's "Canal Street Blues," for instance, all the instruments but the clarinet are either playing head-arranged or written parts during Dodds's solo or improvising within the strict limits of a quite intricate stomp tune. This is precisely what happens not only in the drum corps but also in much other African instrumental music. And besides, when improvisation *was* collective, each instrument had a clear function within the whole. Incidentally, it is sometimes pointed out that improvisation is also found in Europe. But even so, this can only refute an argument that improvisation in jazz was *solely* African-descended. If there is (much restricted) improvisation in Europe, its existence no doubt acted as a reinforcement to the improvisatory techniques in jazz, which plainly spring indirectly both from African patterns of improvisation and from other African-derived practices that have helped to define the terms in which improvisation is expressed.

Harmony in jazz is undoubtedly a strongly European influence. Harmony, in fact, is a European concept. But the European harmony in jazz has always been crossed with African attitudes. In *Early Jazz,* Schuller puts the problem of jazz and European harmony neatly:

> It would . . . be easy to conclude, as most studies of jazz have, that the harmony of jazz derives exclusively from European practices. In one basic sense, this is true, but this conclusion seems to be another one of those over-simplifications in which historians indulge so readily when documentation is scanty. For in another sense . . . the *particular* harmonic choices Negroes made, once they adopted the European harmonic frame of reference, were dictated entirely by their African musical heritage.

This is perhaps putting it a bit too strongly. It might be safer to say that *many* of the harmonic choices in jazz, and also many of the occasions on which jazzmen saw no necessity of a choice, were dictated by musical attitudes that originated in Africa. Clearly, on many other occasions, jazz musicians elected to make use of European harmony, or at least to accord an un-African attention to harmonic implications. The bop era is a case in point. But there are certainly parallels between jazz and African music here, too.

The interweaving roles of the front-line instruments in New Orleans jazz was like much Western Bantu heterophonic singing. One could argue that it was also like the polyphony of pre-Baroque European music, but it would be tough to trace a connection; Monteverdi and his contemporaries were not performed at concerts in turn-of-the-century New Orleans, and Western European popular music had forgotten their polyphonic techniques. An example of

New Orleans' polyphony is Bunk Johnson's recording of "Alexander's Ragtime Band," a fine record by a group first over- and later underrated. Even more interesting are recordings made by Frederic Ramsey of brass bands in the Southern countryside, issued on Folkways.

Listening to these recordings is an almost hallucinatory experience, because the approach of the accompanying instruments, indeed the overall sound, is like nothing so much as the groups of trumpets and shawms found in many parts of West Africa—in Islamic Hausaland, but also among the forest Bantu peoples—in which horns, each producing one or two notes, are played together to make a wind-instrument music that is more rhythmic than melodic. The Haitian *vaccines* work on the same principle; in view of Haiti's intensely African culture, this should not be surprising (see Chapter 4). But to hear the Lapsey Band's euphonium playing a repeated phrase of two blaring notes extraordinarily like the Hausa *kakaki* notes is staggering. Such a close parallel is no coincidence. And if it exists in brass-and-drum ensembles— albeit reinterpreted, and with a wide African catchment area—one must wonder what other discoveries are still to be made. The Lapsey band represents a very early stage. But even in much later jazz, European notions of harmony have often been ignored. Schuller analyzes a riff pattern that is in full agreement with the underlying chords in only two out of six bars, which he finds in a "developed" form of jazz that had been heavily affected by white show-business music!

Incidentally, the idea that making an "arrangement" is a "decidedly 'white' influence," as Schuller put it, on jazz is inaccurate as far as African music is concerned. African music is organized, and usually the roles of the participants are mapped out beforehand by an "arranger"—in the case of the Ewe music on which Schuller leans so heavily, the master drummer usually. Indeed, some African groups compose major orchestral forms. The Chopi of Mozambique play xylophone and choral dance symphonies (if I may use the expression) that comprise several contrasting and linked movements. The same is true of the Ewe themselves, as attested by the very quotations from A. M. Jones used by Schuller when he is discussing form. If this is not "arrangement," what is?

Jazz, then, is rich in African elements, which have fused with its European content to produce a new and major music. Craig McGregor with justice has called it "the black man's classical music." Kmen amply documents the European end of the events that turned New Orleans into a catalyst, combining into one rich style the ragtime, jazzlike marches, and blues that were being played elsewhere. March music was an important ingredient in the blend. Just before the birth of jazz, as many as a dozen black brass bands took part in the funeral procession for President Garfield in 1881. Even before that, residents complained that bands were "going about the city early on Sunday mornings, squeaking and rattle-te-banging away . . . and waking everybody." New Orleans became brass-crazy in the 1830s, when rival theaters presented famous virtuosos of the trumpet and trombone running concurrently in an attempt to outdraw each other: The trumpeters were Alessandro Gambati and John T. Norton, who had already engaged in contests in New York; the trombonist was Felippe Cioffi, and a famous clarinetist, James Kendall, was also featured.

New Orleans also was accustomed early to the notion of bands that could serve as both march and dance groups, as was common in the early jazz days. In 1840, the Neptune Band advertised that it was available for quadrilles and also as a military band, if required. So, whatever the merits of the dispute over New Orleans's claim to be the founder-city of jazz—which depends largely on how one defines ragtime, brass-band music, and jazz—it certainly had a very rich mix ready to pour into the new black music at the turn of the century. Adding to it, New Orleans at times had as many as three opera houses going at once before the Civil War, and this in a town with a population of 60,000, of whom only 25,000 were white. The blacks, including slaves, formed an essential part of the public of these opera houses.

Nor were black brass bands restricted to New Orleans. Peter Van der Merwe's *Origins of the Popular Style* mentions that African-Americans were members of military bands by the mid-eighteenth century (often, though by no means always, drummers), and comments that by the 1830s the all-black band was a familiar feature of the northern cities. These bands seem to have sprung into existence wherever there were cities or large towns with a fair-sized population of free blacks, whether in the North, the upper South, or New Orleans.

Remember that jazz was never a music entirely by or for blacks, despite black musicians' overwhelming dominance both in sheer numbers and as leaders in most jazz developments. Nor were white musicians always mere imitators. Some were innovators, as LeRoi Jones said of Bix Beiderbecke. Some relatively minor white figures influenced important black musicians: Frankie Trumbauer influenced Coleman Hawkins, and for a while Harlem saxophone styling took on features of Guy Lombardo's saxophone section. From Beiderbecke to soul guitarist/composer Steve Cropper, virtually all forms of black music except gospel music have been shared by whites, though not usually as leaders, and most commonly as junior partners.

After each period of emphasis on the "European" technical elements absent from early jazz, there has been a wave of movement away from

European factors; there has not usually been a conscious attempt to be more "African," though since the 1950s that has sometimes been part of it. An example of a procedure exactly the same as West Africa drummers employed was the way in which, in the 1930s, Tatum used to anticipate chord changes by switching just before the rhythm section, a trick Coleman Hawkins copied in, for example, the Mound City Blues Blower recordings of "Hello Lola" and "What Is This Thing Called Love." Why did it happen? Not because jazz musicians knew what Ghanaian drummers were up to: writing about it in a 1966 *DownBeat*, trumpeter Rex Stewart called it "then new."

The bop movement and even more the cool jazz period that followed it were on the whole examples of Europeanization. Though such Africanisms as personal instrumental tone and the vocalization of instrumental technique persisted, both involved a greater focus on harmonic concepts, both (particularly cool jazz) involved musicians who had been studying in the highly Eurocentric world of the conservatories, and both tended to adopt the notion of music as self-expression, which is not only European but was introduced to Europe less than 200 years ago. The 1950s saw even more Eurocentric tendencies, thanks to the large number of musicians who studied music at university or conservatory (thanks in good part to the G.I. Bill). Contrary to jazz mythology, this did not only involve a bunch of supposedly pantywaist white Californians.

The reaction came pretty quickly, with the tougher, more rhythmically oriented hard bop and soul–jazz, and with Miles Davis's and John Coltrane's experiments in abandoning harmonic changes and improvisation on the scale. The use of very African circular ostinatos in much of pianist McCoy Tyner's work with Coltrane may have derived most directly from Latin piano, but it's still an Africanism at however many removes. This, rather than the abandonment of the song, as Garland claimed, "opened up the music, enabling it to move in all directions." In fact Coltrane, like Sonny Rollins, had an ear for a good melody in odd places (such as his reinterpretation of a couple of show tunes, most notably "My Favorite Things") that has at times embarrassed his more solemn admirers.

Still, always there has been a clear continuity in jazz. Coltrane himself worked with boppers Eddie "Cleanhead" Vinson, Gillespie, Earl Bostic, and Johnny Hodges. Similarly there was a clear line of development among trumpeters from King Oliver to Armstrong, then to Eldridge, and finally to Gillespie. Shepp's father was a banjoist in a small group, and Shepp himself played in blues bands. Even musical anecdotes have a sort of continuity. Once, when Coltrane announced a number, one of his musicians said, "Man, I've never heard *that* before." Coltrane answered: "Well, you'll be hearing it now."

What with its tuxedos and its mellow chamber-music quality, the Modern Jazz Quartet's playing was a long way from the popular dance music that was jazz until the 1940s, but the
Africanism central to the black American heritage can be distinguished even here—not least in
the fact that Milt Jackson is playing a vibraphone, a descendant of the African marimba!
Photo courtesy of Columbia Records

In the 1920s the pianist Lil Armstrong auditioned with King Oliver. "Hit it,"
they said. "What key?" "Never mind about keys," they said, "just hit it."
Jazzmen's procedures—and perhaps their sense of humor—have stayed
pretty constant.

One thing has changed. Jazz for the first forty or fifty years of its life was a
people's music and a dance music. Now, in McGregor's words, it has become a
"classical" music. The change is reflected in the attitude of many musicians.
Davis put it bluntly in a 1970 *Newsweek* interview: "We don't play to be seen.
I'm addicted to music, not audiences." According to Alice Coltrane, John
Coltrane felt much the same: "One point he made above all others, and that
was 'Don't ever play *down* to anyone. Play just what you feel yourself.' He did-
n't believe in playing what people might want to hear."

Whether as a cause or as an effect, one important factor in the progress of
jazz from a black popular to an avant-garde music was the increasing exposure
of jazz musicians in the last twenty years or so to European conservatory
music. To take only one example, Coltrane himself studied at Granoff Studios
and the Ornstein School of Music, besides serving a more traditional appren-
ticeship in the bands led by Gillespie, Vinson, and Hodges. Attacking the

absurd tendency of journalists to write of the younger jazz musicians as "unlettered geniuses" (he was thinking particularly of Coleman), Fred Kofsky wrote in *Jazz and Pop* for November 1970: "By 1960 . . . the typical young black jazz musician was likely to be at the very minimum a high school graduate with extensive private musical study; many, like the iconoclastic pianist Cecil Taylor, had conservatory training or the equivalent."

The new attitude to jazz on the part of some of its players has undoubtedly been influenced by contact with the solemnity of too many "classical" musicians. Not that this attitude is altogether new, nor is it entirely conservatory-spawned. According to the jazz critic Barry Ulanov, Tatum once stood up and asked a buzzing audience, "Do I have to perform a major operation in here to get quiet?" An objection to general babble is understandable; a disdain for dancers is a different matter. It has recently been said that the supposed resistance of musicians to playing for dancing seems to have been overstated; the growth of the jazz buff, the cabaret tax, and the higher return to be made by putting tables on a former dance floor seem to have had more to do with it. And certainly many musicians were highly flexible. Trumpeter Leonard Goines has told me of playing a free-jazz gig one night, a black dance with rhythm and blues elements the next, and a Latin gig the third. But to the extent that any jazzman resented dancers he was abandoning an enduring (and to my mind creatively important) Africanism in jazz: the interaction between musician and dancer.

This attitude contributed as much as anything else to the split in the 1940s between blues and jazz bands. Louis Jordan, for instance, said of the bebop musicians, "those guys . . . really wanted to play mostly for themselves, and I still wanted to play for the people. I just like to sing my blues and swing." And many fine but ebullient and dance-oriented saxophonists found themselves written out of the jazz canon. Some of them—like Illinois Jacquet—have quite recently been rehabilitated. Others, like Bostic, were relegated to rhythm and blues to its great benefit. And yet the number of "progressive" jazz players with one foot in rhythm and blues, from Coleman back and forward, is considerable.

To the extent that jazz, like many a major idiom before it, become an "art" music rather than a "people" music, it has left behind the greatest Africanism of all; because African music, with few exceptions, is a "people" as well as gods' music. This is not to deny the existence of courtly music in Africa that has claim to be called "classical." Nor is it to make value judgments. There is not merely room for both but a desperate need for both. Avant-garde musicians of the 1960s used to claim that "the people" would like their music if it weren't kept from them by ill-defined but malevolent forces. But the evidence is all the other way. The popular musical heroes, the folk mythmakers, have not been in the jazz world for at least a generation. They are in the world of blues and soul, of funk and rap—in the world that tells a story people relate to or that moves their feet, not that expresses a musician's sacred (or maybe at times quite superficial) self. They are the descendants of Louis Jordan, not of Charlie Parker.

In a popular culture with so much left that is African, the reason may well be partly functional: jazz is no longer a dance music, and dance music is central to African culture everywhere. This fact was recognized, consciously or unconsciously, by the musicians involved in the jazz-funk wave of the 1970s, a parallel to the 1950s soul-jazz. The fact that, by 1971 many musicians were tiring of the evident failure of most free-form jazz to communicate or even to express anything that struck the man in the street as relevant to him, was clearly expressed in the title number of Freddie Hubbard's album *Backlash*, which went back to a soul beat and feeling. And whatever the excesses of the Latinate jazz-funk period, it produced a handful of instrumental hits, gaining a popularity for jazz that it had not achieved since bossa-jazz came on the scene a decade before. (Late '70s jazz-funk is a part of jazz history—along with the extraordinary flowering of both Cuban- and Brazilian-based Latin jazz that has taken over from it and become such an accepted part of the 1990s jazz—that I will explore in Chapter 7.)

The most significant developments in "straight" or non-Latin jazz in the '80s and '90s have relatively little to do with the subject of this book. One is the re-assertion of the "straight 4/4" or shuffle bass that was an endangered species twenty years ago. Another is the remarkable and to many depressing rise of a tradition-conscious generation of young jazzman. And the third is the steady removal of jazz from entertainment and the music business to education and the music establishment of which the steady proliferation of college courses and the Jazz at Lincoln Center program are emblematic.

The reassertion of "straight 4/4" is, I think, due to the discovery that the rich rhythms and percussion sections of Latin music can act as something of a straitjacket to the soloists. The second is to my mind simply another perfectly healthy example of the flux and reflux, the exploration and consolidation that have always succeeded each other in the history of popular and indeed all music. As to the third, if those who feel it is the death knell of straight jazz as a lively art form prove to be right, at least they can take comfort from the liveliness and relative ungovernability of the jazz fusions (see Chapter 7).

Fusions

Jazz, Latin America, and Africa

From its earliest days, the Afro-American music of some parts of the United States has had connections with the very different styles of the Caribbean. I have shown how Louisiana, which at various times was under Spanish and (much more significantly) French rule, was musically closer to the French islands to the south than to the rest of the U.S. mainland (see Chapter 5). Not only were New Orleans creole songs sung in French *patois*, but their tune-types and their rhythms were Caribbean. These Caribbean qualities spread out, though much reduced in degree, into other parts of the South. The juba, the neo-African dance popular in Haiti, Martinique, Guadeloupe, and other French-influenced islands, was found not only in New Orleans but also in Georgia and the Carolinas.

Creole music became part of the heritage of New Orleans and passed as one element into jazz, to which the creole musicians, especially the clarinetists, brought a French touch. The "creole tone," inherited from French reed technique, instantly distinguished clarinetists like Albert Nicholas, Sidney Bechet, or Alphonse Picou from the much bluer and more African-derived sound of black New Orleans musicians. Creoles like Nicholas, Picou, Paul Barbarin, Danny Barker (also of the Barbarin family), Ferdinand "Jelly Roll" Morton, and Kid Ory brought to jazz a degree of "legitimate" musicianship, which allowed it to broaden its base without swamping the more earthy elements. There were also a few creole songs in the jazz repertoire; the most famous, perhaps, is "Eh Là Bas," which Ory made popular during the New Orleans revival of the 1940s. Something of the Caribbean-creole touch remained in these tunes, but not as a major ingredient. A band would rather uneasily play one chorus with a "Caribbean" creole beat and then launch with relief into four-four. What might have happened if the creole songs had been present in New Orleans jazz in larger numbers and if the rhythm had been preserved can be heard on a recording of "Eh Là Bas" in which the creole beat is maintained throughout, and in which Barker plays a fine and very "West Indian" banjo solo.

The issue of an indigenous New Orleans creole (that is, Afro-French) tradition is complicated by two fairly substantial influences that jazz historians have pretty well entirely ignored. One, the Cuban/Mexican strain and the presence of many Latin musicians in New Orleans in the crucial years of jazz, I've already discussed (see Chapter 6). The other is an equally neglected possibility: a substantial Haitian strain, which of course would considerably muddy the waters, being itself Afro-French. I have only ever seen this discussed in one place: In an article in the journal *Popular Music,* Thomas Fiehrer points out that in 1809–1810, New Orleans took in 10,000 Haitian refugees deported from Cuba, where they had first taken refuge, and who were about equally divided between black (slave and free), white, and mulatto. Among other less relevant examples, Jelly Roll Morton, despite his claims of pure French ancestry, was of 100 percent Haitian ancestry, according to Fiehrer.

Whether indigenous or Haitian, the Afro-French element in New Orleans jazz—some classic compositions of the early period aside—acted largely as a facilitator for a larger Latin-Caribbean influence. The habanera rhythm, the tango, the rumba, and various other Afro-Spanish rhythmic devices seem never to have ceased interacting with jazz: sometimes as a major element; sometimes as part of a more general musical background, as when in the 1930s swing musicians played rumbas and tangos as part of regular gigs at dance halls like Harlem's Savoy Ballroom; sometimes simply taken over or adapted from "Latin" music; and sometimes developed separately. In the 1930s, the boogie-woogie pianist Jimmy Yancey often used versions of the same figure in his left hand, especially on slow numbers like "Five O'Clock Blues." Writers on jazz have referred to this as a habanera rhythm. Given that Yancey was a vaudeville dancer as a child, and that he retired from the stage at the time the tango craze was at its peak, it seems more likely that this was a direct influence from popular music rather than some esoteric pass-along that affected this one man.

The relationship of jazz to popular music in general and the recurring enthusiasms for Latin dance rhythms in particular is an odd one. Early-jazz and ragtime buffs have tended to talk as if their beloved music were some entirely separate entity. Many jazz writers used to go to great lengths to make a distinction between "folk" (good) and "popular" (bad) material. What they called "folk" was usually simply popular music of which they did not know the history. There is a story (apocryphal or not) about William Russell's horror when, having resurrected the early jazz trumpeter Bunk Johnson, Johnson's first choice to record was "The Yellow Rose of Texas" (then in the Top Ten). Whether it was a local hit like "Pretty Baby" or some newfangled blues, early jazz was trendy, up to the minute, and musically aware.

That being so, it isn't surprising that jazz was strongly influenced by Latin music. What is odd (particularly given the Latin elements in the prejazz era), is how long it took—or appeared to take. True, Jelly Roll Morton, the most famous exponent of a Latin streak in early jazz, went so far as to claim that a "Spanish tinge" was an essential ingredient in jazz music (remember that "Spanish" was and is still frequently used to mean "Latin"). Over a period of some fifteen years, Morton composed several pieces using a habanera bass including "New Orleans Blues," "Mama Nita," and "The Crave," besides using a habanera section in one of his best known works, "Jelly Roll Blues."

But despite the creole element in jazz and the direct influence of habanera in the prejazz period, the Spanish tinge in its various forms seems mostly to have resulted from the fact that during most of the history of jazz the United States has gone through one Latin dance vogue or another. Because, in reality, there are hints that the connections were closer than has until recently been admitted. Early African-American composers in New York—notably William H. Tyers—wrote habanera-based numbers as early as the 1890s (the forgotten "La Trocha" and the bizarrely named "Maori," which was around long enough for Duke Ellington to record it in the 1930s), and Tyers' habanera "Panama," in a de-Latinized form, became something of an early jazz classic. The 1902 show tune "Under the Bamboo Tree" (which originally had a habaneralike bass) became enough of a New Orleans hit that veteran trombonist Kid Ory recorded it in the 1940s. True, later jazz groups ironed out the Latin bass line, but the Cuban-influenced patterns of the melodies remained. W. C. Handy's "Memphis Blues" from 1912, just before the tango hit, had a section that he called "tangana" but was essentially a habanera. Similarly, his "St. Louis Blues" (which dates from the tango craze) famously opens with a brief tango section. And "Egyptian Fantasy," the long-forgotten 1915 theme tune of the Original Creole Jazz Band, did much the same thing.

To comb the jazz books, you would think that Jelly Roll Morton and Jimmy Yancey were it for Latin rhythms in jazz until the Afro-Cuban era of the 1950s; if this were true it would not amount to much. In fact jazz musicians, African-American popular composers, and Latin music existed cheek by jowl at least from the first tango craze of 1913 and 1914 onward. Harlem was as tango-crazy then as midtown, and offers of tango lessons, tango teas, and tango competitions were rife. According to Jervis Anderson in *This Was Harlem,* middle-class African-Americans danced the tango to ragtime music. Moreover, the music at Harlem tango teas was not confined to the standard downtown compositions. According to Jervis it included titles like "I'm Crazy About My Tango Man," "That's Why I'm Loving Someone Else Today," "Back to the Carolina I Love," and "Every Girl Is My Girl." (Note: these were tango teas, not some more general junket with a tango or two thrown in.) If jazz musicians—who at the time were *dance* musicians, even if of a special sort—went though the teens and '20s oblivious to the tango, they were clearly operating in some alternative universe.

Jazz, in fact, did not just share a universe with the tango: from the early 1920s, a number of Latin musicians performed in major jazz bands. Ellington trombonist Juan Tizol is mentioned as if he was some unique species, but in fact many of the bigger and more polished African-American bands used Puerto Rican musicians, mostly recruited from James Reese Europe's big World War I military band, around half of whose members seem to have been Puerto Rican. (The reason was simple: almost no African-American musicians hornplayers at the time had a high degree of formal skill—sight-reading ability and so forth.) And what is regarded as the first jazz flute solo, on Clarence Williams's 1928 "Have You Ever Felt That Way?," was played by Cuban flutist Alberto Socarras.

What was true of the tango was also true of the rumba, which hit the United States around 1930; like the tango, Paris and London were both onto it before New York. True, jazz was a little slow on the uptake. While a version of "The Peanut Vendor" by Cuban bandleader Don Azpiazu was a huge national hit (and led to the sale of various Cuban percussion instruments in the United States for the first time), it apparently took jazz musicians—with the one exception of a 1931 Ellington recording—fifteen years to catch up. But a passing remark by white trumpeter Wild Bill Davison in W. Royal Stokes's *The Jazz Scene* mentions that the classier nightclubs had a band for dancing, a band for the show, and a Latin band for rumbas and tangos; something similar was true in the black clubs and dance halls. Harlem was certainly exposed to the rumba; in July 1931 a show at the Lafayette Vaudeville Theater called "Rhumba-land" starred Antonio Machin (lead singer on Azpiazu's "Peanut Vendor") along with vaudeville blues singer Mamie Smith and drummer Kaiser Marshall. A little later an *Amsterdam News* columnist referred to rumba dancers at the Savoy Ballroom, where the Lindy was created; in Chicago, Margo Webb and Harold Norton, a well-known black cabaret dance duo of the era with both tangos and rumbas in their repertoire, were backed for years by the band of the great jazz pianist Earl Hines.

It should not be necessary to labor the point, but Latin music and jazz existed side by side throughout most of jazz's history, and it strains credulity to maintain that there was no mutual interaction even before jazz musicians began recording Latin-influenced numbers. This in fact happened surprisingly late, whether because jazzmen wanted it that way or because of the notions of the recording companies. Benny Moten's band recorded a "Rumba Negro" partly composed by Count Basie in 1929, and in the mid-1930s Spencer Williams recorded a number called "Runenae Papa" that was borrowed from the chorus of an Azpiazu piece. But it was in the late 1930s that what one might call proto–Latin-jazz numbers became more common in the repertoires of both black and white jazz groups. In 1939 Artie Shaw recorded the Mexican ballad "Frenesi" and a neo-*maxixe*, "Carioca" (only six years after the pop dance groups had picked it up from the movie *Flying Down to Rio*!) The following year Dizzy Gillespie wrote for Cab Calloway a piece called "Pickin' the Cabbage" whose bass rhythm foreshadowed his famous "Night in Tunisia." In 1941 and 1942, Calloway recorded several congas with a strong Cuban element, thanks to his Cuban trumpeter Mario Bauza. And in 1942, Bauza jumped ship to a band run by his brother-in-law, Frank "Machito" Grillo, Jr.

Another important development in the 1930s was a great increase in the number of citizens and resident aliens from various Latin American countries: Puerto Ricans most of all, of course, because as U.S. citizens they had automatic right of passage, but also Cubans and other nationals, and in the Southwest, Mexicans joining the Mexican-American communities who had often been there longer than their dominant Anglo neighbors. The Mexican influence (except purely locally) was diffuse, but I think it no coincidence that Mexican songs were (again) beginning to creep into the mainstream. In New York, meanwhile, East Harlem was turning from Jewish to Latino throughout the 1930s, and other less famous *barrios* were also growing. East Harlem provided an important audience for the Latin bands that were crossing over into the mainstream.

The bands that played the Latino uptown scene were not necessarily more "authentic"—whatever that means in dance musics where novelty was at a premium. In fact "uptown" bands like Augusto Coen's were sometimes less rootsy than midtown bands (even Xavier Cugat's) because Anglo rumba fans wanted something new and exotic, and uptown dancers wanted something sophisticated, which meant swing-influenced. But East Harlem groups provided backup work for musicians, so that they stuck around, and in general a wider Latin-music pool was established. Most fundamentally, a substantial number of Cuban and Puerto Rican musicians established themselves in East Harlem, providing not only music but role models for New York-born Latinos.

Thus, by the 1940s there were really two major Afro-American styles of dance music in the United States (or at least in certain big cities). One was jazz, and the other was basically Cuban, though increasingly with jazz elements. The most famous representative of the Cuban-jazz trend at the time was probably Machito's orchestra. About 1946, the two styles began to come together. The leader of this trend from the jazz side is commonly assumed to have been Dizzy Gillespie, but as always the truth is more complex. Even if only because he launched his band rather earlier, the white bandleader Stan Kenton preceded Gillespie in frequent recording of Latin-tinged numbers.

Gillespie's innovation was to draw on a different level of Afro-Cuban music than the dance-band idioms that had provided the earlier inspiration to jazz musicians. In the winter of 1947, Gillespie began playing with a conga-player who had been a drummer with the Cuban Lucumí sect, Chano Pozo. Pozo burst upon an unsuspecting world at a concert in New York's Town Hall, soloing with the Gillespie band, an event frequently taken as the start of the Afro-Cuban period of jazz. But in fact, Kenton had begun to use Latin rhythms by 1941–42 as part of the general drift of the time, and was doing so quite seriously in 1946. Not all of Kenton's pieces were Cuban: in July 1946, he recorded a number called "Ecuador"; and early in the spring of 1947, he recorded "Machito" using a couple of the percussionists from Machito's band. In September 1947, Kenton had a new band that included the Brazilian guitarist Laurindo Almeida, who was later to be involved with Stan Getz in another jazz-Latin fusion, the U.S. version of the bossa nova. Kenton is apt to be dismissed these days as variously a pretentious and insignificant bandleader, but he played a leading part in the "Afro-Cuban" period of jazz. His arrangement of "Peanut Vendor," made in 1947, was possibly his best-known number, and the arrangement is remarkable.

The so-called Cubop style was essentially a branch of jazz rather than of Latin music, but it was the presence of Latin musicians that gave it weight and conviction. In particular, the large number of recordings that Machito made with jazzmen stand out. The basis of Cuban rhythm is an offbeat two-measure phrase (crudely represented by the old phrase "shave and a hair cut, bay rum") called a *clave* rhythm. *Clave* comes in various forms, but it always has a call-and-response feel, uses a contrast of three and two (or two and three) beats, and is a direct descendant of the patterns of beats and silence that are a basic building block of West African rhythm. *Clave* fits neatly into jazz, which itself builds on multiples of four measures (twelve-bar blues, six-teen- and thirty-two-bar popular songs). But the second measure in every *clave* phrase feels different from the first. The importance of *clave* becomes obvious when you listen to some of the early 1950s neo–Latin-jazz that con-sisted of a conventional jazz group with a conga added. Without *clave*, a con-ventional Afro-Cuban conga-player is reduced to playing a depressing picka-packa-picka-packa: a fifth wheel, and with a flat tire at that.

The earliest Latin jazz, and much of what has been played ever since, basi-cally consisted of jazz solos over Afro-Cuban rhythm sections. Whether the pianist played jazz or Cuban-style patterns became more important in the overall sound than you might expect. Jazz soloists like Charlie Parker or trum-peter Doc Cheatham—who played on and off with many Latin bands, includ-ing Machito—normally did not try to play "Latin" themselves, but learned to adapt to *clave* and the complex rhythms of the percussion, a job made easier by an underlying two-four or four-four in almost all Cuban (and, when it became relevant, Brazilian) dance music. Only a few soloists, Gillespie among them, modified their playing to suit the surroundings.

While Cubop, especially in the collaborations with Machito, was taking on a level of Cubanism unimagined in earlier times, the booming Latin dance scene was also affected by jazz. The big mambo bands of the 1950s were in no sense poor relations of the jazz big bands, though they drew from them. In fact there was a remarkable back and forth which produced two distinct idioms that were clearly related. Just as Kenton and later jazz musicians (including the long-lasting Latin jazz vibraphonist, Cal Tjader) had been inspired by the big band mambo of Machito, so Damasiano Pérez Prado, the mambo bandleader best known to America as a whole, was influenced by Kenton (and at times used a jazz musician, Maynard Ferguson, as his lead trumpet player). And while mambo kept its Cuban roots throughout all its acquisition of jazz trimmings, the two way-flow of musicians—black and white—continued. The roster of horn players with experience in both the Herman or Kenton and the Machito or Tito Puente bands grew ever longer, in part because Latin bands often provided steadier money than their jazz equiv-alent. And of course this mutual back and forth laid the groundwork for a more generalized Latin jazz by giving Latino and non–Latino musicians extensive experience with both idioms.

By the early 1950s, a fusion between Latino and Afro-American musics was developing—a fusion that had been in the making for more than half a century. Even since then, Latin jazz of one form or another has been a major part of the jazz scene. And, as you might expect, the fusion began to produce new styles, or substyles at least. These almost always produced howls from the

Raised in the Cuban street-drumming tradition, Mongo Santamaria formed Latin-soul crossover groups in the early 1960s that have influenced two generations of African-American music.

Photo by Steve Maruta, courtesy of Milestone Records

tradition-minded—who play an important part in keeping any music healthy, submitting every new development to test and helping avoid a slide to the merely trendy. One of the first developments was a mini-generation of percussionists who learned to play with jazz without being thrown by the absence of *clave*. As you might expect, some of these were U.S. Latinos, notably conga players Ray Barretto and Sabu Martínez, and *timbalero* Willy Bobo, all born in New York. But though their strong sense of tradition of Cuban conga-players often inhibited them, many of them too became so-to-speak musically bilingual, notably Candido Camero and Carlos "Patato" Valdes; Francisco Aguabella, a masterly secular and sacred drummer, went even further, becoming a key member of Santana's rock band at one point; Cuban-born Mongo Santamaria, as will be seen, took a different path.

Cubop itself faded in the mid to late 1950s, but the Latin element in jazz has never been absent. The tough groove-oriented rhythms of hard bop or soul-jazz—a reaction against bebop's somewhat Eurocentric emphasis on virtuosity and harmonic sophistication—was a mix of Cuban *clave* with the driving rhythms of gospel music, themselves descendants of Sanctified piano playing. The essential difference is that hard bop, as well as the later versions like jazz-funk, moved the two-measure feel of *clave* back onto the beat, syncopated or not. The hard bop of the 1950s gained a second Cuban charge during the 1960s, both from the virtually unknown black groups who played Latin-derived music for African-Americans such as Hugo Dickens's and Pucho's bands, and most significantly (because they recorded extensively) from the various Latin-jazz-funk groups run by Santamaria and Willy Bobo. Both, especially Santamaria, were important not just because they were good but because they were popular.

Santamaria in particular influenced the entire funk generation of the 1970s, providing a second-remove Latin tinge for groups like Brass Construction. He was the only musician playing any form of hyphenated-Latin music to have two recordings in the Top 40, "Watermelon Man" at the beginning and "Cloud Nine" at the end of the 1960s. And his "Afro Blue" is an enduring classic, almost as widely played as Gillespie's "Night in Tunisia." Santamaria's constant touring was part of the gradual process by which the mainstream United States was becoming ever more familiar with Latin and Latinate rhythms. These days one tends to be so used to them, whether pure or in various Americanized guises, that it is hard to imagine what a contrast they were with the universal "straight" or shuffle four-four of virtually all U.S. popular music, including jazz, until the late 1950s. The Latin-funk approach was not simply Africanizing U.S. music as a whole in an obvious way, by introducing rhythms which, even at second or third remove, were nearer to Africa than the European common time (four-four) that had been predominant. Funk of all kinds reemphasized the importance of rhythm as a major component in the pleasure of the music, to the extent that rhythmic interest alone could carry the audience. It also introduced the slight dissociation with which African dance music dispelled fatigue to a listening as well as a dancing audience.

Though it was several degrees removed from African or Afro-American roots, the success of bossa nova in the early 1960s added another ingredient to the pot. Bossa nova itself was an extremely "white" music in that very few Afro-Brazilians were in its forefront (guitarist Djalma de Andrade, known as Bola Sete, was the major exception) and that its considerable jazz influences were mostly from the (largely white) West Coast cool school. Nevertheless, it rested on a rhythmic tradition with a high African component, and a tradition moreover quite different in many ways from the Latin-Caribbean traditions to which the United States was gradually becoming accustomed. Unmeasurable though it is, Brazilian rhythmic procedures of most sorts have a different basic "feel," which Carlos Santana once summed up to me in passing as "Brazilian

Santana's blend of Afro-Cuban and rock elements in his early music was only one of a multiplicity of new experiments in combining what had been separate styles.
Courtesy of Cinerama Releasing

rhythms are lifting, Cuban rhythms drive down." More (though admittedly not very) importantly, bossa nova brought this peculiarly Brazilian feel—perhaps a legacy of the Portuguese, who even in Europe made music so different from the Spanish out of much the same ingredients—in a far more complex package than the simplified samba that the United States knew in the 1940s.

But perhaps the most important African rhythmic legacy of bossa nova, as it transmuted in a new U.S. substyle generally called jazz-bossa, was one of subtlety and obliqueness. East African guitar researcher John Low once told me he only mastered a seemingly simple acoustic guitar groove when he realized that (like the Ghanaian drumming I mentioned earlier) it "started" on what to European ears was the fourth and final beat of the "previous" measure. This effect can produce a remarkable mix of subtlety and propulsion which is at the heart of bossa-nova guitar playing in the hands of one of its major creators, João Gilberto.

Bossa nova is truly all-American music: largely European-derived overt material thoroughly soaked in an underlying Africanism. And it affected jazz and American music in two ways: first, the bossa-nova rhythm was subtle and yet unaggressive enough that it provided an ideal underpinning for ballads of

The jazz-bossa of the 1960s was an important movement, but it was the arrival of a second wave of roots-conscious Brazilians in the late 1960s who consolidated Brazilian music on the U.S. scene. Flora Purim's experimental group paired (left to right) African-Americans George Duke, Ndugu Leon Chancler, and Alphonso Johnson with Brazilians David Amaro, Hermeto Pascoal, and Airto (himself a crucial figure in U.S.-Brazilian fusions).
Courtesy of Fantasy Records

all sorts; and second, it led to the arrival of more avant-garde Brazilians from the jazz singer Flora Purim to the very different but equally important percussionists Airto Moreiro and Paulinho Da Costa, all of whom became a permanent part of the U.S. jazz scene, Brazilianizing it from within.

As far as the relationship of Latin music to jazz was concerned, the 1960s was mostly the era of jazz-bossa, but the post-hardbop Latin-funk movement also continued, fueled in part by an attempt to keep a popular audience that was slipping away from jazz. Meanwhile in Latin New York and Los Angeles, a new idiom was growing out of the first large generation of U.S.-born Latinos with the multicultural experience of the public schools. This was loosely called *bugalú*, and it mixed Cuban rhythms with the earlier black doo-wop vocal style (whose New York version had involved quite a few Puerto Ricans) and jazz-oriented brass solos and piano. *Bugalú* itself did not last all that long; nor did its younger brother, the Latin-soul of singers like Ralfi Pagan and Joe Bataan. Nor was it all that was happening in Latin New York music; this was also the first major era of one of the individual greats, pianist Eddie Palmieri, who was to be influenced by McCoy Tyner while maintaining a lifelong passion for Cuban music.

Manny Oquendo has been a significant figure in New York Latin music since the 1940s. His band Libre creates a bridge between Latin jazz and trombone-frontline New York salsa based on talented musicians as knowledgeable about jazz as they are about Cuban-derived idioms.
Photo by John Abbot, courtesy of Milestone Records

Both the pop-funk and jazz-funk of the 1970s continued to instill in the United States a music that was essentially rhythm-oriented, and this tradition has continued into rap, despite rap's relative lack of variety. Indeed, by the end of the 1970s, it seemed as though the Afro-Latin-funk rhythms had taken over jazz completely. But the complexity and sophistication of a multipercussion approach has its own limitations and has tended to lock in soloists used to far more freedom: four-to-the-bar may be limited, but it is the reverse of limiting to the soloists above it.

Meanwhile, hard-core Latin music in the United States, which around the early 1970s had come to be called salsa—a word as reviled by some as jazz had been, and as useful and thus durable—was going through renewal process. After the intermingling of the 1950s and 1960s, salsa groups returned to the Cuban source in a *típico* (downhome) wave that ensured it did not just vanish into American music as a whole.

Another movement of some significance, though begun without fanfare, was the mixing of Cuban dance music with the deep Afro-Cuban percussion of the *guaguancó* and even the religious rituals, a phenomenon that went along with a considerable revival of Afro-Cuban religion in New York (with which several important Latin musicians were involved). This affected dance-hall salsa less than it did a generation of Latino Latin-jazz musicians who were to

Nigerian expatriate Orlando Julius Ekemode playing in a Mississippi club. Whether resident or on tour, African bands have become a regular part of the U.S. music scene, bringing with them influences that are still in the formative stage but can only grow stronger.
Photo by Don Hill

become prominent in the 1980s and 1990s, notably the Gonzalez brothers (who, along with their peers in the newer Latin jazz, had extensive experience with both jazz and Latin groups), and introduced a direct infusion of neo-Africanism into the more avant-garde fringes of the Latin jazz world.

By the 1990s, the two major strains—Brazilian and Cuban—had become so much a part of jazz as to provide perhaps half of its impetus in ways direct and indirect. And they did so in somewhat different ways. The subtler Brazilian tinge had pretty much become a part of mainstream jazz, notably as an underpinning to ballads, while the more aggressively distinctive Cuban strain contributed to a separate and extremely healthy Latin-jazz substyle. Meanwhile a few artists like the innovative pianist Michele Rosewoman, notably in her New Yor-Uba big band, were going beyond the Africanism inherent in Cuban music to mix both Afro-Cuban and African-Yoruba elements.

The relationship between jazz and African music has somewhat paralleled the connection between jazz and Latin music, though it has been marked—and at times distorted—by the tendency among some African-American musicians to see Africa as a blend of Golden Age and Garden of Eden. The whole other order of Africanism in jazz has been covered by Norman Weinstein in his important though little-noticed study, *A Night in Tunisia*.

Africa long represented a source of exotica for jazz musicians. This arose in the 1920s out of the nearly universal perception—on the part of blacks as well as whites—of African music as something extraordinarily unusual. Ellington, particularly when he had the resident band at the Cotton Club, provided "jungle" music for the floor shows. (One of his records from the period is entitled "Jungle Fantasy.") The audiences of the time were hardly likely to know the difference between Bubber Miley's plunger-mute growls and African music. No doubt they were put vaguely in mind of lions, and the fact that lions do not live in jungles was not allowed to spoil their fun. And certainly Ellington knew no more about African music than his audiences—and would probably not have been deflected if he had.

Serious interest in African music among jazz musicians began to develop just after, and to some extent in connection with, the rise of Afro-Cuban jazz. In London, drummer Kenny Baker's Afro-Cubists (seemingly the first group in the world to play entirely Afro-Cuban and Afro-Caribbean jazz) actually used two African drummers, Ginger Johnson and Guy Warren. By the late 1950s there were quite a number of African musicians in the United States. Meanwhile, the black consciousness movement was turning people's minds toward Africa as a source of pride; thus the two elements fused. Max Roach went to Haiti to study neo-African drumming styles, and like many other jazz musicians began to listen to the available recordings of African drumming. Roach, Art Blakey, and other drummers began making a serious attempt to relate African drumming to their own tradition. Other jazz players have consciously turned to Africa for inspiration. Art Farmer made a disc in the mid-1950s called "Uam Uam," which is "Mau Mau" backward. Somewhat later, Coltrane recorded "Africa." There have been a number of jazz recordings of the Cuban musician Mongo Santamaria's "Afro-Blue"; and, of course, Ellington's *Liberian Suite* is a prime instance. The degree of African-ness in these examples varied, of course. Sometimes it showed in little more than a name. But, whether through listening to records, through the influence of the South African Miriam Makeba, who introduced Johannesburg pop styles to the United States, or merely through a feeling of mystical rapport, African music—or the idea of it—became important to the jazz scene in the mid-1960s.

An important Blakey experiment was *The African Beat*, with the Afro-Drum Ensemble. Here the numbers were all African or composed by Africans, and many of the musicians were African. The album contains some fine things (although again Blakey tends to be the odd man out; one might suppose that the drum kit is the problem, were it not for the fact that many modern African dance groups combine drum kit and conga drums). The numbers composed by Africans are all in the modern African styles (see

Chapter 8), which themselves contain Afro-American elements. Thus, a degree of common ground existed. Moreover, the presence of Africans in considerable force helped, especially that of the Nigerian Solomon G. Ilori, who did the singing. The embarrassing vocals of Art Blakey's *Holiday for Skins* were absent from this record. The jazzman Yusuf Lateef showed a genius for gap-bridging; he was at his best in the highlife track "Ayiko Ayiko," to which his tenor playing made a major contribution, and even when he provided little more than a musical joke, as on his hand-piano solos, the joke was good. In fact, the only real drawback of *The African Beat* was the failure of Blakey's style to blend with the rest.

The interest in Africa was not entirely confined to African-American jazzmen. Kenny Baker aside, the white flutist Herbie Mann, better known for his Latin-jazz work, hired African musicians for his excellent Afro-Jazz Sextet in the late 1950s. But the movement, which has never taken on the broad-based nature of Latin jazz, found extra resonance for African-American musicians with a leaning to black nationalism, and is in an early stage. At times the connection remained purely conceptual. The sleeve notes to *Accent on Africa*, by the Cannonball Adderley Quintet, for instance, make no claim that Adderley is playing African music, but suggest that the album is meant to "show the influence." The music, however, is too often reminiscent of Hollywood's Africa, and certainly far further from its inspiration than the Latin-jazz of the period was from Cuban music.

Much, but not all, of the Afro-jazz recording has been in the Islamic tradition, whose rhythmic approach made for easier absorption into jazz. Several times in the 1950s, Blakey recorded with African as well as Latino drummers, among them Yoruba percussionist Babatunde Olatunji, a long-time Harlem resident who also has worked with many other jazzmen. And in 1996 percussionist Bill Summers recently recorded an almost purely Yoruba CD with Cuban drummer Lararo Galancaga and the group, Iroko. Nevertheless, most of the Afro-jazz mixes, and pretty much all the successful ones, have involved Afro-Islamic regions. One of the factors that freed jazz players up to cope with the complexities of African music was their experience with 1940s and 1950s Cubop, and the hidden Middle Eastern element seems to facilitate Euro-African blends in the United States as well as in Latin America. Some players have gone further than others in integrating African music into jazz. Lateef and pianist Randy Weston have lived greater or lesser periods in Africa (Weston in Morocco, Lateef in northern Nigeria). And Weston has played over the years with Ghanaian drummer Obo Addy and other Africans. Lateef taught at Nigeria's Ahmadu Bello University and organized an experimental group there, mixing jazz with Afro-Islamic elements and instruments.

During more than three decades based in Harlem, Nigerian percussionist Babatunde Olatunji has been a major element in the Africanization of jazz, notably through his classic *Drums of Passion* album.

Photo by John Werner, courtesy of Rykodisc Records

So far, the relatively recent conscious jazz-African fusions have been a rather small part of jazz compared with their Latin equivalents. Whether that will change is unknown. On the one hand, Latinos greatly outnumber Africans in the United States. However, a considerable African minority in the United States is growing rapidly. In the late 1990s, there are around 20,000 Nigerians alone in the D.C. area, and sizable Ghanaian and Nigerian populations in Chicago. They include a number of notable African musicians: not just Yoruba percussionist Babatunde Olatunji, who has been teaching and playing for his Harlem base for more than a quarter-century, but also Ghanaian singer Pat Thomas, and many others.

Once the jazz world gets past a fixation on African traditional music and starts finding out what has been happening across the South Atlantic over the past four decades, a whole new fusion could enrich jazz considerably in the next century.

8

Modern Urban Popular Styles

New World music was born of the encounter between African and European concepts of music, which intermingled, interwove, and fought their way into a relationship that produced major new contributions to the world. There was, however, another area in which Western and African music came into contact and produced a series of new styles: Africa itself. For in Africa, as in the New World, the meeting of local and non-African music caused an enormous creative ferment. Some of this foreign music was European. A great deal of it—whether centuries old or recently arrived—was Middle-Eastern through the spread of Islam. And some fed back across the Atlantic, which was far from a one-way street.

Africa has never been isolated from the rest of the world, and its music has taken in aspects of other traditions as the circumstances have dictated, sometimes extensively, sometimes in small degrees. The foremost outside influence in the past was Arabic, or at all events Islamic, but others may have preceded it. One school of thought, in fact, holds that the xylophone came to Africa via two large-scale immigrations of peoples from Oceania a couple of thousand years B.C., and that other musical and nonmusical cultural elements widespread in certain parts of Africa, including western Africa, started in Southeast Asia or the Pacific—which, as far as the island of Madagascar is concerned, is certainly possible. There is also an opposing and more plausible theory that Southeast Asia at least was influenced from Africa through Middle Eastern slave-trading in West Africa. Either way, the arguments for contact between the two areas are impressive. Moreover, there are Indian influences on the East coast through centuries of trading and settlement, and elsewhere through the great popularity in Africa of Indian movie musicals.

The influence with which this chapter is concerned, however, is much more recent. It began with the contact between Europeans and Africans either before or during the colonial era and has resulted in the development in this century of a number of modern urban popular styles. Music in these styles is played on Western or a mixture of African and Western instruments and contains material from both cultures. The styles exist in most parts of Africa, but the best known are the highlife of anglophone West Africa, Congolese dance music, and the styles of South Africa.

There has always been popular music in Africa, of course, and there are types of African music showing no European influence, or almost none, that are both modern and popular. "Traditional" musical modes, in the words of the Nigerian composer Akin Euba, "not only flourish, but are the main musical fare of most Africans." This is probably true of Africa as a whole, though less so perhaps of East, East Central, and southern Africa than of the West and the Congo-Angola region.

Most discussions of modern African pop music have concentrated on one or another of the main forms, but despite sharp contrasts in styles between one area and another, it is clear that certain processes have taken place in much the same way everywhere. These are, not necessarily in chronological order:

1. The increasing accessibility to Africans of music from other parts of the world, through the radio and recordings
2. The introduction and, more important, wide availability of Western instruments, in particular very cheap guitars
3. The invention of new forms of popular music by young people

Obviously, the final step was influenced by the first two.

This process did not happen in the same way everywhere, nor at the same time. Apparently random happenings came together in one place and stayed separate in others. A widespread, dynamic, and confusing situation was complicated by several factors. First, what was taking place in popular music was usually disapproved of by people who might have been in a position to analyze it. Second, it was only partially documented in some of its phases by commercial phonograph records. Third, most anthropologists and musicologists regarded the birth of new popular forms—until recently—as a disaster rather than an interesting phenomenon of social change. As a result, the evidence, which consists mainly of people's often inaccurate memories of something to which they did not pay much mind at the time, is only just beginning to be sifted.

A living symbol of African guitar's deep roots, rural Zambian guitarist Spokes Chola has no access to pop trimmings or even an electric socket. But it is with teenagers like him that the whole phenomenon started.

Photo by John Low

Roughly speaking, African *traditional* popular music can be divided into two kinds: group or communal music—made, at least in West Africa, by the basic complement of three drummers plus other percussion, and produced for an audience of dancer-singers—and more personal music, in which one or maybe two people play largely for their own self-expression and amusement. An example of the more private music might be a man singing about his troubles with his wife to an audience of two or three fellow husbands and accompanying himself on a hand-piano. One of his listeners might be tapping a couple of sticks, and another clapping gently. These categories shade into each other at times, but mostly they produced different types of music.

New World music began influencing Africa in the nineteenth century, as new research in this very underresearched area is beginning to show. Much of this influence was caused by freed slaves returning home. To give just a few examples, Jamaica expert Kenneth Bilby and highlife student John Collins have established that there is evidence the *goombay* or *gumbe* drum—a distinctive Jamaican neo-African instrument—had been brought to the West African coast by the 1820s. There is an entire area of Lagos inhabited by "Brazilian" Yoruba, descendants of freed slaves who settled together in the city and brought back Brazilianized music that has gradually melted into the enormously complex patterns of urban Yoruba percussion styles. And Trinidadian members of the West India Regiment stationed in Sierra Leone and Accra may have brought songs that are part of the roots of the very distinctive Sierra Leonean creole or Krio palmwine style—the very popular "Everybody Loves Saturday Night" is supposed to be an example—though I believe calypso and palmwine (discussed later in the chapter) may well have developed separately out of similar elements in both countries. And Collins has shown that the guitar work of the Kru of Liberia, who produced a very large number of sailors, spread into early Ghanaian guitar and probably then (at second hand via Ghanaian Ashanti sailors) up the Congo River to form part of the basis for Congolese guitar. What the relationship between Kru music and any influence from the Americo-Liberian community of freed and resettled U.S. slaves may be is still very unclear, but it is certainly possible that this is another example of trans-Atlantic feedback.

On the European side, military bands were also a major though forgotten element, whose importance to African/Afro-American interaction is that they provided a corps of African musicians able to take and adapt jazz and Latin playing. Ghana and Sierra Leona have a coastal fife-and-drum style that may be a re-Africanization of eighteenth-century British marching groups. Toward the end of the nineteenth century and later on the East Coast, African musicians in colonial military brass bands began adapting local melodies in their spare time. Moreover, the up-country Christian missions also funded brass bands to provide their converts with an alternative to local dance-oriented festivities; they did not disapprove of the local music except when it was in the service of non-Christian worship, but did disapprove of all dancing, African or Western. For a while there was a flowering of African brass bands, both urban and rural in Ghana, and there have been revivals at various times (including the 1990s).*

As in Ghana, so in Nigeria, where the so-called Calabar Brass Bands of eastern Nigeria supplied horn players for urban dance music, and the village brass bands became more and more indigenized as brass instruments broke and local drums were introduced. The contemporary Nigerian *fuji* style, which tends to use one bugle along with drums, may be a distant memory of the village brass ensembles; in East Africa, too, there was a brass band tradition, albeit not so entrenched and long-lasting as in West Africa. And, in many of these traditions, even when the bands had not reverted to largely traditional groupings, they were not merely imitations of European ensembles. Traditional drumming might be blended with full brass sections, and

* The best account of the Ghanaian brass bands I have seen is in the notes to the Pan Records CD *Frozen Brass: Africa and Latin America*, which also has splendid examples of Ghanaian brass bands.

fairly traditional singing added to what in Europe is almost entirely an instrumental tradition.

But the appearance of modern African pop music was symbolized, when it was not actually precipitated, by the guitar. There has been dispute about when the European guitar—that is to say, either the modern six-stringed, so-called Spanish guitar or any of the variants that existed before it became standardized—reached Africa. The most likely date would seem to lie between the sixteenth and twentieth centuries, and I do not mean that face-tiously. It is inconceivable that the Portuguese should not have introduced the guitar into Mozambique and Angola early on, and yet in Ghana (the for-mer Gold Coast) good guitarists were rare enough in the 1930s to attract a good deal of admiration.

Actually, the guitar was not the only European instrument to be adopted by African musicians. Other European stringed instruments have also been commercially recorded in Africa: the mandolin cropped up in 1930s Nigerian recordings, and the fiddle has taken root in the South African countryside. So has the accordion, which was also quite widespread for a considerable time. It gave birth to a very distinctive local sound in southern Africa, where it is still played (perhaps under Afrikaner influence). It was in the Congo before World War I; I have seen postcards that included one of a war dance with a seemingly incongruous concertinist in and among the spears and feather headdresses. Hugh Tracey recorded Malawian and Kenyan rural accordionists in the 1950s. And a Sierra Leonean accordionist, Salliah Koroma, recorded quite fre-quently in the 1950s (a Malawian cut and an example of Koroma's playing are on my own compilation *Africa Dances*). And an accordion analogue, the har-monica, was played in South Africa in semitraditional music, by musicians who switched between the European instrument and the musical bow, some-times in alternating numbers. Nevertheless, the guitar spread further and lasted longer than any of these other instruments.

Accounts cited by Collins and others make it clear that sailors' dives in the big West African coastal ports hosted all sorts of impromptu music-making involving both African and Western sailors, including, in all likelihood, African-Americans. This would probably have involved both the universal sailor's instruments—concertina, mandolin, guitar—and ad hoc percussion. The Kru sailors from Liberia were a factor in this. Not only were there "Krutowns" in Freetown and other ports where Kru colonies settled, but Collins has shown that Kru guitar had four standard grooves or ostinato pat-terns (with names like "stoker" that betray their nautical link), that the 1920s and 1930s Ghanaian palmwine guitarists borrowed these, and that at least one, called *amponsah* in Ghana, is still being played today.

There is, of course, a good deal of difference between the presence of a few accordions or guitars in a few coastal cities and widespread diffusion in town and country all (or almost all) over the continent. There is no evidence of the *customary* use of the European guitar, or any version of it, before the twentieth century, with the possible exception of the *ramkie,* a guitarlike instrument found in the Cape area of South Africa. There are a few examples of West African instruments influenced by European guitars, such as a hybrid form of guitar-fiddle photographed in the Congo. But there is no sign that the European details on these—mainly a matter of guitarlike tuning pegs and a flat fingerboard, as opposed to the normal African sticklike fingerboard and tuning rings—are old.

The adoption of the guitar by musicians all over Africa, which began taking place in the 1930s, led to one of two main generic styles of modern pop music. The first and most common was typically played by a group consisting of one or two guitars (or guitar and mandolin in a few cases) and some sort of percussion, almost always a bottle tapped with a knife to give a high chinking note, which filled the role of the *gankogui* in Ewe music or the *claves* in Cuban; by a single guitar; or by a guitar with another instrument, usually African, with or without percussion. The second style came about through the addition of European instruments (usually, at first, guitar) to a traditional percussion dance ensemble. Insofar as such categories have any significance in African music, the first was a "song" or "listening" style, in which the words were important, and the second a dance style. The other major division—perhaps even more important—is between acoustic and electric guitar styles.

The music played by the small acoustic-guitar–based groups varied widely. The essential factor for change at first was that the European guitar gave an African string-player a much larger number of notes than he had had before. The big Guinean *seron* has nineteen strings, and the Senegalese *kora* twenty-one. Most African stringed instruments have far fewer: The Luya *lidungu,* from Kenya, has six, for example. The important factor is not the number of strings, however, but the fact that very few African plucked instruments are stopped or fretted; that is to say, each string produces only one note, like a traditional European harp string. In most parts, stringed instruments have played a semirhythmic role, in which a small choice of notes is not a limitation. But music suitable for an instrument with half a dozen notes or so and no fretting system clearly wastes much of the capability of the guitar, which can produce more than a hundred notes. Therefore, one important factor in the development of the new music was the greater range of the guitar.

Some African musicians who took up the guitar began by playing on it patterns much like the ones they had played on whatever stringed instruments were traditional for them. It is reasonable to assume that this was, in fact, the first step for most musicians. As a result, there are recordings from all over Africa of rural songs accompanied by guitar, and often bottle-and-knife, of an extremely traditional kind. Many Africans who, like most people anywhere, tend to notice the song rather than the style, appear to regard this type of music as truly traditional, though of course it is really only partly so. A good example is a recording made in Sierra Leone of a Mandingo song to Sumailia accompanied by a guitar and a traditional *kora* and sung by two women in a traditional style.

The way in which the extraordinary array of African guitar styles developed was spectacularly illustrated by a Congolese guitarist who became popular for a short time throughout East Africa and is regarded by buffs as one of the most original of all African players. A clerk called Mwenda Jean Bosco was recorded by Tracey in 1951. Consciously or not, Bosco transferred certain characteristic elements of his own tribe's traditional music onto the new instrument. Specifically, he took rhythms and melodic patterns used on hand-pianos and played them on the guitar. The short, repeated, tumbling, rather bell-like phrases and the trick of using a phrase early as a secondary theme, then making it the major theme later on, are typical of the hand-piano music of the Sanga tribe, to which Bosco belonged. Just how close his guitar was to the hand-piano playing of his area can only be grasped by comparison.* Besides the guitar/hand-piano links, "Masanga" showed some interesting features in the singing. The general quality of the vocal line was indigenous, with short phrases, a descending tune, and a fairly straightforward rhythm against which the complications of the guitar rhythm were set off, somewhat as if the voice were accompanying the guitar rather than the other way around (a common tendency in earlier African music). But Bosco departed from local tradition by singing in a kind of semi-Swahili, apparently to explore the freedoms offered by melodies unrestricted by tonal considerations.

Bosco was only one of a school of guitarists playing in and around the Copper belt of southeastern Congo and northern Zambia, and he was but slightly unusual. But recordings of other Congolese and Zambian Copperbelt musicians show that there were basically two approaches: consciously or unconsciously imitating local elements—notably the tinkling, tumbling finger-piano idioms—by using a capo to raise the pitch of the instrument; or borrowing the foreign elements that caught the musician's fancy, most commonly the bass runs and rhythms of Cuban music. A new form of street-guitar music

---

* Fortunately, there are examples of Sanga hand-piano in Tracey's immense series of records of African music, *Sounds of Africa*, while Bosco's "Masanga" was issued on the *Music of Africa* series, also overseen by Tracey and released in the United States on the Kaleidophone label.

grew up when musicians began using the guitar to do what Nigerian and other street drummers had done with a traditional instrument. This procedure has been most common in the regions where strolling musicians are still numerous. A particularly fine set of examples was recorded by Tracey in the 1950s among the acoustic guitarists who wandered from mine to mine on the Zambian Copperbelt, entertaining the workers and their families in the mine compounds.*

A more mixed style that probably existed in many coastal cities but is specially well-documented on the West African coast was the so-called palmwine music, which took its name from the cheap bars that sold palm wine. Though the name only got attached to the music in West Africa, there were also examples in eastern Africa. In Ghana, Sam of Sam's Trio; in Cameroun, Jean Bikoko; in Sierra Leone, Ebenezer Callendar; and in Kenya, the influential early guitarist Fundi Konde all played a fairly simple but intensely beguiling guitar style backed by small percussion, and in Callendar's case an irresistible tuba. That said, these styles were not equally developed at any one time. Even in eastern Africa, which lagged for various reasons, backings to Konde's songs of the late 1940s to early 1950s already were clearly early versions of a lasting Kenyan idiom. Zambia's Alice Nkhata by contrast was still finding his way at that time.

These professional and semiprofessional musicians emerged out of an enormous number of amateur players, some of them very fine, many of them rural. John Low once recorded an excellent Tanzanian guitarist, Francis Mwakitime, who played only for friends. And some of the finest and most original pieces of African acoustic guitar playing that I have ever heard were recorded by a South African known only as Citaumvano, sitting on the porch of a Pondoland general store. At one time, in fact, the acoustic guitar was widespread in rural areas, and for a short period appeared on record. This was perhaps most true in Kenya, where the music of relatively small language groups was recorded during the 1950s. And the so-called dry (acoustic) guitar styles of the large western Kenyan Luo and Luhya groups was still being recorded in the late 1960s. This was a parallel to palmwine music, although, as up-country Kenya is quite chilly after dark, there was nothing there equivalent to the rich ad hoc nightlife of West and Central Africa.

Kenyan (and Tanzanian) dry guitar was entirely different in sound from West African equivalents. Though some of its rhythms appear to stem from Cuban import discs, there are also precedents for the peculiar phrasing and instrumental interplay of the guitars in Luya and Luo traditional string techniques. Moreover, up-country Kenyan music is not nearly as drum-oriented as

---

* Some of these appeared on the Original Music CD *From the Copperbelt*.

Nigerian and Ghanaian styles, and the favorite percussion for dry-guitar music was one or two Fanta soda bottles, tapped and/or scraped with a knife blade.

This local element in African guitar styles is more obvious in some countries than others. One very large and special case is the music of the large Afro-Muslim cultures of both West and East, particularly the countries of the so-called Sahel, which runs across Africa just south of the Sahara. To outside ears this music can sound almost entirely Middle Eastern; yet further acquaintance reveals that despite the theoretically common bases both in Muslim and traditional African procedures, the pop music of every one of these countries is instantly identifiable. True, the Arabic elements in the music of Mali, Guinea, and Senegal—influenced by Moroccan and Algerian music—are different from those in Sudan, Somalia, and the East African coast, where the influences are from the Arabian peninsula, notably Yemen and Oman.

Yet the localization goes beyond these broad regions—there is no mistaking a Somali recording from Kenyan or Tanzanian *taarab*—for very varied reasons. Language always affects melodic line, even though East African languages are only marginally tonal compared with Yoruba, Ewe, or even the Lingala of the Congo. In contemporary electric music, Mali, Guinea, and Senegal have taken very different paths. Major Malian bands like Super Biton have always used an extremely strong infusion of traditional melody and rhythm, and often played electric guitars almost like koras; Senegalese musicians have tended to be fascinated by electronics, and bands like Xalam were experimenting with jazz when it was far from popular locally; and Guinean groups, like the famous women policemen's band, Les Amazones, have tended to split the difference. Traditionalist or no, Mali, Guinea, and Senegal have also picked up on foreign influence.

The countries of francophone coastal West Africa—Togo, Benin, and to a lesser extent the larger Cameroun—at one time were very heavily influenced by French pop, and that influence has persisted. In Mali, Senegal, and Guinea this was less true, perhaps for the reason Paul Oliver argued that the African element in U.S. blues came from these regions: the local music was already strongly string-based and eminently translatable to guitar. In addition, Mali was overwhelmingly more rural than urban and many of its inland towns hardly saw a Frenchman except the odd administrator.

The major French influence in these countries, in fact, was indirect. While they were strongly affected by Cuban music, like everybody else in Central Africa, the French brought recordings of the Franco-African *biguine* and other Franco-Caribbean music, including Haitian ones. And the echoes remain, notably in a saxophone playing strongly reminiscent of the lovely older Antillean solo saxophone idiom.

A vital factor in African guitar music from the 1930s on was the availability of foreign records. Naturally, many African musicians copied what they liked from these. At the opposite end of the scale from the semitribal "folk" songs were many recordings that were almost straight translations of foreign styles. I have on tape an old 78-rpm record in Venda, a South African language, that is a lift from Jimmie Rodgers, the white American singer of the 1920s and 1930s. The language is Venda, but the vocal tune and the guitar style are pure Rodgers. (There's a more mixed South African song—pure Rodgers yodel, more ambiguous melody—on the compilation *Marabi Nights.*) The Zambian singer Alick Nkhata also recorded at least one song with Rodgers-style yodeling and guitar bass-lines. And there were plenty of other examples. I have a Kenyan disc from around 1952 that offers a highly lugubrious version of the Inkspots' style (it is on the Original Music CD *Kenya Dry*), and the Kenyan guitarist Fadhili William was strongly influenced by the British guitar group, the Shadows. But the recordings that most influenced Africa—known by older musicians from Cameroun to Kenya as the "GV" series after their numerical prefix—were Victor recordings by Cuban groups such as the Trio Matamoros and even Don Azpiazu. The classic *montuno* of "The Peanut Vendor" still surfaces in improbable seeming contexts: I have a recording of a semitraditional Malian group that was performing it in the 1970s.

The Cuban influence was strongest, naturally enough, in the more mainstream and novelty-oriented forms of African music. But even in culturally separate and theoretically traditional forms like the *taarab* of the East African coast—a Yemeni-influenced wedding music known to all Swahili and very few other residents even of the big cities—it would sometimes surface. My Original Music *taarab* compilation, *Songs the Swahili Sing,* includes one of the world's most idiosyncratic *chachachás*.

In the long run, the Cuban, like other foreign, influences was in the Sahel (as much as elsewhere) a mechanism for the discovery of new, African ways of remaking local tradition to suit new circumstances in which the only other option was for the tradition to die out. In the case of few individual artists is this as easy to track as in Senegalese singer Youssou Ndour, because Ndour's international success has brought the reissue of older local recordings. From 1960, long before he joined it, the Star Band essentially played Senegalese takes on Cuban music. Even as a teenager, Ndour's singing was strongly Senegalese in vocal tone and style, and with his arrival the band began to indigenize—a process speeded up with the importation of a local talking drum, the *tama*, to give the rhythm section a voice. In 1977, N'dour (at a ripe 18 years old!) took the band over and renamed it Etoile de Dakar. Now the process was almost complete and a new and strictly Senegalese style that Ndour called

Typical of Mali's strongly tradition-based Sahelian sound is Al Farka Touré, whose guitar work would be almost that of a *kora* if it weren't for the influences from bluesman John Lee Hooker! But even his traditional elements are original, mixing elements from several ethnic groups.
Photo by Jon Mided, courtesy of Rykodisc

mbalax was affirmed, in which the horns still played music recognizably influenced by Afro-America, but were integrated into a whole that only the terminally obtuse would call, pejoratively, "westernized."

Indeed, there is a process at work. The earliest guitarists, presented with the new possibilities of a new instrument, tended either simply to transfer what they were doing before, or to borrow from overseas recordings. The second phase was a more complex version of the borrowing in which musicians tried to reproduce, or modified, foreign styles seen as sophisticated and hip. These were sometimes European, but the effect of the colonizing power seems to have been minor and transitory. More important were Cuban music, which combined the attraction of the foreign with a general familiarity, jazz in South Africa, and later soul and funk. (Blues was never such a major influence, though it was important in 1950s South African *kwela*, and the Malian guitarist Ali Farka Touré was influenced by bluesman John Lee Hooker.) But fairly soon the modification procedure began to produce a new music, a process that usually started with the vocal lines, because Spanish melodies (for example) often clashed with the sound patterns of tonal languages. An obvious and documented example was the way in which the Congolese developed their own melodies—neither traditional nor imported—while still playing rumbas, though rumbas modified by playing on a guitar what might be a fiddle part in the Cuban record being imitated.

The third phase began when enough of a local history was built up that African national styles began building on themselves, and developing their own rhythms and dances. This happened at different times in different areas. West African highlife had essentially developed its own rhythms by the 1950s, even though overseas or other-African rhythms might have a passing success (as Congo music did in the mid-1960s and soul in the early 1970s). Congolese music used the rumba, with passing excursions into the *chachachá* and *pachanga,* until new and local rhythms like the *boucher* and most influentially the *soukous* developed in the late 1960s and early 1970s.

In reality, the whole process was more complex than this and involved factors ranging from geography to patterns of importation. As a generalization, Zimbabwean music drew either from eastern African or South African music; one of its most popular bands of the 1980s, the Real Sounds, originated in East Africa. Even though the term *jit* was used for all Zimbabwean pop, the Bhundu Boys for example hew largely to an eastern African sound, and the Four Brothers more to South Africa. But as an illustration of the danger of generalization, Zimbabwe has also produced perhaps the most creative of all African musicians, Thomas Mapfumo, whose mix of traditional material with some reggae influence is entirely personal and nonderivative. And where traditional instruments are ignored by the pop musicians of most African countries, Zimbabwean musicians like Stella Chiweshe have turned the *mbira* finger-piano into an important contemporary instrument.

But despite the almost universal creativity of local styles, the most internationally important contemporary music in Africa has been the Congolese music that has come to be called *soukous* (after a dance of the mid-1970s). *Soukous* and its predecessors influenced to a greater or lesser extent every other African pop style in the last ten years, because of its brilliance, its relatively nonlocal sound, and, during the crucial period of the 1960s and 1970s, the political chaos in the Congo which sent waves of musicians both east and west.

Indeed, *soukous*'s pan-African influence goes back almost to its own beginnings. Congolese modern modes of music, like those of other countries in Africa, can be divided into the guitar-song and dance-band forms. The most immediately noticeable fact about Congo dance music since the late 1950s is its heavy debt to Afro-Cuban music, specifically its rhythm, derived

Kanda Bongo Man, second-generation star of *soukous*, the Congolese music that swept Africa with its sophisticated sound originally based on blending local and Cuban elements in both vocals and guitar.

Photo by J. R. Rost, courtesy of Rykodisc

from various versions of the rumba. In an article in *Africa Report,* Pierre Kazadi states that what he calls the "rumba" style began in the early 1950s with a dance called the *maringa,* which used traditional or "folk" tunes backed by a rectangular drum, a hand-piano, and a bottle playing the *claves* part. Soon new instruments began to be added, and a period of great musical adventurousness set in, when lineups such as fiddle, guitar, drum, and two hand-pianos, or even kazoos, were recorded. But in reality, the famous GV series of Cuban recordings was a major influence: some early recordings copy elements of Cuban *sones* almost exactly. And the *biguines* out of Paris were another clear influence: as late as 1953, a group was recorded in Stanleyville that played *biguines* using two clarinets (in general, wind instruments seem to have been rare in that period). There was even then a clear preference for foreign elements that corresponded in some way to local ones. A purported *biguine,* for instance, might in fact be played with a basic rhythm of fast triplets. On the other hand, some groups were as imitative as they could manage to be of the *biguines* they copied. A feature that seems to have become standardized from Cuban music at the time, in Congo pop and in East Africa as well, was the use of parallel thirds for most vocals. Wherever found in modern African pop music, it appears to be a sign of Congolese influence.

By the late 1950s, a period of consolidation was underway. The *biguines* had dropped out, and the definitive foreign ingredient was Cuban, or at least Afro-Cuban. The early discs of Congo music using fiddles may well be a response to such groups as the Orquesta Aragón and the Cuban *charanga* ensembles, and one element of Congolese guitar was demonstrably the result of playing *charanga* fiddle riffs on guitars. Another influence—inferred from the jazz-style entries to solos that soon evolved—may have been Cab Calloway, whose records were very popular with Belgians in the Congo of the 1940s.

The choice of the rumba, a strongly neo-African form in its Cuban version, had several important results. First, the rumba has built-in possibilities for improvisation in its second section, or *montuno*. This gave Congo lead guitarists a chance to develop their music and to shine when they did so. Moreover, the use of a rhythm that was basically generalized African but was not associated with any one part of Africa (as was Ghanaian and Nigerian highlife) accounted to some degree at least for the remarkable spread of Congo music. Highlife never caught on in East Africa, because it was too. *West* African. The rumba—at least as reinterpreted by Central Africans—was, paradoxically, less foreign to East Africans.

Stylistically, Congo music shows a number of interesting features (apart, that is, from the development of a highly original and influential guitar style). One of them is its way of getting around the melodically limiting factor of a tonal language without disrupting a two-voice vocal using basically parallel-third harmony. The first voice follows the speech-tone pattern, while the second voice departs from it. This resolved a problem faced by earlier Congolese musicians, who had either to ignore the tone patterns, with often peculiar results, or allow themselves to be restricted by them (although "restricted" could be the wrong word; the tone patterns may well have helped Congolese groups to break away quickly from overly Cuban-style melodies).

Much the greater part of African acoustic-guitar music, wherever it came from, falls between the two extremes of imitation-Western and traditional-on-a-new-instrument. At the same time that Bosco recorded "Masanga," Nono Ngoi and Anastase Kabongo, also Congolese, recorded equally semitraditional music in a very different style, one more reminiscent of East African lute-playing. Another couple, Patrice Ilunga and Victor Misomba, recorded music based on imported Cuban records, with all the various Cuban characteristics transposed for guitar, which was the acoustic-guitar ancestor of the Congolese dance music to be discussed below. Mozambican examples of this acoustic style show slight (never strong) Portuguese elements. More particularly, there are traits that are apparently Brazilian, whereas the common Latin influence (direct or indirect) in other areas is practically always Cuban, except in the early days in the Congo, where there was some *biguine* influence (the Congo being Belgian, and thus francophone).

While one contribution to dry-guitar music was local and traditional, the other was not simply "Western," but Afro-American. In the Congo, and in West Africa to a lesser extent, it was Cuban, while in South Africa it was jazz. There is no mystery about why different Afro-American styles were influential in different parts of Africa. Cuban music had strong roots in West Africa and the Congo, and so there was the most natural of affinities. South African traditional music is quite different from West African and Congo-Angolan. As a generalization, it tends toward rhythmic complexity of singing voices over a regular beat; its polyrhythms come from the voices, which vary their accentuation relative to the basic rhythm. This is remarkably like jazz, especially the 1930s and 1940s music of Count Basie and others, who riffed and soloed against a rock-solid four-four beat. Another important influence was inter-African. Kenya, for example, has an extremely strong tradition of dry-guitar playing and singing, which appears to owe a good deal to imported records of the early Congolese musicians. But the plain fact is that a wide range of unmistakably African guitar music exists, and although foreign influences can be discerned—some strong, some weak—the national styles are overriding: One can never mistake a Kenyan record for a Congolese, let alone a Nigerian.

A crucial moment in all African pop music was the adoption of electric guitars. Until about 1958, Congo bands were playing in a fairly skilled Cuban-derived style, in which elements of an original guitar technique (going back to the music of Ilunga and others in the early 1950s) and an Africanization of melody lines were offset by fairly Cuban rhythm lines and saxophone or clarinet influence on the guitar part. The electrification of the guitar brought into prominence the Congolese guitar style, which had already shown its originality and ability to modify other African styles. This style, of immense force and flexibility, at first sounds somewhat Latin American, but there is actually nothing like it in the New World. It seems to have grown partly from localizing techniques like Bosco's, and partly from the playing on guitar of lines that, in Cuban music, were brass or saxophone lines. Certainly Congolese records from the early 1960s, like Rocherau's "Afrika Mokili Mobimba," suggest this essentially Afro-Cuban brass sound in their guitar work.

The crucial decade for almost all these dance styles was the late 1950s and early 1960s. In the mid-1950s styles were jelling, and usually showing undigested foreign influences. In the two Congos, the early recordings by the great Franco and the Bantous de la Capitale still gave off a strong whiff of Cuba, for all that the future of *soukous* was also foreshadowed. In Ghana, E. T. Mensah's early trumpet playing was strongly influenced by British sweet trumpeter Eddie Calvert. And while the Kenyan guitar style was already jelling, Fundi Konde and Ester John were experimenting with limited clarinet and European-sounding accordion backings as well as version of the Congo tinge.* By 1963 or so, the major styles were clearly set. Occasionally, as with a Congolese *chachachá* and bolero rage, unfamiliar styles would cause something of a reversion. But in the Congo, classics were being recorded by 1962 or so (among them the pan-African hit, "Afrika Mokili Mobimba").

Another important outside influence in the late '60s was the popularity of African-American soul music, common to most parts of Africa. The introduction of soul produced some slightly odd results in places, just as all the other imported elements did before becoming acclimated. Musically speaking, the Afrobeat idiom that developed in the late 1960s as a reaction to the arrival of U.S. soul records, was also in a sense a version of pidgin highlife. Its best-known exponent, the late singer-saxophonist Fela Anikulapo Kuti (born Fela Ransome Kuti) extended its range with a particularly heavy U.S. jazz/soul influence, and carried the tradition of songs rebuking erring leaders—a common way of letting traditional chiefs know what the man in the compound thought about things—to lengths that made him an icon of Western progressives. But musically he was in a strong tradition, and never the most popular exponent of it locally, though his strong foreign elements gave him a cachet of hipness (this was also true of the Camerounian *makossa* saxophonist, Manu Dibango).

Other Afrobeat pioneers included the Dahomeyan trumpeter Ignace de Souza, who hired a then-unknown Fela in 1968 to appear in his Accra nightclub, and later moved to Nigeria and recorded a number of Afrobeat titles. Another popular group was a Gambian band, the Super Eagles, which played Afrobeat versions of James Brown and Aretha Franklin hits (it has since changed its name to Ifang Bondi and gone neotraditional in Mandingo vein). Though it is not often mentioned, West Africa is full of what are locally called "copyright" bands, which in the United States would be known as cover groups or bands. Sometimes they were brilliant: Ghanaian Charlotte Dada's

---

* One problem with assessing early Kenyan, South African, and Zambian recordings is that English musicians were sometimes included on them.

version of "Don't Let Me Down" (included on the Original Music CD *Money No Be Sand*) is in my sacrilegious view better than the Beatles original.

Afrobeat is a style with more strong overseas (specifically African-American) following than most, which explains why—despite international hype—artists like Fela were outsold tenfold locally by many musicians, even in styles unknown in the West. But the highlife of which it is—in the long view—a minor part, is one of the oldest "westernized" styles on the continent. Earlier writers on highlife were at odds on its origins, partly because—like the wise men and the elephant—they mistook partial influences for the whole thing, and partly because of a basic semantic disagreement as to what formed part of highlife and what did not. J. H. Kwabena Nketia claimed that highlife grew up as a street music, and J. E. Casely-Hayford argued that, as its name suggests, it started among the African middle class. Some Sierra Leoneans believe that the large West Indian garrison in Freetown brought the style to Africa and that all the Ghanaians did was get it on record first. This endemic bickering results from the fact that there was no single original highlife, but a wide range of dances of differing names and similar natures, for which highlife was always—or rapidly became—a vague generic label that has been applied differently by different people to a complex of styles, urban and rural, working-class and elite. This is not the only example of the same name being used to describe very different music in different places. *Ashiko,* for example, was in Cameroun the local name for an acoustic-guitar form somewhere between palmwine and highlife; in Nigeria, it was a percussion music associated mostly with Christian Yoruba; and in Ghana it was a brass band style!

Wherever it came from, by the late 1940s highlife had become a highly developed group of forms. In both Ghana and Nigeria, two distinct styles developed: the guitar band (mostly rural and often associated with traveling "concert parties"), and urban dance bands with a front line of horns. The guitar bands developed, though not perhaps directly, from 1930s palmwine bands, and particularly Sam's Trio (which introduced the *amponsah* groove I mentioned earlier in this chapter). Another important musician was Onyina, who in the 1940s introduced jazz chordings into what had been largely a single-string style.

Until the late 1960s, the horn bands of the big cities were the most prestigious. Stylistically they were quite varied. One of the earlier postwar groups, the West African Rhythm Brothers (formed in 1946), chose its personnel from traditional musicians and trained them in Western instruments, so that traditional or at least indigenous elements remained strong. Highlife was also intertribal, at least to the degree permitted by the multiplicity of languages. Nigerian bands like Victor Olaiya's Cool Cats, Eric "Show Boy" Akaeze's

Back in the 1950s, Sierra Leone's Famous Scruggs used a banjo in a highly personal version of palmwine calypso.
Courtesy of West Africa Magazine

Azagas, and Charles Iwegbue's Archibogs had Yoruba, Ibo, Hausa, and other tribes represented among their musicians, and E. K. Nyame's influential Ghanaian guitar band at one time or another employed players from most Ghanaian tribes as did most other guitar bands from Ghana. Indeed, one of highlife's strengths is that the groups combined constant renewal of contact with traditional material, "modern" trends in pop music, and intertribalism. Thus, the midwestern guitar band of Sir Victor Uwaifo—an important musician essentially unknown in the West—was highly polished with a good deal of soul-type showmanship; and yet Uwaifo introduced the Calabari *akwete* rhythm into highlife and used a traditional xylophone in his lineup.

Accra and the western Ghanaian mining capital of Takoradi were awash with fine dance bands. In the 1950s, most famous and influential throughout West Africa was trumpeter E. T. Mensah's Tempos. In the 1960s a slew of bands grew up, including Broadway, the Ramblers, and the bands run by de Souza, who introduced Congo music to Accra in the mid-1960s and later was an early Afrobeat proponent. In Nigeria, the first band of note was run by the

West African highlife comes in many forms. The eastern Nigerian version, in the hands of guitarists like Dan Satch Opara, is built on ferocious guitar riffing.
Courtesy of Original Music

legendary Bobby Benson. In the early 1960s Lagos was home to many fine
bands. These usually involved an ethnic mix of musicians (their recordings
often had a Yoruba song on one side and an Ibo song on the other), but many
of the best-known bandleaders—Eddy Okonta and Charles Iwegbue among
them—were Ibo from the area that tried to break away as Biafra. When the
Nigerian Civil War broke out in 1967, the horn-band highlife scene of Lagos
pretty much collapsed. In Lagos the Yoruba style called *jujú* took over, and in
West Africa as in the world generally, a new generation regarded jazz-
influenced trumpets and saxophones as corny and the guitar as king.

But Lagos was not the only city in which the horn bands fell on hard
times. A new generation brought a major revolution that followed the international pattern of rejecting the parents' music, including jazz or jazz-based
forms, and taking to the guitar (and to rock and roll) as part of one phenomenon. In West Africa the process was slowed: in Nigeria by the rise of Afrobeat
and in particular of Fela; and in Ghana by the success of the Ramblers Dance
Band. But in the 1970s a passion for soul and particularly James Brown swept

First of the 1960s–1980s Nigerian *juju* triumvirate, E. K. Dairo M.B.E. introduced the accordion and more importantly the superb *Aladura* Church vocal style to *juju*.
Courtesy of Graviton Productions

Ghana, influencing singers like Pat Thomas, and by the end of the 1970s, Nana Ampadu and similar bands in Ghana were all guitar or guitar-and-keyboard based. In Nigeria, *juju* swept the western area. Where highlife clung on—notably in the Ibo areas of the East—it either developed into a fierce guitar groove exemplified by the various Oriental Brothers groupings, or took on a tinge of Camerounian *makossa* like the band of Prince Nico Mbarga. Only in the mid-'90s has a classic, 1960-style horn band, the Western Diamonds, begun recording in Ghana.

Highlife produced many local offshoots, some of which developed into very strongly individual styles, often through a process of re-Africanization and localization. The best known is perhaps the Yoruba *juju*, a guitar music with rather more obvious traditional content than Ghanaian guitar music. The intensely individual sound of *juju* stems less from the guitar work (which falls into the general highlife-like pattern of simple chording and single-string picking) than from the use of Yoruba percussion, such as talking drums, and from a singing style akin to the highly distinctive traditional Yoruba style.

Christopher Waterman traces *juju* from a palmwine/highlife-like style of the 1930s. Many Nigerians date the beginning of *juju* to the early 1960s, when the bandleader I. K. Dairo became famous. But it would be more accurate to say that Dairo altered and "modernized" *jujú,* thus widening its appeal. A less famous musician, Tunde Nightingale, was already playing a very similar music in 1944–1945, though it was Dairo who introduced the gorgeous *jujú* vocal choral style from the indigenous Christian Yoruba *Aladura* church, besides using an accordion as well as a guitar (the introduction of the talking drum which gave *jujú* rhythm sections such power and individuality was also credited to Dairo, but apparently wrongly). Dairo turned *jujú* into a music that went beyond the Yoruba people, and yet he also incorporated more Yoruba traditional material. This is less of a paradox than it seems. Dairo's procedure in fact reflects an abiding dualism in African music of all kinds. He has produced music that is new but that asserts its newness in a framework of the past, thus supplying both novelty and continuity to a people who value both. Dairo was one of three major innovators in the past forty years; he was followed in the 1970s by Ebenezer Obey, who was heavily influenced by modern Congolese guitar styles, and in the 1980s by King Sunny Adé, who expanded the front line to four or five guitars, used a Hawaiian guitar, and moved *jujú* into the electronic age by using synthesizers. Here is another example of African pop music's dualism: electronics and traditional drumming!

The guitar has been the basic instrument of contemporary nontraditional African music—the tool of the revolution. But the common Western categorizations of guitar = modern; percussion = traditional—or even guitar = urban; percussion = rural—can be misleading. There are also urban twentieth-century percussion styles. The Yoruba, whose culture was quite urban well before colonization, developed an array of percussion music in this century which are the true popular music of Lagos and Ibadan. Stars of the Muslim idioms, *apala, waka,* and sakara (all of which are purely Yoruba in inspiration, though fairly new), far outsell figures famous in the west like Fela. Nor were they alone; in the 1960s the teenagers of Accra developed an idiom called *kpanlogo* which earned all the parental obloquy showered on any teenage phenomenon, and earlier largely teenage styles like Ghanaian *konkoma* and Malawian *chiwoda* were also novelties to their first public. Moreover, even this music of vocals and drums, so local-sounding to outside ears, has some Afro-American influence. I have mentioned *ashiko,* which in Lagos is a drummed idiom mostly associated with Christian Yoruba. Though it sounds entirely Yoruba to outside ears, it in fact is apparently influenced by the music of freed slaves returned from Brazil. Players of the mostly Muslim Lagos idiom called *agidigbo* have specifically cited Afro-Cuban music as one of its inspirations. And *konkoma* and particularly *chiwoda* were semiparade styles influenced by brass band music.

The music most thoroughly and permanently influenced by soul and funk comes from Ethiopia. A very early example, from the late 1960s, was included on the Original Music CD *Africa Dances*. Bands like Mahmoud Ahmed continued the tradition, which is not one of dilution for a foreign market, but music made by Ethiopians for Ethiopians with a typical soul/funk electric bass line but a strongly Ethiopian singing style.

Before dealing with the last of the major modern style areas of Africa—South Africa—it is worth returning to East Africa for a look at two countries that have been deeply affected by Congo music while retaining an individuality of manner not achieved by the rest of francophone Africa (with the possible exception of Cameroun). Tanzanian dance music in the 1950s and early 1960s, as represented by groups like the Cuban Marimba Band with Salim Abdulla, showed strong Congolese influence, but with an Arab element due to the Islamic civilization of the coast. Certain Tanzanian pop discs were almost purely Afro-Arab in singing style, and Abdulla once brought off the stylistic coup of using an Arab-style bridge between one Congo-type section and another. Later, the Arab content seemed to vanish, except perhaps for a certain quality in Tanzanian vocal tone, a gentle but not sloppy sadness. The Tanzanian bands continued to evolve under the influence of Congo music—any rhythm fashionable in Kinshasa would be fashionable in Dar es Salaam a couple of months later—yet with unquantifiable differences that make a Tanzanian record instantly distinguishable from a Congolese. Even the Tanzanian guitar styles, though it is impossible to analyze how they differ from Congolese, are unmistakable. Certain groups, such as the Western Jazz, experimented with such things as trumpet solos, but this was relatively rare. The most obvious variant, the use of Swahili, is the least important, and besides, the Congo groups out of Kisangani also used to use Swahili, which is one of the country's official languages.

Kenya's pop music underwent very major changes during the 1970s. Like most African pop music, the earliest examples were strongly Western in influence. During the early period it was noteworthy for its charm and its large degree of non-Kenyan components, despite which it contrived to sound entirely nonderivative. There were, until about 1966, two fundamental Kenyan beats. One, vaguely Latin, was introduced via the Congo but was given idiosyncrasy by the Kenyan two-voice, two-guitar formula. Also distinct was the song form, consisting of three verses, each made up of a couplet that is repeated, and then the whole thing is repeated. The other beat, the so-called African twist, was a version of the South African *kwela*, which a European producer who had worked in South Africa introduced to certain bands in Kenya at the time of the twist craze. The Kenyan style has always been

Even local styles had their international aspect. The sound at this 1960s Nairobi recording session was pure Kenyan, but the popular vocal duo consisted of Nashil Pichen (Zambia) and Peter Tsotsi (Congo). Behind them is Kenyan guitarist/vocalist Fadhili William of "Malaika" fame.
Photo by John Storm Roberts

song-oriented, rhythmically simple, and very jaunty. For a while around 1966, bands like the Ashantis became very Congo-oriented, in part under the influence of a large number of Congolese refugee musicians in East Africa.

But during the 1970s and 1980s, a revolution—or counter-revolution—took place. Until then, the language of Kenyan pop was Swahili, spoken not only in Kenya but in Tanzania, eastern Congo, and Uganda. But the Swahili-language phase turned out to be quite shortlived. I have mentioned that in the 1950s, more local guitar-backed styles were recorded in various ethnic languages. Even in the Swahili heyday of the late 1960s, occasional records would be produced in the language of the Luo, Kenya's second largest ethnic group, whose melody lines, rhythms, and guitar playing were closer to Luo traditional music. In the 1970s and 1980s, both the Luo and their western neighbors the Luya (two tribes with strong string elements in their traditional music) began to dominate with a new idiom called *benga*. By the late 1980s, there were several *benga* styles, each drawing from its own traditional music. The reasons were partly political; the days when musicians sang optimistically

A century and a half after the Jamaican *goombay* drum moved to Africa, reggae hit the continent in the work of singers such as Nigerian Sonny Okosuns.
Photo by Gary Stewart

of East African federation were long gone. But I think they were also human. Swahili is a nearly universal second language in Kenya, but Luo, Luya, Kikuyu, and so on are the first languages of most Kenyans, and thus the languages most emotionally suited to personal expression.

If both Kenya and Tanzania had strongly derivative elements in their music, Uganda has a pop style that lies mostly in a set of vocal-line characteristics, including melodies modified by Luganda speech-patterns and a cool vocal tone stemming, I think, from widespread mission-school education. This singing is backed by one or two foreign styles, Congolese or Kenyan, and the reasons for this reflect economic realities in the African music business, as well as a dash of past politics. Partly owing to the Congolese political crises of the early 1960s, Uganda was full of Congolese musicians looking for peace and quiet and a job. As a result, the Congo band style swamped Kampala's night clubs early and thoroughly. On the other hand, the recording industry was in Nairobi. The Ugandan singer therefore found himself backed by a Congo sound in club dates, but when he made a record he had to go to Nairobi to do it, and Nairobi record companies were not about to pay session men's fares when they had their own resident groups. The dark period of Idi Amin and his successors basically killed all but very local expressions of Ugandan urban dance music, and though several bands are now playing, the interruption has been great enough that the overseas elements—reggae, soul, rock—still dominate a music only beginning to recuperate from twenty years of political repression.

So far, all the regions I have been discussing have been tied together in one way or another. South Africa is something else again. South African traditional music is quite dissimilar in many respects from that of the rest of Africa. Most important, from the point of view of the evolution of South African modern pop music, its rhythmic approach is different. Instead of instrumental polyrhythms, with the vocal line simply supplying another rhythmic layer, South African music, which is short on instruments—partly because the South African ecology is on the whole short on materials out of which to make them—tends toward a pattern of complex sung rhythms set off against a steady beat, whether from hand-clapping, drum, or rattle. (This is, of course, a tendency, not a universal rule.) The effect on South African pop music is twofold: First, it has supplied a local element very different from those of other African pop forms; and second, Afro-Cuban music has meant relatively little to South Africans, and certainly very little to the development of their pop music. Jazz, on the other hand, has meant a good deal.

Though it in fact consisted of many styles and/or substyles, Westerners know South African music under two headings which make a good place to start: the vocal *mbube* or *iscathamiya* exemplified by Ladysmith Black Mambazo, and the township jive or *mbaqanga*, which often also backs vocals related to *iscathamiya*'s lead singing. Both, as elsewhere in Africa, mix strong local elements with overseas elements. The contact with African-American music in South Africa was with a more developed version than the earlier contributions of returned slaves in West Africa. As Veit Erlmann has documented in *African Stars: Studies in Black South African performance*, an African-American minstrel group, the Virginia Jubilee Singers run by Orpheus M. MacAdoo (a former member of the Fisk Jubilee Singers), spent a total of almost five years in South Africa in the 1890s. Thus vocal influences on South Africa are the oldest. They have varied very much over time, and depend considerably on the type of group singing.

There are no available records from before the 1930s of vaudeville groups like Motsieloa's Pitch Black follies and the Bantu Glee Singers. These tended to be backed by British village-hall piano (possibly white studio musicians, though earlier recordings by Reuben Caluza have much the same feeling), and sometimes banjo. But their singing was already strongly South African in feeling. Motsieloa's Pitch Black Follies' 1939 "Tsaba Tsaba ke No.1" (reissued on Christian Ballantine's *Marabi Roots* book/cassette set) is very clearly a forerunner of the great female vocal groups of later periods. And the big Zulu and

Despite a brief vogue in Britain, South Africa's blues-influenced 1950s pennywhistle *kwela* was a street music at its heart, and one of its most famous exponents was a shoeshine boy.
Photo by David Rycroft

Xhosa choirs draw largely from traditional group singing, as well as from church choirs, and sometimes seemingly from other mission influences (some had an odd German/Austrian sound, perhaps from the Moravian missions).

But quartets and other small vocal ensembles have often contained much more African-American quartet singing. This influence is particularly obvious in Ladysmith Mambazo, which sometimes shows the strong influence of the Golden Gate Quartet, very popular in South Africa. The seminal "Wimoweh" by Solomon Linda (popularized by Miriam Makeba and an international hit) also has obvious U.S. quartet elements. Even though the sensational "groaning" of Mahlathini, lead singer with the Mahotella Queens, has strong roots in *iscathamiya*, I'm not sure it is a coincidence that it surfaced some time after the popularity of "hard" gospel groups like the Mighty Clouds of Joy and soul shouters like James Brown.

By the mid-1940s, vaudeville vocal groups were begin backed by jazzlike combos of piano, bass, guitar, and drums, in which the piano—an instrument very rare in other parts of Africa, incidently—was playing grooves that clearly stemmed from the driving repetitions of the vocals, and foreshadowed township jive and provided a link with more instrumentally slanted styles. Jazz became a part of South Africa's modern urban music because it blends in a number of ways with certain inclinations in the indigenous traditional music. The strongly swing-oriented township jazz of the 1940s was essentially the solid, Count Basie-type four-four rhythm of black swing bands. But the *kwela* beat of the 1950s blues-tinged pennywhistle *kwela* bands had a light, lifting beat between the main beats—an eight-to-the-bar effect, but quite distinct from the barrelhouse eight-to-the-bar. It owed its existence to the fact that many traditional rhythms also had a pattern of firm beats with light, lifting beats in between—particularly musical bow rhythms, to which a second light tap on the string was often basic.

A big increase in the foreign records available to black South Africans, either to buy or to hear on the radio, occurred in the 1940s, when big-band sounds with a steady, driving beat and the singing of Ella Fitzgerald and her imitators were the best-selling black American music. The influence of Fitzgerald cannot be doubted if you listen to a very early recording, made in South Africa, of Mireiam Makeba singing "Rocking in Rhythm" or a singer called Toko Tomo singing "Zulu Boy *Kwela*."* Many of the turns of the highly distinctive group-singing style of "township jazz" of the 1950s were vocalizations of U.S. big-band arrangers' tricks.

In the mid-1950s the Americanization of South African pop music was such that some of the pennywhistle *kwela* tunes of the time used twelve-bar blues patterns, and some singers were backed not by the *kwela* beat, with its lilting shuffle, but by a straight four-four beat. This underscores the importance of an apparently small traditional element, for while the *kwela* beat was incredibly lilting and swinging, the examples of straight jazz rhythms plodded.

South Africa is also arguably the only country outside the United States that has developed its own form of pure jazz. Pianist Abdullah Ibrahim (Dollar Brand), saxophonist Dudu Pukwana, trombonist Jonas Gwangwa, and trumpeter Hugh Masekela have all made their mark in the U.S. jazz scene during years of exile, as of course has vocalist Makeba, with her strong roots in the women jazz singers. And they are only the best known of an entire class of musicians who flavored jazz with South African elements to make it their own. But this was only part of the jazz influence. The idea that the South African township jazz is simply an imitation of American jazz (even though many of the South African jazz musicians came out of it) would be just as false as the notion that Congo pop is merely pseudo-Cuban. The basic instruments of this style, like all the others, are human voice and guitar. The singing, when it is not solo, is almost always call-and-response, a root Africanism in this area as everywhere else. But more significant, the very characteristic relationship of leader and chorus—with its interweaving of voices in the choral part and more overlapping of solo and group than is common in other parts of Africa—is not

---

* Both songs were reissued on a U.S. London LP, *Something New from Africa*.

a foreign feature. Like *mbube,* it is a version, "urbanized" and probably generalized slightly, of a choral singing style common to most of the big South African ethnic groups, though it varies a good deal in detail from one to another. It happens that some techniques of big-band jazz, with the soloist riding a pattern of riffs, fuse with this South African vocal pattern. All this means that there are some components that resemble each other in jazz and South African music, seen in very general terms. It does not, however, mean that there was a direct link in the past between the two, as there was between Cuban music and West African and Congo-Angolan styles.

The jazz–South African pop connections had some ongoing results, including a greater emphasis on instrumental music (despite the fundamental guitar-voice complex). The instrumental sector, naturally enough, tended to show slightly stronger jazz characteristics than the vocal, because there was not much South African traditional instrumental technique to carry over. Yet there are striking similarities of phrasing between some traditional South African flute playing and the pennywhistle style of the mid-1950s. The pennywhistle was just the first of many passing instrumental crazes; others included mouth organ, accordion (apparently an Afrikaner influence), and more recently saxophone. Each has shown the influence of reinterpreted jazz in its playing style, especially when first introduced. The fairly new saxophone sound, generically called "sax-jive," is a pop phenomenon not to be confused with the use of saxophones for backing or section work by the bigger and more "sophisticated" groups, or their use by the South Africans—of whom there were quite a few—who played "pure jazz." The jazz influence on township jazz is slight; it is typical that a record called "Charlie the Bird" had no detectable trace of the Parker touch.

The successive pop styles went beyond mere fashions in instruments to reflect more fundamental crazes in dance rhythms. *Kwela* and *phatha-phatha* are two that, it so happens, have been heard of outside South Africa. But there are plenty of others: monkey-jive, *'smodern,* on and on. All these rhythms, of course, differed from each other noticeably, but the overall stylistic continuity of South African popular music overrides the variations. Obvious Africanisms abound even in the instrumental pop, such as versions of call-and-response, a tendency toward extreme repetition (deliberate and functional, as has been shown), and the direction of all musical endeavor toward polyrhythmic rather than melodic ends.

There were also marked differences between urban and rural styles, and between the music of the mining areas. Along with the more urban sounds, vocal and instrumental, have grown up rougher, more earthy idioms like the so-called "traditional" fiddle and accordion groups of the Zulu and Shangaan, which is of course not traditional but is very much a music of the rural migrants who work in the big mines. Shangaan music in particular, which bridges South Africa and Mozambique, is special; the Original Music release *Kerestina* documents some of the grassroots music on which the semiprofessional groups who make commercial recordings have built.

As should be abundantly clear from this sketchy portrait of a continent as musically rich now as it has ever been, the old and usually pejorative concept of "Westernized" pop music entirely misses the point of a reality that might equally (as might its analogue in the New World) be called the Africanization of Western music. The root of all African pop styles is a blend of reinterpreted traditional—or at least local—elements with any foreign ingredients that may enhance them (besides, of course, impressing people in any particular time and place as desirably new and "sophisticated"). Even if one excepts Islam, which though older is originally just as foreign, many—perhaps most—of these foreign elements are almost all Afro-American (Cuban, other Caribbean, black U.S.), and many of the apparently non–Afro-American influences have themselves been influenced by black music.

The more recent concept of "Third World" cultures being ravaged by wicked Western ways is, in my view, equally off the mark and insulting. It essentially sees African cultures as too reactive and too feeble to revive or change, where in fact they have always used new influences to build on their traditions and—like every other culture—emerged richer. The whole idea suggests that the musicians who have in fact reacted enthusiastically to new ideas and transmuted them into something of their own are mere straws in the winds of change. It is like the occasional allegation that Afro-American music is "all African music"—which besides clearly being untrue except in the most vaguely mystical sense, suggests that in 200 years of suffering and a very varied cultural environment black U.S. musicians have been incapable of coming up with any original ideas. Such theories are not only as demeaning to the artists involved as any of the old white-racist incomprehension, but quite as oblivious to the musical realities. Modern African pop music, in fact, completes a very satisfactory black-music circle binding together the Old World and the New, in which Europe and Africa have provided Afro-Americans with the fundamentals to create much of the greatest popular music ever conceived.

Selected Discography

Compared with 1972, when I wrote the first edition of *Black Music of Two Worlds*, an enormous amount of material is at least theoretically available, though there are also some significant gaps in Western releases (and even more so in United States releases). Moreover, "available" is a weasel word. The fact that a record is in print does not make it easy to find, and many fairly recent issues have disappeared again. All the records listed here are, or have been, issued in the West and are therefore theoretically findable, if not in regular stores then through specialists. Surf the Web and also contact the list of sources (pages 307 to 309) for a number of reliable specialist mail-order sources (but be prepared for them to go out of business—it's a tough period for people selling outside the Top 100). The Latin record market is a largely separate entity (except for Latin recordings on "mainstream" labels). If you live in a big city with a barrio there will be at least one large record store there. Otherwise see my source list. I have not indicated what recordings are in or out of print because that will have changed before this book hits the stores. All the LPs are out of print; with the CDs, the situation keeps changing. Finally, don't expect logic: field recordings of Yoruba traditional music from Nigeria are almost unavailable, but there are several releases of Yoruba music from the much smaller group in the much smaller country of Benin.

General

The old Columbia World Library of Folk and Primitive Music, overseen by Alan Lomax, was not ideal (cuts tend to be faded after a minute or so) but contained some music you wouldn't find anywhere else. Though long gone and sought after, you may occasionally find a relevant volume in the second-hand bins.

Europe

Belgium

Ballads Songs and Dances of Flanders and Wallonia. Ocora 580061.

Britain

The Folk Songs of Britain Ten LPs: Topic 12T1257-161 and 12T194-198.
Boscastle Breakdown. Topic LP 12T244.
Bob Roberts, *Songs from the Sailing Barges.* Topic LP 12TS361.
Sam Larner, *Now Is the Time for Fishing.* Musical Traditions Cassette MTC203.
Songs of the Travelling People, Saydisc CD SDL407.
Hidden English. Topic CD TSCD600.
Bob Hart, *Songs from Suffolk.* Topic LP 12TS225.

France

Folk Music of France. Folkways LP FE4414.
Musique Traditionnelle des Pays de France. Chant du Monde LP LDX74516.
Violoneux et Chanteurs Traditionnels en Auvergne. Chant du Monde LP LDX74635.
Musique Traditionnel du Berry. Chant du Monde LP LDX74653.
Violoneux et Chanteurs Traditionnels du Dauphiné. Chant du Monde LDX74687.
Chants Tradittionels des Marins Pêcheurs de Fécamp. Chant du Monde LP LDX74704.

Italy

Organetto & Tarantelle. SudNord CD SNCD0028.
Traditional Dances in Umbria. SudNord CD SNCD0030.
Festival Music of Calabria. Inédit CD W260051.

All these compilations include examples of accordion and singing styles that fetched up in Argentina during the tango's formative years.

Portugal

Musical Traditions of Portugal. Smithsonian-Folkways CD 40435.
Portuguese Traditional Music. Auvidis CD D8008.

Corridinhos. Playa Sound CD PS65093.
Fado de Lisboa, 1928–1936. Heritage CD HTCD14.
Fados from Portugal Vol 2 (Coimbra). Heritage CD HTCD15.

Spain

Antología del Folclor Musical de España. Hispavox 10-107 to 110; also at one time available in the
    United States as Everest 3286/4.
Aledo: Sones de Fiesta. Auvidis/Ethnic CD B6798.

African Traditional

Regional

The most important collection of eastern, southern, and central African music
is Hugh Tracey's set of some 200 LPs issued by the International Library of
African Music in South Africa. These are not on general sale but any major
ethnolomusicological library ought to have them. A set of ten LPs called
"Music of Africa," culled from the larger collection, has appeared in various
guises, in the United States most recently on the small Kaleidophone label.

Africa South of the Sahara. Folkways FE 4503.
Music of Equatorial Africa. Folkways FE 4402.
Musique d'Afrique du Nord: Maroc, Algérie, Tunisie. Vogue Contrepoint MC 20.016.
Musique d'Afrique Occidentale. Contrepoint LP MC20.045 France.

By Country

Benin (formerly Dahomey)

Yoruba Drums from Benin, West Africa. Smithsonian-Folkways CD 40440.
Bariba and Somba Music. Auvidis/UNESCO CD D8057.
Rhythms and Songs for the Vodun. VDE-Gallo CD VDE612.
Music of the Princes of Dahomey. Counterpoint Esoteric 537.
Musiques Dahoméennes. Ocora LP OCR 17.
Ogun: God of Iron. Vogue Contrepoint LP MC20159.
Rhythms of Life, Songs of Wisdom. Smithsonian-Folkways 40463.

Cameroun

Flutes and Rhythms of Cameroun. Buda CD 824602.
Danses et Chants Bamoun: Musique de la République Fédérale du Cameroun. Ocora SCR 3.
Musiques du Cameroun. Ocora OCR 25.
Nord Cameroun: Musique Fali. Ocora; no number.

Cape Verde

Kode Di Dona. Ocora CD 560100.
Cesaria Evora. Nonesuch CD 79379.
Travadinha: The Violin of Cape Verde. Buda 92556.
The Roots. Playa Sound PS65061.

Central African Republic

Sanza Music in the Land of the Gbaya. VDE-Gallo CD VDE755.
Kongo Drums. Buda CD 925252.
Music for Xylophones. Chant du Monde CD 274932.
Xylophones of the Ouam-Pende. Ocora CD 560094.

Congo (both)

Mongo Polyphony. Ocora 580050.

Gambia

Alhaji Bai Konte, *Kora Melodies.* Rounder CD CD5001.
The Art of Jali Nyama Suso. Ocora CD 580027.

Ghana

Master Drummers of Dagbon. Vol. 1 and Vol. 2. Rounder CD5016/CD5046.
Oboade, *Kpanlogo Party.* Lyrichord CD LYRCD7251.
Ewe Music of Ghana. Asch AHM 4222.

Guinea

Musics of Fouta Djalon. Playa Sound CD PS65028.
Jali Musa Jawara Yasimika. Hannibal CD HNCD1355.

Liberia

Music of the Kpelle of Nigeria. Folkways FE4385.
Folk Music of Liberia. Folkways FE 4465.

Mali

Drums of Mali. Djenne CD DJCD1001.
Ancient Strings. Musicaphon LP BM2505.
The Steppes and Savannahs of Mali: The Mandingo. Musicaphon LP BM2501.
Fluvial Mali: The Peul. Musicaphon LP BM2502.
Les Dogon Mali. Ocora OCR 33.

Morocco

Berber Music from the High Atlas and the Anti-Atlas. Chant du Monde CD 274991.
B'Net Houariyat. Al Sur CD ALCD126.

Drums of Morocco: Aadat. Al Sur CD ALCD121.
Hadra of the Gnawa of Essaouira. Ocora CD 560006.
Sacred and Secular Music of the Middle-Atlas. Ocora CD 559057.

Niger

Anthology of Music from Niger. Ocora CD 559056.

Nigeria

Music of the Fulani. Auvidis/Unesco CD D8006.
Drums of the Yoruba of Nigeria. Ethnic Folkways FE 4441.
The Igede of Nigeria. Music of the World CD CDT117.

Senegal

Fulani and Tenda Music. Ocora 560043.

Sierra Leone

Traditional Musics. Ocora CD 580036.

South Africa

See the note on Hugh Tracey recordings at the head of the Africa section
(page 289).

Togo

Music from West Africa. Rounder CD5004.
Musique Kabrè du Nord-Togo. Ocora OCR16.

Tunisia

Tunisie. Philips 844 924 BY.
Lotfi Bouchnak, *Malouf Tunisien.* Inédit CD W260053.
Malouf Tunisien: Nuba al-Dhil. Inedit CD W260044.
RBAIBIYA Artistes. *Arabes Associés.* CD AAA073.

African Non-Traditional and Pop

General

Africa Dances. Original Music OMCD002.
Guitar Songs: Tanzania, Zaire & Zambia. Original Music OMCD023.
West African Instrumental Quintet 1929. Heritage CD HTCD16.

Afro-Reggae

Black Star Liner: Reggae from Africa. Heartbeat CD HBCD16.
Alpha Blondy, *The Best of . . .* Shanachie Cassette SH43075.
Lucky Dube Prisoner. Shanachie CD DSH43073.
Sonny Okosuns Liberation. Shanachie CD DSHAN43019.

Cameroun

Makossa Connection Vol. 1. TJR Music CD CDAT107.
Moni Bile, *10e Anniversaire.* Mad Production CD CD52711.
Sam Fan Thomas, *Si Tcha.* MST Productions CD 59801.
Têtes Brulées, *Hot Heads.* Shanachie CD DSHAN64030.

Cape Verde

Travadinha: The Violin of Cape Verde. Buda CD 92556.
The Roots. Playa Sound CD PS65061.

Ethiopia

Ethiopian Groove: The Golden Seventies. Blue Silver CD BSCD002.
Mahmoud Ahmed, *Era Era.* Hannibal CD HNCD1354.

Ghana

Kumasi Trio 1928 [Sam's Trio]. Heritage HTCD22.
Giants of Danceband Highlife 1950s–1970. Original Music OMCD011.
Black Beats/Mensah/Rhythm Aces/Etc., Telephone Lobi. Original Music OMCD033.
Ignace de Souza. Original Music OMCD026.
I've Found My Love: 1960s Guitar Band Highlife. Original Music OMCD019.
E.T. Mensah, *All for You.* RetroAfric CD Retro1CD.
Koo Nimo, *Osabarima.* Adasa Records CD ADCD102.

Guinea

Bembeya Jazz National. Esperance CD 8491.
Les Amazones du Guinée/M'Mah Sylla. Bolibana CD 420762.

Kenya

Fundi Konde, *Retrospective* Vol. 1. RetroAfric RETRO8CD.
Various Artists, *Kenya Dry.* Original Music OMCD021.
The Nairobi Sound. Original Music OMCD022.
Kenya Dance Mania. Earthworks CD 310242.
The Nairobi Beat. Rounder CD5030.
Misiani and Shirati Band: Benga Blast. Earthworks/Virgin CD STEW13CD.

Selected Discography

Malawi

Alan Namoko & Chimvu Jazz, *Ana Osiidwa*. Pamtondo CD PAM004.

Mali

Ambassadeurs Internationaux. Rounder CD CD5053.
Kante Manfila, *Tradition*. Celluloid CD 66860.
Salif Keita, *Soro*. Mango CD CD9808.
Super Biton de Ségou, *Afro Jazz du Mali*. Bolibana CD 42013.
The Wassoulou Sound: Women of Mali. Sterns CD STCD1035.

Nigeria

Juju Roots 1930s-1950s. Rounder CD CD5017.
Cardinal Rex Lawson, *Greatest Hits*. Flametree CD531.
Fela Anikulapo Kuti, *Beasts of No Nation*. Shanachie CD DSHAN43070.
I. K. Dairo, *Ashiko*. Green Linnet/Xenophile CD XCD4018.
Sunny Ade, *The Return of the Juju King*. Mercury 832522.
Ebenezer Obey, *Juju Jubilee*. Shanachie CD DSHAN43031.
Sikiru Ayinde Barrister, *Fuji Garbage*. Globestyle CD ORBCD067.
Kabaka's Oriental Brothers International, *Do Better If You Can*. Original Music OMCD034.
Money No Be Sand. Original Music OMCD031.
I. K. Dairo M.B.E., *The Glory Years*. Original Music OMCD009.
Yoruba Street Percussion. Original Music OMCD016.
Azagas & Archibogs. Original Music OMCD014.

Senegal

Youssou Ndour/Etoile de Dakar, *Thiapathioly*. Stern's CD STCD3006.
Youssou Ndour, *Set*. Virgin CD WEA91426.
Mamadou Ly, *Mandinka Drum Master*. Village Pulse CD VP1001.
Tabala Wolof, *Sufi Drumming of Senegal*. Village Pulse CD VP1002.
Sabar Wolof, *Dance Drumming of Senegal*. Village Pulse CD VP1003.
Orchestre Baobab, *On Verra Ça*. World Circuit CD WCD027.

Sierra Leone

Sierra Leone Music. Zensor CD ZSCD41.
Ebenezer Callender et al., *African Elegant*. Original Music OMCD015.

Somalia

Jamiila, *Songs of a Somali City*. Original Music OMCD007.

South Africa

Caluza's Double Quartet 1930. Heritage CD HTCD19.

Siya Hamba. Original Music OMCD003.
Dark City Sisters/ Flying Jazz Queens. Earthworks CD STEW31.
Homeland: Black South African Music. Rounder CD11549.
Jive Soweto. Earthworks CD STEW26.
Dudu Pukwana & Spear, *In the Townships.* Earthworks CD STEW05.
Mahlathini, *The Lion of Soweto.* Earthworks CD STEW04.
Iscathamiya. Heritage LP HT313.
Boyoyo Boys, *Back in Town.* Rounder CD 5026.
Ladysmith Black Mambazo, *Induku Zethu.* Shanachie CD DSHAN43021.
Black Mfolosi, *Unity.* World Circuit WCD020.
Mbube Roots. Rounder CD CD5025.
Seshwe, *The Sound of the Mines.* Rounder CD CD5031.
Singing in an Open Space. Rounder CD CD5027.
Spokes Mashiyane, *King Kwela.* Celluloid CD 668912.
Township Swing Jazz 1954–1958. Vol. 1. Harlequin CD HQCD08.
Hugh Masekela, *Stimela.* Connoisseur Collection CD VSOPCD200.
Miriam Makeba & the Skylarks, *African Heritage.* Teal TELCD2302.

Sudan

Rain in the Hills. Original Music OMCD029.
Abdel Aziz el Mubarak, *Straight from the Heart.* World Circuit WCD010.

Tanzania

Dada Kidawa. Original Music OMCD032.
Mlimani Park Orchestra, *Sikinde.* Africassette CD MSCD900202.

Uganda

The Kampala Sound. Original Music OMCD013.

Zaire/Congo (both nations)

Note: Many hundreds of CDs of Congolese music are available, mostly of French issue. I have mentioned here only a few of the most significant. The series on African/Sonodisc is particularly important. The LP prefix was 300-. The CD prefix is 360-.

Kasongo. Capitol T10005.
The Kinshasa Sound. Original Music OMCD010.
Franco & T.P.OK Jazz, *Originalité 1957–1959.* RetroAfric CD RETRO2CD.
African Fiesta, Nico, Rochereau & Roger 1962–1963. Sonodisc CD 36509.
Bantous de la Capitale, 1963–1969. Sonodisc CD 36527.
Compilation Musique Congolo-Zairoise 1972–1973. Sonodisc CD 36531.
Grand Kallé & L'African Jazz 1961–1962. Sonodisc CD 36506.
Kanda Bongo Man, *Zing Zong.* Hannibal CD HNCD1366.

Mwenda Jean Bosco, *Mwenda wa Bayeke*. Rounder CD5061.
Zaiko Langa Langa, *Zaire-Ghana*. Retroafric CD RETRO5.

Zambia

From the Copperbelt. Original Music OMCD004.
Alick Nkhata, *Shalapo*. RetroAfric CD RETRO4.

Zimbabwe

Jit. Earthworks CD: 310232.
Real Sounds, *Wende Zako*. Rounder CD5029.
Thomas Mapfumo & Blacks Unlimited, *Hondo*. Zimbob CD TMBU13.
Thomas Mapfumo, *Chimurenga Singles*. Meadowlark CD DSHAN43066.
Bhundu Boys, *Shabini*. Discafrique AFRICD02.
Zimbabwe Frontline. Earthworks EWVCD9.

New World General

Africa in America. Corason 3 CDs: MTCD115-7.

Caribbean

General

Caribbean Revels: Haitian Rara & Dominican Gaga. Smithsonian-Folkways 40402.
Caribbean Island Music. Nonesuch CD 72047.
West Indies: An Island Carnival. Nonesuch CD 72091.
Brown Girl in the Ring: Game and Pass Play Songs. Rounder CD1716.
Caribbean Dances. Folkways FW 6840.
Caribbean Folk Music. Folkways FA 4533.

Bahamas

Kneeling Down inside the Gate. Rounder 5035.
The Real Bahamas. Nonesuch H-72013.
Joseph Spense, *Living on the Hallelujah Side*. Rounder CD2021.
Religious Songs and Drums in the Bahamas. Ethnic Folkways FE 4440.

Belize

Mr. Peters Boom & Chime, *Haul Up Your Foot You Fool*. Fire Ant CD FACD1006.
Shine Eye Gal. Corason CD COCD118.

Costa Rica

Calypsos: Afro–Limonese Music. Lyrichord CD LYRCD7412.

Dutch Antilles

Tumba Cuarta & Ka'i. Original Music LP OMC201.
ABC of the Antilles. Philips PHI 444.

French Antilles

Biguine, Valse et Mazurka Créoles 1929–1940. Frémeaux 2 CDs: FA007.
Dede Saint Prix, *Mi Se Sa.* Mango CD 5398132.
Diapason vol. 3. Hibiscus Records CD 92003.
Eugène Mona, *Blanc Mangé.* Hibiscus CD 880372.
Eugène Mona, *Vol. 1 1975–1978.* Hibiscus CD 88050.
Génération Cadence. Hibiscus CD 191174.
Gramacks / Jeff Joseph, Best of, Vol. 1. Joseph Prods CD CDS7238.
Guadeloupe: Gwoka in Cacao. Ocora CD 560031.
Guy Konket et Le Groupe Ka. Bolibana CD BIP96.
J. B. B. / Vincent Gama Collection Antholojika Sonodisc CD CDS7258.
Kali Racines. Coco Sound CD 88020-2.
Kassav Live au Zénith. SONY / Tristar CD WK57777.
Kassav Eva & No. 3. Hibiscus CD 88056-2.
Malavoi, *L'Autre Style 1975–1982.* Hibiscus CD 88052-2.
Malavoi, *La Belle Epoque.* Hibiscus CD 191162-2.
Marce & Toumpak, Best of . . . Sodipro CD 65663.
Pakatak, *Pa Fè Wôl.* Hibiscus CD 191175-2.
Sartana, *Ostilité.* Polidisc CD 64101.
Stellio 1929–1931. Frémeaux 2 CDs: FA023.
Ti Ken Bonb'La Kaliko. Hibiscus CD 88043-2.
Ti Emile Roi du Bel-Air. Hibiscus CD 191170-2.
Vikings de Guadeloupe, *Les Précurseurs du Zouk.* Hibiscus CD 880542.
Zouk Attack. Rounder CD CD5037.

Guyane

Musique de Guyane. Boite à Musique LP308.

Haiti

Rhythms of Rapture: Sacred Music of Haitian Vodou. Smithsonian-Folkways 40463.
Drums of Haiti. Ethnic Folkways FE 4403.
Fabre Duroseau, *Haitian Piano.* Folkways FW 6837.
Songs and Dances of Haiti. Ethnic Folkways FE 4432.
Althiery Dorival, *An Ba Tonelle.* Mini Records CD MRSD1072.
Méringue: Haiti Chérie. Corason COCD107.
Bossa Combo, *Accolade.* Mini Records CD MRSD1069.

Ska Shah #1, *For Ever.* Mini Records CD MRSD1111.
Boukman Eksperiens, *Vodou Adjae.* Mango CD 539899.
Coupé Cloué, *Maximum Compas from Haiti.* Earthworks CD EWCD2426.
Nemours Jean Baptiste, *Musical Tour of Haiti.* Ansonia CD HGCD1280.
Rara Machine, *Break the Chain.* Shanachie CD DSH64038.
Roots of Haiti Voodoo, Vols. 1 & 2. Mini Records CDs MRSD1063/4.
Shleu-Shleu, *Cé La ou Yé.* Mini Records CD MRSD1004.
Gypsies de Pétionville, *L'Age D'Or.* Rubicolor CD: RVCD75050.
Tabou Combo, *8e Sacrement.* Mini Records CD MRSD1044.
Tabou Combo, *Live au Zenith.* Esperance TD8057.

Jamaica

A Dee-Jay Explosion Inna Dance Hall Style. Heartbeat CDHB04.
Ska Bonanza. Heartbeat CDHB86/87.
Abyssinians, *Satta Massagana.* Heartbeat CD HBCD120.
Augustus Pablo, *King Tubby's Meets The Rockers Uptown.* Message CD MESS1007.
Bob Marley, *In Memoriam.* Trojan 2 CDs: CDTALL400.
Wailers, *Reggae Greats.* Mango CD 539795.
Drums of Defiance. Smithsonian/Folkways CD SFCD40412.
Ethiopians. Trojan CD TRCD228.
John Crow Say . . . Smithsonian/Folkways Cassette FE4228.
Jolly Boys, *Pop'n'Mento.* Rykodisc/First Warning CD RCD10185.
Keep on Coming Through the Door. Trojan TRCD255.
Lititz Mento Band, *Dance Music & Working songs from Jamaica.* Wergo CD SM1512.
Rudies All Round. Trojan CD TRCD322.
Peter Tosh, *The Toughest.* Heartbeat CDHB150.
Churchical Chants of the Nyabinghi. Heartbeat CDHB20.
Folk Music of Jamaica. Ethnic Folkways FE 4453.
From the Grass Roots of Jamaica. Dynamic 3305.
Jamaican Cult Music. Ethnic Folkways FE 4461.

Martinique (see French Antilles)

Small Islands

Under the Coconut Tree. Original Music CD OMCD201.
Blinky and the Roadmasters, *Crucian Scratch Band Music.* Rounder CD CD5047.
Zoop Zoop Zoop. New World CD 80427.
Musical Traditions of St. Lucia. Smithsonian-Folkways CD 40416.

Suriname

William Souvenir, *A Tin Télé.* Music & Words MWCD3010.
Carlo Jones & the Surinam Kaseko Troubadours. MW Records MWCD3011.
Switi: Hot! Kaseko Music SPN Records SPN010.
Ghabiang, *Tanapu in De Rij.* Artie ARCD210770.

Trinidad

Calypso Breakaway 1927–1941. Rounder CD1054.
Calypso Carnival 1936–1941. Rounder CD1077.
Ah Feel to Party. Rounder CD 5066/7.
Heat in De Place: Soca Music from Trinidad. Rounder CD5041.
Say What? Double-Entendre Soca from Trinidad. Rounder CD5042.
Brother Resistance, *De Power of Resistance.* Tonga CD TNGCD9302.
Bamboo-Tamboo, Bongo and the Belair. Cook 5017.
Grand Curucaye String Orchestra of Trinidad, *Epilogue to the String Band Tradition.* Cook/Road Runner 5020.
Jump Up Carnival. Cook 1072.
Nancy Stories—West Indies. Cook E105.
Peter Was a Fisherman. Rounder CD1114.

Latin Continuum

General/Miscellaneous

Oxala: Black Music of South America. Nonesuch 72036 LP.
Harps and Guitars of Latin America. Playa Sound CD PS65043.

Argentina

Historia del Tango. Music Hall MH100102.
Instrumental Tangos of the Golden Age. Harlequin HQCD45.
Tango Ladies: El Tango Hecho Carne. Harlequin CD HQCD34.
Astor Piazzolla, *Tristezas de Un Doble A.* Messidor CD 159702.
Mercedes Sosa, *Amigos Mios.* Polygram CD8422032.

Brazil

Capoeira Angola. Smithsonian-Folkways 40465.
Songs and Dances of Brazil. Folkways FW 6953.
Afro-Brazilian Religious Songs. Lyrichord LYRCD7315.
Amazonia: Cult Music of Northern Brazil. Lyrichord LYRCD7300.
Batucadas and Music of the Northeast. Playa Sound PS65098.
O Samba. Luaka Bop 260192.
Bossa Nova Trinta Anos Depois. Brazilian Verve 8268702.
Brazil Roots Samba. Rounder CD5045.
Carmen Miranda: The Brazilian Recordings. Harlequin HQCD33.
Chico Buarque, *Convite Para Ouvir . . .* Parrot G2207.
Forro: Music for Maids and Taxi-Drivers. Rounder CD5044.
Historia del Carnaval de Brasil 1902–1952 Vols. 1–3. Ubatuqui CDs: UBCD20003-5.
Jacob do Bandolim, *Mandolin Master of Brazil.* Acoustic Disc CD ACD3.
Olodum, *Revolution in Motion World.* Circuit CD WCD031.

Velha Guarda da Portela, *Grandes Sambistas*. Auvidis CD A6132.
Folk Music of Brazil: Afro-Bahian Religious Songs. Library of Congress AFS L13.

Colombia

Porros Solo Porros. Vedisco 1218-2.
Alejandro Duran, *Interpreta a Escalona*. Fuentes CD D16097.
Calixto Ochoa, *Folclor Costeño de Colombia*. Fuentes CD D10055.
Pacho Galan, *El Rey del Merecumbe*. Fuentes SD16029.
Cumbia Cumbia. World Circuit CD WCD016.
Cumbias, Bambucos & Pasillos. Playa Sound CD PS65123.
Cumbias y Gaitas Famosas. Fuentes CD D10034.
Grupo Niche, *Cielo de Tambores*. CBS Discos CD 805082.
Lisandro Meza, *Lisandro's Cumbia*. World Circuit CD WCD026.
Joe Arroyo y La Verdad, *16 Exitos*. Fuentes SOF5648.
Toto La Momposina, *Music of the Atlantic Coast*. ASPIC X55509.
La Ceiba. ASPIC X55504.
Vallenato. Ocora CD 559039.
Afro-Hispanic Music from Western Colombia and Ecuador. Ethnic Folkways FE 4376.
Cancionero Noble de Colombia. Universidad de los Andes LP 501-3 Col.

Cuba

Sacred Rhythms of Cuban Santería. Smithsonian-Folkways 40419.
Afro-Cuba: A Musical Anthology. Rounder CD CD1088.
Real Rumba from Cuba. CD Corason 110.
Lazaro Ros & Olorun, *Songs for Eleguá*. Ashé CD2001.
Antonio Machin, *Cuarteto*, Vol. 1. Harlequin CD HQCD24.
Orquesta Aragon, *Danzones de Ayer y de Hoy*. Discuba CD CDD515.
Arsenio Rodriguez, *A Todos Los Barrios*. RCA Latino CD 33362RL.
Beny Moré, *Y Hoy Como Ayer*. RCA Tropical CD 32032RL.
Cachao y Su Conjunto, *Descarga*. Maype CD MCD168.
Celia Cruz, *Homenaje a los Santos*. TH-Rodven CD CD136.
Cha Cha Cha Epoca de Oro del . . . Orfeon CD CDTR812.
Chappottin y Sus Estrellas. Antilla CD ACD594.
Cuban Counterpoint: History of the Son Montuno. Rounder, CD CD1078.
Dan Den, *Viejo Lázaro*. QBADisc CD DQB9009.
Dances of the Gods. Ocora CD 559051.
Don Azpiazu and His Havana Casino Orchestra. Harlequin CD HQCD10.
Fajardo Danzones Completos Instrumentales. Antilla CD566.
Irakere Misa Negra. Messidor 15972.
Melodias del 40, *Me Voy Pa' Moron*. Antilla CD ACD5.
Muñequitos de Matanzas, *Congo Yambumba*. QBADisc CD DQB9014.
Musica Campesina. Auvidis CD B6758.
Orquesta Casino de la Playa, *Memories of Cuba 1937–44*. Tumbao CD TCD1503.
Orquesta Ritmo Oriental. Globestyle CD ORBCD034.
Los Papines, *Tambores Cubanos*. Egrem CD EGCD0037.
Pello el Afrokan, *Un Sabor Que Canta*. Vitral CD VCD4122.

Rumba. SudNord, Italy CD SNCD0037.
Oru. SudNord, Italy CD SNCD0038.
Septeto Nacional, *Sones Cubanos.* Seeco CD SCCD9278.
Septetos Cubanos. Corason 2CDs: MTCD113/4.
Sexteto Habanero, *Son Cubano.* Tumbao CD TCD001.
Trio Matamoros, *20 Exitos Inolvidables.* Kubaney CD CDK150.
Van Van, *Azúcar.* Green Linnet/Xenophile CD GLCD4025.

Dominican Republic

Stripping the Parrots: Essential Merengue. Corason CD COCD122.
Milly, Jocelyn y Los Vecinos, *Ahora Es!* Musical Productions CD MPCD6021.
Pochi y Su Cocoband, *La Faldita.* Kubaney CD KCD224.
Juan Luis Guerra, *Bachata Rosa.* Karen CD KCD136.
Johnny Ventura Y Su Combo. Kubaney CD117.
Pura Bachata. Kubaney CD KCD244.
Wilfrido Vargas, *Wilfrido 86.* Karen KCD95.
Los Grandes del Merengue Típico. Jose Luis Records CD JL093.
Angel Viloria/Dioris Valladares/Ramon Garcia, *Merengues.* Ansonia Records HGCD1206.
El Cieguito de Nagua, *Aprovechate.* José Luis CD JCD02.
Fefita la Grande, *Vamonos Pal Can.* Guitarra Records CD G1013.

Ecuador

Música de Ecuador. Caprice 2CDs: CAP22031.

Honduras

The Black Caribs of Honduras. Ethnic Folkways FE 4435.
La Guerra de las Puntas. Musical Productions CD MP6063.
Los Roland's, *Los Reyes de la Punta.* Musical Productions CD MPCD6049.

Latin Jazz

Bola Sete, *Bossa Nova.* Fantasy CD OJCCD286.
Bola Sete, *Trio Autentico.* Fantasy LP OJCCD290.
Cal Tjader, *Primo.* Original Jazz Classics CD OJCCD76223.
Stan Getz/Charlie Byrd, *Jazz Samba.* Verve CD810061.
Mongo Santamaria, *Afro-Roots.* Prestige CD PD240182.
Damasiano Perez Prado, *Havana 3 a.m.* RCA CD 24442RL.

Mexico

Antologia del Son de México. 3CDs/bklt Corason MTCD101/3.
Festival of San Miguel Tzinacapan. Ocora 560099.
La Negra Graciana & Trio Silva, *Sones Jarochos.* Corason CD COCD109.
Fiestas of Chiapas & Oaxaca. Nonesuch CD: 720702.
Mexican Revolution. Folklyric 9041/4.

Pregoneros del Puerto, *Sones Jarochos*. Rounder CD R5048.
El Caiman: Sones Huastecos. Corason COCD129.

New York

Ray Barretto, *Acid*. Fania SLP346.
Ray Barretto, *Hand Prints*. Concord Picante CD CCD4473.
Milton Cardona, *Bembe!* American Clave CD AC1004.
Johnny Colón, *Boogaloo Blues*. Cotique CD CSCD1004.
Willie Colón, *El Malo*. Fania CD SLPCD337.
Willie Colón, *Tiempo Pa' Matar*. Fania CD JMCD631.
Cortijo y Kako, *Ritmos Callejeros*. Ansonia CD HGCD1477.
Cortijo, *Time Machine*. Musical Productions CD MP3108.
Celia Cruz & Johnny Pacheco, *Celia & Johnny*. Vaya CD VS31.
Celia Cruz, *Azucar Negro*. RMM Productions CD RMCD80985.
José Curbelo & His Orchestra, *Rumba Gallega*. Tumbao CD TCD042.
Johnny Pacheco & El Conde, *Compadres*. Fania CD JMCD400.
Mongo Santamaria's Afro Cubans, *Drums and Chants*. Vaya CD VS56.
Machito, *Mucho Macho*. Pablo CD PACD2625.
Eddie Palmieri, *Mozambique*. Tico SLP1126.
Eddie Palmieri, *Sun of Latin Music*. MP Productions 3109.
Tito Puente, *Sensación*. Concord Picante CD CD4301.
Tito Puente *Dance Mania*. RCA Tropical 2467RL.

Panama

Street Music of Panama. Original Music OMCD008.
Danzas Panama: Instrumental Folk Music of Panama. JVC CD VICG5338.

Peru

Huayno Music of Peru, Vol.1. Arhoolie CD CD320.
Chocolate. Lyrichord CD LYRCD7417.
Afro-Peruvian Classics. Luaka Bop 45672.

Puerto Rico

Early Music of the North Caribbean 1916–1920. Harlequin CD HQCD67.
The Music of Puerto Rico 1929–1947. Harlequin CD HQCD22.
Canario y Sus Pleneros. Ansonia CD HGCD1232.
Tierra Adentro. Ansonia CD ANSCD1537.
Pleneros de la 21 / Conjunto Melodia. Shanachie CD DSHAN65001.

Tejas

Pioneer Recording Artists 1928–1958. Folklyric CD FLCD7001.
Flaco Jimenez, *Arriba el Norte*. Rounder CD6032.
Narciso Martinez. Folklyric CD FLCD9017.
San Antonio's Conjuntos in the 1950s. Arhoolie CD ARHO376.

Venezuela

Songs and Drums of the Black Brotherhoods. Ocora CD 560085.
Los Grandes del Cuatro. Leon CD LEON1131.
Folk Music of Venezuela. Library of Congress AFS L15.
Music of Venezuela. LP High Water LP1303.

United States Vocal

It would be the proverbial drop in the bucket to try to select from the thousands of major-label releases of jazz, blues, r & b soul, rap, and other mainstream styles relevant to this book. Here I have listed some of the less familiar recordings, either because their artists are less well known or because the labels on which they appear are relatively hard to find.

General

Voices from the American South: Blues, Ballads, Hymns, Reels, Shouts, Chanteys and Work Songs. Rounder 1701.
Sheep Sheep Don'tcha Know the Road. Rounder 1706.

African-American Roots

Murderous Home: Prison songs from Parchman Farm, Vol.1. Rounder CD1714.
Don'tcha hear Poor Mother Calling? Prison Songs from Parchman Farm, Vol.2. Rounder CD1715.
Negro Work Songs and Calls. Library of Congress AAFS L8.
Play and Dance Songs and Tunes. Library of Congress AAFS L9.
Georgia Sea Island Songs. New World CD 802782.
The Roots of Rap. Yazoo CD YD2018.
Cannon's Jug Stompers. Yazoo CD YD1082/3.
Wake Up Dead Man. Rounder CD CD2013.
Roots of the Blues. New World CD 802522.
Been in the Storm So Long. Smithsonian/Folkways CD CDSF40031.
Earliest Times: Georgia Sea Islands Songs for Everyday Living. Rounder 1713.

Religious: Collections

Wade in the Water, Vols.1–4. Smithsonian-Folkways CD SFCD40072-5.
Georgia Sea Islands: Biblical Songs and Spirituals. Rounder CD1712.
Memphis Sanctified Jug Bands 1928–1930. Document CD DOCD5300.
Negro Spirituals and Gospel Songs 1926–1942. Fremeaux 2 CDs FA008.
Gospel Quartets 1921–1942. Fremeaux 2 CDs FA026.
The Great Gospel Women. Shanachie CD DSH6004.
The Great Gospel Men. Shanachie CD DSH6005.

Selected Discography

Religious: Groups and Singers

Wiregrass Sacred Harp Singers, *The Colored Sacred Harp*. New World CD 80433.
Blind William Johnson, *Praise God I'm Satisfied*. Yazoo CD YCD1058.
Sister Rosetta Tharpe, *Gospel 1938–1943*. Frémeaux CD FA017.
Mahalia Jackson, *Gospels, Spirituals & Hymns*. Columbia 2 CDs 470832.
Rev. Cleophus Robinson, *A Better Place Somewhere* [Sermon]. Nashboro LP 7086.
Swan Silvertones, *My Rock/Love Lifted Me*. Specialty CD SPCD72022.
Sam Cook with the Soul-Stirrers. Specialty CD SPCD70092.
Graceland McCullough Tigers, *Heaven Fire*. Ant CD FACD1005.

Blues: Collections

61 Highway Mississippi. Rounder CD1703.
Bad Men Ballads. Rounder CD1705.
Texas Piano Blues. Story of the Blues CD SOB3509.
Barrelhouse Blues 1927–1936. Yazoo CD YD1028.

Secular Individuals

Lightnin' Hopkins. Smithsonian-Folkways 40019.
Sleepy John Estes, *I Ain't Gonna Be Worried No More*. Yazoo CD YD2004.
Leroy Carr, *Southbound Blues*. Drive CD DRIVE3215.
Tampa Red 1928–1942 (Story of the Blues). CD SOB3505.
Blind Lemon Jefferson. Milestone CD MCD470222.
Blind Blake. Yazoo CD YD1068.
Bessie Smith, *The Complete Recordings*. Columbia/Legacy 470912 and 474712.
John Lee Hooker, *Everybody's Blues*. Specialty CD SPCD7035.
Robert Johnson, *The Complete Recordings*. Columbia 2 CDs 46222.
Huddie Ledbetter, *Leadbelly, Library of Congress Recordings*. 6 CDs Rounder 1045-7/Rounder
   1097-9.
Mance Lipscomb. Arhoolie CDs 101 & 306.
Howlin' Wolf, *Cadillac Daddy*. Rounder CDSS28.

Zydeco

Amédé Ardoin, *I'm Never Comin' Back*. Folklyric FLCD7007.
Clifton Chenier, *60 Minutes with the King of Zydeco*. Arhoolie CD ARHO30155.
Clifton Chenier, *Zodico Blues & Boogie*. Specialty CD SPCD7039.
Boozoo Chavis, *The Lake Charles Atom Bomb*. Rounder CD2097.
Beau Jocque & the Zydeco Hi-Rollers. Rounder CD CD2120.

African-American Instrumental Collections

Altamont: Black String Band Music from the LIbrary of Congress. Rounder CD0238.
Country Brass Bands. Folkways FA 2650.
New Orleans Brass Bands. Rounder CD 11562.
New Orleans: The Music of the Streets, the Music of Mardi Gras. Folkways FA 2461.

Selected Discography

Parlor Piano 1917–27. Biograph BCD1001.
Ragtime: 1. The City; 2. The Country, Folkways RBF 17 and 18.
Boogie Woogie Special. Topaz CD TPZ1025.

African-American Instrumental Groups and Musicians

Eubie Blake, *Memories of You.* Biograph CD BCD112.
Freddie Keppard, *The Legend.* Topaz YPZ1052.
*Johnny Dodds 1926.*Classics Records CD 589.
Ferdinand "Jelly Roll" Morton, *The Pearls.* Bluebird CD 65882RB.
Jimmy Yancey 1939. Masters of Jazz CD MJCD91.
George Lewis, *Trios & Bands.* American Music CD AMCD4.
Earl Bostic. Charly CD CHCD241.
Dizzy Gillespie, *Dizzy's Diamonds.* 4 CDs/Bklt Verve 314 513 875.
Sidney Bechet, *Chronological 1923–1936.* Classic CD 583.
Cannonball Adderley Quintet, *Accent on Africa.* Capitol ST 2987.
Art Blakey, *Holiday for Skins.* Blue Note BST 84004.
Art Blakey and the Afro-Drum Ensemble, *The African Beat.* Blue Note BLP 84097.
Blind James Campbell and His Nashville Street Band. Arhoolie CD438.
Cannonball and Coltrane. Limelight LS 86009.
Rosewoman, Michele, *Harvest.* Enja ENJ7069.
Professor Longhair, *The Lost Sessions 1971–72.* Rounder 2057.
Ferdinand "Jelly Roll" Morton. *Winin' Boy Blues.* Rounder CD1094.
New Orleans Ragtime Orchestra, *Instrumental Rags.* Arhoolie 1058.
King Oliver's Creole Jazz Band. 2CDs Retrieval RTR79007.

Anglo-American

Brethren We Meet Again—Southern White Spirituals. Rounder CD1704.
Mountain Music of Kentucky. Smithsonian-Folkways CD SFCD40077.
White Spirituals from the Sacred Harp. New World CD 802052.
The Bristol Session. CMF Records 2 CDs CMF011.
Anglo-American Ballads. Library of Congress AAFS L7.
Anglo-American Shanties, Lyric Songs, Dance Tunes and Spirituals. Library of Congress AAFS
    L2.
Anglo-American Songs and Ballads. Library of Congress AAFS L12, L14, and L20.
Cowboy Songs, Ballads, and Cattle Calls from Texas. Library of Congress AAFS L28.
Play and Dance Songs and Tunes. Library of Congress AAFS L9.
Sacred Harp Singing. Library of Congress AAFS L11.

Videos/Films

Beats of the Heart

Roots Rock Reggae. Shanachie Video V1201.
Salsa! Shanachie Video V1202.

Rhythm of Resistance. Shanachie Video V1203.
Konkombe. Shanachie Video V1204.
Shotguns & Accordions. Shanachie Video V1205.
African Guitar. Vestapol V13017.
Dudu Ndaiye Rose, *Djaboté*. Multicultural Media MCM1006.
Juju Music. Rhapsody Films 9016.

Repercussions: A Celebration of African-American Music

Vol.1: *Born Musicians/On the Battlefield*. VREP01.
Vol.2: *Legends of Rhythm & Blues/The Max Roach Story*. VREP02.
Vol.3: *The Drums of Dagbon/Caribbean Crucible*. VREP03.
Vol.4: *Africa Come Back*. VREP04.
One Hand Don't Clap. Rhapsody Films 9018.
Jobim: An All Star Tribute. View Video 1349.
Poncho Sanchez, *A Night at Kimball's East*. Concord Picante CVC8001.
Bossa Nova: Music and Reminiscences. Multicultural Media MCM1005.
The Return of Rubén Blades. Rhapsody Films 9032.
Milly, Jocelyn y Los Vecinos, *Ahora Es!* MP Video.
Sworn to the Drum: A Tribute to Francisco Aguabella. Flower Films.
Alejandro Duran: El Inmortal. Guajira Productions.
Talking Feet. Flower Films.
A Singing Stream. Davenport Films.
Legends of the Delta Blues. Vestapol 13038.
Born for Hard Luck. Davenport Films.
Ladies Sing the Blues. View Video.
Zydeco Gumbo. Rhapsody Films 8062.
Always for Pleasure. Flower Films.

Sources for the Recordings

Library of Congress

Motion Picture, Broadcasting and Recorded Sound Division
Library of Congress
Washington, D.C. 20540
Much of the Library of Congress Archive of Folk Culture, including the remarkable archive of Alan Lomax recordings is, gradually being issued on CD by Rounder Records or Smithsonian Folkways. But the Library of Congress itself still sells cassette copies of many of the recordings cited in my discography.

Descarga

328 Flatbush Ave, #180
Brooklyn, NY 11238
Tel: 1-800-377-2647
Fax: 1-718-693-1316
The leading U.S. mail-order source for in-print Latin CDs, books (including how-to), and videos.

World Music Institute

49 West 27th Street
New York, NY 10001
Tel: 1-212-545-7536
Fax: 1-212-889-2771
Excellent for traditional musics from all over the world, they also carry a fair amount of contemporary styles.

Stern's Music USA

598 Broadway
New York, NY 10012
Tel: 1-212-925-1648
Fax: 1-212-925-1689
The best U.S. mail-order source for African recordings, as well as the Harlequin and Heritage line and some other Latin and Caribbean material.

Dusty Groove America

1180 N. Milwaukee Ave, 2nd Floor
Chicago, Il 60622
Tel: 1-773-645-1200
Fax: 1-773-645-3160
E-mail: jp@dustygroove.com
The best source I have found for out-of-print Latin LPs and Japanese CD re-releases of Latin material.

Roundup Records

One Camp Street,
Cambridge, MA 02140
Tel: 1-617-354-0700
Fax: 1-617-491-1970
E-mail: info@rounder.com
The mail-order source for Rounder Records and its "family," which include

several important Latin labels including Messidor, as well as a lot of music from Africa and the Afro-American diaspora.

House of Musical Traditions

7030 Carroll Avenue
Takoma Park, MD
Tel: 1-800-540-3794
Fax: 1-301-270-3010
E-mail: hmtrad@hmtrad.com

Euclid Records

4906 LaClede Ave
St. Louis, MO 63108
Tel: 1-314-961-8978
Fax: 1-314-961-8206
E-mail: euclid@icon-stl.net
The best source I've found, as a ratio of availability to price, for out-of-print jazz LPs and imported CDs. Also carries some Latin material (including some Japanese rarities).

Smithsonian Tapes

416 Hungerford Drive
Rockville, MD 20850
Tel: 1-301-443-2314
Folkways and Cook Records material that has not been issued on CD is available to order on cassette, along with photocopies of the original notes. This is the place to order them.

Selected Bibliography

(In all categories, see also accompanying notes to records listed in Discography.)

General

Black Music Research Journal.

Lomax, Alan. *Folk Song Style and Culture.* Washington, D.C., American Association for the Advancement of Science, 1968.

Manuel, Peter. *Popular Musics of the Non-Western World.* New York: Oxford University Press, 1988.

Nettl, Bruno. *Folk and Traditional Music of the Western Continents.* Englewood Cliffs, N.J.: Prentice-Hall, 1965.

Small, Christopher. *Music of the Common Tongue.* New York: Riverrun Press, 1987.

Van der Merwe, Peter. *Origins of the Popular Style.* New York: Oxford University Press, 1989.

Ethnomusicology.

The Beat.

Africa

Africa magazine.

Africa Report.

Andersson, Muff. *Music in the Mix.* Johannesburg: Ravan Press, 1981.

Ballantine Christopher. *Marabi Nights.* Johannesburg: Ravan Press, 1993. Monograph/Cassette.

Bascom, W. R., and M. J. Herskovits, eds. *Continuity and Change in African Cultures.* Chicago: University of Chicago Press, 1959.

Selected Bibliography

Beattie, John, and John Middleton, eds. *Spirit Mediumship and Society in Africa*. Africana, 1969.

Bebey, Francis. *African Music a People's Art*. Westport, Conn.: Lawrence Hill.

Bender, Wolfgang. *Sweet Mother*. Chicago: University of Chicago Press, 1991.

Carrington, J. F. *Talking Drums of Africa*. Chicago: Negro Universities Press, 1969.

Chernoff, John Miller. *African Rhythm and African Sensibility*. Chicago: University of Chicago Press, 1979.

Chilivumbo, Alifeyo. "Malawi's Lively Art Form," *Africa Report*, October 1971.

Collins, John. *Musicmakers of West Africa*. Washington, D.C.: Three Continents Press, 1985.

Colloquium on Negro Art. Présence Africaine, 1968.

Coplan, David B. *In Township Tonight*. New York: Longman, 1985.

———. *In the Time of Cannibals*. Chicago: University of Chicago Press, 1994.

Drum magazine. 1964–70 passim.

Edet, E. M. "Music of Nigeria." *African Music*, vol. 3, no. 3 (1964).

Erlmann, Veit. *African Stars*. Chicago: University of Chicago Press, 1991.

Euba, Akin. "Music Adapts to a Changed World." *Africa Report*, November 1970.

Ewens, Graeme. *Congo Colossus*. Buku Press, 1994.

Graham, Ronnie. *Da Capo Guide to Contemporary African Music*. Da Capo, 1988.

———. *The World of African Music*. Pluto Press, 1992.

Jahn, Janheinz. *Geschichte der Neoafrikanischen Literatur*. Düsseldorf & Cologne: Eugen Diederichs Verlag, 1967.

Jones, A. M. *Studies in African Music*. London: Oxford University Press, 1961.

———. Article on Indonesia/Africa. *African Music*, vol. 2, no. 3 (rebuttal by Jeffreys, *African Music*, vol. 2, no. 4).

Kazadi, Pierre. "Congo Music: Africa's Favorite Beat." *Africa Report*, April 1971.

Kivnik, Helen Q. *Where Is the Way*. New York: Penguin, 1990.

Lee, Hélène. *Rockers d'Afrique*. Paris: Albin Michel, 1988.

Low, John. *Shaba Diary*. Stiglmayer, Austria, 1982.

Mensah, Atta Annan. "Music Education in Modern Ghana," *East African Journal*, 1971.

Merriam, Alan P. "Music" columns in *Africa Report*, 1962–69.

Nikiprowetzky, Tolia, ed. *La Musique dans la Vie*, vol. 1. Paris: OCORA, 1967; vol. 2, ORTF, 1969.

Nketia, J. H. Kwabena. "Modern Trends in Ghana Music," *African Music*, vol. 1, no. 4 (1957).

———. *Our Drums and Drummers*. Legon: Ghana Publishing House, 1968.

Papers in African Studies, 3. Legon: Ghana Publishing Corporation, for Institute of African Studies.

Roberts, John Storm. "Songs to Live By," *Africa Report*, August 1965.

Rycroft, David. "The Guitar Improvisations of Mwenda Jean Bosco," parts I and II. *African Music*, vol. 2, no. 4 (1961), vol. 3, no. 1 (1962).

Smith, Edna M. "Popular Music in West Africa," *African Music*, vol. 3, no. 1 (1962).

Stapleton, Chris, and Chris May. *African Rock*. London and New York: Penguin, 1990.

Stewart, Gary. *Breakout: Profiles in African Rhythm*. Chicago University of Chicago Press, 1992.

Tracey, Hugh. *Chopi Musicians*. New York: Oxford University Press, 1970.

Van Everbroeck, René. *Lingála Dictionary*. Kinshasa: Editions l'Epiphanie, 1985.

Vansina, Jan. *Kingdoms of the Savanna*. Madison: University of Wisconsin Press, 1966.

Waterman, Christopher. *Jùjú*. Chicago: University of Chicago Press, 1990.

European and Arabic

Anglés, Higini. "Hispanic Musical Culture from the Sixth to the Fourteenth Century," *Musical Quarterly* (1940).

Bouali, Sid-Ahmed. *Petite Introduction à la Musique Classique Algérienne*. Algiers: SNED, 1968.

Chase, Gilbert. *The Music of Spain*. New York: Dover, 1959.

Encyclopédie de la Musique et Dictionnaire du Conservatoire, vol. 4: *Music of Spain and Portugal*.

Knosp, Gaston. *Encyclopédie de la Musique et Dictionnaire du Conservatoire*, vol. 5: *Canary Isles*.

Lambertini, Michel'angelo. *Encyclopédie de la Musique et Dictionnaire du Conservatoire*, vol. 4: *Popular Music of Portugal*.

Lloyd, A. L. *Folk Song in England*. International Publishers, 1967.

Rouaret, Jules. *Encyclopédie de la Musique et Dictionnaire du Conservatoire: Arab Music of the Maghreb*.

Vaughan Williams, Ralph, and A. L. Lloyd, eds. *The Penguin Book of English Folk Songs*. Baltimore: Penguin, 1959.

Afro-American General

Bastide, Roger. *Les Amériques Noires*. Paris: Payot, 1967.

Curtin, Philip D. *The Atlantic Slave Trade: A Census*. Madison: University of Wisconsin Press, 1970.

Hammond, Peter B. "West Africa and the Afro-Americans," in *The African Experience*, ed. John N. Paden and Edward W. Soja. Evanston, Ill.: Northwestern University Press, 1970.

Herskovits, Melville J. *The Myth of the Negro Past*. Boston: Beacon Press, 1941.

———. *The New World Negro*, ed. Frances S. Herskovits. Bloomington: Indiana University Press, 1966.

Howard, Joseph H. *Drums in the Americas*. Oak Publications, 1967.

Whitten, Norman E., Jr., and John F. Szwed, eds. *Afro-American Anthropology*. New York: The Free Press, 1970.

Latin America, General

Salinas Rodriguez, José Luis. *Jazz, Flamenco, Tango: Las Orillas de un Ancho Río*. Catriel Ensayo, 1994.

Zoila Gómez García, ed. *Musicologia en Latinoamerica*. Havana: Editorial Arte y Literatura, 1985.

South America

Alvarenga, Oneyda. *Música Popular Brasileña*. Mexico City: Fondo de Cultura Económica, 1947.

Bossa Brazilian Jazz World Guide (newsletter, Boston).

Cancionero Noble de Colombia, record liner notes (see Selected Discography).

Freyre, Gilberto. *The Mansions and the Shanties: The Making of Modern Brazil.* Knopf, 1963.

Garay, Narcisco. *Tradiciones y Cantares de Panama.* Panama City: n.p. 1930.

Hague, Eleanor. *Latin American Music.* Fine Arts Press, 1934.

Harris, Marvin. *Town and Country in Brazil.* New York: Norton, 1971 (reprint of 1956 ed.).

Herskovits, Melville J. *Surinam Folklore.* New York: Columbia University Press, 1936.

McGowan, Chris, and Ricardo Pessanha. *The Brazilian Sound.* Billboard Books 1991.

Ortiz Oderigo, Nestor R. "Negro Rhythm in the Americas," *African Music,* vol. 1, no. 3 (1956).

Perdomo Escobar, J. I. *Historia de la Música en Colombia.* Bogotá: Biblioteca Popular de Cultura Colombiana, 1945.

Ramon y Rivera, L. *Música Folklórica y Popular de Venezuela.* Caracas: Ministry of Education, 1963.

———. "Rhythm and Melodic Elements in Negro Music of Venezuela," in *Journal of the International Folk Music Council,* 1962.

Slonimsky, Nicholas. *Music of Latin America.* New York: Crowell, 1945.

Various authors. *Música Tropical y Salsa En Colombia.* Medellín: Ediciones Fuentes, 1992.

Caribbean/Central American

Austerlitz, Paul. *Merengue: Dominican Music and Dominican Identity.* Philadelphia: Temple University Press, 1997.

Averill, Gage. *A Day for the Hunter, a Day for the Prey: Popular Music and Power in Haiti.* Chicago: University of Chicago Press, 1997.

Beltran, Gonzalo A. *Cuijla: Esbozo Etnográfico de un Pueblo Negro.* Mexico City: Fondo de Cultura Económica, 1958.

Bowles, Paul. "Calypso—Music of the Antilles," *Modern Music,* March-April 1940.

Brathwaite, Edward. *Folk Culture of the Slaves in Jamaica.* Boston: New Beacon Books, 1970.

Cabrera, Lydia. *El Monte: Igbo, Finda, Ewe Orisha, Vititi Nfinda.* Miami: Ediciones C.R., 1971.

———. *La Sociedad Secreta Abakuá.* Miami: Ediciones C.R., 1970.

Carpentier, Alejandro. *La Música Cubana.* Mexico City: Fondo de Cultura Económica, 1946.

Courlander, Harold. *The Drum and the Hoe.* Berkeley and Los Angeles: University of California Press, 1939.

———. "Musical Instruments of Cuba," *Musical Quarterly,* April 1942.

———. "Musical Instruments of Haiti," *Musical Quarterly,* July 1941.

Crowley, Daniel J. "Towards a Definition of 'Calypso,'" *Ethnomusicology,* vol. 3, nos. 2 and 3 (1959).

Cruz, Francisco Lopez. *La Música Folklórica en Puerto Rico.* Troutman Press, 1967.

Daniel, Yvonne. *Rumba: Dance and Social Change in Contemporary Cuba.* Bloomington: Indiana University Press, 1995.

Demorizi, Emilio R. *Música y Baile en Santo Domingo.* Santo Domingo: Librería Hispaniola, 1971.

Díaz Ayala, Cristóbal. *Discografia de la Música Cubana Vol.1 1898–1925.* San Juan, PR: Fundación Musicalia 1994.

———. *Música Cubana del Areyto a la Nueva Trova.* Havana: Editorial Cubanacan 1981.

Edwards, Paul, ed. *Equiano's Travels*. New York: Praeger, 1967 (reprint, first published in 1789).

Espinet, Charles S., and Harry Pitts. *Land of the Calypso*. Trinidad: n.p., 1944.

González-Wippler, Migene. *Santería*. New York: Anchor, 1975.

Guilbault, Jocelyne, et al. *Zouk: World Music in the West Indies*. Chicago: University of Chicago Press, 1993.

Hernandez, Julio Alberto. *Música Tradicional Dominicana*. Santo Domingo: Julio D. Postigo, 1969.

Hill, Donald R. *Calypso Callalou*. Gainesville: University of Florida Press, 1993.

Jallier, Maurice, and Yollen Lossen. *Musique aux Antilles*. Paris: Editions Caribéennes 1985.

Jekyll, Walter, ed. *Jamaican Song and Story*. New York: Dover, 1966.

Kaptain, Laurence. *The Wood That Sings: The Marimba in Chiapas, Mexico*. Honeyrock Press, 1992.

Knight, Franklin W. *Slave Society in Cuba During the Nineteenth Century*. Madison: University of Wisconsin Press, 1970.

Labat, R. P. *Voyage aux Iles de l'Amérique*. Paris: Lacharte, 1931 (reprint).

Leon, Argiliers. *Música Folklórica Cubana*. Havana: Biblioteca Nacional José Martí, 1964.

Ligon, Richard. *A True and Exact History of the Island of Barbadoes*. London, 1673 (Facsimile edition, London: Frank Cass, 1970).

Manuel, Peter. *Caribbean Currents*. Philadelphia: Temple University Press 1995.

————, ed. *Essays on Cuban Music*. University Press of America, 1991.

Métraux, Alfred. *Haiti: Black Peasants and Their Religion*. London: Harrap, 1960.

Moore, Robin. *Nationalizing Blackness: Afrocubanismo and Artistic Revolution in Cuba*. Pittsburgh: University of Pittsburgh Press, 1997.

Muñoz, Maria Luisa. *La Música en Puerto Rico*. Troutman Press, 1966.

Ortiz, Fernando. *La Africanía de la Música Folklórica de Cuba*. Havana: Cardenas, n.d.

————. *Los Negros Brujos*. Ed. Universal, 1973.

————. *Los Bailes y el Teatro de los negros en el Folklore de Cuba*. Ed. Letras Cubanas, 1951.

Pacini Hernández, Deborah. *Bachata*. Philadelphia: Temple University Press, 1995.

Pearse, Andrew. "Aspects of Change in Caribbean Folk Music," *Journal of the International Folk Music Council*, 1955.

Perrone, Charles A. *Masters of Contemporary Brazilian Song*. Austin: University of Texas Press, 1989.

Potash, Chris, ed. *Reggae, Rasta, Revolution*. New York: Schirmer Books.

Quevedo, Raymond, ed. *Victory Calypsos*. Trinidad: n.p., n.d.

Roberts, Helen H. "Possible Survivals of African Song in Jamaica," *Musical Quarterly*, July 1926.

Rosemain, Jacqueline. *La Musique dans La Société Antillaise 1635–1902*. L'Harmattan 1986.

Saldivar, Gabriel. *Historia de la Música en México*. SEP, 1934.

Seabrook, W. B. *The Magic Island*. New York: Harcourt, Brace, 1929.

Serra, Otto Mayer. *Panorama de la Música Mexicana*. Colegio de México, 1941.

Stuempfle, Stephen. *The Steelband Movement*. Philadelphia: University of Pennsylvania Press, 1995.

Thomson, Kelvin. *Background of Trinidad's Carnival and Calypso*. Trinidad: n.p., n.d.

Van Dam, Theodore. "Influence of the West African Songs of Derision in the New World," *African Music*, vol. 1, no. 1.

Warner, Keith Q. *Kaiso!* Three Continents Press, 1982.

Wilcken, Lois. *The Drums of Vodou*. White Cliffs Media, 1992.

United States

Allen, Ray, and Lois Wilcken, eds. *Island Sounds in the Global City: Caribbean Popular Music and Identity in New York City.* Institute for Studies in American Music, 1998.

Allen, W. F., C. P. Ware, and L. M. Garrison. *Slave Songs of the United States.* Oak Publications, 1965.

Anderson, Jervis. *This Was Harlem.* New York: Farrar Strauss Giroux.

Berendt, Joachim E. *The Jazz Book.* Lawrence Hill, 1982.

Berry, Jason, Jonathan Foose, and Tad Jones. *Up from the Cradle of Jazz.* University of Georgia Press, 1986.

Blesh, Rudi. *Shining Trumpets.* New York: Knopf, 1946.

———. *Combo USA.* New York: Chilton Books, 1971.

———, and Harriet Janis. *They All Played Ragtime.* New York: Grove Press, 1970.

Boggs, Vernon W. *Salsiology.* Westport, Conn.: Greenwood Press, 1992.

Bornemann, Ernest. *A Critic Looks at Jazz.* Workers' Music Association, n.d.

Bradford, Perry. *Born with the Blues.* Oak Publications, 1965.

Broonzy, William, and Yannick Bruynoghe. *Big Bill Blues.* Cassell, 1955.

Broven, John. *Rhythm & Blues in New Orleans.* New York: Pelican, 1974.

Brown, James, with Bruce Tucker. *James Brown: The Godfather of Soul.* New York: Macmillan, 1986.

Cantwell, Robert. *Bluegrass Breakdown: The Making of the Old Southern Sound.* Bloomington: University of Illinois Press, 1984.

Chapman, Abraham, ed. *Steal Away: Stories of the Runaway Slaves.* New York: Praeger, 1971.

Charles, Ray, and David Ritz. *Brother Ray: Ray Charles' Own Story.* New York: Dial, 1978.

Charters, Samuel. *The Bluesmen.* Oak Publications, 1967.

———. *The Poetry of the Blues.* Oak Publications, 1963.

Chase, Gilbert. *America's Music from the Pilgrims to the Present.* New York: McGraw-Hill, 1966.

Collier, John Lincoln. *The Making of Jazz.* New York: Dell, 1978.

Courlander, Harold. *Negro Folk Music, U.S.A.* New York: Columbia University Press, 1963.

Dance, Helen. *Stormy Monday: The T-Bone Walker Story.* Baton Rouge: Louisiana State University Press, 1987.

Davis, Gerald I. *I Got the Word in Me and I Can Sing It You Know.* Philadelphia: University of Pennsylvania Press, 1985.

Dickerson, James. *Goin' Back to Memphis.* New York: Schirmer Books, 1996.

Dixon, Robert, and John Godrich. *Recording the Blues.* Stein & Day, 1970.

Dubois, W. E. B. *Souls of Black Folk.* Reprint of 1903 ed. Johnson Reprints, 1969.

Ducas, George, ed. *Great Documents in Black American History.* New York: Praeger, 1970.

Epstein, Dena J. *Sinful Tunes and Spirituals.* Bloomington: University of Illinois Press, 1977.

Evans, David. *Big Road Blues.* Berkeley: University of California Press, 1982.

Feather, Leonard. *The Book of Jazz.* New York: Horizon Press, 1965.

———. *Encyclopedia of Jazz.* Da Capo Press.

———. *Encyclopedia of Jazz Yearbooks.* Da Capo Press, 1993.

———. *Encyclopedia of Jazz in the 60s.* Da Capo Press.

———. *Encyclopedia of Jazz in the 70s.* Da Capo Press.

Ferris, William. *Blues from the Delta.* New York: Anchor, 1979.

Fiehrer, Thomas. "From Quadrille to Stomp: the Creole Origins of Jazz," *Popular Music,* vol. 10, no. 1, 1991.

Floyd, Samuel A., Jr. *The Power of Black Music.* New York: Oxford University Press, 1995.

Frazier, E. Franklin. *The Negro Church in America*. Liverpool: Liverpool University Press, 1964.

Garland, Phyl. *The Sound of Soul*. New York: Regnery, 1969.

Gerard, Charley, with Marty Sheller. *Salsa! The Rhythm of Latin Music*. Tempe, Ariz: White Cliffs Media.

Gillespie, Dizzy, and Al Fraser. *To Be or Not to Bop*. New York: Doubleday, 1979.

Gillett, Charlie. *The Sound of the City*. Outerbridge & Dienstfrey, 1970.

Glasser, Ruth. *My Music Is My Flag*. Berkeley: University of California Press 1995.

Gospel Music Jubilee magazine.

Guralnik, Peter. *Feel Like Going Home*. New York: Vintage, 1981.

——— *Searching for Robert Johnson*. New York: Obelisk 1989.

Handy, W. C. *Father of the Blues*. New York: Collier Paperbacks, 1970.

Harris, Michael W. *The Rise of Gospel Blues*. New York: Oxford University Press, 1992.

Haskins, James, with Kathleen Benson. *Scott Joplin: The Man Who Made Ragtime*. New York: Doubleday, 1978.

Hasse, John Edward. *Beyond Category*. Da Capo, 1995.

Hazzard-Gordon, Katrina. *Jookin'*. Philadelphia: Temple University Press, 1990.

Holloway, Joseph E., and Winifred K. Vass. *The African Heritage of American English*. Bloomington: Indiana University Press, 1993.

Heilbut, Anthony. *The Gospel Sound*. Limelight, 1985.

Jasen, David A., and Trebor J. Tichenor. *Rags & Ragtime*. New York: Dover, 1978.

Johnson, J. Weldon, ed. *The Book of American Negro Spirituals*. New York: Viking Press, 1964.

Jones, LeRoi. *Black Music*. New York: William Morrow, 1968.

———. *Blues People*. New York: William Morrow, 1963.

Jones, Max, and John Chilton. *Louis: The Louis Armstrong Story, 1900–1971*. Boston: Little, Brown, 1971.

Keil, Charles. *Urban Blues*. 2nd ed. Chicago: University of Chicago Press, 1991.

Kirkeby, Ed. *Ain't Misbehavin': The Story of Fats Waller*. London: Peter Davies, 1966.

Kmen, Henry A. *Music in New Orleans: The Formative Years, 1791–1841*. Baton Rouge: Louisiana State University Press, 1966.

Kofsky, Frank. "Ornette Coleman: Jazz Musician," *Jazz and Pop*, November 1970.

Krehbiel, Henry Edward. *Afro-American Folksongs*. New York: Ungar, 1962.

Latrobe, Benjamin. *Impressions Respecting New Orleans: Diary & Sketches, 1818–1820*. New York: Columbia University Press, 1951.

Lincoln, C. Eric, and Milton Meltzer. *A Pictorial History of the Negro in America*. 3d ed. New York: Crown, 1968.

Linn, Karen. *That Half-Barbaric Twang: The Banjo in American Popular Culture*. Urbana: University of Illinois Press, 1991.

Lomax, Alan. *The Land Where the Blues Began*. New York: Pantheon, 1993.

———. *Mister Jelly Roll*. New York: Duell, 1950.

Lomax, John A. *Adventures of a Ballad Hunter*. New York: Macmillan, 1947.

Lovell, John, Jr. *Black Song: The Forge and the Flame*. New York: Macmillan, 1972.

Loza, Steven. *Barrio Rhythm: Mexican Music in Los Angeles*. Bloomington: University of Illinois Press, 1993.

McCarthy, Albert, et al. *Jazz on Record: The First Fifty Years, 1917 to 1967*. Oak Publications, 1969.

Malone, Bill. *Country Music U.S.A.* Austin: University of Texas Press, 1968.

Monson, Ingrid. *Saying Something: Jazz Improvisation and Interaction*. Chicago: University of Chicago Press, 1966.

Murray, Albert. *The Omni-Americans*. Da Capo Press.

———. *Stompin' the Blues*. New York: Vintage, 1982.

Newell, William Wells. *Games and Songs of American Children*. New York: Dover, 1963.

Odum, Howard W., and Guy B. Johnson. *The Negro and His Songs*. New York: New American Library, 1969.

Oliver, Paul. *The Blues Tradition*. Oak Publications, 1970.

———. *Savannah Syncopators: African Retentions in the Blues*. New York: Stein & Day, 1970.

———. *The Story of the Blues*. Chilton, 1969.

———. *Songsters and Saints*. Cambridge University Press, 1984.

Owens, Thomas. *Bebop: The Music and Its Players*. New York: Oxford University Press, 1995.

Parrish, Lydia. *Slave Songs of the Georgia Sea Islands*. Creative Age, 1942.

Pearson, Barry Lee. *Sounds So Good to Me*. Philadelphia: University of Pennsylvania Press, 1984.

Roberts, John Storm. *The Latin Tinge*. New York: Oxford University Press, 1979.

Rosenberg, Bruce A. *The Art of the American Folk Preacher*. New York: Oxford University Press, 1970.

Russell, Ross. *Jazz Style in Kansas City and the South-West*. Berkeley: University of California Press, 1971.

Russell, Tony. *Blacks Whites and Blues*. New York: Stein & Day, 1970.

Salazar, Max. "The History of the Up-Tempo Latin American Music in New York City" (unpublished study).

———. *Latin New York* and *Latin Beat* magazines.

Sargeant, Winthrop. *Jazz: Hot and Hybrid*. New York: Dutton, 1946.

Sawyer, Charles. *The Arrival of B. B. King*. Da Capo 1980.

Schafer, William J., and Johannes Riedel. *The Art of Ragtime*. Baton Rouge: Louisiana State University Press, 1973.

Schuller, Gunther. *Early Jazz*. New York: Oxford University Press, 1968.

Shapiro, Nat, and Nat Hentoff, eds. *Hear Me Talkin' to Ya*. New York: Rinehart, 1955.

Shaw, Arnold. *Black Popular Music in America*. New York: Schirmer Books, 1986.

———. *Honkers and Shouters*. New York: Schirmer Books, 1986.

Silvester, Peter J. *A Left Hand Like God: A Hstory of Boogie-Woogie Piano*. Da Capo, 1989.

Southern, Eileen. *The Music of Black Americans*. New York: Norton, 1971.

Spellman, A. B. *Four Lives in the Bebop Business*. New York: Pantheon, 1966.

Stancell, Steven. *Rap Whoz Who*. New York: Schirmer Books, 1996.

Stearns, Marshall, W. *The Story of Jazz*. New York: Oxford University Press, 1970.

———, and Jean Stearns. *Jazz Dance*. Da Capo Press. 1994 (re-issue).

Stokes, W. Royal *The Jazz Scene*. New York: Oxford University Press, 1991.

Thomas, J. C. *Chasin' the Trane*. Da Capo, 1975.

Titon, Jeff Todd. *Early Downhome Blues*. 2nd ed. Chapel Hill: University of North Carolina Press, 1994.

Ulanov, Barry. *A History of Jazz in America*. Da Capo Press, 1971.

Weinstein, Norman C. *A Night in Tunisia*. New York: Limelight, 1994.

Williams, Martin T., ed. *The Art of Jazz*. New York: Oxford University Press, 1959.

———. *The Jazz Tradition*. New York: Oxford University Press, 1983.

———. *Jazz Heritage*. New York: Oxford University Press, 1985.

Work, John W. *American Negro Songs and Spirituals*. Bonanza Books, 1940.

Wynn, Ron, ed. *All Music Guide to Jazz*. Miller Freeman, 1994.

Index

Page numbers in italics refer to illustrations.

Index

creole music, 241–42
criolla, 117
Critic Looks at Jazz, A (Bornemann), 57–58
Cropper, Steve, 236
crossover, *188*, 211
Crowley, Daniel, 122, 129
Crusaders, xxxiii
Cruz, Celia, *99*, 100
Cuarteto Machin, 104
cuartetos, 104
cuatros, 91, 92, 109, 123, 131
Cuba, 2, 6–7, *14*, 15–21, 24–26, *28*, 56, 76–77, 102–9, 110
Cubop style, 246–49
Cuffee, Ed, 61
cumbé, 87
cumbia, x, 15, 87–88, 89, 90, 92
cumbiamba, 88, 90
currulaos, x, 12, 15, 88, 89

Dabney, Ford, 218
Dahomeyan tribes, xxiii, xxiv, 2, 16, 20, 22, 176
Dairo, I. K., *276*, 277
dance-dramas, 92
dances, xxiv, xxvi, 7–8, 31, 36, 42
    country, 214–15
    drums for, 6, 15, 17, 25, 29–30, 39, 75, 78, 80–81, *80*, 94–95
    European influences on, 53–54, 56, *68*
    mime, 77, 105
    national, 92
    urban popular, xxv, 76–77, 213–40
    See also specific dances
"Dancing in the Street," 203
danzas, 50, 109, 112, 217
danzón, 106
Davies, John, 175–76
Davies, Samuel, 175
Davis, Aubrey, 134
Davis, Gary, 206
Davis, General, 93
Davis, Miles, 237, 238
Davison, Wild Bill, 244
décima verse form, 53, 76, 91, 104, 106, 131
Decimus, Pierre-Edouard, 152
Deija Falar, 78
Dekker, Desmond, 144
Dessalines, Jean-Jacques, 20
"Devil and the Tailor, The," *119*
"Devil's Honey-Dram," 136
"Devil's Nine Questions, The," 134
Dhrupati, 127
Diabate, Toumani, *197*
"Diana," 130
Dibango, Manu, 152
Dickens, Charles, 41
Diddley Bow, 15, *60*
Difficiles de Pétionville, Les, 149–50
digging songs, x, 32, *136*, 137–38, 140
dikgambo, 176
disco, 144
Dixie Hummingbirds, 185
Dixieland, 225
Dixon Brothers, 171
Dixon-Gottschild, Brenda, 57

Dodds, Baby, 225–26
Dodds, Johnny, 229
Dogon peoples, xxiv, 16
Dominguinhos, *83*
Dominican Republic, 13, *14*, 15, 33–34, 46, 47, *49*, 52–53, 54, 71, 113–18, 146, 147, 223
Domino, Fats, 202
Donaldson, Eric, 144, 145
Donayre, Manuel, *98*
"Donkey City," 138
Dorival, Althiery, 147
Dorsey, Georgia Tom, *184*, 185, 187
double basses, 48, 107
"Dozens, The," 71, 125, 203, 210
DP Express, 149–50
Dranes, Arizona, 185
"Dream, The," 220
"Drop Down Mama," 201
drums, xxiii, xxvi, xxxi–xxxii
    banning of, 22, 173
    for dancing, 6, 15, 17, 25, 29–30, 39, 75, 78, 80–81, *80*, 94–95
    ensembles of, x, 4–7, 10–11, 36, 48
    religious use of, xiv, 7, 17, 18, 19, 22, 33–34
    talking, xxv, *xxv*, 206
    types of, xxxiv, 4–7, *5*, *6*, 11, 13, 15–16, 18, 19, 27, *28*, 39, 47, 75, 84, 87
Du Bois, W. E. B., 63, 64–65, 67
Duran, Alejandro, 90
"Dust my Broom," 199

Early Jazz (Schuller), 217, 224–25, 234
earthbow, 13, 47, *60*
East Africa, xxi, xxii, xxviii
Eccles, Clancy, 143
Ecuador, 73, 86
"Edna," 51
"Eh Là Bas," 241–42
Ekemode, Orlando Julius, *253*
"El Frijolar," 94
El General, 153
"El Jardinero," 116
"Ella Gift," 132
Ellington, Duke, 109, 228, 230, 243, 244, 254
Emancipation, 173–74, 175, 187
"Emmanuel Road," 139
"Empty Bed Blues," 167
"Entertainer, The," 219
Epstein, Dena, 3, 12–13, 15, 37, 38, 41, 66, 70
Equiano, 70
Erlmann, Veit, 281
Espinet, Charles, 122, 123–24
Estes, Sleepy John, 201
estribillo, 103–4
Ethiopians, 145
ethnomusicology, ix–xiii, xv–xvi, xxiii
Ethnomusicology, 122
Euba, Akin, 258
Eubanks, Horace, 150
Europe, James Reese, 218, 244
"Everybody Loves Saturday Night," 260
Ewe peoples, xxxii, 1–2, 27, 30, 48, 61, 94, 140, 158, 225
Ezell, Will, 222

322

vvvvvv

Index

Roberts, Luckey, 218, 220
Roberts, Oral, 142
Robeson, Paul, 175
Robinson, Cleophus, 180, 185
Robinson, Jim, 232
rock, x, xii–xiii, 90
rocksteady, xii, 32, 142, 143, 144, 145
Rodgers, Jimmie, 266
Rolling Stone, 201
Rollins, Sonny, 239
Roman Catholic Church, 18–19, 44–46, 63, 65, 176
Romao, Dom Um, 15
Roots of Rap, 203
Rosario, Félix del, 115
"Rose Leaf Rag," 220
Rosewoman, Michelle, 253
"Rosey," 167
Rousseau, Jean Jacques, xxi
Rude Boys of Kingston, 143, 144
"Rudies Is Tough," 143, 144
rumba-box, *14*, 15
rumbas, 27–29, 47, 90, 108, 109, 117, 244–45, 270
Rumbas de Tiempo' España, 27
"Run, Old Jeremiah," 186
Rushing, Jimmy, 208
Russell, Ross, 226
Russell, William, 222, 243
Ryco Jazz, 155

Sahelian tradition, xxvii
saint's houses, 18
"Sally's in the Skiff," 166
"Sally Water," 71, 139
salsa, 22, 88, 100, 102, 109, 110, 112, 115, 151, 252
salves, 53, 117
samba, 29–30, 56–57, 76, 77–82, 113
samba-choro, 84
samba malato, 100
samba schools (*escolas de samba*), 78, *79*, 81
sambas da roda, 29, 78
sambas de enredo, 29, 78
"Sammy Beatin' Suzanna," 132
Sam's Trio, 264
"Santa Maria," 112
Santamaria, Mongo, 248–49, *248*, 254
Santana, Carlos, 249–50, *250*
Santería, 16, 65
saradunga, 117
"Satta Amasa Gana," 145
Savannah Syncopators (Oliver), 59–61, 173
saxophones, 110, 115, 132, 148
Saying Something (Monson), 48
"Say It Loud, I'm Black and Proud," 66
scales, xxxvi–xxxvii, 16, 38–39, 74, 178, 204–5
scat singing, 108
Schaeffner, André, 38–39
Schafer, William J., 218
School of Oriental and African Studies, 161
schottische, 140
Schuller, Gunther, 204, 217, 224–25, 229, 234, 235
scratch bands, 118, 119, 132
sea-chanteys, 32, 163
Seeger, Pete, 159
seis, 112

seis del toro, 77
"Selah," 145
Sencación, 109
Senegambian culture, 2, 59–61
Senghor, Léopold, 206
Septeto Habanero, 47
septetos, 104, 107
Sexteto Habanero, 104, *105*
Sexteto Nacional, 104
sextetos, 104
Shango, 17, 18, 63, 65, 121, 131
Shango Rada cult music, 7
Shaw, Artie, 245
Shelley, Percy Bysshe, 162–63
Shepp, Archie, 227, 233, 237
Shirley and Lee, 143
Shleu Shleu, 149
"Shortening Bread," 167
"Short of Breath," 226
Shorty, Lord, 126–27
Sicot, Webert, 148
Sierra Leone, 2, 55, 260, 273
Silva, Robertinho, *80*
Simone, Nina, 185, 208
"Simpson," 126
"Simpson the Funeral Agency Man," 126
Sinful Tunes and Spirituals (Epstein), 15, 37, 70
Singers of Joy, *184*
singing, xxiii, xxxi
    call-and-response, xxiii, xxx, 7, 17, 19, 25, 27,
      33, 36, 52–53, 74, 81–82, 89, 91–92, 94, 104,
      124, 135–37, *136*, 161, 176, 185, 196–99
    choral, xxii, xxvi, xxxii, 17, 19, 29, 75, 110,
      178–79
    falsetto, 9, 17, 33, 130, 136, 206–7
    hockett, 206, 207
    religious and festival, 9–10, 17, 45–47
    social commentary in, 7–8, 9, 69–70, 110,
      125–26
    storytelling, xxvi, 8
    styles and techniques of, xxviii, xxxii–xxxiii, 9,
      17, 33, 75, 108, 206–9
    unaccompanied, 53
Sissle, Noble, 223
ska, xii, 142, 143
skiffle bands, 215
slaves, 102
    escape of, 40, 44, 69
    freed, 39, 41, 70, 95
    "nations" and secret societies of, 22–25, 46, 65,
      70, 96, 130
    origins of, 1–3
    religious conversion of, 64–65
    revolts of, 20, 22
    trade in, ix, xxix, 38
    white styles used by, 165–74
Slave Songs of the Georgia Sea Islands (Parrish), 66, 168
Sloan, Hans, 13
Sly and the Family Stone, 203
Small, Millie, 143
Smith, Bessie, 167, 194, *195*, 196, 198, 202
Smith, Jabbo, 231
Smith, Jimmy, 144
Smith, Pinetop, 222